TERM PAPER RESOURCE GUIDE TO TWENTIETH-CENTURY WORLD HISTORY

Michael D. Richards
and Philip F. Riley

Greenwood Press
Westport, Connecticut • London

Library of Congress Cataloging-in-Publication Data

Richards, Michael D.
    Term paper resource guide to twentieth-century world history / Michael D.
Richards and Philip F. Riley.
      p. cm.
    Includes bibliographical references and index.
    ISBN 0–313–30559–5 (alk. paper)
    1. History, Modern—20th century. 2. History, Modern—20th century—
Bibliography. 3. History, Modern—20th century—Sources—Bibliography.
I. Riley, Philip F. II. Title.
D421.R47 2000
909.82—dc21   99–088458

British Library Cataloguing in Publication Data is available.

Library of Congress Catalog Card Number: 99–088458
ISBN: 0–313–30559–5

First published in 2000

Greenwood Press, 88 Post Road West, Westport, CT 06881
An imprint of Greenwood Publishing Group, Inc.
www.greenwood.com

Printed in the United States of America

The paper used in this book complies with the
Permanent Paper Standard issued by the National
Information Standards Organization (Z39.48–1984).

10 9 8 7 6 5 4 3 2 1

Contents

Preface

The history of the twentieth-century world is a rapidly expanding field that no one person can hope to master. We believe, however, that it is possible to construct a historical research guide for the twentieth-century world that will provide high school students, undergraduates, and their teachers with a useful introduction to world history in this century.

This text examines one hundred events that have shaped the twentieth century, beginning with the first manned flight in 1903 and ending with the economic uncertainties of China in 1999. Because the contribution of the United States is fully covered in Greenwood Press's *Term Paper Resource Guide to Twentieth-Century United States History* (1999), we have focused this guide primarily on non-American events, while providing coverage of the American involvement wherever appropriate.

Any list of one hundred important events is subject to criticism, second thoughts, and revision. We have worked to construct a list that reflects recommendations for teaching world history on the high school and undergraduate level. To this end, we have consulted Charlotte Crabtree and Gary B. Nash, eds., *National Standards for World History: Exploring Paths to the Present*, expanded edition (Los Angeles: National Center for History in the Schools, 1994). We have also made use of the Standards of Learning recently instituted by the state of Virginia. And, not surprisingly, we have chosen topics we have taught and to which students have responded in our courses. Finally, we have made a special effort to include topics on science and technology in this century that owes so much to those areas.

Three overriding concerns have shaped our approach to this guide. First, this is a book for students and teachers, although we hope people without term papers to write will find it useful and enjoyable as well. Each entry is accompanied by suggestions for term papers and a bibliography of the standard works on the event, more recent recommended books and articles, and, where possible, audiovisual and World Wide Web (WWW) resources. In constructing bibliographies, we began either with the bibliographies of widely used histories of the twentieth-century world or with books recognized as standard sources for particular topics. Additionally, we made a conscious effort to note new books and articles that appeared to be important contributions to the literature. Our aim in all this was to assemble a list of books and articles highly recommended by scholars and teachers. In the case of many entries, one or both of us were personally familiar with the major sources. Some entries, of course, covered material new to us. While we relied on experts in the field to guide us, we nevertheless also made it a point to evaluate all the items listed ourselves. Finally, we have viewed all of the recommended audiovisual sources, often more than once, and have worked extensively with the WWW resources to ensure their appropriateness. In most cases, we have used the audiovisual and the WWW resources in our courses.

Second, to show the connections within twentieth-century world history, we have included after each entry a listing of all events in the guide related to that entry. Finally, to underscore our belief that men and women make history, we have emphasized biography and autobiography in our entries and in the annotated bibliographies.

COMPOSITION OF THE GUIDE

Each of the one-hundred entries offers a brief narrative of the event and an indication of the major issues associated with it. Boldfaced keywords will help the student with further research.

The "Suggestions for Term Papers" section usually lists six suggestions designed to assist the student in developing a theme or question to pursue as a project or paper. "Research Suggestions" notes related entries in the guide. It also contains suggestions about additional keyword searches.

The "Suggested Sources" sections include lists of primary and secondary sources, as well as Web sites where appropriate. Under "Primary Sources" the student can find annotated entries for memoirs, autobiographies, collections of documents, and other kinds of primary source material that furnish the raw material for historical investigation and interpretation. The section on "Secondary Sources" contains annotated entries for books, articles, and audiovisual resources that we feel are useful and reliable. All Web site addresses were current at time of printing. Unfortunately, audiovisual and World Wide Web resources do not exist for every entry.

Acknowledgments

We would like to thank our colleagues for assistance of various kinds with this work, especially Brad Arnold, Jack Butt, Michael J. Galgano, Frank Gerome, Caroline T. Marshall, David Owusu-Ansah, and Chong K. Yoon at James Madison University, and Jim Alouf, Gerald Berg, the late Joan Kent, and Christopher Witcombe at Sweet Briar College. Paul Deslandes, now at Texas Tech University, also provided help. Sweet Briar students in History 147, "The 20th-Century World," reviewed earlier versions of some entries and in other ways helped with the project.

We owe a particularly large debt to Dr. Barbara A. Rader, the Executive Editor of the Broad Reference Program. Her support and advice were welcome contributions to the project. We also wish to thank David Palmer, the production editor, and Barbara Goodhouse, the copy editor, for valuable assistance.

In an area that is growing as rapidly as twentieth-century world history, there will inevitably be new interpretations and new resources. We would welcome any comments, criticisms, or suggestions our readers might have. Please send them to Michael Richards, Department of History, Sweet Briar College, Sweet Briar, Virginia 24595, or by e-mail to *richards@sbc.edu*.

1. THE FIRST MANNED FLIGHT, 1903

In the latter half of the nineteenth century several people had experimented with airships or dirigible balloons, that is, balloons that had a means of propulsion and could be steered. At the turn of the century, some concentrated on heavier-than-air flight. One of the foremost experimenters of the time was **Samuel P. Langley**, who had succeeded in testing unmanned scale models of his airplane design as early as 1896. Attempts in 1903 to launch manned flights off a houseboat in the Potomac ended both times in failure.

Wilbur and Orville Wright had also been working on manned flight. Although neither had attended college, they were well educated and sophisticated about technology. By 1899 they had both the technical skills and the income, through their print shop and bicycle repair and sales shop, to allow them to experiment in a serious, sustained way with heavier-than-air flight.

In addition to being familiar with Samuel Langley's work, the Wright brothers had studied the work of **Otto Lilienthal**, a German and the foremost expert on gliders of his day. Using a United States Weather Service list of windy sites, the brothers picked **Kitty Hawk, North Carolina**, a little village in the Outer Banks. There they experimented with gliders in 1900 and 1901. Because of their experience with bicycles, they focused on the problem of controlling the airplane. After the 1901 tests, they designed and used a wind tunnel to test dozens of wing designs. The 1902 tests were much more successful than earlier tests had been. Ailerons (movable flaps on the wings) and a rudder helped considerably with the problem of control.

In 1903 at Kill Devils Hill, the Wright brothers made one attempt on 14 December, but the plane stalled and was damaged. After repairs, they tried again on 17 December. Orville Wright flew 120 feet in 12 seconds on the first flight. There were four flights in all that day, the last, by Wilbur, the longest. It covered 852 feet in 59 seconds.

The Wright brothers continued to work on the design of their plane over the next two years. By 1905 they were flying for as long as 39 minutes at a time. In October they stopped flying and began working to secure patents and contracts.

In 1908 Wilbur Wright went to France, where he captured the

imaginations of Europeans. France was the center of aviation at that point, with both **Louis Bleriot**, who flew over the English Channel the following year, and the Brazilian **Alberto Santos-Dumont** working to catch up with the Wright brothers.

The technology of the airplane developed rapidly over the next few decades. Wilbur died in 1912, but Orville, who lived until 1948, witnessed the extraordinary changes that had come about since he first flew on a windy day in December 1903.

Suggestions for Term Papers

1. Investigate the way the Wright brothers worked between 1899 and 1903 and determine what factors might account for their success on 17 December 1903.
2. Report on the various attempts to fly across the English Channel in 1908. Why did Wilbur Wright decline to attempt the flight?
3. Count Ferdinand von Zeppelin, who had served in the Union army in the Civil War, took aviation in a different direction than the Wright Brothers. What did he accomplish in the first decade of the twentieth century and what did this lead to in the period after World War I? (see Suggested Sources)
4. How much interest in the military potential of airplanes did the various military establishments show in the period before World War I?
5. In 1908 H. G. Wells, already a well-known writer, published a book entitled *The War in the Air*. Read Wells's book or another similar book published about the same time and report on how the author portrayed airplanes and pilots.
6. Samuel P. Langley seemed destined to be the first person to fly successfully a manned, heavier-than-air machine. Why was he not successful? Use *The American Heritage History of Flight* and *The National Air and Space Museum* as starting points (see Suggested Sources).

Research Suggestions

In addition to the boldfaced items, search under **Octave Chanute, Lord Northcliffe (Alfred Harmsworth), H. G. Wells,** and **Count Ferdinand von Zeppelin.**

SUGGESTED SOURCES

Primary Sources

The Papers of Wilbur and Orville Wright. 2 vol. Edited by Marvin W. McFarland. New York: Arno Press, 1990. Reprint of the 1953 edition. Provides an excellent picture of the careful way in which the Wright brothers worked.

Wright, Orville. *How We Invented the Aeroplane.* New York: F. C. Kelly, 1953. A firsthand account.

Secondary Sources

The American Heritage History of Flight. Narrative by Arthur Gordon. New York: American Heritage, 1962. A good introduction to the topic.

Angelucci, Enzo, ed. *World Encyclopedia of Civil Aircraft: From Leonardo Da Vinci to the Present.* New York: Crown, 1982. The first two chapters offer an extensive introduction to those who came before the Wright brothers and to the brothers and their contemporaries. Many illustrations, often with detailed commentary.

Crouch, Tom D. *The Bishop's Boys.* New York: W. W. Norton, 1989. The best biography. Good coverage of technical issues but also useful biographical insights into the lives of Wilbur and Orville.

Jakab, Peter L. *Visions of a Flying Machine: The Wright Brothers and the Process of Invention.* Washington, D.C.: Smithsonian Institution, 1990. The book emphasizes how the Wright brothers solved the problems encountered in designing an airplane that would fly.

Myer, Henry Cord. *Airshipmen, Businessmen, and Politics, 1890–1940.* Washington, D.C.: Smithsonian Institute Press, 1991. A comprehensive source on the Zeppelin airships, including both commercial and political aspects.

The National Air and Space Museum. Text by C.D.B. Bryan. New York: Harry N. Abrams, 1979. A survey of the history of aviation illustrated by hundreds of photographs.

Taylor, John W. R., and Kenneth Munson. *History of Aviation.* New York: Crown, 1977. Divided into topics such as "Dirigibility" and "Alberto Santos-Dumont," with many illustrations.

Wohl, Robert. *A Passion for Wings: Aviation and the Western Imagination, 1908–1918.* New Haven: Yale University Press, 1994. A fascinating, beautifully illustrated book that discusses how Europeans, particularly artists and intellectuals, responded to the airplane.

The Wright Stuff [videocassette]. New York: Shanachie Entertainment, 1996. Part of the American Experience series.

World Wide Web

"The Wright Stuff." *www.pbs.org/wgbh/pages/amex/wright/index.html*. This
   Web site includes the transcript of the program and other features.
"Zeppelin." *http://spot.colorado.edu/~dziadeck/zf/htmls/introduction.htm*.
   A well-designed Web site with information on all aspects of the Zep-
   pelin airships and links to other Web sites.

2. THE REVOLUTION OF 1905 IN RUSSIA

Often thought of as a dress rehearsal for the revolutionary events of
1917 in Russia, the Revolution of 1905 was a full-fledged revolution
in its own right. In part, it stemmed from the economic downturn
at the end of the nineteenth century and political dissent and disorders at the beginning of the twentieth. Russian losses in the initial
stages of the **Russo-Japanese War** furnished a more immediate cause.
Finally, **"Bloody Sunday"** (9 January 1905), the massacre of workers
attempting peacefully to petition **Tsar Nicholas II** in St. Petersburg,
provided the catalyst.

The government failed to respond adequately to Bloody Sunday or
to calls for reform. In particular, reformers called for a **duma**, a representative body that would share in the process of governing the
empire. The government, attempting to fight a war 6,000 miles from
the capital, was also hampered by nationalist movements. In the summer, sailors on the battleship *Potemkin* mutinied, adding fuel to the
revolutionary fires.

The government suggested the establishment of a consultative
duma in August, but it was an inadequate gesture. In September,
railroad workers led a general strike that paralyzed the country's economy. In October, the **St. Petersburg Soviet** or council of workers
formed.

The tsar asked **Count Sergei Witte** to deal with the crisis. Witte
recommended either a military dictatorship or political concessions.
The tsar, not finding anyone willing to undertake the first option,
was forced to issue the **October Manifesto**, which promised an
elected parliamentary assembly and various civic freedoms.

The revolutionary movement, which had consisted of students, middle-class liberals, workers, and socialists, fragmented. Liberals and moderates decided to work with the tsarist government. The socialists worked to continue the revolution.

Over the next two years, the government regained control and severely limited the concessions originally made. The Revolution of 1905 headed the Russian Empire toward constitutional monarchy, but the tsarist government effectively did everything possible after 1905 to avoid taking that path.

Suggestions for Term Papers

1. Examine the causes and the course of the Russo-Japanese War. Why was the Japanese military successful?
2. "Bloody Sunday" was the catalyst for the Revolution of 1905, an event that caused large numbers of Russians to question the legitimacy of the government. Investigate the responses of the government to the event and suggest how these responses affected public opinion.
3. Why was the mutiny of the battleship *Potemkin* such an important part of the Revolution of 1905?
4. Count Sergei Witte played an enormously important role in saving the Russian Empire from collapse in 1905. Discuss his activities in that year.
5. The Constitutional Democrats (or Kadets), mostly liberals, were a very important political party in 1905. What did the party hope to gain from the October Manifesto?
6. How did Nicholas II view the Revolution of 1905? The October Manifesto?

Research Suggestions

In addition to boldfaced terms, look under the entry for "The 1917 Russian Revolution" (#10). Search under **Bolsheviks, Mensheviks, Socialist Revolutionaries, Octobrists, V. I. Lenin,** and **Piotr Stolypin**.

SUGGESTED SOURCES

Primary Sources

Miliukov, Pavel. *Political Memoirs 1905–1917.* 1955. Ann Arbor: University of Michigan Press, 1967. Miliukov was one of the most important political figures in this period.

Trotsky, Leon. *1905.* 1922. New York: Random House, 1971. A brilliant Marxist analysis of the events by a prominent participant.

Witte, Sergei. *The Memoirs of Count Witte.* Garden City, N.Y.: Doubleday, Page. 1921. A fascinating discussion of the 1905 Revolution and many other topics by the man who was the most able governmental official in the reign of Nicholas II.

Secondary Sources

Ascher, Abraham. *The Revolution of 1905.* 2 vols. Stanford: Stanford University Press, 1988, 1992. The best discussion of the Revolution of 1905 available.

Engelstein, Laura. *Moscow, 1905: Working-Class Organization and Political Conflict.* Stanford: Stanford University Press, 1982. An important book on a major center of revolutionary politics in 1905.

Ferro, Marc. *Nicholas II: The Last of the Tsars.* New York: Oxford University Press, 1993. An excellent recent study of Nicholas.

Galai, Shmuel. *The Liberation Movement in Russia, 1900–1905.* Cambridge: Cambridge University Press, 1973. A good analysis of the important liberal movements active before the Revolution of 1905.

Harcave, Sidney. *First Blood: The Russian Revolution of 1905.* New York: Macmillan, 1964. A solid history of the event. A good starting point for further work.

Hough, Richard. *The Potemkin Mutiny.* Annapolis, Md.: Naval Institute Press, 1996. A fine discussion of a central event in 1905.

Manning, Roberta Thompson. *The Crisis of the Old Order in Russia: Gentry and Government.* Princeton: Princeton University Press, 1982. A very important discussion of the failure of reform elements in the tsarist government.

Mehlinger, Howard D., and John M. Thompson. *Count Witte and the Tsarist Government in the 1905 Revolution.* Bloomington: Indiana University Press, 1972. A helpful discussion of the crucial role played by Count Sergei Witte in the events of 1905.

Morgan, Anne. "Revolution of 1905 in Russia." *The Modern Encyclopedia of Russian and Soviet History,* vol. 31, pp. 57–69. Gulf Breeze, Fla.:

Academic International Press, 1983. An up-to-date and concise overview.

Riha, Thomas. *A Russian European: Paul Miliukov in Russian Politics.* Notre Dame, Ind.: University of Notre Dame Press, 1969. A useful political biography of a major political actor.

Sablinsky, Walter. *The Road to Bloody Sunday: Father Gapon and the St. Petersburg Massacre of 1905.* Princeton: Princeton University Press, 1976. The definitive account of this event.

Suhr, Gerald D. *1905 in St. Petersburg: Labor, Society, and Revolution.* Stanford: Stanford University Press, 1989. A close look at the revolution in Imperial Russia's most important city.

Weinberg, Robert. *The Revolution of 1905 in Odessa: Blood on the Steps.* Bloomington: Indiana University Press, 1993. A careful study of 1905 in an important provincial city.

3. PABLO PICASSO AND CUBISM, 1907

In 1907 **Pablo Picasso** painted one of his most famous paintings, *Les Demoiselles d'Avignon*. Although the painting was not widely appreciated at the time or even seen by that many people before Picasso rolled up the canvas and put it away, it nonetheless marked the beginnings of **Cubism**, a seminal form of modern art. It also marked a new stage in the career of the man who became the twentieth century's best-known artist.

Picasso was born in Spain in 1881. He studied first with his father, a professor of drawing. In the 1890s he studied in Barcelona, but in 1899 broke with his art school training. The following year Picasso came to Paris to see the 1900 World's Fair and to become acquainted with what was then regarded as the center of the art world.

Over the next several years, Picasso often returned to Spain, but he began to regard Paris as his home. He went through a **Blue Period** between 1901 and 1904, so called because of the colors he used in his paintings and also because of his response to the suicide of a good friend. The next period, the **Rose Period** from 1904 to 1905, corresponded with his involvement with **Fernande Olivier** and the use of entirely different colors.

In the meantime, Picasso had become the center of a circle of friends including the French poet **Guillaume Apollinaire** and the

American writer **Gertrude Stein**. Also, like many painters at this time, he increasingly was influenced by the paintings of **Paul Cézanne**. He remained, however, deeply influenced by Iberian art, particularly the great Spanish painter **El Greco** and primitive Iberian sculptures. Picasso's *Portrait de Gertrude Stein* (1906) marked the rapid progress he had made in his first few years in Paris.

At the end of 1906, Picasso began working on *Les Demoiselles d'Avignon*, which he finished the next year. It was a radical departure in style. He no longer attempted to provide an illusion of depth. Instead, he used harsh, angular planes in his composition. The faces of the women in the painting took on a masklike quality. The painting marked the beginnings of Cubism, which emphasized the use of geometric forms and often presented subjects from several angles at once.

Over the next several years, Picasso and **Georges Braque** experimented with different forms of Cubism. Their work was probably the most radical of several efforts to break with ideas about art from the late nineteenth century. Picasso himself enjoyed a long and amazingly productive career, reinventing himself again and again and establishing his reputation as the artistic genius of the century.

Suggestions for Term Papers

1. Investigate Picasso's activities in Barcelona before he visited Paris for the first time in 1900.

2. Trace Picasso's activities in his Blue Period and his Rose Period. How significant were these periods for his artistic development?

3. Why had Cézanne become such a compelling influence early in the twentieth century not only for Picasso but for virtually all artists working in Paris? Begin with H. W. Janson's *History of Art* (see Suggested Sources).

4. Write a paper on Henri Matisse, a painter who was also emerging as a major figure in the art world in this period. Begin with H. W. Janson's *History of Art* (see Suggested Sources).

5. Read Gertrude Stein's study of Picasso (see Suggested Sources) and comment on her approach to his art.

6. What did Georges Braque contribute to the development of Cub-

ism as an artistic movement? Begin with H. W. Janson's *History of Art* (see Suggested Sources).

Research Suggestions

In addition to the boldfaced items, search under **Paul Gauguin, Post-Impressionists, Henri de Toulouse-Lautrec, Henri Matisse, The Fauvres**, and the **1905 Salon d'Automne**.

SUGGESTED SOURCES

Primary Sources

McCully, Marilyn, ed. *A Picasso Anthology: Documents, Criticism, Reminiscences.* Princeton: Princeton University Press, 1997. A very useful collection of material.

Stein, Gertrude. *Picasso.* London: B. T. Batsford, 1938. Stein was a good friend, and she and her brother bought many of Picasso's paintings. The book contains her reflections on him and his work.

Secondary Sources

Daix, Pierre, and Georges Boudaille, with the collaboration of Joan Rosselet. *Picasso: The Blue and Rose Periods; A Catalogue Raisonné of the Paintings, 1900–1906.* Greenwich, Conn.: New York Graphic Society, 1967. A revision of the original French version. An exhaustive and beautifully illustrated examination of Picasso's early career.

Faerna, Jose Maria, ed. *Picasso.* New York: Harry N. Abrams, 1995. Part of the Great Modern Masters series. An introduction to Picasso's work by way of more than sixty plates.

Fitzgerald, Michael C. *Making Modernism: Picasso and the Creation of the Market for Twentieth-Century Art.* New York: Farrar, Straus and Giroux, 1995. Fitzgerald examines Picasso as a businessman, focusing on the interwar period. He contends that Picasso was always pragmatic about making money.

Gardner, Howard. *Creating Minds: An Anatomy of Creativity Seen Through the Lives of Freud, Einstein, Picasso, Stravinsky, Eliot, Graham and Gandhi.* New York: Basic Books, 1994. A fascinating attempt to analyze creativity by examining a number of extraordinary figures from the twentieth century, including Picasso.

Janson, H. W., and Anthony F. Janson, *History of Art*, 5th ed., rev. New York: Harry N. Abrams. Widely regarded as the best single-volume history. A good place to begin a research project.

McCully, Marilyn, ed. *Picasso: The Early Years, 1892–1906.* Boston: Boston Museum of Fine Arts, 1997. A useful collection of essays on various aspects of Picasso's early career and a large assortment of illustrations of his works.

O'Brian, Patrick. *Pablo Ruiz Picasso: A Biography.* New York: G. P. Putnam's Sons, 1976. A readable, dependable single-volume biography.

Richardson, John. "Picasso's Apocalyptic Whorehouse." *New York Review of Books* 34, no. 2 (23 April 1987): 40–47. Richardson stresses the Spanish roots of *Les Demoiselles d'Avignon* and Cubism, especially the influence of El Greco.

Richardson, John, with the collaboration of Marilyn McCully. *A Life of Picasso, 1881–1906.* Vol. 1. New York: Random House, 1991. Now the best biography of Picasso available. Vol. 1 covers Picasso's life up to the point where he begins work on *Les Demoiselles d'Avignon.*

———. *A Life of Picasso, 1907–1917: The Painter of Modern Life.* Vol. 2. New York: Random House, 1996. Vol. 2 covers the painting of *Les Demoiselles d'Avignon* and Picasso's Cubist period.

Rubin, William S., Helene Seckel, and Judith Cousins. *Les Demoiselles d'Avignon.* New York: Museum of Modern Art, 1994. The definitive study of Picasso's famous painting.

World Wide Web

"Museo Picasso Virtual." *http://www.tamu.edu/mocl/picasso.* A very fine Web site with an extensive biography, bibliography, and many other features.

4. THE MEXICAN REVOLUTION, 1910–1920

The first major revolution of the twentieth century, the Mexican Revolution spanned the decade from 1910 to 1920. Its roots lay in the rapid economic and social changes during the 1890s and the first part of the twentieth century under **Porfirio Díaz**. The more immediate cause was Díaz's plan to run for president again in 1910. Díaz had been in power since 1876. **Francisco Madero**, a liberal, began the revolution by publishing the **Plan of San Luis Potosí**.

Initially, Madero enjoyed wide backing, not only from members of provincial elites like himself and from liberal intellectuals but also from cowboys, farmers, and miners from the north and agrarian rebels in the south like **Emiliano Zapata**, who led a movement to recover communal lands. Zapata published his own plan, the **Plan of Ayala**, in 1911. Díaz left the country in 1911 and Madero became president.

With the help of the U.S. ambassador to Mexico, **Victoriano Huerta** overthrew Madero in 1913. Madero was later assassinated. Huerta was mainly an opportunist, and his seizure of power provoked a civil war. He was opposed by Zapata and also by **Pancho Villa**, an important leader of popular forces from the north. Even more important was **Venustiano Carranza**, the leader of the Constitutionalist forces. Carranza enjoyed the help of **Alvaro Obregón**, who contributed much to the military success of the Constitutionalists. Obregón was a careful student of the new patterns of warfare being developed in Europe in World War I.

In 1914, at the **Convention of Aguascalientes**, Villa and Zapata met with representatives of Carranza and Obregón, but they could find no basis for a lasting agreement. In 1915 Carranza used his control of export earnings to rebuild his army. Obregón led the army to victory over Villa. In 1916–1917 another meeting resulted in the **Constitution of 1917**. Zapata and Villa were not represented, but Obregón was able to place in the constitution clauses that later furnished a basis for land reform, for labor rights, and for national control of subsoil resources. Carranza served as president between 1917 and 1920.

By 1920 the revolution was over and most of the major figures had met violent deaths. Over the next two decades, however, the revolution took on institutional forms that included a near-monopoly of political life by the revolutionary party (the PRI since 1946). Only in the last few years have changes begun to appear in the system that was set in place by 1940.

Suggestions for Term Papers

1. During the last decade of Díaz's regime, many different forms of opposition appeared and attempted to find supporters. Investigate the activities of these oppositional groups, the forms their opposition took, and whether there were American connections.

2. Compare the Plan of San Luis Potosí and the Plan of Ayala.

3. Read a biography of Zapata (Womack's is the best—see Suggested Sources) and compare its presentation of Zapata with that of *Viva*

Zapata!, the film directed by Elia Kazan with a script by the novelist John Steinbeck.

4. What did Pancho Villa hope to achieve in the Mexican Revolution?

5. The United States played a very important role in the Mexican Revolution, intervening on a number of occasions. Review American involvement and draw conclusions about why the United States paid so much attention to events in Mexico in this period. John Mason Hart's *Revolutionary Mexico* (see Suggested Sources) contains much useful information on this topic.

6. The Mexican Revolution was a costly and traumatic event for Mexicans. What are some of the reasons they participated in it? (Azuela's *The Underdogs* will be helpful in this regard—see Suggested Sources.)

Research Suggestions

In addition to the boldfaced items, look under the entries for "The Revolution of 1905 in Russia" (#2) and "The 1911 Revolution in China" (#5). Search under **Porfiriato** (1876–1910), **Pascual Orozco, Cristero Rebellion** (1926–1929), and **Lazaro Cardenas** (president, 1934–1940).

SUGGESTED SOURCES

Primary Sources

Guzman, Martin Luis. *The Eagle and the Serpent*. Gloucester, Mass.: Peter Smith, 1969. A firsthand account by a young Mexican liberal who began as a supporter of Francisco Madero and after his assassination became associated with Pancho Villa.

Reed, John. *Insurgent Mexico*. New York: International Publishers, 1994. First published in 1914. Classic reporting from a famous American journalist whose specialty was revolution.

Wilkie, James W., and Albert L. Michaels, eds. *Revolution in Mexico: Years of Upheaval, 1910–1940*. Tucson: University of Arizona Press, 1984. First published by Knopf, 1969. A very useful anthology containing many documents and reports by journalists as well as some secondary source material.

Secondary Sources

Azuela, Mariano. *The Underdogs*. Translated by E. Munguia, Jr. New York: New American Library, 1962. A short novel. Helpful in understanding the motives of participants in the revolution.

Brunk, Samuel. *Emiliano Zapata: Revolution and Betrayal in Mexico*. Albuquerque: University of New Mexico Press, 1995. A recent biography of one of the most important leaders in the Mexican Revolution.

Cockcroft, James. *Intellectual Precursors of the Mexican Revolution, 1900–1913*. Austin: University of Texas Press, 1968. The standard work on the liberal opposition to Porfirio Díaz.

Cumberland, Charles C. *Mexican Revolution: Genesis under Madero*. Austin: University of Texas Press, 1952. A dependable account of the beginnings of the Mexican Revolution.

Dunn, John. *Modern Revolutions: An Introduction to the Analysis of a Political Phenomenon*. Cambridge: Cambridge University Press, 1972. The chapter on the Mexican Revolution is well worth reading.

Fuentes, Carlos. *The Death of Artemio Cruz*. Translated by Alfred MacAdam. New York: Farrar, Straus and Giroux, 1991. A wonderful novel that manages to convey some of the ways in which the Mexican Revolution has echoed through the history of Mexico in the twentieth century.

Hall, Linda. *Alvaro Obregón: Power and Revolution in Mexico, 1911–1920*. College Station: Texas A&M University Press, 1981. A good biographical study of one of the most important figures in the Mexican Revolution.

Hart, John Mason. *Revolutionary Mexico: The Coming and Process of the Mexican Revolution*. Berkeley: University of California Press, 1987. An excellent history of the Mexican Revolution that places it in the context of Mexican history and also compares it in very useful ways with events in early twentieth-century Russia, China, and Iran.

Katz, Friedrich. *The Life and Times of Pancho Villa*. Stanford: Stanford University Press, 1998. A highly regarded study of a central figure in the Mexican Revolution, one usually shrouded in legend and myth.

Knight, Alan. *The Mexican Revolution*. 2 vols. London: Cambridge University Press, 1986. A major study.

Meyer, Michael C., William L. Sherman, and Susan M. Deeds. *The Course of Mexican History*. 6th ed. New York: Oxford University Press, 1998. Among other things, offers a fine introduction to the Mexican Revolution.

Niemeyer, Victor E. *Revolution at Querétaro: The Mexican Constitutional*

Convention of 1916–1917. Austin: University of Texas Press, 1974. The best book on this important topic.

Quirk, Robert H. *An Affair of Honor: Woodrow Wilson and the Occupation of Veracruz.* New York: W. W. Norton, 1962. An excellent study of one of the most important interventions by the United States in the Mexican Revolution.

Richmond, Douglas. *Venustiano Carranza's Nationalist Struggle, 1893– 1920.* Lincoln: University of Nebraska Press, 1983. A useful study of a central figure in the Mexican Revolution.

Ross, Stanley R. *Francisco I. Madero, Apostle of Mexican Democracy.* New York: Columbia University Press, 1955. A useful biography of Madero.

Ruiz, Ramon E. *The Great Rebellion: Mexico, 1905–1924.* New York: W. W. Norton, 1980. An important survey based on a lifetime of research.

Tutino, John. *From Insurrection to Revolution in Mexico: Social Bases of Agrarian Violence, 1750–1940.* Princeton: Princeton University Press, 1986. A careful study of an important factor in the Mexican Revolution.

Viva Zapata! [videotape]. Livonia, Mich.: Key Video, a division of CBS/ Fox Video, 1987. 112 minutes. Directed by Elia Kazan, written by John Steinbeck, and starring Marlon Brando. An interesting but somewhat Hollywoodish effort to present the life of Zapata.

Womack, John, Jr. *Zapata and the Mexican Revolution.* New York: Knopf, 1969. A superb biography of Zapata.

World Wide Web

"The Mexican Revolution." *http://northcoast.com/~spdtom/rev.html.* A well-organized Web site featuring a time line, bibliography, capsule biographies, and many links.

5. THE 1911 REVOLUTION IN CHINA

In the early twentieth century the **Qing dynasty** struggled to preserve its empire in China. Nineteenth-century attempts to match the military strength of Western nations had been mostly unsuccessful. In 1900 several European nations and Japan combined to defeat the so-called **Boxer Rebellion**, a movement directed against missionaries and foreign businessmen.

After the Boxer Rebellion, the Qing government began several reforms. In order to encourage education along Western lines it ended the examination system based on the Confucian classics and moved toward the establishment of a constitutional system of government. Additionally, it founded the **New Army**, which was organized and equipped along Western lines.

Despite reform efforts, mass protests continued among the urban and rural poor, and revolutionaries organized to overthrow the regime. The most prominent revolutionary was **Sun Yat-sen**, educated in Guangzhou and Hong Kong as a doctor. Sun advanced what he termed the **"Three People's Principles"**: nationalism, democracy, and "people's livelihood," a vaguely socialist approach to the improvement of living standards. Sun's party, the **Revolutionary Alliance (Tongmeng hui)**, had organized several revolutions before 1911, but all had been suppressed.

The 1911 Revolution began by accident with a bomb explosion in Hankou, Hubei province. The revolutionaries realized that the government officials investigating the explosion would soon track them down, so they acted first by seizing nearby Wuhan on 10 October 1911. The revolution quickly spread to other parts of southern China, then north. New Army officers and provincial elites joined the revolution. The Qing counterattacked, but foreign powers, worried about trade, wanted a cease-fire. After the cease-fire in December, a provisional government was established and Sun was elected president. The Qing emperor abdicated on 12 February 1912. Sun soon turned the presidency over to **Yuan Shikai**, a powerful Qing official who had negotiated the abdication of the emperor.

Yuan declared himself emperor in 1915, but China was already slipping into warlordism, a situation where local or provincial military leaders ruled without regard to the national government. In 1916 Yuan died, but it took several more years for Sun and his party, now called the **Guomindang**, to become powerful enough to begin thinking about uniting China once again.

Suggestions for Term Papers

1. Investigate the Boxer Rebellion, the methods used, and what those involved hoped to accomplish, and evaluate its significance for the history of China in the early twentieth century.

2. One of the most important contemporaries of Sun Yat-sen was Liang Qichao, a nationalist and reformer. Trace his political activ-

ities in the 1890s and the first part of the twentieth century and compare them with those of Sun.

3. Review the efforts of the Qing dynasty between the end of the Boxer Rebellion and the start of the 1911 Revolution to bring change to China. Why did these efforts fail?

4. Read Sun Yat-sen's writings on the "Three People's Principles." What did he appear to want for China, and why?

5. Examine Yuan Shikai's career before and after the 1911 Revolution. How had he become powerful enough to emerge as the major figure in the aftermath of the 1911 Revolution? Why was he not able to rule China effectively as president?

6. After the 1911 Revolution China was ruled by a number of warlords, some with good intentions, others not. Find out more about one warlord and evaluate his time in power.

Research Suggestions

In addition to the boldfaced items, look under the entries for "The Revolution of 1905 in Russia" (#2), "The Mexican Revolution, 1910–1920" (#4), "The May 4th Movement in China, 1919" (#12), and "The Northern Expedition in China, 1926–1928" (#16). Search under **Kang Youwei** (*Book of the Great Community*), **Emperor Guangxu, Zou Rong** (*The Revolutionary Army*), **Qui Jin, Lu Xun**, and **Emperor Puyi** (*The Last Emperor*).

SUGGESTED SOURCES

Primary Sources

Schurmann, Franz, and Orville Schell, eds. *Republican China: Nationalism, War, and the Rise of Communism, 1911–1949*. Volume 2 of *The China Reader*. New York: Random House, 1967. Contains a few documents on the 1911 Revolution and the early Republic of China.

Teng, Ssu-yü and John K. Fairbank, eds. *China's Response to the West: A Documentary Survey, 1839–1923*. Cambridge, Mass.: Harvard University Press, 1954. A convenient source of several important documents.

Sun, Yat-sen. *Prescriptions for Saving China: Selected Writings of Sun Yat-sen*. Wei, Julie Lee, Ramon H. Myers, and Donald G. Gillin, eds.

Stanford: Hoover Institution, 1994. A useful collection of Sun's political writings.

Secondary Sources

Cohen, Paul A. *History in Three Keys: The Boxers as Event, Experience, and Myth*. New York: Columbia University Press, 1997. A very important study of the Boxer Rebellion.

Dunn, John. *Modern Revolutions: An Introduction to the Analysis of a Political Phenomenon*. Cambridge: Cambridge University Press, 1972. The chapter on China is a good introduction.

Esherick, Joseph W. *Reform and Revolution in China: The 1911 Revolution in Hunan and Hubei*. 2nd ed. Ann Arbor: University of Michigan Press, 1998. An investigation of the 1911 Revolution focused on two important centers of revolution.

Gasster, Michael. *Chinese Intellectuals and the Revolution of 1911: The Birth of Modern Chinese Radicalism*. Seattle: University of Washington Press, 1969. A good overview.

Gillin, Donald. *Warlord: Yen Hsi-shan in Shansi Province, 1911–1949*. Princeton: Princeton University Press, 1967. One of several fascinating studies of warlords.

Levenson, Joseph. *Liang Ch'i-ch'ao and the Mind of Modern China*. Cambridge, Mass.: Harvard University Press, 1953. A very useful study of the most influential spokesman for change before the 1911 Revolution.

MacKinnon, Stephen. *Power and Politics in Late Imperial China: Yuan Shi-Kai in Beijing and Tianjin, 1901–1908*. Berkeley: University of California Press, 1980. An investigation of the early activities of the most powerful figure to emerge from the 1911 Revolution.

Rankin, Mary. *Early Chinese Revolutionaries: Radical Intellectuals in Shanghai and Chekiang, 1902–1911*. Cambridge, Mass.: Harvard University Press, 1971. A scholarly study of key figures in the events leading up to the 1911 Revolution.

Rhoads, Edward. *China's Republican Revolution: The Case of Kwangtung, 1895–1913*. Cambridge, Mass.: Harvard University Press, 1975. Kwangtung was an important center of early revolutionary activity.

Schiffrin, Harold Z. *Sun Yat-sen and the Origins of the Chinese Revolution*. Berkeley: University of California Press, 1970. A useful introduction to Sun and his role in the 1911 Revolution.

Spence, Jonathan D. *The Gate of Heavenly Peace: The Chinese and Their Revolution, 1895–1980*. New York: Viking Press, 1981. A highly readable book that discusses revolution in twentieth-century China largely from the standpoint of writers. The early chapters contain much information on the 1911 Revolution and the period leading up to it.

————. *The Search for Modern China*. New York: W. W. Norton, 1990. A masterful survey of Chinese history since the late Ming dynasty. Chapters 11 and 12 provide a good introduction to the 1911 Revolution and the new republic.

Wilbur, C. Martin. *Sun Yat-sen, Frustrated Patriot*. New York: Columbia University Press, 1976. A useful study of Sun.

Wright, Mary C., ed. *China in Revolution: The First Phase, 1900–1913*. New Haven: Yale University Press, 1968. An important collection of essays on the 1911 Revolution.

Young, Ernest. *The Presidency of Yuan Shih-k'ai: Liberalism and Dictatorship in Early Republican China*. Ann Arbor: University of Michigan Press, 1977. A study of the most powerful figure after the 1911 Revolution.

6. THE SUFFRAGE MOVEMENT IN BRITAIN BEFORE WORLD WAR I, 1906–1914

In the nineteenth century British women gained many rights concerning property, education, and marriage. In terms of the vote, however, they could only vote locally. From 1906 to 1914, they campaigned vigorously for the vote in national elections.

Two groups dominated the British suffrage movement. One, the **National Union of Women's Suffrage Societies (NUWSS)**, led by **Millicent Garrett Fawcett**, favored the use of political means to gain the vote. The other, the **Women's Social and Political Union (WSPU)**, founded by **Emmeline Pankhurst** and her daughters **Christabel** and **Sylvia**, followed a more radical path. Working-class women also participated in the suffrage movement in large numbers.

Mrs. Pankhurst argued that men would only respond to threats to property and to violence. "The argument of the broken pane of glass is the most valuable argument in modern politics," she said in 1912. She and her daughters led suffragists in campaigns that featured parades, suffragists chaining themselves to the gates of Parliament, and acts of violence that included smashing plate-glass windows and slashing works of art. When arrested, suffragists staged hunger strikes. The authorities countered by using painful techniques to force-feed them.

The most dramatic moment of the campaign came on Derby Day, 31 May 1913, when a WSPU activist threw herself in front of the King's horse and was trampled to death.

World War I interrupted the suffrage movement. Both the Pankhursts and Millicent Garrett Fawcett devoted themselves to war work. They were rewarded with the extension of suffrage to women over the age of thirty in 1918 (women between twenty-one and thirty could not vote until 1928).

In Germany, where women also achieved the vote after World War I, the situation before the war was complicated. The women's movement within the **German Social Democratic Party (SPD)** subordinated work for the vote for women to the larger goal of the defeat of capitalism. Radicals within the mainstream women's movement created controversy by adopting causes such as the legalization of abortion.

In Russia, the women's movement was similarly divided between socialist women working for the overthrow of the tsarist government and middle-class women who pursued more modest demands. Russian women gained extensive rights after the war and the Revolution of 1917. The nature of the Soviet system, however, meant that many rights existed only on paper.

Suggestions for Term Papers

1. Investigate the life of Millicent Garrett Fawcett. What led her to become involved in the women's movement in Britain, and what factors enabled her to become the head of that movement?

2. Review the political atmosphere that prevailed in Britain between 1906 and 1914. On the basis of this review, present arguments for and against Emmeline Pankhurst's "argument of the broken [window] pane."

3. What arguments did the opponents, both men and women, use against the idea of women's suffrage? Why, in particular, would women oppose suffrage for women?

4. In both Germany and Russia, socialists strongly supported women's movements, yet insisted that women support the defeat of capitalism as the prerequisite to women's liberation. Report on the relationship in either Germany or Russia between the women's movement and socialism.

5. To what extent was the experience of World War I crucial in the decision in Britain to grant suffrage to women (see the book by Arthur Marwick in Suggested Sources)?

6. Read *Three Guineas* by Virginia Woolf (see Suggested Sources) and present a report on ways in which she extended the arguments put forth by women's movements in their campaigns for the vote.

Research Suggestions

In addition to boldfaced terms, look under the entries for "The Home Front in World War I, 1914–1918" (#9) and "The 1917 Russian Revolution" (#10). Search under **"Cat and Mouse Act"** (Britain), **Hubertine Auclert, Clara Zetkin, Lily Braun**, and **Alexandra Kollontai**.

SUGGESTED SOURCES

Primary Sources

Fawcett, Millicent Garrett. *What I Remember*. Westport, Conn.: Hyperion Press, 1976. Originally published in 1925. The story of the struggle for women's suffrage from a moderate perspective.

Pankhurst, Emmeline. *My Own Story*. New York: Source Book Press, 1970. Originally published in 1914. Mrs. Pankhurst's version of the suffrage campaign.

Woolf, Virginia. *Three Guineas*. New York: Harcourt, Brace and World, 1966. Originally published in 1938. Woolf argues that women should have the possibility of influencing all aspects of life. Merely voting is, in her opinion, insufficient.

Secondary Sources

Edmondson, Linda H. *Feminism in Russia, 1900–1917*. Stanford: Stanford University Press, 1984. A study of the middle-class women's movement in Russia.

Evans, Richard S. *The Feminists: Women's Emancipation Movements in Europe, America and Australasia, 1840–1920*. London: Croom Helm, 1977. A good introduction.

Harrison, Brian. *Separate Spheres: The Opposition to Women's Suffrage in Britain*. New York: Holmes and Meier, 1978. A useful study of the many who opposed suffrage for women.

Hause, Steven. *Hubertine Auclert: The French Suffragette*. New Haven: Yale University Press, 1987. The suffrage movement in France as viewed through one of its most important activists.

Kent, Susan Kingsley. *Sex and Suffrage in Britain, 1860–1914*. Princeton: Princeton University Press, 1987. A major study of the suffrage movement.

Liddington, Jill, and Jill Norris. *One Hand Tied Behind Us: The Rise of the Women's Suffrage Movement*. London: Virago, 1984. An important source of information on working women and the suffrage movement.

Mackenzie, Midge, ed. *Shoulder to Shoulder: A Documentary*. New York: Knopf, 1975. A very useful collection of documents related to the suffrage campaign.

Marwick, Arthur. *The Deluge: British Society and the First World War*. New York: W.W. Norton, 1965. Marwick sees the experience of World War I as fundamentally important in the decision to grant suffrage to women after the war.

Quataert, Jean H. *Reluctant Feminists in the German Social Democracy, 1885–1917*. Princeton: Princeton University Press, 1979. Feminism and socialism in Imperial Germany.

Stites, Richard. *The Women's Liberation Movement in Russia: Feminism, Nihilism, and Bolshevism, 1860–1930*. Princeton: Princeton University Press, 1978. An excellent book on the women's movement in Russia and socialism.

Tickner, Lisa. *The Spectacle of Women: Imagery of the Suffrage Campaign, 1907–14*. Chicago: University of Chicago Press, 1988. An original and insightful book. Tickner discusses the images generated by the suffrage movement, by its opponents, and by commentators.

7. THE BATTLE OF THE SOMME, 1916

By the summer of 1915 it was clear that World War I, the war between the **Allied Powers** (France, Great Britain, Italy, and Russia) and the **Central Powers** (Germany, Austria-Hungary, Bulgaria, and Turkey), would be long, especially on the **Western Front**. To break the stalemate both sides planned offensives for 1916. **General Erich von Falkenhayn**, the German chief of staff, selected the fortress system of **Verdun** in northeastern France as his target. The German plan aimed at drawing the French army into Verdun and bleeding it to death. Between February and August 1916, a horrific battle raged at Verdun, resulting in French losses of 315,000 and German losses of 282,000.

Meanwhile, in December 1915 France's **Marshal Joseph Joffre** met with Britain's **General Douglas Haig** to plan the Allied spring offensive. Unaware at that time of Falkenhayn's plans for Verdun, Joffre and Haig decided upon a July offensive in northwestern France where the British and French trenches met astride the **Somme River**. On 24 June 1916, British artillery erupted along an eighteen-mile front in a continuous eight-day barrage of more than 1.5 million shells that supposedly would obliterate the German trenches. On 1 July, 200,000 British and French soldiers clambered "over the top" of their trenches and crossed 500 yards of **no man's land** toward the eleven battle-hardened German divisions of General Fritz von Below. Immediately, things went terribly wrong for the untested all-volunteer **New British Army**. Despite the massive artillery barrage, the German trenches were not obliterated. Suddenly German machine gun squads appeared and took deadly aim at the exposed British infantry, weighted down with sixty pounds of equipment. The British soldiers who survived the German gunners and reached the German lines found that their wire cutters could not cut the German barbed wire. Hundreds caught on the wire were easy targets for German guns. Some British officers kicked soccer balls across no man's land to inspire their troops, but by sunset of 1 July, the British army suffered 57,470 casualties and counted 20,000 dead. Never in the history of the British army had there been such a terrible day.

The offensive ended on 18 November 1916. The British army lost 419,00 men, the French more than 204,000, and the Germans some 500,000. The Somme offensive was a murderous battle of attrition. The failure to break the German defenses and the conquest of only 125 square kilometers chilled enthusiasm for future offensive attacks and affirmed for many the value of defensive strategy for the next two years.

Suggestions for Term Papers

1. Read Wilfred Owen's famous poem "Dulce et Decorum Est." Investigate his experiences in World War I and write a paper analyzing the last two lines of the poem.

2. Compare John Keegan's chapter on the Somme in his *The Face of Battle* with parts 3 and 4 of *The Great War and the Shaping of the Twentieth Century* (see Suggested Sources).

3. Read Robert Graves's chapters on the Battle of the Somme in his *Good-Bye to All That* and present a report on his experiences in combat (see Suggested Sources).

4. Based on reading and viewing, draw a detailed, annotated plan for trenches of the kind British or French soldiers might have constructed. An alternative project would be the actual construction of a short section of a front-line trench.

5. In a research paper on the history of the machine-gun, discuss why Europeans were surprised at the way in which it changed the style of warfare in World War I.

6. Investigate the life of General Douglas Haig and evaluate his handling of the Somme campaign.

Research Suggestions

In addition to the boldfaced items, look under the entry for "The French Army Mutinies, 1917" (#8). Search under **World War I, Field Marshall Kitchener**, and **Field Marshall Paul von Hindenburg**.

SUGGESTED SOURCES

Primary Sources

Graves, Robert. *Good-Bye to All That*. New York: Doubleday, 1985. First published in 1929. Despite fictionalized parts, this memoir remains one of the most poignant accounts of the fighting.

Sassoon, Siegfried. *Memoirs of an Infantry Officer*. New York: Coward-McCann, 1930. One of many memoirs that illustrate the futility of the fighting and the bravery of the combatants.

Silkin, Jon, ed. *First World War Poetry*. New York: Viking Penguin, 1997. An excellent collection of poetry from the war.

Secondary Sources

De Groot, Gerard J. *Douglas Haig, 1861–1928*. London: Unwin Hyman, 1988. An accessible, recent full-length study.

Ferguson, Niall. *The Pity of War: Explaining World War I*. New York: Basic

Books, 1999. The most important reevaluation of Britain's role in World War I in fifty years.

Fussell, Paul. *The Great War and Modern Memory.* New York: Oxford University Press, 1975. An imaginative account of the "troglodyte world" of the trenches showing in great detail how the prose and poetry of World War I forever changed the English language.

The Great War and the Shaping of the Twentieth Century. [videorecording] A KCET/BBC co-production in association with the Imperial War Museum. Distributed by PBS Video, 1996. Excellent contemporary footage of the fighting on the Western Front together with insightful comments by British, American, and French historians.

Horne, Alistair. *Death of a Generation: Neuve Chapelle to Verdun and the Somme.* New York: American Heritage Press, 1970. A crisp introduction to the great battles of 1916. The photographs, maps, and artwork capture the horrific style of fighting.

Keegan, John. *The Face of Battle: A Study of Agincourt, Waterloo and the Somme.* New York: Random House, 1967. A masterly analysis of the battle that shows its significance for modern military history.

McDonald, Lyn. *Somme.* London: Michael Joseph, 1983. Based on the diaries of the men who fought in Lord Kitchener's New Army, this study includes large selections from soldiers' diaries in the text.

Middlebrook, Martin. *The First Day on the Somme, 1 July 1916.* New York: W. W. Norton, 1972. The best single source, complete with pictures, maps, and charts.

World Wide Web

"World War I: Trenches on the Web." *http://www.worldwar1.com*. Battlefield maps are one of the strengths of this site, and there are good photographs of the trenches.

8. THE FRENCH ARMY MUTINIES, 1917

By 1917 France had been at war for three years and had suffered 3 million casualties. **Marshal Joseph Joffre**, who led France through the first two years of World War I, was replaced late in 1916 by **General Georges Nivelle**. Brimming with confidence, Nivelle assured the **Allied Powers** (France, Great Britain, Italy, and Russia) that he could defeat the **Central Powers** (Germany, Austria-Hungary, Bulgaria, and Turkey) in a 1917 spring offensive aimed at the Chemin-des-Dames salient of the **Siegfried/Hindenburg line**.

Nivelle's plan called for a massive artillery barrage to pulverize the German trenches, followed by a quick, violent infantry assault. On 16 April 1917, some 120,000 French soldiers opened the offensive by advancing on an eighty-mile front. However, **General Erich von Ludendorff**, the German commander, had learned of Nivelle's plans and taken countermeasures. Immediately German aircraft and artillery targeted French artillery communication, thereby nullifying the accuracy of the artillery barrages. After crossing 1.5 miles of no man's land, the French infantry found the German outer defenses abandoned. Instead, Ludendorff had prepared hundreds of fortified machine-guns deployed to direct the French into "killing zones" where prepositioned German gunners inflicted murderous fire.

By 25 April the French had suffered 100,000 casualties. When Nivelle mercifully halted the offensive on 9 May, 30,000 French soldiers had been killed and more than 100,000 wounded. Starting on 17 April, "collective disorders" had broken out in rear echelon assembly areas. Initially, elements of the French 6th Army refused to follow their officers. Within days these "collective disorders" had spread to other units; by May more than 30,000 soldiers were refusing to follow orders.

Shaken by the extent of these mutinies, the government fired Nivelle and on 15 May named **General Philippe Pétain** commander-in-chief. Immediately Pétain assured his officers that there would be no more Nivelle-style offensives. The mutinies, which lasted until 14 July 1917, were the most serious threat to France since the German invasion of 1914. Military courts convicted 3,427 mutineers; 554 men received the death penalty, and 49 were executed. Official records of the mutinies were subsequently closed to the public for nearly fifty years.

Suggestions for Term Papers

1. As a defense attorney for one of the mutineers at a French court-martial, how would you argue the defense of your client?
2. View episode 5 of *The Great War and the Shaping of the Twentieth Century* (see Suggested Sources) and write a paper explaining the significance of the mutinies.
3. Compare the mutinies in the Russian army in 1917 with those in the French army and explain why the French mutinies failed to result in political upheaval.

4. Investigate General Philippe Pétain's policies for improving the morale of the French army after the mutinies and assess Pétain's role in stopping the mutinies.

5. The British and the German armies also experienced problems in 1917, although not on the same scale as the French and the Russian armies. Review the situation in either the British or the German army and discuss reasons why their difficulties were not as severe as those of the French or the Russians.

6. General Pétain emerged from World War I as a great hero for the French. In the terrible defeat of 1940 in World War II, France again turned to Maréchal Pétain. Evaluate his efforts during the war in the government of Vichy France.

Research Suggestions

In addition to the boldfaced items, look under the entries for "The Battle of the Somme, 1916" (#7), "The Home Front in World War I, 1914–1918" (#9), and "The 1917 Russian Revolution" (#10).

SUGGESTED SOURCES

Primary Sources

Cru, Jean Norton. *War Books: A Study in Historical Criticism.* Translated by Stanley J. Pincetl. San Diego: San Diego State University Press, 1988. A good collection of French soldiers' eyewitness accounts of the fighting on the Western Front, particularly in 1917.

Pedroncini, Guy. *Les Mutineries de 1917.* Paris: Presses Universitaires de France, 1967. Although this is a secondary account, the author includes extensive quotes from heretofore sealed French archives. He also includes a helpful set of maps showing the outbreaks of the mutinies.

Spears, Edward. *Two Men Who Saved France: Pétain and de Gaulle.* New York: Stein and Day, 1966. In 1926 General Pétain gave Spears his recollections of the mutinies. These have been translated and are printed here as "A Crisis of Morale in the French Nation at War by General Pétain."

Secondary Sources

Atkin, Nicholas. *Pétain.* London: Longman, 1997. A reliable biography with helpful bibliographical leads.

The Great War and the Shaping of the Twentieth Century. [videorecording] A KCET/BBC co-production in association with the Imperial War Museum. Distributed by PBS Video, 1996. Excellent contemporary footage of the Verdun sector together with insightful comments by British, American, and French historians.

Keegan, John. *The First World War.* New York: Alfred L. Knopf, 1999. A comprehensive and well written account of World War I.

Smith, Leonard V. *Between Mutiny and Obedience: The Case of the French Fifth Infantry Division During World War I.* Princeton: Princeton University Press, 1994. The most authoritative English language account, incorporating Pedroncini's arguments as well as the author's important research from the French Army Archives.

Szaluta, Jacques. "Marshall Pétain and the French Army Mutiny of 1917: A Study in Military Leadership and Political Personality." *Third Republic/Troisième République* 6 (1978): 181–210. A good overview of the mutinies stressing Pétain's calming influence in the summer of 1917.

Watt, Richard. *Dare Call It Treason.* New York: Simon and Schuster, 1963. A well-written though dated account that could not incorporate the research of Guy Pedroncini's *Les Mutineries de 1917* (1967).

World Wide Web

"The Second Battle of the Marne River." *http://perso.club-internet.fr/ batmarn2.* Good links to other sites.

"World War I: Trenches on the Web." *http.//www.worldwar1.com.* Battlefield maps are one of the strengths of this site, and there are good photographs of the trenches.

9. THE HOME FRONT IN WORLD WAR I, 1914–1918

World War I ushered in a century of **total war**, a form of warfare that increasingly blurred the distinction between soldiers at the battlefront and civilians at the home front. By the end of the war in 1918 the patterns of daily life at home had changed forever. The staggering losses of men and material had forced all belligerents to adopt conscription, rationing, and economic planning. In addition to putting men into uniform, in Germany conscription also meant **obligatory labor service** for all men between the ages of seventeen and sixty. But these measures were not enough to meet demands. In Britain, France, and Germany, women joined the work force in record numbers. The labor force at **Krupp**, Germany's premier munitions maker, was nearly 40 percent female in 1916, and in Britain more than 2 million women were in the labor force.

By 1916 France and Germany had issued 67 million people **ration cards**, limiting their consumption of meat, sugar, bread, and fuel. German bakers sold "war bread" made from wheat mixed with potatoes. French workers were asked to give up meat two days a week and forgo pastry one day a week. Britain did not issue ration cards, but the government imposed voluntary rationing of butter and controlled the sale of sugar. Wartime pressures also convinced the British government to regulate closely the hours pubs could remain open. "Queuing" became the new word for waiting in line for goods and services in wartime Britain. Food scarcities on the home front spiked mortality rates. Civilian death rates in 1918 were 37 percent higher than pre-1914 rates, and the European birth rate in 1918 was 40 percent below that of 1914. In Russia, Austria-Hungary, Turkey, Serbia, and Bulgaria, home front conditions were much worse; bread riots in Russia in 1917 triggered the **Russian Revolution** and the eventual exit of Russia from the war.

If the feminization of the work force was the most visible change on the home front during World War I, two other wartime experiences helped to shape the postwar world. First, to meet wartime demands, governments grew enormously. France added 291 new **war commissions** to oversee wartime production, while Germany employed 4,000 bureaucrats just to regulate foreign commerce. Second, all governments encouraged the growth of large-scale businesses. Companies such as **I. G. Farben** in Germany, **Vickers** in England, and **Renault** in France not only provided weapons for the war, but now became the principal manufacturing centers for peacetime production, employing thousands of workers in the postwar world.

Suggestions for Term Papers

1. Research the ration system for civilians used in World War I. Many nutritionists believe reduced rations actually resulted in a healthier diet. Agree or disagree, providing reasons for your position.
2. The opening and closing hours of English pubs, established dur-

ing the war, extended well into the 1990s. Why did the British government continue these regulations? What are the closing hours of pubs today?

3. "Queuing" is but one reminder of words associated with the home front that continue to be used today. Use Paul Fussell's *The Great War and Modern Memory* (see Suggested Sources) and other sources to write a paper on ways in which World War I changed the English language.

4. Investigate the role of women in World War I. What were the most significant political and social consequences of the feminization of work during the war?

5. Trace the development of one of the large World War I arms manufacturers such as Krupp, Vickers, I.G. Farben or Renault. Use Gerd Hardach, *The First World War, 1914–1918* and William Manchester, *The Arms of Krupp: 1587–1968* (see Suggested Sources).

6. Read Vera Brittain's *Testament of Youth* (see Suggested Sources) and write an essay on how she viewed life in England during the war.

Research Suggestions

In addition to the boldfaced items, look under the entries for "The Suffrage Movement in Britain Before World War I, 1906–1914" (#6), "The Battle of the Somme, 1916" (#7), and "The 1917 Russian Revolution" (#10). Search under **labor unions, women's rights**, and **pacifism**.

SUGGESTED SOURCES

Primary Sources

Brittain, Vera. *Testament of Youth: An Autobiographical Study of the Years 1900–1925*. New York: Macmillan, 1933. A most readable account of the home front in England.

Carlotti, François. "World War I: A Frenchman's Recollections." *American Scholar* 57 (Spring 1988): 283–89. A vivid memoir of a little French boy living in wartime France.

Secondary Sources

Becker, Jean-Jacques. *The Great War and the French People*. Translated by Arnold Pomerans. Dover, N.H.: Berg, 1985. The most complete account of the French home front.

Fussell, Paul. *The Great War and Modern Memory*. New York: Oxford University Press, 1975. An imaginative account of how the prose and poetry of World War I forever changed the English language.

The Great War and the Shaping of the Twentieth Century. [videorecording] A KCET/BBC co-production in association with the Imperial War Museum. Distributed by PBS Video, 1996. Includes very good contemporary footage of everyday life for civilians during the war.

Hardach, Gerd. *The First World War, 1914–1918*. Berkeley: University of California Press, 1977. A solid economic analysis that is particularly good on the German home front.

Kochka, Jürgen. "The First World War and the 'Mittlestand': German Artisans and White Collar Workers." *Journal of Contemporary History* 8 (1973): 101–24. A good portrayal of how middle-class Germans were affected by the war.

Manchester, William. *The Arms of Krupp: 1587–1968*. Boston: Little, Brown, 1968. A well written study of Germany's leading arms manufacturer.

Marwick, Arthur. *The Deluge: British Society and the First World War*. Boston: Little, Brown, 1965. A good starting point for the British home front.

Williams, John. *The Other Battleground: The Home Fronts: Britain, France and Germany, 1914–1918*. Chicago: Henry Regnery, 1972. A solid account for Britain and France.

10. THE 1917 RUSSIAN REVOLUTION

The year 1917 was an eventful one in Russian and world history. The **February Revolution** (which took place in February according to the calendar then in use in Russia, but in March according to the calendar in use in the West) ended the **Romanov** dynasty. The **October** or **Bolshevik Revolution** brought **V. I. Lenin** and his party to power.

The collapse of the Russian Empire in World War I led to the February Revolution. Russia, battered by defeats, was close to economic disintegration early in 1917. Large numbers of people thronged the streets of Petrograd (St. Petersburg) beginning on 23 February. Over the next few days, the crowds grew larger. Eventually the soldiers sent to control the crowds made common cause with them.

A **Provisional Government**, led by **Prince Georgy Lvov**, an **Octobrist**, formed at the end of February. Its most influential members were **Alexander Guchkov**, minister of war and also an Octobrist, and **Paul Miliukov**, foreign minister and a **Constitutional Democrat (Kadet)**. At the same time, the **Petrograd Soviet of Soldiers and Workers** appeared. People spoke of **"dual power,"** the idea that the Soviet represented public opinion and therefore had a great deal of leverage on the Provisional Government.

In the first heady months of freedom, the Provisional Government overestimated the patience of the average Russian and insisted on continuing the war effort. This required postponing vital decisions on the form of government and on land reform. Failure to end Russia's participation in the war and to resolve vital questions doomed the government.

For several months after the February Revolution, however, the Provisional Government maintained power in Russia. **Alexander Kerensky**, a moderate socialist, quickly emerged as the most powerful figure in the government, becoming prime minister in the summer of 1917. Kerensky's main challenger was Lenin. When Lenin returned to Russia from Switzerland in April, he set out in the **April Theses** a position that marked his party, the **Bolsheviks**, off from all other political parties in Russia. He called boldly for a peace without annexations or indemnities, land for the peasants, and all power to the Soviets.

By the fall of 1917 Lenin believed conditions were ripe for revolution in Russia. The **Central Committee (CC)** of the Bolsheviks was reluctant to take action, but Lenin eventually persuaded them to subscribe to the idea of revolution. **Leon Trotsky**, by then an influential figure in the Petrograd Soviet, made preparations to block any attempts the Provisional Government might make to destroy the revolution. **Red Guard** units, workers' militias, and soldiers and sailors in the area overthrew the Provisional Government in October when it appeared it was beginning a counterrevolution. The **Second All-Russian Congress of Soviets**, then meeting in Petrograd, approved the formation of a government by the Bolsheviks, the only party at that time prepared to take power. The seizure of power was accomplished with relatively little bloodshed, but the civil war that followed would be bloody and cruel. The Soviet Union emerged victorious in 1921 with fateful consequences for world history in the twentieth century.

Suggestions for Term Papers

1. Investigate the origins of the February Revolution. You may wish to look at long-term factors such as Russia's participation in World War I and difficulties in supplying the army, or you may prefer to focus on the events of the February Revolution itself.

2. Paul Miliukov, the foreign minister, wanted to achieve the war aims of the tsarist government. To what extent did his efforts to achieve these aims contribute to the end of the first Provisional Government?

3. Lenin returned to Russia from exile in Switzerland courtesy of the German government. Why were the Germans willing to help Lenin return to Russia, and what were his motives in accepting German help and money?

4. For much of 1917, Kerensky seemed to be the man of the hour. Evaluate his performance as prime minister and discuss why he fell from power so quickly and decisively in October.

5. In later years, Josif Stalin presented himself as Lenin's indispensable right-hand man in the events of 1917. What was his actual role?

6. It was often said that there would not have been an October Revolution without Lenin. Read about Trotsky's activities in 1917 and determine whether one might say the same about Trotsky.

Research Suggestions

In addition to boldfaced items, look under the entry for "The Revolution of 1905 in Russia" (#2). Search under **Nicholas II, Rasputin, Mikhail Rodzianko, Fourth Duma, Mensheviks, Socialist Revolutionaries, July Days, Josif Stalin**, and **Winter Palace**.

SUGGESTED SOURCES

Primary Sources

Browder, R. P., and A. F. Kerensky, eds. *The Russian Provisional Government, 1917.* 3 vols. Stanford: Stanford University Press, 1961. An excellent source of documents on 1917.

Reed, John. *Ten Days that Shook the World.* New York: Viking Press, 1990. First published in 1919. A classic although not always accurate account of 1917.

Steinberg, Mark D., and Vladimir M. Khrustakev, eds. *The Fall of the Romanovs: Political Dreams and Personal Struggles in a Time of Revolution.* New Haven: Yale University Press, 1995. An excellent collection of documents made available after the collapse of the Soviet Union in 1991.

Sukhanov, Nikolai N. *The Russian Revolution, 1917: A Personal Record.* 1922. 2 vols. New York: Oxford University Press, 1955. A classic memoir of 1917 by a man who seemed to have been nearly everywhere.

Trotsky, Leon. *The History of the Russian Revolution.* 3 vols. New York: Simon and Schuster, 1932. A fascinating version of the history of the revolution by one of its most prominent actors.

Secondary Sources

Daniels, Robert V. *Red October: The Bolshevik Revolution of 1917.* New York: Scribner, 1967. An excellent discussion of the October Revolution.

Deutscher, Isaac. *The Prophet Armed: Trotsky, 1879–1921.* New York: Oxford University Press. 1954. The first of three volumes on Trotsky by a major Marxist historian. Still probably the best single book on Trotsky.

Elwood, Ralph C. "Bolshevik Revolution of 1917." *The Modern Encyclopedia of Russian and Soviet History*, vol. 5, pp. 85–93. Gulf Breeze, Fla.: Academic International Press, 1977. A useful brief discussion of the October Revolution.

Ferro, Marc. *October 1917: A Social History of the Russian Revolution.* Boston: Routledge and Kegan Paul, 1980. A readable and solid history by a leading French historian.

———. *The Russian Revolution of February 1917.* Englewood Cliffs, N.J.: Prentice-Hall, 1972. Also readable and useful.

Figes, Orlando. *A People's Tragedy: A History of the Russian Revolution.* New York: Viking, 1996. A well-written narrative history.

Fitzpatrick, Sheila. *The Russian Revolution*. 2nd ed. New York: Oxford University Press, 1994. An excellent introduction that covers not only 1917 but also the decades of the 1920s and 1930s.

Keep, John L.H. *The Russian Revolution: A Study in Mass Mobilization*. New York: W. W. Norton, 1976. One of the few books that looks at 1917 outside of Petrograd and Moscow.

Koenker, Diane. *Moscow Workers and the 1917 Revolution*. Princeton: Princeton University Press, 1981. One of the best of several studies that look at the working class in 1917.

Pipes, Richard. *A Concise History of the Russian Revolution*. New York: Knopf, 1995. An up-to-date and well-informed study. Pipes is very critical of Lenin and the Bolsheviks.

Rabinowitch, Alexander. *The Bolsheviks Come to Power: The Revolution of 1917 in Petrograd*. New York: W. W. Norton, 1976. An excellent study of October 1917.

————. *Prelude to Revolution: The Petrograd Bolsheviks and the July 1917 Uprising*. Bloomington: Indiana University Press, 1968. An important book on an event that usually gets little attention.

Skinner, Frederick W. "February Revolution of 1917." *The Modern Encyclopedia of Russian and Soviet History*, vol. 11, pp. 67–74. Gulf Breeze, Fla.: Academic International Press, 1979. A fine overview of the February Revolution.

Stockdale, Melissa Kirshke. *Paul Miliukov and the Quest for a Liberal Russia, 1880–1918*. Ithaca, N.Y.: Cornell University Press, 1996. A recent political biography of one of the most important figures in the first part of 1917.

Ulam, Adam B. *The Bolsheviks: The Intellectual, Personal, and Political History of the Triumph of Communism in Russia*. Cambridge, Mass.: Harvard University Press, 1998 (reissue of the 1965 publication with a new preface). Essentially a biography of Lenin.

11. THE PARIS PEACE CONFERENCE, 1919

On 18 January 1919, representatives of twenty-seven nations met in Paris to draft the peace treaties ending **World War I** (1914–1918). Although all delegates would sign the peace treaties, an **Allied Council of Four**, consisting of **David Lloyd George**, prime minister of Great Britain; **Georges Clemenceau**, premier of France; **Vittorio Orlando**, premier of Italy; and **Woodrow Wilson**, president of the United States, presided over the conference. The **Big Four Powers** decided all matters dealing with the defeated **Central Powers** of Germany, Austria-Hungary, Bulgaria, and Turkey.

All sides had expected President Wilson's proposals to frame the peace, but four issues overshadowed his **Fourteen Points** and shaped the treaties. First, although allied leaders respected Wilson, they found him difficult to work with. Wilson, for his part, was troubled by the secret wartime agreements between the allies that violated his Fourteen Points. Increasingly, bickering and mistrust soured the relations among the four allied leaders.

A second issue was the question of European security. To ensure a compliant Germany, its army was reduced to 100,000. France occupied the **Saarland** coal fields, and Germany's **Rhineland** was demilitarized. Yet, France did not believe these measures would guarantee its own security. Having little faith in Wilson's **League of Nations**, France took the position that European security must be linked to German **war reparations**.

The linking of security and reparations resulted in a third issue—certainly one of the most contentious of the Peace Conference. **Article 231** of the Treaty of Versailles charged that Germany and its allies were solely responsible for "causing all the loss and damage" of the war. **Article 232** required that Germany "make compensation for all damage" done to civilians and property during the war. These **"war guilt" articles** stipulated that Germany was responsible for the war and that ultimately it must pay reparations.

Finally, the conference was keenly aware that the collapse of the German, Austro-Hungarian, Russian, and Turkish empires left a power vacuum in the heart of Europe. Boundaries for seven new countries had to be drawn and a **mandate system** established to govern former German and Turkish colonies.

After the Big Four decided all issues, they required the defeated Central Powers to sign five separate treaties: the **Treaty of Versailles** with Germany (28 June 1919), the **Treaty Saint-Germain-en-Laye** with Austria (10 September 1919), the **Treaty of Neuilly** with Bulgaria (27 November 1919), the **Treaty of Trianon** with Hungary (4 June 1920), and the **Treaty of Sèvres** with Turkey (10 August 1920).

Suggestions for Term Papers

1. Using an atlas, find one of the new countries established by the Paris Peace Conference and give a brief account of its history in the 1920s and 1930s.

2. Read Articles 231 and 232 of the Treaty of Versailles as part of a research project on the "war guilt" issue. Discuss whether the concept of German war guilt was correct.

3. Why didn't the Paris Peace Conference design a more durable peace? Was this a peace doomed to failure?

4. Investigate the mandate system and see how it was applied to Germany's former colonies in China.

5. The Soviet Union was not invited to the Paris Peace Conference and probably would not have attended even if invited. What difference do you think its absence made?

6. Perhaps too much attention has been focused on Woodrow Wilson at the Paris Peace Conference. What roles did David Lloyd George and Georges Clemenceau play?

Research Suggestions

In addition to the boldfaced items, look under the entries for "The 1917 Russian Revolution" (#10), "The May 4th Movement in China, 1919" (#12), "The British Mandate of Palestine, 1922" (#13), "Mustafa Kemal Atatürk and the Founding of the Republic of Turkey, 1923" (#15), and "The Nazi 'Seizure of Power' in 1933" (#24). Search under **Versailles System**.

SUGGESTED SOURCES

Primary Sources

Link, Arthur, et al., eds. *The Papers of Woodrow Wilson.* 67 vols. Princeton: Princeton University Press, 1966–1993. A full account of Wilson's views on peacemaking.

Mantoux, Paul, ed. *The Deliberations of the Council of Four (March 24–June 28, 1919): Notes of the Official Interpreter, Paul Mantoux.* 2 vols. Translated and edited by Arthur S. Link, with the assistance of Manfred F. Boemeke. Princeton: Princeton University Press, 1992. A bird's-eye-view of the inner workings of the Council of Four.

Nicolson, Harold. *Peacemaking 1919.* New York: Grosset and Dunlap, 1965. Insightful comments on the diplomacy and the participants by a member of the British delegation.

Temperley, Harold, et al., eds. *History of the Peace Conference of Paris.* 6 vols. Oxford: Oxford University Press, 1920. An exhaustive collection of documentation in English covering all aspects of the treaty.

U.S. Department of State. *Papers Relating to the Foreign Relations of the United States: The Paris Peace Conference of 1919.* 13 vols. Washington, D.C.: Government Printing Office, 1943. 13 vols. A comprehensive collection of documents on America's role in peacemaking.

Secondary Sources

Boemeke, Manfred E., et al., eds. *The Treaty of Versailles: A Reassessment after Seventy-Five Years.* Cambridge: Cambridge University Press, 1998. Leading German scholars have contributed the major essays in this collection.

Kent, Bruce. *The Spoils of War: The Politics, Economics and Diplomacy of Reparations, 1918–1932.* Oxford: Oxford University Press, 1989. One of the most recent studies to focus on the importance of the treaties during the 1920s.

Keylor, William R., ed. *The Legacy of the Great War: Peacemaking 1919.* New York: Houghton Mifflin, 1998. An up-to-date collection of the key interpretations of the Paris Conference.

Link, Arthur. *Woodrow Wilson: War, Revolution and Peace.* Princeton: Princeton University Press, 1979. The best study of Wilson at the Paris Peace Conference.

Sharp, Alan. *The Versailles Settlement: Peacemaking in Paris, 1919.* New York: St. Martin's Press, 1991. A succinct analysis of all aspects of peacemaking, including a summary of eight decades of scholarly debate on the treaties.

Sontag, Raymond. *A Broken World, 1919–1939.* New York: Harper and Row, 1971. The first chapter of this text is a masterly summary of the Peace of Paris. The remainder of the book traces the effects of the treaties on Europe in the 1920s and 1930s.

World Wide Web

"The Versailles Treaty." *http://ac.acusd/edu/History/text/versaillestreaty/vercontents.html.* All of the articles of the Versailles treaty are here.

12. THE MAY 4TH MOVEMENT IN CHINA, 1919

On the afternoon of 4 May 1919, 3,000 students assembled in Peking's **Tiananmen Square** near the **Gate of Heavenly Peace** to protest the decision of the **Versailles Treaty** ending **World War I** to give Japan control of the former German colonial possessions in China's **Shandong province**. The students had assumed that because Germany had been defeated, China would take control of Shandong province. They were indignant that Japan, the country that in 1915 levied the infamous **Twenty-one Demands** giving Japan economic monopolies in China, was again violating Chinese sovereignty.

To protest the Treaty of Versailles, the students decided to march from Tiananmen to the foreign-legation quarter of Peking and present their grievances to the Western powers. Armed riot police intervened, killing one student and arresting hundreds of demonstrators. Yet, the students did not lose heart. They continued the protests, so that each day more students and even senior faculty from Peking National University joined the demonstrations. By June 1919 the Chinese government was so shaken by the protests that it refused to sign the Treaty of Versailles.

Not only did the protesters denounce the Treaty of Versailles, but they also called for a more relaxed social model and attacked the strict **Confucian social hierarchy** that promoted **filial piety** (the obligatory respect for elders) and a patriarchal society. Furthermore, they advocated that spoken vernacular Chinese, not the highly stylized classical Chinese, become China's national language. The protesters also demanded that women be admitted to universities and free to marry whom they chose, and that **female foot-binding** be outlawed.

Although initially directed at foreigners, May 4th-style demonstrations spread to 200 cities and quickly became a comprehensive reform movement affecting China well beyond the summer of 1919. Intellectuals such as the famous short-story writer **Lu Xun**, the vibrant female poet **Ding Ling**, and the Columbia University trained philosopher **Hu Shih** enthusiastically joined the protests and repeatedly wrote of May 4th throughout their distinguished careers. Political leaders such as communists **Mao Zedong** and **Zhou Enlai** and

Guomindang leader **Chiang Kai-shek** were also inspired by May 4th's idealism and social reforms.

Suggestions for Term Papers

1. Investigate Sino-Japanese relations during the period 1895 to 1919 and write a paper examining how young Chinese viewed Japan during that time.
2. On 4 May 1989, China held elaborate commemorative celebrations marking the seventieth anniversary of the May 4th demonstration. As a research project, analyze their style and significance. In what ways were they connected to the Tiananmen Square massacre of June 1989? Use James A. Miles, *The Legacy of Tiananmen: China in Disarray* (see Suggested Sources).
3. Discuss why the Chinese considered the Twenty-one Demands Japan made in 1915 to be "infamous."
4. In June 1998, President Clinton visited Peking University and invoked the name Hu Shih, one of the leaders of May 4th, to remind Chinese students of the importance of this scholar and reformer. Read Hu Shih's *The Chinese Renaissance* (see Suggested Sources) and write a report on his views of early twentieth-century China.
5. The May 4th movement gave special emphasis to women's rights, especially to the anti–foot-binding leagues' efforts to end that practice. What success did reformers have over the next three decades in their efforts?
6. The poet Ding Ling is but one of many writers who found inspiration in the idealism of the May 4th movement. Read some of her poetry (see Suggested Sources) and write about her life as a dissident poet.

Research Suggestions

In addition to the boldfaced items, look under the entries for "The Northern Expedition in China, 1926–1928" (#16), "Mao Zedong's 'Report on an Investigation of the Peasant Movement in Hunan, March 1927'" (#17), "Mao Zedong and the Long March, 1934–1935" (#25), "The Rape of Nanking, 1937" (#28), and "The Victory of the Chinese Communist Party, 1949" (#46). Search under **Sun Yat-Sen, mandate system,** and **Anglo-Japanese Alliance**.

SUGGESTED SOURCES

Primary Sources

Chiang Kai-shek. *China's Destiny.* Translated by Wang Chung-hui. New York: Da Capo Press, 1976. A view of May 4th by the leader of the Guomindang (Nationalist Party).

Ding Ling. *I Myself Am a Woman: Selected Writings of Ding Ling.* Edited by Tani E. Barlow with Gary J. Bjorge. Boston: Beacon Press, 1989. A representative anthology of one of twentieth-century China's major female writers.

Hu Shih. *The Chinese Renaissance.* Chicago: University of Chicago Press, 1934. A scholarly appraisal by one of May 4th's leading intellectuals.

Mao Tse-tung. "The May Fourth Movement." In Mao Tse-tung, *Selected Works.* 5 vols. New York: International Publishers, 1955, 3: 9–12. Mao's analysis of how the movement connected with Marxism.

Secondary Sources

Bergère, Marie-Claire. *Sun Yat-sen.* Translated by Janet Lloyd. Stanford: Stanford University Press, 1998. A fresh treatment of the effects of May 4th on one of the most important leaders of the Chinese Republic.

Cho Tse-tsung. *The May Fourth Movement: Intellectual Revolution in Modern China.* Cambridge, Mass.: Harvard University Press, 1960. This remains the definitive study of the event.

———. *Research Guide to the May Fourth Movement: Intellectual Revolution in Modern China, 1915–1924.* Cambridge, Mass.: Harvard University Press, 1963. The starting place for all research. This annotated bibliography is a supplement to the author's classic study of May 4th.

Miles, James A. *The Legacy of Tiananmen: China in Disarray.* Ann Arbor: University of Michigan Press, 1996. A useful summary of political and social conditions before and after Tiananmen.

Spence, Jonathan D. *The Gate of Heavenly Peace: The Chinese and Their Revolution, 1895–1980.* New York: Viking, 1981. Chapter 5 is focused on the principal insurrectionists who took part in May 4th. The remainder of the book shows the influence of the May 4th movement on modern China.

13. THE BRITISH MANDATE OF PALESTINE, 1922

Palestine, the land from which the modern state of Israel later emerged, had been under Turkish control since the sixteenth century. In the course of **World War I** (1914–1918), **Great Britain**, an enemy of **Turkey**, sponsored the dashing **T. E. Lawrence**'s guerrilla-style raids against Turkish military installations in Palestine. In 1917, hoping to gain support from the international Jewish community, Britain's foreign secretary, **Arthur Balfour**, publicly pledged (the **Balfour Declaration**) that "His Majesty's Government view with favour the establishment in Palestine of a national home for the Jewish people."

The Balfour Declaration was of special interest to those Jews who had supported the call of **Theodor Herzl**'s **World Zionist Congress** (1897) for an independent Jewish state. After the defeat of Turkey in World War I, France and Britain stripped Turkey of its possessions in the Middle East. France took control of **Syria** and **Lebanon** while Britain took control of **Iraq**, **Transjordan**, and **Palestine**. In 1920 Sir **Herbert Samuel** was appointed **British High Commissioner for Palestine**, and in 1922 the **League of Nations** gave Great Britain the mandate to rule Palestine. Under terms of the mandate Great Britain was not to view Palestine as a British colony but was to prepare it for independence and self-governance.

In exercising its mandate Britain moved cautiously, especially because it was quite difficult to know precisely how many people lived in Palestine. In 1922 Britain estimated that 620,00 **Arab Muslims**, 70,000 **Arab Christians**, and 60,000 Jews lived in Palestine. During the 1920s few Jews immigrated to Palestine, but by the 1930s, particularly after Hitler came to power in Germany, Jewish immigration and land ownership in Palestine accelerated. Tensions between Palestinians and the growing Jewish community came to a flash point in 1936 when anti-Jewish riots broke out. In the wake of the riots **Lord Robert Peel**, who headed a commission of inquiry charged with investigating the riots, issued a report concluding that the only way to prevent further bloodshed was to divide Palestine into three parts: a Jewish state, a Palestinian state, and the holy cities of Jerusalem and

Bethlehem under British control. Both the Jewish and Palestinian communities rejected the **Peel Commission**'s recommendations.

As war threatened in Europe, Britain, fearful of losing access to its oil supplies, sought to strengthen ties with the Arab world. In May 1939 it issued a new policy severely limiting Jewish immigration to Palestine and announced that it would withdraw from Palestine in 1949, thereby assuring that the Arab majority would govern an independent Palestine. With the outbreak of war in Europe in 1939, Britain's mandate in Palestine came under increasing attack from Jews who felt that Britain was not doing enough to assist Jews fleeing Germany. After the defeat of Germany in 1945, Britain continued to rule Palestine and to limit immigration of Jewish refugees of the **Holocaust**. In 1947 Britain requested that the **United Nations** devise a settlement for Palestine because Britain intended to give up its mandate on 15 May 1948.

Suggestions for Term Papers

1. Investigate the Gallipoli campaign in World War I (see Suggested Sources) and write a paper on the ways in which it influenced British strategy in the Middle East.

2. How did the Arab inhabitants of Palestine view the British mandate? What were their views on the Balfour Declaration and Zionism?

3. Explore the situation in Palestine between 1936 and 1939 and draft a script for a short documentary presenting the perspectives of Arabs, Jews, and British officials.

4. Discuss Britain's reasons for limiting Jewish immigration to Palestine before, during, and after World War II and the efforts of the Jewish community to reverse the restrictions.

5. Do a research project on the career of Chaim Weizmann (see Suggested Sources) and his influence on British policy in Palestine.

6. Examine the role of the United Nations in attempting to find a solution to the Palestinian problem in 1947–1948.

Research Suggestions

In addition to the boldfaced items, look under the entries for "The Paris Peace Conference, 1919" (#11), "The Holocaust, 1941–1945"

(#34), "The Establishment of the State of Israel, 1948" (#43), "Gamal Abdel Nasser and the Suez Crisis, 1956" (#52), "The Six-Day War, 1967" (#66), and "Terrorism in the 1970s" (#78). Search under **Menachem Begin, Exodus, Haganah, Irgun, Jewish Agency, League of Arab States**, and **Sykes-Picot Treaty**.

SUGGESTED SOURCES

Primary Sources

Esco Foundation for Palestine. *Palestine: A Study of Jewish, Arab, and British Policies.* 2 vols. New Haven: Yale University Press, 1947. An eclectic collection of materials focused on the mandate period.

Khalidi, Walid, ed. *From Haven to Conquest: Readings in Zionism and the Palestine Problem until 1948.* Beirut: Institute for Palestine Studies, 1971. Excellent documentation from the Palestinian perspective.

Laqueur, Walter, and Barry Rubin, eds. *The Israeli-Arab Reader: A Documentary History of the Middle East Conflict.* New York: Penguin Books, 1984. More than thirty key documents on the British mandate are in this collection.

Moore, John N., ed. *The Arab Israeli Conflict.* 3 vols. Princeton: Princeton University Press, 1974. A wide-ranging collection of government documents and personal accounts of the mandate period.

Weizmann, Chaim. *Trial and Error: The Autobiography of Chaim Weizmann.* New York: Harper, 1949. Autobiography of the key Zionist leader and drafter of the Balfour Declaration.

Secondary Sources

Abu-Lughon, Ibrahim, ed. *The Transformation of Palestine: Essays on the Origin and Development of Arab-Israel Conflict.* Evanston, Ill.: Northwestern University Press, 1971. Sixteen essays on the mandate period.

Cohen, Michael J. *The Origins and Evolution of the Arab-Zionist Conflict.* Berkeley: University of California Press, 1987. A solid treatment of conflict during the period of the British mandate.

Lesch, Ann Mosely, and Dan Tschirgi. *Origins and Development of the Arab-Israeli Conflict.* Westport, Conn.: Greenwood Press, 1998. Analysis, biographical profiles, and primary documents for the entire period.

Ovendale, Ritchie. *The Origins of the Arab-Israeli Wars.* 2nd ed. New York: Longman, 1992. A good account of the tensions between Arabs and Jews during the mandate years.

Stein, Kenneth W. "A Historiographic Review of Literature on the Origins of the Arab-Israeli Conflict." *American Historical Review* 96 (1991):

1450–1465. A most useful summary of interpretations of the mandate period.

14. THE NEW ECONOMIC POLICY (NEP) IN RUSSIA, 1921–1928

By 1921 the **Bolshevik Party** had triumphed in the Civil War following the **Russian Revolution in 1917**. But the country still faced severe challenges—a collapsing economy, widespread famine, peasant rebellions, and the revolt of the sailors at the **Kronstadt Naval Base**. All this indicated a dangerous level of popular dissatisfaction with the Bolshevik government.

At the Tenth Party Congress in March 1921, **V. I. Lenin** convinced the Bolsheviks to accept the **New Economic Policy (NEP)**. This new approach to the economy called for peasants to pay a percentage of their harvest as a tax instead of having most of it requisitioned by the state. It allowed a return to retail trade and small-scale manufacture as well. The Bolsheviks retained control of the "commanding heights" of the economy: wholesale trade, foreign trade, banking, and insurance. The partial return to capitalism was meant to encourage farmers to produce more food and artisans and small businessmen to make more consumer goods available.

The NEP remained in place until 1928. That year the Russian economy achieved approximately the same levels of production as in 1913, the last full year before World War I. Art, literature, and film flourished during this time, although hampered by lack of funds and shortages of materials. It was also a period of new ideas and radical schemes in areas like education, architecture, design, law, and city planning.

The year 1927 was the tenth anniversary of the October Revolution, and many idealistic revolutionaries worried that the Soviet Union was drifting toward capitalism and that socialism would never be achieved. Stalin, after winning out over his main rivals in the period after Lenin's death in 1924, appealed to the energy and enthusiasm of many Russians with a call for the fulfillment of the **First Five-Year Plan**, which was an attempt to use economic planning by the state to achieve an industrialized economy. The stage was set for the transformation of the **Soviet Union** over the next decade.

Suggestions for Term Papers

1. Events at the Tenth Party Congress in 1921 were crucial for the 1920s and beyond. The congress not only produced the New Economic Policy but also a policy against the formation of factions in the Communist Party. Trace the ways in which this policy was used by Stalin in the 1920s.

2. Lenin seemed to adopt a gradualist approach to development in the Soviet Union in the 1920s. Read some of his articles from this period (see *The Lenin Anthology* in the Suggested Sources) and write about his views in this period.

3. Investigate the lives of the peasantry in the 1920s and assess the impact of NEP on how they lived and farmed.

4. What was life like for women in the Soviet Union in the 1920s? Begin with Richard Stites, *The Women's Liberation Movement in Russia* (see Suggested Sources).

5. Soviet cinema quickly became well known in the 1920s among film critics. View a Soviet film from the period by Sergei Eisenstein, Vsevolod Pudovkin, or Aleksandr Dovzhenko and write about the tensions between art and the need to create propaganda for the Soviet state.

6. Compare the novel *We* by Evgeny Zamyatin (see Suggested Sources) and George Orwell's novel *1984*. What similarities and differences do you find in the two novels?

Research Suggestions

In addition to the boldfaced items, look under the entries for "The 1917 Russian Revolution" (#10) and "Stalin's First Five-Year Plan, 1928–1932" (#23). Search under **Communist International (Comintern), Nepmen, People's Commissariat of Enlightenment, Aleksandra Kollontai**, and **Evgeny Zamyatin**.

SUGGESTED SOURCES

Primary Sources

Lenin, Vladimir Ilich. *The Lenin Anthology*. Edited by Robert C. Tucker. New York: W. W. Norton, 1975. The best single-volume collection of Lenin's writings. Approximately half the book consists of post-1917 material.

Stalin, Joseph. *The Essential Stalin: Major Theoretical Writings, 1905–1952.* Edited by H. Bruce Franklin. Garden City, N.Y.: Doubleday, 1972. A convenient source of Stalin's writings, including some important material from the 1920s.

Trotsky, Leon. *The Basic Writings of Trotsky.* Edited by Irving Howe. New York: Random House, 1963. Contains a few useful articles from the 1920s.

Zamyatin, Evgeny. *We.* New York: Bantam Books, 1972. A novel that satirized the new Soviet state. George Orwell's *1984* was based in part on Zamyatin's book.

Secondary Sources

Ball, A. M. *Russia's Last Capitalists.* Berkeley: University of California Press, 1987. An excellent discussion of NEP and the "nepmen," those retailers and small manufacturers who used NEP to return to capitalism.

Clark, Katerina. *Petersburg: Crucible of Cultural Revolution.* Cambridge, Mass.: Harvard University Press, 1995. A very interesting study of Soviet culture in the 1920s as seen from St. Petersburg (later Leningrad).

Deutscher, Isaac. *The Prophet Unarmed: Trotsky, 1921–1929.* Oxford: Oxford University Press, 1959. One of three volumes of Deutscher's biography of Trotsky, this volume traces Trotsky's fall from power in the Soviet Union.

Kenez, Peter. *The Birth of the Propaganda State: Soviet Methods of Mass Mobilization, 1917–1929.* Cambridge: Cambridge University Press, 1985. A thorough study of Bolshevik attempts to reach the masses in the 1920s.

Stites, Richard. *Revolutionary Dreams: Utopian Vision and Experimental Life in the Russian Revolution.* New York: Oxford University Press, 1989. A discussion of efforts to create a revolutionary society in the Soviet Union in the 1920s.

———. *The Women's Liberation Movement in Russia: Feminism, Nihilism, and Bolshevism, 1860–1930.* Princeton: Princeton University Press, 1990. Part four of this standard source deals with the liberation of women in the Soviet Union in the 1920s.

Tucker, Robert C. *Stalin as Revolutionary, 1879–1929.* New York: W. W. Norton, 1973. An outstanding study of Stalin's rise to prominence in this period.

Tumarkin, Nina. *Lenin Lives! The Lenin Cult in Russia.* Cambridge, Mass.: Harvard University Press, 1983. An important book on one of the major ways in which Stalin achieved enormous power in the Soviet Union by the end of the 1920s.

15. MUSTAFA KEMAL ATATÜRK AND THE FOUNDING OF THE REPUBLIC OF TURKEY, 1923

Mustafa Kemal Atatürk (1881–1938), the founder of modern Turkey, was born in Salonika, which is today part of Greece, but then was part of the **Ottoman Turkish Empire**. He trained as a soldier and in 1905 was commissioned as an officer in the Turkish army. As a young officer he was drawn to the political reform program formulated by a group of military leaders called the **Committee of Union and Progress (CUP)**. Better known as the **"Young Turks,"** these officers seized power in a 1913 coup d'état.

When World War I broke out in 1914, Turkey allied with the **Central Powers** (Germany, Austria-Hungary, Bulgaria, and Turkey). Kemal distinguished himself as a military leader in the battle of **Gallipoli** (1915) against the **Allied Powers** (France, Great Britain, Italy, and Russia). By war's end in 1918, Kemal was commanding the Seventh Army Corps in **Syria**, where he had acquired a reputation for bravery, leadership under fire, and careful strategic planning.

The victorious allies treated Turkey, a defeated power, harshly. The **Treaty of Sèvres** (1920) provided for cessation of parts of Turkey to Greece, creation of an independent **Armenia**, internationalization of the **Dardanelles**, and division of **Anatolia** into British, French, and Italian zones of occupation. While these humiliating provisions were being implemented, civil strife, rebellion, and war against the allied occupation forces broke out in Turkey. In 1921 Mustafa Kemal was named commander-in-chief of all Turkish forces. Two years later all foreign troops had been evacuated from Turkey, and on 29 October 1923 the **National Assembly** declared the birth of the **Turkish Republic**. Mustafa Kemal was elected president.

After becoming president, Kemal took the name **Atatürk** or "Father of all Turks" to emphasize his determination to educate, modernize, and secularize Turkey's 13 million citizens. Much like **Peter the Great** of Russia, he inaugurated a series of administrative, economic, and legal reforms aimed at modernizing every aspect of Turkish life. He abolished all religious courts, adopted a new legal code, and introduced the Latin alphabet. Turkish women were given the right to divorce their husbands. Turkish men were forbidden to wear the traditional hat, the fez. He also outlawed polygamy, introduced free public education, and encouraged a new Western-style Turkish nationalism. Through state-sponsored universities he promoted Western medicine, architecture, and music. Diplomatically, he sought close relations with the West but stayed clear of close military alliances. Although committed to progressive reform, Kemal was intolerant of dissent and ruthless in suppressing opposition. In 1925 he smashed a revolt of the **Kurdish minority**, and in 1926 he executed several members of the CUP party who had opposed his policies.

His fifteen-year rule energized the Turkish economy and left a stable legacy of republican-style government, ensuring that Turkey would modernize rapidly and become the model for secular-minded reformers throughout the Middle East.

Suggestions for Term Papers

1. Ottoman Turkey at the time of Atatürk's birth was often described as "the sick man of Europe." Read about the history of the Ottoman Empire in the late nineteenth century and determine if it deserved this description.

2. Atatürk gained his early military experience in the First Balkan War of 1912. Write a paper discussing the significance of this war for Turkey and for the Balkan countries.

3. Investigate the Gallipoli campaign of 1915 and write a paper explaining why Atatürk and the Turkish military were able to defeat the allied forces.

4. How did Atatürk's legal, social, and educational reforms affect Turkish women?

5. Atatürk was relentless in his repression of the Kurdish minority. Why was this? How does Atatürk's policy compare with the present policy of the Turkish government toward the Kurds?

6. Turkey is the only predominantly Muslim state to be a member of NATO. In what ways does this create a special role for Turkey

in NATO? What contributions has Turkey made to NATO since becoming a member?

Research Suggestions

In addition to the boldfaced items, look under the entries for "The Paris Peace Conference, 1919" (#11), "The British Mandate of Palestine, 1922" (#13), and "The Dissolution of Yugoslavia in the 1990s" (#93). Search under **Ankara, Balkan Wars, Lawrence of Arabia** (**T. E. Lawrence**), and **NATO**.

SUGGESTED SOURCES

Primary Sources

Simsir, B. N. *British Documents on Atatürk*. 4 vols. Ankara: Tük Tarih Kurumu Basimevi, 1973–1999. Good summaries of British diplomats' views on Atatürk's rise to power.

Secondary Sources

Bodurgil, Abraham. *Kemal Atatürk: A Centennial Bibliography (1881–1981)*. Washington, D.C.: Government Printing Office, 1984. An accessible and up to date bibliography.

Kinross, Patrick Balfour. *Ataturk: A Biography of Mustafa Kemal, Father of Modern Turkey*. New York: Morrow, 1965. Despite its age this remains the most complete biography available.

Macfie, A. L. *Atatürk*. New York: Longman, 1994. A short biographical study focusing on Atatürk's political reforms and consolidation of power. Good maps, a helpful chronology, and an annotated bibliography are included.

———. *The End of the Ottoman Empire, 1908–1923*. New York: Longman, 1998. A detailed study of the political conditions permitting Atatürk to seize power.

The Great War and the Shaping of the Twentieth Century [videorecording]. A KCET/BBC co-production in association with the Imperial War Museum. Distributed by PBS Video, 1996. Part three has grim footage from the Gallipoli invasion.

Volkan, Vamik, and Norman Itzkowitz. *The Immortal Atatürk: A Psychobiography*. Chicago: University of Chicago Press, 1984. A penetrating psychological study that emphasizes the influence of his early home life on his character.

Zürcher, Erik Jan. *The Unionist Factor: The Rôle of the Committee of Union and Progress in the Turkish National Movement, 1905–1926.* Leiden: J. Brill, 1984. A short study focused on Atatürk's rise to power in the CUP. Excellent bibliography.

World Wide Web

"The World Factbook, 1999." *http://www.odci.gov/cia/publications/ factbook/index.html.* This Central Intelligence Agency site is updated yearly.

16. THE NORTHERN EXPEDITION IN CHINA, 1926–1928

In the early 1920s **Sun Yat-sen** and the **Guomindang** (Nationalist) Party had limited power in a China ruled by warlords and foreign powers. This situation began to change after Sun's talks with Soviet diplomat **Adolf Joffe** in January 1923. The two agreed that China was not ready for communism and that independence and unity were the most important issues. Shortly after the talks, the **Communist International (Comintern)** sent **Mikhail Borodin** to supervise an alliance between the Guomindang and the **Chinese Communist Party (CCP)**, which had just been founded in 1921.

Borodin also helped the Guomindang establish the **Whampoa Military Academy**. Its first commandant was **Chiang Kai-shek**. The first director of the political department was **Zhou Enlai**.

Sun died in 1925. The alliance, together with assistance from the Comintern and the Soviet Union, continued. The Guomindang in this period included not only members who were also communists but many others on the left. A substantial part of the organization, however, began to move to the right. Chiang emerged as the most powerful figure.

In June 1926 Chiang was named commander-in-chief of the **National Revolutionary Army**, and the **Northern Expedition** began. By October, the army had taken the important tri-cities area of **Wuhan** in Hubei province. The question for the Guomindang became where next?

Late in March 1927 a general strike and armed insurrection by the powerful communist-led labor movement broke out in **Shanghai**. The National Revolutionary Army moved quickly to take control of the city. A few days later members of the so-called **Society for Common Progress** (a front for the **Green Gang**) attacked the headquarters of all the large unions in Shanghai. Many people were killed outright. Hundreds were arrested, some of them later executed. Chiang, who had connections to foreign business interests and the Green Gang, did nothing to interfere. He and a large part of the Guomindang moved to the right, splitting the alliance with the CCP.

Josif Stalin, responding to a domestic political struggle with **Leon Trotsky**, used the Comintern to order the CCP to cooperate with a leftist faction of the Guomindang. When this failed, he ordered the CCP to stage an insurrection in Canton (now Guangzhou). This was brutally suppressed by the Guomindang. The CCP suffered unnecessary defeats because of Stalin's use of the Comintern in domestic politics. The Guomindang now controlled a large part of China. By the late 1920s the Chinese Republic appeared to be firmly established.

Suggestions for Term Papers

1. Conduct a research project on Mikhail Borodin and other Comintern agents working in China in the 1920s and assess their contribution to the success of the Guomindang in that period.

2. Chiang Kai-shek was the most important figure in the Guomindang after Sun's death. What had he done before becoming commandant of the Whampoa Military Academy, and how was he viewed in China in the mid-1920s?

3. Review the early history of the Chinese Communist Party before its alliance with the Guomindang. Use the results of this review to evaluate the alliance. To what extent was it in the interests of the CCP?

4. Why did the split in the Guomindang–CCP alliance happen? Was there any way it could have been prevented, or were the inherent differences between the two parties simply too great?

5. Investigate the role played by the Comintern's China policy in Soviet politics in 1927. Examine in particular the views of Comintern agents in China as opposed to ideas Soviet officials had about China.

6. Shanghai in 1927 was a fascinating tangle of conflicting interests.

Identify the major players and assess the actions they took in terms of effectiveness.

Research Suggestions

In addition to the boldfaced items, look under the entries for "The May 4th Movement in China, 1919" (#12), "The New Economic Policy (NEP) in Russia, 1921–1928" (#14), and "Mao Zedong's 'Report on an Investigation of the Peasant Movement in Hunan, March 1927'" (#17). Search under **M. N. Roy, Vasily Blyukher, Chen Duxiu, Li Lisan, Mao Zedong**, and **T. V. Soong**.

SUGGESTED SOURCES

Primary Sources

Roy, M. N. *Revolution and Counter-Revolution in China*. Westport, Conn.: Hyperion Press, 1973. Reprint of the 1946 edition. Roy was an official of the Communist International and active in the 1920s in China.

Wilbur, C. Martin, and Julie How, eds. *Documents on Communism, Nationalism, and Soviet Advisers in China, 1918–1927. Papers Seized in the 1927 Peking Raid*. New York: Columbia University Press, 1956. Useful source material on a central topic.

Secondary Sources

Bergère, Marie-Claire. *Sun Yat-sen*. Translated by Janet Lloyd. Stanford: Stanford University Press, 1998. An excellent biography of Sun by a leading scholar.

Cambridge History of China. Vol. 12, *Republican China, 1912–1949*, Part 1. New York: Cambridge University Press, 1983. Useful essays on aspects of the 1920s by leading scholars of the period.

Eudin, Xenia, and Robert North. *M. N. Roy's Mission to China: The Communist Kuomintang Split of 1927*. Berkeley: University of California Press, 1963. A long introduction to the problems associated with the alliance between nationalists and communists together with thirty-seven documents related to the 1927 split.

Isaacs, Harold. *The Tragedy of the Chinese Revolution*. 2nd rev. ed. Stanford: Stanford University Press, 1961. One of the best books available on the Chinese revolutionary movement in the 1920s.

Jacobs, Dan. *Borodin: Stalin's Man in China*. Cambridge, Mass.: Harvard

University Press, 1981. Borodin was a key figure in the alliance between the Chinese nationalists and communists.

Jordan, Donald. *The Northern Expedition: China's National Revolution of 1926–1928*. Honolulu: University of Hawaii Press, 1976. An excellent study of this important event.

Sheridan, James E. *China in Disintegration: The Republican Era in Chinese History, 1912–1949*. New York: The Free Press, 1975. A useful survey of the period.

Spence, Jonathan D. *The Search for Modern China*. New York: W. W. Norton, 1990. Part 3 covers the period of the Northern Expedition. An excellent place to begin research.

Wilbur, C. Martin. *The Nationalist Revolution in China, 1923–1928*. New York: Cambridge University Press, 1983. A solid study of the topic.

Yu, George T. *Party Politics in Republican China: The Kuomintang, 1912–1924*. Berkeley: University of California Press, 1966. A good discussion of the Guomindang before the period of cooperation with the Chinese communists.

17. MAO ZEDONG'S "REPORT ON AN INVESTIGATION OF THE PEASANT MOVEMENT IN HUNAN, MARCH 1927"

In 1927, as the **Northern Expedition** was conquering large parts of China for the **Guomindang Party, Mao Zedong**, a member of the **Chinese Communist Party (CCP)** and director of the Guomindang's **Peasant Movement Training Institute**, spent time in **Hunan** province observing the peasant movement there. His report stressed the accomplishments the peasant movement had already made and the vast potential yet to be tapped: "To march at their head and lead them? To follow in the rear, gesticulating at them and criticizing them? To face them as opponents? Every Chinese is free to choose among the three."

There was no question where Mao stood. The CCP, its policy virtually dictated from Moscow by **Josif Stalin** to suit his political needs in the struggle with **Leon Trotsky**, failed to take full advantage of possibilities. Only after the moment had passed did Stalin give orders to stir up rebellion in rural areas. Mao tried, but the **"Autumn Harvest Uprising"** of 1927 had no chance of success.

After the failure of the Autumn Harvest Uprising, Mao led survivors first to the Jinggan Mountains on the border between Hunan and Jiangxi and then about a year later to another mountainous area, this between Jiangxi and Fujian provinces. There Mao established the **Jiangxi Soviet**, which survived until 1934, when Guomindang attacks forced Mao and his followers to go on the **Long March**.

In the Jiangxi Soviet Mao learned a great deal more about working with the peasantry. In particular, he experimented with land reform policies, attempting to find the degree of rigor that would provide justice for the poor peasants and yet not alienate potential supporters among the peasants who were better off. In 1930 he studied one county in Jiangxi, **Xunwu**, very carefully and learned a great deal about how peasant society worked. Among other things, Mao became more convinced than ever of the importance of improving the lot of women in the countryside.

With the help of **Zhu De**, a former soldier of fortune and opium addict, Mao developed the Red Army as a guerrilla force. The CCP constantly wanted Mao to send troops to other areas to foster uprisings. Mao opposed this, but could not oppose direct orders to attack a nearby city as part of an ambitious campaign in 1930. The campaign ended in defeat, and Mao and Zhu withdrew their forces without permission rather than see them destroyed.

Despite Mao's success with the Jiangxi Soviet, the CCP leadership was slow to abandon its emphasis on the proletariat and urban insurrection. Only after the Long March and the establishment of a new soviet in **Yan'an**, Shaanxi province, did Mao begin to win converts to his unorthodox ideas about a peasant base for a Marxist revolution.

Suggestions for Term Papers

1. Investigate and report on Mao Zedong's early life (up to his walking tour of Hunan in 1927.)

2. Read Mao's report on the peasant movement in Hunan in 1927. Pay particular attention to his analysis of peasant life, especially his comments on the life of peasant women.

3. Do a research project on the life of Zhu De before, during, and after the Jiangxi Soviet. How much credit should Zhu get for the

ideas about guerrilla warfare we usually associate with Mao? Begin with Agnes Smedley, *The Great Road: The Life and Times of Chu Teh* (see Suggested Sources).

4. Read Mao's report on Xunwu County in Jiangxi and compare it with his earlier report on Hunan.

5. Assess the debates about policy within the Chinese Communist Party between the split with the Guomindang in 1927 and the beginnings of the Long March in 1934. To what extent was the CCP able to reconcile Marxist doctrines with Chinese political and social realities?

6. Trace Mao's activities between his report on the peasant movement in Hunan in 1927 and the beginnings of the Long March in 1934. How important was he in the hierarchy of the CCP?

Research Suggestions

In addition to the boldfaced items, look under the entries for "The May 4th Movement in China, 1919" (#12), "The Northern Expedition in China, 1926–1928" (#16), and "Mao Zedong and the Long March, 1934–1935" (#25). Search under **Chen Duxiu, Li Lisan, "returned students," Zhou Enlai, Deng Xiaoping**, and **Gao Gang**.

SUGGESTED SOURCES

Primary Sources

Mao Zedong. *Mao's Road to Power: Revolutionary Writings: 1912–1949.* Vol. 2, *National Revolution and Social Revolution, December 1920–June 1927.* Edited by Stuart Schram and Nancy Jane Hodes. Armonk, N.Y.: M. E. Sharpe, 1995. Vol. 3, *From the Jinggangshan to the Establishment of the Jiangxi Soviet, July 1927–December 1930.* Edited by Stuart Schram. 1995. Vol. 4, *The Rise and Fall of the Chinese Soviet Republic, 1931–1934.* Edited by Stuart Schram. 1997. Highly useful background material.

———. *Report from Xunwu.* Translated and edited by Roger R. Thompson. Stanford: Stanford University Press, 1990. A much more detailed and elaborate report than the 1927 report. Very useful for measuring the distance Mao had come since 1927.

Secondary Sources

Hofheinz, Roy. *The Broken Wave: The Chinese Communist Peasant Movement, 1922–1928*. Cambridge, Mass.: Harvard University Press, 1977. An important study of the possibilities of peasant unrest in the 1920s.

Hsiao Tso-liang. *Power Relations Within the Chinese Communist Movement, 1930–1934: A Study of Documents*. Seattle: University of Washington Press, 1961. A useful but advanced book.

Kim, Ilpyong. *The Politics of Chinese Communism: Kiangsi under the Soviets*. Berkeley: University of California Press, 1973. A good discussion of the overall operation of the Kiangsi (Jiangxi) Soviet.

McDonald, Angus. *The Urban Origins of Rural Revolution: Elites and the Masses in Hunan Province, China, 1911–1927*. Berkeley: University of California Press, 1978. Presents an important aspect of peasant unrest in the 1920s.

Schram, Stuart. *Mao Tse-tung*. New York: Simon and Schuster, 1966. A good introduction to Mao's life.

Schwartz, Benjamin. *Chinese Communism and the Rise of Mao*. Cambridge, Mass.: Harvard University Press, 1958. One of the best books available on this topic.

Smedley, Agnes. *The Great Road: The Life and Times of Chu Teh*. New York: Monthly Review Press, 1956. An older but still useful biography.

18. ALEXANDER FLEMING AND THE DISCOVERY OF PENICILLIN, 1928

Alexander Fleming was a Scottish bacteriologist who gained worldwide fame as the discoverer of **penicillin,** an **antibiotic** that has saved countless lives since it was first used on a large scale in **World War II**. However, although Fleming discovered penicillin, the story of its development as a life-saving antibiotic is a complicated one involving the dedicated work of two other researchers, **Howard Walter Florey** and **Ernst Boris Chain**.

Fleming graduated from St. Mary's Hospital Medical School, London University, in 1906. For several years, he did research. During **World War I**, he served in the Royal Army Medical Corps. After the war he conducted research and taught at St. Mary's.

In 1928, quite by accident, Fleming noticed a mold that had appeared on a culture plate that had not been washed for two weeks because he had been on vacation. He observed that no bacteria grew near the mold, which he named penicillin (after the Latin name for the mold, *Penicillium notatum*). He experimented further with penicillin, but could neither isolate and identify the compound involved nor produce enough to conduct tests on humans. In 1929 Fleming wrote a paper on his work, then dropped the project.

Howard Florey and Ernst Chain picked up Fleming's work several years later as part of an effort to find an antibacterial substance that was nontoxic to humans. Florey was an Australian. Chain was a German Jew who had been forced to leave Germany in the 1930s. Both were intense and competitive. After years of painstaking work, they were able to isolate the compound and test it. By 1939 they were convinced penicillin was a major pharmaceutical discovery.

World War II provided a situation that made it much easier to convince governments to produce penicillin in large quantities. Nevertheless, Florey still had to fly to the United States in 1941 to present his case before the U.S. government would commit the resources needed for mass production.

Fleming and Florey were knighted in 1944 for their work. All three shared the Nobel Prize in Physiology or Medicine in 1945. Over the years that followed, Fleming, because he enjoyed giving interviews, became identified not simply with the discovery of penicillin but also with the work involved in developing it as a useful product. Florey, who avoided journalists whenever possible, and Chain were never given the public recognition they deserved. For decades the romantic myth about Alexander Fleming's discovery of penicillin obscured the real story. Even now that an accurate account of the discovery and development of penicillin is readily available, the myth persists.

Suggestions for Term Papers

1. Report on Alexander Fleming's career up to the point when he discovered penicillin. What kind of a career had he had?

2. Investigate the life of Howard Walter Florey. How did he deal with Alexander Fleming's great fame and the fact that it rested largely on Florey's work?

3. What did Florey and Ernst Chain actually do in order to develop penicillin as a life-saving drug?

4. Trace the development of the romantic myth of the discovery of penicillin and evaluate those factors that appear to account for it (begin with Macfarlane's biography in Suggested Sources).

5. In what ways did World War II accelerate the development and widespread use of penicillin and other drugs? Begin with Gordon Wright, *The Ordeal of Total War, 1939–1945* and Gwyn Macfarlane's biography of Howard Florey (see Suggested Sources).

6. Interview one or more medical doctors about the current practices and problems associated with the use of antibiotics today.

Research Suggestions

In addition to the boldfaced items, look under the entries for "General Broadcasting of Television in Britain, 1936" (#26), "The Discovery of the Double Helical Structure of DNA, 1953" (#49), and "The Spread of AIDS in the 1980s" (#83). Search under **Louis Pasteur, Joseph Lister, Robert Koch**, and **Sulphonamides**.

SUGGESTED SOURCES

Primary Source

Florey, H. W., et al. *Antibiotics.* Oxford: Oxford University Press, 1949. An exposition of the state of knowledge on antibiotics at that time.

Secondary Sources

Böttcher, Helmuth M. *Wonder Drugs: A History of Antibiotics.* Philadelphia: J. B. Lippincott, 1964. Somewhat dated, but a very interesting and comprehensive account of efforts before Fleming to discover antibiotics as well as considerable coverage of developments afterwards.
Macfarlane, Gwyn. *Alexander Fleming: The Man and the Myth.* Cambridge, Mass.: Harvard University Press, 1984. The best book on the subject.
———. *Howard Florey: The Making of a Great Scientist.* Oxford: Oxford University Press, 1979. An excellent biography of the man instrumental in making penicillin available to the world.
Otfinoski, Steven. *Alexander Fleming: Conquering Disease with Penicillin.* N.Y.: Facts on File, 1992. A recent, concise discussion.
Parshall, Gerland. "The Masters of Discovery: Medicine's Accidental Hero." *U.S. News and World Report,* 17–24 August 1998. A brief, readable account of the contributions of Fleming, Florey, and Chain to the development of penicillin.

Wright, Gordon. *The Ordeal of Total War, 1939–1945.* New York: Harper and Row, 1968. An excellent history of World War II. Includes useful information on medicine in the war.

World Wide Web

"The Nobel Prize in Physiology or Medicine, 1945." *http://nobel.sdsc.edu/ laureates/medicine-1945.html.* An excellent site, part of the larger, official Nobel Prize site. It contains links to biographies of Fleming, Florey, and Chain, and a link to the presentation speech. The latter outlines the work done to discover and develop penicillin.

19. SIGMUND FREUD'S *CIVILIZATION AND ITS DISCONTENTS,* 1930

In the summer of 1929, **Sigmund Freud** wrote a short but powerful book entitled *Civilization and Its Discontents.* Published the following year, the book warned its readers that civilization was a fragile creation requiring constant attention. Its appearance in the early days of the **Depression** and not long before the **Nazis** came to power in Germany, made it into one of the most influential books of the first half of the twentieth century.

By 1930 Freud was widely known in Europe and America as the founder of **psychoanalysis**. His provocative theories of human psychology had gained many adherents and generated much controversy. In his depiction of human nature, Freud emphasized two basic drives: a **death drive** that played itself out in aggression and destructiveness, and a **sexual drive** that manifested itself in terms of love and desire. In the individual, the **id** was the source of these drives. The **ego** was the individual's conscious awareness of himself or herself. The **superego** or conscience acted to restrain the id and remind the ego of the importance of limits.

In *Civilization and Its Discontents,* Freud discussed human society more or less in terms of the individual writ large. Civilization was analogous to the superego, a set of ideas and institutions necessary to keep the instinctual drives of humans from creating chaos.

If civilization provided a means for making life livable, it nonetheless made humans unhappy because it forced them to repress or suppress basic drives. Civilization, then, was a self-imposed compromise between what humans wanted to do and what they should do in order to live more comfortably and securely. One paid a price for living in a civilization, at times a very high price, but the alternative was worse.

Freud may be seen as a gloomy realist. He was hostile to the idea of **utopia**, a perfectly ordered society that featured abundance, peace, and harmony. From his vantage point in Vienna at the end of the 1920s, Freud saw the fallacies in both **communism** and **fascism**. Neither system took into account human nature.

Typically, Freud disparaged what he had accomplished in the book, but it extended his ideas about human psychology to the level of society. The struggles of society to maintain civilization mirrored the struggles of the individual. The last decade of his life provided ample opportunity for observing civilization's struggles. After the **annexation of Austria** by **Nazi Germany**, Freud emigrated to England, where he died shortly after the beginning of **World War II** in September 1939.

Suggestions for Term Papers

1. Investigate the reception of Sigmund Freud's theories in Europe and America in the 1920s. To what extent did people understand and make use of his theories?

2. Compare *Civilization and Its Discontents* with another short, speculative book written a few years earlier, *The Future of an Illusion* (see Suggested Sources).

3. Another important examination of European civilization, José Ortega y Gasset's *Revolt of the Masses*, was also published in 1930. In a comparison of the two, note similarities and differences.

4. Why does Freud find that civilization, however necessary it may be, is also painful for human beings?

5. Perhaps the most controversial parts of *Civilization and Its Discontents* concern his views on women and civilization. Read this material closely together with at least one feminist critique of Freud's views (see Suggested Sources), then assess the validity of his position.

6. As part of a group project, examine contemporary journalism and other writing, music, films, television, and Internet sources to de-

termine whether Freud's perspective on civilization is reflected in contemporary culture.

Research Suggestions

In addition to the boldfaced items, look under the entries for "Stalin's First Five-Year Plan, 1928–1932" (#23), "The Nazi 'Seizure of Power' in 1933" (#24), and "*Kristallnacht* ('The Night of Broken Glass'), 1938" (#31). Search under **Anna Freud, Princess Marie Bonaparte, Lou Andreas-Salome, Carl Jung**, and **Albert Einstein**.

SUGGESTED SOURCES

Primary Sources

Freud, Sigmund. *Civilization and Its Discontents*. Translated and edited by James Strachey. New York: W. W. Norton, 1989. Original edition 1930. Freud's application of psychoanalytic theories to human civilization.

———. *The Freud Reader*. Edited by Peter Gay. New York: W. W. Norton, 1989. A convenient source of Freud's most significant writings.

———. *The Future of an Illusion*. Translated and edited by James Strachey. New York: W. W. Norton, 1989. Original edition 1927. Freud's analysis of religion. Like *Civilization and Its Discontents*, an attempt to use his ideas to address large issues.

———. *The Letters of Sigmund Freud*. Edited by Ernest L. Freud. New York: Basic Books, 1960. A convenient selection. Letter 243 to Lou Andreas-Salome mentions completing *Civilization and Its Discontents* in Freud's typically disparaging style.

Secondary Sources

The Cambridge Companion to Freud. Edited by Jerome Neu. New York: Cambridge University Press, 1991. Useful articles on, among other topics, Freud and women and *Civilization and Its Discontents*.

Clark, Ronald W. *Freud: The Man and the Cause*. New York: Random House, 1980. A good biographical study of Freud.

Gay, Peter. *Freud: A Life for Our Time*. New York: W. W. Norton, 1988. Probably the best biography of Freud now available.

Jones, Ernest. *The Life and Work of Sigmund Freud*. Edited and abridged in one volume by Lionel Trilling and Steven Marcus. New York: Basic Books, 1961. The standard biography in a convenient abridged version.

Kofman, Sara. *The Enigma of Woman: Women in Freud's Writings.* Ithaca, N.Y.: Cornell University Press, 1985. An important feminist discussion of Freud's controversial ideas about women.

Rieff, Philip. *Freud: The Mind of the Moralist.* 3rd ed. Chicago: University of Chicago Press, 1979. See in particular "Politics and the Individual."

Roazen, Paul. *Freud: Political and Social Thought.* New York: Knopf, 1968. A good overview of Freud's ideas on social and political topics.

Stromberg, Roland N. *Makers of Modern Culture: Five Twentieth-Century Thinkers.* Arlington Heights, Ill.: Harlan Davidson, 1991. Includes a good introductory essay on Freud.

20. GANDHI'S SALT MARCH, 1930

In the spring of 1930, **Mohandas K. Gandhi** walked with seventy-eight followers more than 200 miles to the sea, where he symbolically defied the British monopoly on the production and distribution of salt in India. This marked the beginnings of a dramatic nonviolent civil disobedience campaign. Although the British did not grant independence to India until 1947, the **Salt March** may be said to be the beginning of the end of British colonial rule in India.

At the time of the Salt March, Gandhi was sixty-one years old. Educated in England, he gained a reputation as an activist on behalf of the rights of Indians in South Africa. From 1915, he worked in India, transforming the **Congress Party** into a mass movement and conducting his first large nonviolent civil disobedience movement from 1920 to 1922. His method of nonviolent civil disobedience is known as *Satyagraha*, "Hold fast to the truth."

On 12 March 1930, Gandhi and his followers began the march to the sea to challenge the **Salt Act**, which symbolized the injustice of British rule to many Indians. Salt was a necessity in India's hot climate, and the British tax made it much more expensive than it otherwise would have been.

Gandhi hoped not merely to end the salt tax but also to convince the British of the injustice of colonial rule. Marching twelve miles a day, Gandhi and his followers reached the sea on 6 April. Gandhi walked into the surf and picked up a lump of natural salt. In a public statement, he confessed he had broken the law by evading the tax on salt, and he urged Indians to do the same. The government responded with wholesale arrests, finally arresting Gandhi on 4 May.

After Gandhi's release from prison in January 1931, he attended talks with the Viceroy, which led to the **Gandhi-Irwin Pact** in March. Civil disobedience was "discontinued" and Gandhi agreed to attend the second **Round Table Conference** in London.

Very little came out of the conference. A government **White Paper** in 1933, which only slightly reflected the discussions at the Round Table Conference, led to the **Government of India Act** in 1935 and elections in 1937.

The Salt March was the most dramatic, widely publicized, and successful of Gandhi's civil disobedience campaigns. Although it indirectly caused the British to grant a measure of self-government in 1935, yet another campaign from 1940 to 1942 and the effects of **World War II** were needed to convince the British the time had come to grant India independence. Nonetheless, the Salt March effectively displayed Gandhi's talent for symbolic action and probably came closer than the other major campaigns to matching the high standards he set for his followers. It was the beginning of the end of British rule in India and a crucial step toward independence. Gandhi, influenced by the Russian writer **Leo Tolstoy** and the American essayist **Henry David Thoreau,** in his turn served as an inspiration for **Martin Luther King, Jr.,** and the American civil rights movement.

Suggestions for Term Papers

1. Compare the depiction of the Salt March in the 1982 film *Gandhi* with historical accounts. How accurately does the film portray the Salt March and events following it?

2. Investigate Gandhi's daily routine before and after the Salt March and try to determine the reasons for various activities he undertook on a daily basis.

3. How did the British colonial administration in India respond to the Salt March? What were their views on Gandhi?

4. Read about some of the other major figures associated with Gandhi such as Jawaharlal Nehru. What roles did they play in the Salt March and in the activities that followed it?

5. Find out more about Gandhi's years in South Africa. What was the importance of his work there to his later efforts in India?

6. Trace the influence of Gandhi on Martin Luther King, Jr. To what extent did Dr. King model his civil rights campaigns on Gandhi's idea of *Satyagraha*?

Research Suggestions

In addition to the boldfaced items, look under the entry for "The Independence of India and Pakistan, 1947" (#42). Search under **Jawaharlal Nehru, Muhammad Ali Jinnah, London Round Table Conferences**, and **Government of India Act** (1935).

SUGGESTED SOURCES

Primary Sources

Gandhi, Mohandas K. *An Autobiography: The Story of My Experiment with Truth.* Boston: Beacon Press, 1957. Gandhi's own account of his work.

———. *The Essential Gandhi: An Anthology.* Edited by Louis Fischer. New York: Vintage Books, 1962. A useful collection of Gandhi's writings.

———. *The Gandhi Reader: A Source Book of His Life and Writing.* Edited by Homer A. Jack. Bloomington: Indiana University Press, 1956. Another useful collection.

Secondary Sources

Brown, Judith M. *Gandhi and Civil Disobedience: The Mahatma in Indian Politics, 1928–1934.* Cambridge: Cambridge University Press, 1977. An indispensable source for the history of the Salt March and events surrounding it.

Erikson, Erik H. *Gandhi's Truth: On the Origins of Militant Nonviolence.* New York: W. W. Norton, 1969. An influential study of Gandhi's methods. The epilogue provides a short account of the Salt March.

Fischer, Louis. *The Life of Mahatma Gandhi.* New York: Harper and Brothers, 1950. An older but still useful biography of Gandhi.

Gandhi. Directed by David Lean. 1982. An epic film biography of Gandhi. A good introduction to Gandhi as a person and a leader.

Gopal, S. *The Vice-Royalty of Lord Irwin, 1926–1931.* Oxford: Clarendon Press, 1957. Gandhi and the Salt March from the British perspective.

Mehta, Ved. *Mahatma Gandhi and His Apostles.* New Haven: Yale University Press, 1993. A fascinating introduction to Gandhi and his work. Originally published by Viking Press in 1977.

Wolpert, Stanley. *Nehru: A Tryst with Destiny.* New York: Oxford University

Press. 1996. A recent and useful biography of a man who worked closely with Gandhi and was a major figure in the independence movement in his own right.

———. *A New History of India*. 6th ed. New York: Oxford University Press, 2000. The standard history of India. Probably the best starting point for those wishing to investigate Indian history in the twentieth century.

21. THE BAUHAUS IN WEIMAR, GERMANY, 1919–1933

Walter Gropius, a well-known architect, began the **Bauhaus** in 1919 in the city of **Weimar** by merging an academy of art and a school of applied arts. Expanding on prewar artistic concepts, Gropius called for artists and craftsmen to join together to produce the building of the future, a building that would combine function and beauty.

The Bauhaus was simultaneously a course of studies, a series of workshops that accepted architectural and design commissions, and a commentary on political and social issues. The course of studies consisted of an elementary course and training in a workshop. The basic idea was to provide the artist with a mastery of the materials available for work as well as an understanding of aesthetic questions. It was a form of education designed to erase the line separating artists from craftsmen, bringing the two together in building projects that would create the material basis for a good life.

Those involved in the Bauhaus not only designed buildings but also worked in a great variety of other fields: furniture design, lamps, rugs, pottery, typography and book design, even dance and theater. Perhaps the best-known product of the Bauhaus is **Marcel Breuer**'s tubular chair, copies of which may still be found in homes, colleges, and airports around the world. Among the many prominent artists and architects associated with the Bauhaus are **Paul Klee, Wassily Kandinsky, Lyonel Feininger, Oskar Schlemmer**, and **Laszlo Moholy-Nagy**.

The Bauhaus was a controversial institution and the object of considerable hostility both because of its radical design ideas and the bohemian outlook of students and masters. In 1925 the Bauhaus moved from Weimar, an increasingly conservative city, to the indus-

trial town of **Dessau**, a more congenial location. There Gropius designed and built his most famous buildings and the Bauhaus enjoyed
its most productive period. Gropius's primary aim was to make the
most of advantages offered by technology: "Our object was to elim-
inate every drawback of the machine without sacrificing any one of
its real advantages."

Despite Gropius's efforts to keep the Bauhaus nonpolitical, it became associated with communism. The ideas it represented, the work
it carried out, even the existence of the Bauhaus as a community and
way of life—everything about it had political overtones. In 1932,
hampered by both the **Great Depression** and the increasingly conservative political situation, the Bauhaus moved to **Berlin**. It survived
the end of the **Weimar Republic** by only a few months.

Participants in the Bauhaus movement spread its influence around
the world in the 1930s and 1940s. For several decades after World
War II its concepts dominated architecture and design.

Suggestions for Term Papers

1. Find out more about Walter Gropius's career before the founding
   of the Bauhaus and trace the development of the ideas that came
   to be associated with that movement.

2. Investigate the lives and careers of some of the well-known participants in the Bauhaus.

3. Read about the artistic and cultural scene in the Weimar Republic
   more generally and determine the place of the Bauhaus.

4. Compare the ideas about architecture and urban planning associated with the Bauhaus to Nazi ideas, especially those of Adolf
   Hitler and Albert Speer, Hitler's collaborator in his architectural
   projects.

5. Follow the career of Gropius or other well-known participants after the end of the Bauhaus movement.

6. Interview local architects on the extent to which they have been
   influenced by the Bauhaus. Ask if there are any local structures
   that embody some of the principles of the Bauhaus.

Research Suggestions

In addition to the boldfaced items, look under "Pablo Picasso and
Cubism, 1907" (#3), "The New Economic Policy (NEP) in Russia,

1921–1928" (#14), and "The Nazi 'Seizure of Power' in 1933" (#24). Search under **Erich Mendelsohn, Ludwig Mies van der Rohe, Le Corbusier, Frank Lloyd Wright**, **De Stijl** (Dutch group similar to the Bauhaus), and **Vkhutemas** (Russian group similar to the Bauhaus).

SUGGESTED SOURCES

Primary Sources

Gropius, Walter. *The New Architecture and the Bauhaus*. 1935. London: Faber and Faber, 1965. The most complete statement of Gropius's ideas.

————. *Scope of Total Architecture*. 1955. New York: Collier Books, 1962. Shorter pieces.

Kaes, Anton, Martin Jay, and Edward Dimenberg, eds. *The Weimar Sourcebook*. Berkeley: University of California Press, 1994. A comprehensive and very useful selection of documents from the Weimar era, including many related to the Bauhaus.

Secondary Sources

Friedrich, Otto. *Before the Deluge: A Portrait of Berlin in the 1920's*. New York: Harper and Row, 1972. A dependable popular study of the 1920s in Berlin and other parts of Weimar Germany.

Gay, Peter. *Weimar Culture: The Outsider as Insider*. New York: Harper and Row, 1970. An excellent introduction to Weimar culture in general and the Bauhaus in particular by one of America's best historians.

Hughes, Robert. "Trouble in Utopia." *The Shock of the New*. New York: Time-Life Video, 1980. Number 4 in the series places the Bauhaus in the context of architectural and design trends in the 1920s. A companion book to the television series is also available.

Klotz, Heinrich. *Twentieth Century Architecture*. London: Academy Editions, 1989. A highly readable survey that includes a good discussion of the Bauhaus movement.

Lane, Barbara Miller. *Architecture and Politics in Germany, 1918–1945*. Cambridge, Mass.: Harvard University Press, 1985. A useful discussion of architecture and urban planning as a political battleground between left and right. Well illustrated.

Willett, John. *Art and Politics in the Weimar Period: The New Sobriety 1917–1933*. New York: Pantheon Books, 1978. An excellent overview, with over 200 illustrations, that places the Bauhaus not only in a German but also in a European context.

Wingler, H. M. *The Bauhaus.* Cambridge, Mass.: MIT Press, 1969. Considered the standard work on the Bauhaus.

22. THE GREAT DEPRESSION IN THE 1930s

A decade after **World War I** ended the worst economic depression of the twentieth century struck. No country was immune. Triggered by the New York **Stock Market crash of October 1929**, financial markets in Vienna, Berlin, London, Paris, and Tokyo tumbled. This ripple effect in financial markets was expected; what was not expected was the stunning collapse of international trade in manufactured goods and agricultural products. Factory workers had no work, and farmers could not sell their produce. By 1932, 40 million people throughout the world were unemployed.

Initially most governments cut spending, tightened credit, reduced salaries, lowered prices, and raised **tariffs**. Yet by the mid-1930s democratic governments had given up on these traditional remedies and were experimenting with new approaches to jump start their flattened economies. Scandinavian countries, such as **Sweden**, developed very aggressive government-funded **social programs**. Britain, France, and the United States experimented with large government agencies such as the **British Broadcasting Corporation (BBC)** and the **Tennessee Valley Authority (TVA)**, the latter of which produced electricity for the American South. Although these and other similar efforts showed promise, they did not put large numbers of people back to work.

Authoritarian governments were much more successful in battling the Great Depression. The Soviet Union was committed to economic planning, and **Josif Stalin**'s **Five-Year Plans** ensured that Soviet industry enjoyed robust growth during the 1930s. Italy, Germany, and Japan infused their capitalist economies with massive state intervention, particularly in large state-sponsored projects such as the **Volkswagen** automobile, highway and railway construction, and heavy armament manufacturing. In Germany **Adolf Hitler**'s economic policies resulted in full employment. By 1938 the German economy had surpassed the output levels of 1929. In Japan the government overcame a severe agricultural depression by shifting farm workers to heavy industry, especially in armaments and shipbuilding. Between

1929 and 1937 Japan added more than 1 million workers to its factories.

By 1939 three lessons were clear. First, massive state intervention was necessary to combat this Great Depression. Second, the English economist **J. M. Keynes** was correct in arguing in his *The General Theory of Employment, Interest and Money* (1936) that deficit spending, (government spending of borrowed funds), not tight credit, would stimulate business. Third, authoritarian governments were more effective in rescuing capitalist economies than were democracies.

Suggestions for Term Papers

1. Read George Orwell's *Road to Wigan Pier* (see Suggested Sources) and write a paper on his views of England in the Great Depression.
2. Write a research paper on the development of the Volkswagen automobile in Germany. How significant was this project in Nazi Germany's battle against the Great Depression (see Suggested Sources)?
3. Why was Japan able to come out of the Great Depression so quickly? Examine the Japanese government's policies for combating the Depression.
4. John Scott was one of thousands of Americans who immigrated to the Soviet Union during the Great Depression. Investigate his experiences working there during the 1930s (see Suggested Sources).
5. Do a research project on the life and ideas of John Maynard Keynes and evaluate his approach to overcoming the effects of the Great Depression.
6. To what extent did Sweden's embrace of socialism help to overcome the Great Depression (see Suggested Sources)? What are some of the enduring legacies of the Swedish approach?

Research Suggestions

In addition to the boldfaced items, look under the entries for "The New Economic Policy (NEP) in Russia, 1921–1928" (#14), "Stalin's

First Five-Year Plan, 1928–1932" (#23), "The Japanese Economic Miracle in the 1950s" (#47), and "The Asian Economic Meltdown at the End of the 1990s" (#97). Search under **New Deal** and **industrial policy.**

SUGGESTED SOURCES

Primary Sources

Allen, Frederick Lewis. *Since Yesterday: The Nineteen-Thirties in America, September 3, 1929–September 3, 1939.* New York: Harper and Brothers, 1940. The classic social history of Depression-era America.

Fallada, Hans. *Little Man, What Now?* New York: Simon and Schuster, 1933. A powerful evocation of how the Great Depression flattened the German middle class.

Isherwood, Christopher. *The Berlin Stories.* Cambridge, Mass.: R. Bentley, 1954. Although largely fiction, these remain vivid portraits of Depression-era Berlin.

Keynes, John Maynard. *Essays in Persuasion.* London: Macmillan, 1933. Short, accessible essays on Keynes's approach to economics.

Orwell, George. *The Road to Wigan Pier.* New York: Harcourt, Brace, 1958. First published in 1937. A classic depiction of the Great Depression in the British coal fields.

Scott, John. *Behind the Urals: An American Worker in Russia's City of Steel.* First published in 1942. Bloomington: Indiana University Press, 1989. An account of life in Magnitogorsk in the 1930s by an American engineer.

Secondary Sources

Cameron, Rondo. *A Concise Economic History of the World: From Paleolithic Times to the Present.* 3rd ed. New York: Oxford University Press, 1997. A lucid and up-to-date analysis of the worldwide effects of the Depression.

Childs, Marquis William. *Sweden: The Middle Way.* New Haven: Yale University Press, 1936. A classic portrait of Sweden's socialist approach to end the Depression.

Hopfinger, K. B. *The Volkswagen Story.* Cambridge, Mass.: R. Bentley, 1971. A solid account of Hitler's "people's car."

Kennedy, David M. *Freedom from Fear: The American People in Depression and War, 1929–1945.* New York: Oxford University Press, 1999. Well written and comprehensive, the text has an excellent bibliography on the Depression.

Kindleberger, Charles. *The World in Depression, 1929–1939.* Berkeley: University of California Press, 1986. The most authoritative treatment available.

Landes, David S. *The Unbound Prometheus: Technological Change and In-dustrial Development in Western Europe from 1750 to the Present.* London: Cambridge University Press, 1969. Chapter 6 is a good analysis of the European depression.

——. *The Wealth and Poverty of Nations: Why Some Are So Rich and Some Are So Poor.* New York: W. W. Norton, 1998. Comprehensive in approach, with good chapters on Japan.

23. STALIN'S FIRST FIVE-YEAR PLAN, 1928–1932

The first **Five-Year Plan** was a heroic effort to industrialize the Soviet Union. The plan, which emphasized heavy industry and centralized economic planning, was intended to create the economic basis for socialism. Stalin also wanted to prepare the **Soviet Union** for the possibility of war.

Originally, the first plan, officially dated from the latter part of 1928, called for difficult but not impossible goals. Stalin, however, insisted on raising already high targets. He emphasized large-scale projects and speed. **Magnitogorsk**, a new metallurgical complex near the southern end of the Ural Mountains, was a good example of the Stalinist approach to industrialization in that goals for the complex were raised repeatedly.

Another characteristic feature of the Five-Year Plans was the **Sta-khanovite** movement. **Aleksei Stakhanov** devised a way to mine more coal in one shift than miners ordinarily could produce. Stakha-novite workers appeared in many industries, with the result that work-ers were expected to be far more productive than in the past.

The Soviet Union became a major industrial power in the course of the 1930s. The labor force more than doubled, from about 11.5 million to nearly 23 million. Consumer goods were scarce and hous-ing crowded, but many Soviet citizens took great pride in building the new Soviet Union.

Collectivization, which began in 1928, was seen as a vital part of the Five-Year Plan. It resulted by early 1930 in approximately 50 percent of peasant families joining collective farms (where peasants owned the land but pooled their resources and labor and marketed the harvest cooperatively). Many, however, had been forced to join. The level of rebellion was so high that Stalin had to retreat. His March 1930 article, **"Dizzy with Success,"** blamed problems on overzealous subordinates and reassured peasants they would not be forced to join. Many left at that point, but continuous pressure resulted by 1933 in over 90 percent of peasant families joining either collective farms or state farms.

One feature of collectivization was the hunt for **kulaks**, the so-called rich peasants. Often these were simply the most independent peasants in a village. They were sometimes shot on the spot; at best, they might be given an hour to pack and then sent out to some desolate spot to begin again.

Collectivization was a failure as an economic policy. In 1932 there was a massive famine in the **Ukraine** and the northern Caucasus region. Perhaps as many as 7 million peasants died. Collectivization, intended to mechanize agriculture and to increase productivity, became the Achilles' heel of the Five-Year Plan. Soviet agriculture never fully recovered from the experience.

Suggestions for Term Papers

1. Compare the First Five-Year Plan with the Second Five-Year Plan in terms of goals and achievements.

2. Investigate the construction of Magnitogorsk and describe the hardships endured by ordinary workers there.

3. How accurately did Stalin's report to the Seventeenth Party Congress in 1934 present the accomplishments of the Five-Year Plans?

4. What was life like for peasants before the collectivization of agriculture?

5. What was life like for peasants on the new collective farms?

6. Read about the circumstances of the death of Stalin's wife, Nadezhda Alliluyeva, in 1932. Some believe she committed suicide as a protest against the harshness of the Five-Year Plan. Review the evidence and state your reasons for accepting or rejecting this interpretation of the event.

Research Suggestions

In addition to the boldfaced items, look under the entry for "The New Economic Policy (NEP) in Russia, 1921–1928" (#14). Search under **Gosplan** (state planning agency), **Lazar Kaganovich, Sergei Kirov, Kolkhoz** (collective farm), and **MTS** (machine-tractor stations).

SUGGESTED SOURCES

Primary Sources

Garros, V. N. Korenevskaya, and T. Lahusen, eds. *Intimacy and Terror.* New York: New Press, 1995. A collection of diaries from the 1930s.

Hindus, Maurice. *Red Bread.* Bloomington: Indiana University Press, 1988. A reissue of an eyewitness account of collectivization.

Scott, John. *Behind the Urals: An American Worker in Russia's City of Steel.* Bloomington: Indiana University Press, 1989. First published in 1942. An account of life in Magnitogorsk in the 1930s by an American engineer.

Stalin, Joseph. *The Essential Stalin: Major Theoretical Writings, 1905–1952.* Edited by H. Bruce Franklin. Garden City, N.Y.: Doubleday, 1972. A selection of Stalin's writings, including reports to the 1934 and 1939 party congresses.

Secondary Sources

Conquest, Robert. *The Harvest of Sorrow: Soviet Collectivization and the Terror-Famine.* New York: Oxford University Press, 1986. A careful study of the famine of 1932 and collectivization policies.

Davies, R. W. *The Industrialization of Soviet Russia.* 3 vols. Cambridge, Mass.: Harvard University Press, 1980–1991. A standard history of industrialization in the 1930s in the tradition of E. H. Carr's multivolume series on the Soviet Union.

Fitzpatrick, Sheila. *Everyday Stalinism: Ordinary Life in Extraordinary Times. Soviet Russia in the 1930s.* Oxford: Oxford University Press, 1999. A fascinating discussion of the social history from the bottom up.

———. *Stalin's Peasants.* Oxford: Oxford University Press, 1994. An examination of peasant response to collectivization based on new archival material.

Hunter, Holland. "The Overambitious First Five-Year Plan." *Slavic Review*

32 (1973): 237–57. An influential discussion of the problems brought about by inflating the goals of the Five-Year Plan.

Kotkin, S. *Magnetic Mountain.* Berkeley: University of California Press, 1995. An important study of Magnitogorsk, one of the show projects of the First Five-Year Plan.

Siegelbaum, L. H. *Stakhanovism and the Politics of Productivity in the USSR, 1935–1941.* Cambridge, Mass.: Harvard University Press, 1986. A very interesting study of the Stakhanovite movement in particular and labor relations more generally.

Tucker, Robert C. *Stalin in Power: The Revolution from Above, 1928–1941.* New York: W. W. Norton, 1990. The second volume of a major biography of Stalin.

Viola, Lynne. *The Best Sons of the Fatherland: Workers in the Vanguard of Soviet Collectivization.* New York: Oxford University Press, 1987. A fine study of efforts by urban communists to carry out the collectivization policy in the countryside.

———. *Peasant Rebels under Stalin.* New York: Oxford University Press, 1996. A very useful study of peasant resistance to collectivization.

Volkogonov, Dmitrii. *Stalin.* New York: Grove Weidenfeld, 1991. An excellent biography based on an unrivaled access to the archival sources.

24. THE NAZI "SEIZURE OF POWER" IN 1933

Adolf Hitler did not seize power in 1933. Rather, he was appointed by **President Paul von Hindenburg** to be chancellor of the **Weimar Republic** (the government that replaced the monarchy in Germany after **World War I**). The idea that the Nazis had come to power by the use of force nevertheless became part of the Nazi political myth.

Had it not been for the **Great Depression**, the **German National Socialist Worker's Party (NSDAP or Nazi Party)** would never have been in a position to enter the government in 1933. Mounting unemployment and the threat of complete economic collapse led many Germans to vote for extremist parties. In the election for the **Reichstag** (parliament) in 1930, the Nazi Party emerged as the second largest political party.

Over the next two years, the government, unable to secure a majority in the Reichstag, used President Hindenburg's emergency decree powers, but failed to find a way out of the Depression. In 1932 a number of elections were held. In the presidential campaign, Hindenburg won the run-off election, but Hitler ran a respectable second and attracted millions of votes. There were two elections to the Reichstag that year. In the first, in July, the Nazi Party won 230 seats. In November another election was held; this time the Nazi Party won only 196 seats.

Some thought the Nazi Party had peaked and was now declining. Hitler, offered the post of vice-chancellor, refused it. He was only willing to become chancellor. Conservative politicians made overtures to a popular colleague of Hitler's, Gregor Strasser, but Strasser did not respond.

Finally, in January 1933, Franz von Papen, a former chancellor who was intriguing against the current chancellor, convinced Hindenburg to appoint Hitler as chancellor and himself as vice-chancellor. He was convinced the conservatives could use Hitler and the Nazi Party, then discard them once they had served their purpose. The underestimation of Hitler turned out to be fatal, not only to the political system of the Weimar Republic but also to Germany. Within a year and a half, Hitler managed to disolve every other political party and to gain control over or destroy organizations ranging from trade unions to sports clubs, choral societies, and groups for hobbyists. Only the churches and the army still had independent positions, and the army, after the death of President Hindenburg in August 1934, pledged personal loyalty to Hitler. In 1935 Hitler began a campaign of intimidation and violence that led directly to World War II.

Suggestions for Term Papers

1. Hitler was an innovative campaigner and used both the radio and the airplane in the 1930s in his campaigns. Using accounts of his electoral campaigns, discuss Hitler's weaknesses and strengths as a campaigner.

2. On the local level, the Nazi Party pursued an energetic campaigning style that supplemented the national efforts of the party in crucial ways. Using local studies by William S. Allen (see Suggested Sources) and others, investigate the way the party worked on the local level.

3. President Paul von Hindenburg had been the great hero of World War I for Germans. As president, he was a symbol of trust and stability. Evaluate his role in Hitler's rise to power.

4. Soon after Hitler was named chancellor, a mysterious fire broke out in the Reichstag building. The communists were blamed and the incident was used to convince Hindenburg to suspend the guarantee of civil liberty. The Nazis were also accused of setting the fire. Examine the evidence available for each and stage a mock trial (you may either consult accounts of the actual trial and re-create it or put on your own version based on the facts you have established).

5. The Nazi Party consolidated its power after Hitler became chancellor through a process termed *Gleichschaltung*. This might be understood as the process of making something conform to the Nazi viewpoint. Imagine what it would be like if you were living in Germany in 1933 and your student government association and other organizations you were a part of underwent a process of *Gleichschaltung*.

6. The S.A. (Stormtroopers), the paramilitary wing of the Nazi Party, although loyal to Hitler, was a source of problems after he became chancellor. It wanted to move directly to a revolution featuring anti-Semitism and measures directed against big business. Hitler reluctantly agreed to a campaign of assassination against the leaders of the S.A. and other enemies of the Nazis in June 1934, the "Night of the Long Knives." Why would he decide to turn on people who had been staunch supporters? What role did the German army play? Begin with "The Night of the Long Knives" in David Clay Large's *Between Two Fires* (see Suggested Sources).

Research Suggestions

In addition to the boldfaced items, look under the entries for "The Paris Peace Conference, 1919" (#11) and "The Great Depression in the 1930s" (#22). Search under **Reichstag Fire, Enabling Act, Night of the Long Knives, Hermann Göring,** and **Heinrich Himmler.**

SUGGESTED SOURCES

Primary Sources

Noakes, J., and G. Pridham, eds. *Nazism 1919–1945*. Vol. 1, *The Rise to Power, 1919–1934*. Exeter, U.K.: University of Exeter Press, 1983.

One of three volumes of documents and analysis in the series. A comprehensive and valuable collection.

Sax, Benjamin, and Dieter Kuntz, eds. *Inside Hitler's Germany: A Documentary History of Life in the Third Reich.* Lexington, Mass.: D. C. Heath, 1992. The first four chapters present documents on the Weimar Republic, the rise of the Nazi Party, the "seizure of power," and *Gleichschaltung* in 1933–1934.

Secondary Sources

Allen, William S. *The Nazi Seizure of Power: The Experience of a Single German Town, 1922–1945.* New York: Franklin Watts, 1984. Rev. ed. A grass-roots study of the Nazi Party in action. A very useful source.

Blum, George. *The Rise of Fascism in Europe.* Westport, Conn.: Greenwood Press, 1998. A good overview for students with accompanying biographical profiles and primary documents.

Broszat, Martin. *Hitler and the Collapse of Weimar Germany.* New York: St. Martin's Press, 1987. A careful discussion of Hitler's role in the failure of the Weimar Republic.

Bullock, Alan. *Hitler and Stalin: Parallel Lives.* New York: Knopf, 1992. Although Bullock's earlier work, *Hitler: A Study in Tyranny* (1964), is more detailed, the dual biography reflects recent scholarship.

Large, David Clay. *Between Two Fires: Europe's Path in the 1930s.* New York: W. W. Norton, 1991. A good starting point for the history of Europe in the 1930s.

Nicholls, A. P. *Weimar and the Rise of Hitler.* New York: St. Martin's Press, 1991. A good introduction to the topic.

Orlow, Dietrich. *The History of the Nazi Party, 1919–1933.* Pittsburgh: University of Pittsburgh Press, 1969. An excellent analysis of the formative years of the Nazi Party.

Turner, Henry A., Jr. *Hitler's Thirty Days to Power.* Reading, Mass.: Addison Wesley Longman, 1996. The best study currently available of the "seizure of power." Turner stresses that it never had to happen.

25. MAO ZEDONG AND THE LONG MARCH, 1934–1935

A heroic journey of about 6,000 miles, the **Long March** took Chinese Communist forces from the encircled **Jiangxi Soviet** in the south to a new base at **Yan'an** in the northwestern province of

Shaanxi. During the march, **Mao Zedong (Mao Tse-tung)** emerged as the leader of the **Chinese Communist Party (CCP)**.

In 1934 **Zhu De (Chu Teh)**, the Red Army commander-in-chief for the Jiangxi Soviet, met with Communist Party leaders and decided to abandon the soviet. The **Chinese Nationalists (Guomindang)** under **Chiang Kai-shek** seemed on the verge of conquering the area. **Zhou Enlai (Chou En-lai)** planned the breakout strategy. The commander of one of the army corps leading the breakout was **Lin Biao (Lin Piao)**. Many of those who would become the Chinese Communist Party's most important leaders over the following four decades participated in the Long March.

Some 80,000 men and about 35 women, each carrying about a two-week ration of rice and salt, started the march on 16 October 1934. Among the women was Mao's pregnant second wife, **He Zizhen**. The communist forces had to break through four lines of defense before they could reach and take the city of **Zunyi** in Guizhou province in January 1935. Later that month a high-level party conference took place in Zunyi. The resolutions issued after the conference reflected Mao's criticism of the leadership of the Jiangxi Soviet. It was an important step in his rise to power in the party.

Perhaps the most extraordinary adventure experienced by participants was securing the **Luding Bridge**, the last across the Datong River. Nationalist forces had removed most of the planks from the chain suspension bridge. Twenty soldiers crawled across and routed the defenders, making it possible for their comrades to cross safely. Another difficult segment of the journey involved crossing the "Great Snow" mountain range with some passes as high as 16,000 feet. Mao, ill with malaria, had to be carried at times on a litter.

By June 1935 the communists had lost half their original force. Mao nevertheless pressed them to continue on to Shaanxi. Thousands died, however, from illness and exhaustion crossing a large marshy area on the way.

Between 8,000 and 9,000 communists finished the march on 20 October 1935 in Shaanxi. More than 70,000 died or slipped away during the march. In the course of the march, Mao had become the leader of the Chinese Communist Party. Simply by surviving, the party had won a great moral victory over the Chinese Nationalists. The Long March served as an inspiring saga for party members for decades to come. It was a key event in the eventual victory in 1949 of the Chinese Communists over the Chinese Nationalists.

Suggestions for Term Papers

1. Investigate Mao's career in the early 1930s. Why did he have only limited success in winning party members over to his ideas about the peasantry?

2. Trace the route taken by the communists on the Long March and describe some of the different cultures they came across in the course of their journey.

3. Some scholars believe Chiang Kai-shek avoided destroying the communist forces on purpose. Supposedly, chasing them allowed him to extend his influence into new areas. Draw your own conclusions on the basis of your reading.

4. Write a one-act play based on the discussions that took place at the Zunyi Conference.

5. Compare the activities of other top leaders before the Long March with those of Mao.

6. How was the story of the Long March used in the Great Proletarian Cultural Revolution some thirty years later?

Research Suggestions

In addition to boldfaced items, look under the entries for "Mao Zedong's 'Report on an Investigation of the Peasant Movement in Hunan, March 1927' " (#17), "The Victory of the Chinese Communist Party, 1949" (#46), and "The Great Proletarian Cultural Revolution in China, 1966–1976" (#73). Search under **Communist International (Comintern)**.

SUGGESTED SOURCES

Primary Sources

Braun, Otto. *A Comintern Agent in China, 1932–1939.* Stanford: Stanford University Press, 1982. An inside perspective on the Long March and events leading up to it from the Comintern representative in China.

Mao Zedong. *Mao's Road to Power: Revolutionary Writings: 1912–1949.* Vol. 3, *From the Jinggangshan to the Establishment of the Jiangxi Soviet, July 1927–December 1930.* Edited by Stuart Schram. Armonk, N.Y.: M. E. Sharpe, 1995. Vol. 4, *The Rise and Fall of the Chinese*

Soviet Republic, 1931–1934. Edited by Stuart Schram, 1997. Highly useful background material.

Snow, Edgar. *Red Star over China.* New York: Grove/Atlantic, 1989. Rev. ed. The original was published in 1938. A famous contemporary report from a journalist highly sympathetic to Mao and the Chinese Communist Party.

Secondary Sources

Ch'en, Jerome. *Mao and the Chinese Revolution.* New York: Oxford University Press, 1965. A useful and thorough biographical study.

Salisburg, Harrison. *The Long March.* New York: HarperCollins, 1985. A readable account by a well-informed journalist.

Schram, Stuart. *Mao Tse-tung.* New York: Simon and Schuster, 1966. A good introduction.

Schwartz, Benjamin. *Chinese Communism and the Rise of Mao.* Cambridge, Mass.: Harvard University Press, 1958. An excellent discussion of Mao's struggle to gain acceptance for his ideas.

Smedley, Agnes. *The Great Road: The Life and Times of Chu Teh.* New York: Monthly Review Press, 1972. Originally published in 1956. A dated but still useful biography of Zhu De by a writer sympathetic to the CCP.

Spence, Jonathan D. *The Search for Modern China.* New York: W. W. Norton, 1990. A wonderful synthesis of modern Chinese history. Probably the best starting point for any paper on China.

Wilson, Dick. *The Long March of 1935: The Epic of Chinese Communism's Survival.* London: Hamilton, 1971. A detailed and dependable account of the Long March.

Yang, Benjamin. *From Revolution to Politics: Chinese Communists on the Long March.* Boulder: Westview Press, 1990. A recent scholarly analysis by an expert on the period.

26. GENERAL BROADCASTING OF TELEVISION IN BRITAIN, 1936

Scientists and interested laymen began to talk about the possibilities of transmitting pictures in the latter part of the nineteenth century. The use of the telegraph and the telephone to transmit sound suggested the analogous possibility of a machine to transmit images.

The first important development came in 1883 when **Paul Nipkow** invented a mechanical scanning device. Although he abandoned the idea, others later used it in the first efforts to develop television. By the 1920s both **John Logie Baird** in England and **Charles Francis Jenkins** in the United States were using the Nipkow disk to transmit and receive images. By the late 1920s **Ernst Alexanderson**, a Swedish American scientist at General Electric, was also broadcasting. In 1928 he broadcast an announcement by Governor Al Smith of New York that he was running for president. Alexanderson also broadcast a play that year. Despite his successes, he never attracted the major financial backing he needed.

Also in 1928, Baird successfully sent a television signal across the Atlantic Ocean and demonstrated color television. In the 1930s he worked with the BBC in Britain and participated in the first official television broadcasts in 1936. Probably fewer than 1,000 television sets were available in Britain to receive the transmissions.

The real contest to make television commercially feasible involved three Americans: **David Sarnoff, Vladimir Kosmo Zworykin**, and **Philo Taylor Farnsworth**. Farnsworth, whose breakthrough idea came to him as a teenager while he was plowing, probably had the strongest claim to be considered the father of electronic television.

Zworykin had the advantage of support from Sarnoff and **RCA (Radio Corporation of America)**. His **cathode-ray picture tube**, the **Kinescope**, "was the most important single technical advancement ever made in the history of television," according to one historian of the medium. Farnsworth, always strapped for cash, in the meantime developed a superior camera in his **Image Dissector** (he used magnetized beams of electrons to scan line by line at electronic speed; the image produced was far sharper than one produced by mechanical scanners).

Sarnoff visited Farnsworth in 1931 and offered to purchase his ideas for $100,000, but Farnsworth declined the offer. Farnsworth actually was awarded the key patents for electronic television. Sarnoff seemed ready to concede defeat and pay royalties, but **World War II** caused television to be set aside for the duration of the war. After the war, with Farnsworth's patents about to expire, RCA, Sarnoff, and Zworykin turned television into a commercial success. By the 1960s, television had become a major factor in American life.

Suggestions for Term Papers

1. Although the United States successfully developed television as a commercial enterprise, the invention of television was an international effort. Investigate the early history of television, begin-

ning with the coining of the word by a Frenchman in 1900, and write an essay on the international origins of television.

2. Organize a group project to explain the physics of television. This might include building working models of some of the early devices such as the Nipkow disk used in the development of television, or it might result in a television documentary on the physics of television.

3. Philo Farnsworth was a great American original, the self-taught inventor. Examine his life, especially the period after World War II when Sarnoff and Zworykin became known as the fathers of television, and write a short biography of him.

4. What kind of working relationship did John Logie Baird have with the BBC in the 1930s? Why was he unable to make a commercial success of television in the 1930s?

5. Develop a time line for the development of television after World War II including such milestones as color television broadcasts, the development of videocassette recorders, commercial telecommunications satellites, and high-definition television.

Research Suggestions

In addition to the boldfaced items, look under the entries for "The Invention of the Computer, 1944–1946" (#39) and "The Internet in the 1990s" (#99). Search under **BBC (British Broadcasting Corporation)**.

SUGGESTED SOURCES

Primary Sources

Baird, John Logie. *Sermons, Soap and Television*. Croydon, England: Royal Television Society, 1990. Baird's autobiography.

Farnsworth, Elma G. *Distant Vision—Romance and Discovery on an Invisible Frontier*. Salt Lake City: Pemberley Kent, 1990. The memoirs of Farnsworth's wife.

Kisseloff, Jeff. *The Box: An Oral History of Television (1920–1961)*. New York: Viking, 1995. More concerned with television broadcasting than the invention of the process, it nonetheless contains many fascinating and relevant interviews.

Secondary Sources

Abramson, Albert. *The History of Television, 1880 to 1941.* Jefferson, N.C.: McFarland, 1987. A useful discussion of the development of television.

————. *Zworykin: Pioneer of Television.* Champaign: University of Illinois Press, 1995. The definitive biography of one of the most important figures in the development of television.

Baird, Margaret. *Baird of Television.* Cape Town, South Africa: Haum, 1973. A biography of Baird by his wife.

"Big Dream, Small Screen." PBS, 1997. Part of the American Experience series. This is an excellent biography of Philo Farnsworth.

Burns, R. W. *British Television: The Formative Years.* London: P. Peregrinus, 1986. A standard work on the topic.

Fisher, David E., and Marshall Jon Fisher. *Tube: The Invention of Television.* Washington, D.C.: Counterpoint, 1996. A solid, readable history of the invention of television, concentrating mostly on the 1920s and 1930s.

McArthur, Tom, and Peter Waddell. *Vision Warrior.* Orkney, Scotland: Orkney Press, 1990. A useful biography of Baird with much new information.

Norman, Bruce. *Here's Looking at You: The Story of British Television, 1908–1939.* London: BBC and Royal Television Society, 1984. An official history of the period.

Ritchie, Michael. *One Moment Please: A Prehistory of Television.* Woodstock, N.Y.: Overlook Press, 1994. A good introduction to the topic.

Smith, Anthony, ed. *Television: An International History.* Oxford: Oxford University Press, 1995. An authoritative collection of essays.

World Wide Web

Baird, Malcolm H.I. "Eye of the World: John Logie Baird and Television" [Part II]. *Kinema*, Web edition, Fall 1996. *arts.uwaterloo.ca/FINE/juhde/baird962.htm.* Baird's career from 1926 to his death in 1946. The author of the article is Baird's son.

Hills, Adrian R. "Eye of the World: John Logie Baird and Television" [Part I]. *Kinema*, Web edition, Spring 1996. *arts.uwaterloo.ca/FINE/juhde/hills961.htm.* An excellent overview of Baird's early life.

"Big Dream, Small Screen." *http://www.pbs.org/wgbh/amex/technology/bigdream.* The Web site for the PBS production. Several valuable features including the transcript of the program.

27. KITA IKKI AND ULTRANATIONALISM IN JAPAN, 1936–1937

Nationalism dominated Japanese politics in the decades following **World War I**. By the late 1920s Japanese nationalists embraced a belief in Japanese racial superiority, not only toward westerners but also toward fellow Asians. Nationalists also promoted the idea of Japanese territorial expansion, particularly in the Chinese province of **Manchuria**. By the 1930s many Japanese nationalists insisted that Japan could achieve greatness only through war and that civilian politicians who opposed the military were traitors.

Kita Ikki (1883–1937) was one of the most authoritative voices of Japanese nationalism. As a young man he had studied in China and witnessed the fervent outpouring of Chinese nationalism in the **May 4, 1919** demonstrations against the **Treaty of Versailles**. Although often labeled a fascist, Kita Ikki considered himself a modernizer. Ikki insisted that the **Emperor of Japan** was the keystone of the Japanese state. He argued that the men of commerce currently running Japan should be replaced by new "pure-hearted" elites (presumably from the military) who would lead Japan to greatness.

During the 1920s only a few Japanese read Kita Ikki, but in the 1930s his writings, particularly *Outline for the Reconstruction of Japan* (1919) became very popular among the ultranationalists. In this text, Ikki called for a three-year suspension of the constitution, dissolution of parliament, and the assumption of power by "pure-hearted" elites. Under his plan Japan not only had the absolute right to start a war to protect its own national interests, it also had the right to declare war to protect the interests of other Asian countries.

Although not a clear or logical thinker, Kita Ikki was an inspirational writer who was particularly influential among junior army officers, many of whom had little formal education. Although he had no part in the **Tokyo coup d'état**, on **26 February 1936**, his name was linked with the young army officers captured after the failed coup. Arrested and charged with treason, Ikki was executed in 1937. Ironically, the military government of **General Hideki Tojo** that came to power in 1941 adopted many of Kita Ikki's ideas.

Suggestions for Term Papers

1. Ikki insisted that, of all the European countries, Germany was the most appropriate model for Japan. Why would Germany's political and military institutions be so popular in early twentienth-century Japan?

2. Although he insisted he was not a fascist, Kita Ikki has often been called Japan's premier fascist thinker. Investigate the meaning of the term "fascist" and based on your understanding of the term determine whether Ikki was a fascist.

3. Many of the young army officers executed in the failed coup d'état in 1936 insisted they were imitating the chivalric ideals of the ancient Japanese Samurai warriors, the revered Forty-Seven Ronin, who had sacrificed their lives to avenge the honor of the Emperor of Japan. After reading the story of the Forty-Seven Ronin (see Suggested Sources), do you agree?

4. Investigate the failure of parliamentary government in Japan in the 1930s and determine the various factors in addition to Ikki's ultranationalist ideas that contributed to that failure.

5. The governments of China, South Korea, and the Philippines have insisted that Japan must pay indemnities to their citizens for "the racially motivated ultranationalist conduct of Japanese military during World War II." Examine the Japanese occupation policies in one of these countries and write a paper analyzing the legitimacy of these claims for indemnity.

6. To ensure that Japan's military would not be able to repeat its ultranationalist policies of the 1930s, the 1946 Japanese Constitution incorporated special measures to restrict the military. Read the constitution (see Suggested Sources) and assess the constitutional role of the military in contemporary Japan.

Research Suggestions

In addition to the boldfaced items, look under the entries for "The Paris Peace Conference, 1919" (#11), "The Rape of Nanking, 1937" (#28), "The Use of Atomic Bombs in World War II, 1945" (#37), and "The Japanese Economic Miracle in the 1950s" (#47). Search under **fascism, Shinto**, and **International Military Tribunal for the Far East**.

SUGGESTED SOURCES

Primary Sources

Kita Ikki. "Outline for the Reconstruction of Japan." In *Sources of Japanese History*, vol. 2. Edited by David Lu. New York: McGraw-Hill, 1974.

Writers and Revolutionaries: The Pacific Century [videorecording]. Seattle: Nihon Hoso Kyokai and KCTS: Annenberg/CPB Project, 1992. The film examines the lives of Lu Xun, China's greatest modern writer, and Kita Ikki. George M. Wilson, one of the premier American scholars of Kita Ikki, reads from Ikki's works and comments on his writings.

Secondary Sources

Chikamatsu, Monzaemon. *Four Major Plays of Chikamatsu*. Trans. Donald Keene. New York: Columbia University Press, 1998. These English selections have the story of the "Forty-Seven Ronin" who avenged the honor of their lord.

Ineaga, Saburo. *The Pacific War: 1931–1941*. Translated by Frank Baldwin. New York: Pantheon Books, 1978. Written by a leading Japanese scholar who insists that too many Japanese accounts gloss over the "naked realities" of Japanese aggression.

Inoue, Kyoko. *MacArthur's Japanese Constitution: A Linguistic and Cultural Study of Its Making*. Chicago: The University of Chicago Press, 1991. A detailed examination of the English and Japanese versions of the 1946 constitution.

Iriye, Akira. *The Origins of the Second World War in Asia and the Pacific*. London: Longman, 1987. Written by the leading American authority, this book has a very helpful bibliography of all aspects of the period.

———. *Pearl Harbor and the Coming of the Pacific War: A Brief History with Documents and Essays*. Boston: St. Martin's Press, 1999. The best introduction to Japanese strategic planning for the Pacific War and the Japanese military's role in pressing for war.

"Kita Ikki, 1883–1937." In *The Routledge Dictionary of Twentieth-Century Political Thinkers*. 2nd ed. Edited by Robert Benewick and Philip Green, 129–30. London: Routledge, 1992. A crisp summary of Ikki's ideas.

Reischauer, Edwin, and Albert M. Craig. *Japan: Tradition and Transformation*. Boston: Houghton Mifflin, 1989. Although this is a general textbook, it is very good on the interwar years.

Wilson, George M. *Radical Nationalist in Japan: Kita Ikki, 1883–1937.*
    Cambridge, Mass.: Harvard University Press, 1969. The most acces-
    sible English language study of Ikki and his writings. Wilson hesitates
    to label Ikki a fascist.

28. THE RAPE OF NANKING, 1937

During the 1920s, Japan launched an aggressive economic penetra-
tion of the Chinese province of **Manchuria**. To protect their investments in Manchuria, the Japanese government established a new
Manchurian army command, the **Kwantung Army**.

The Kwantung Army enjoyed considerable autonomy in Manchuria; it reported directly to Japanese **Emperor Hirohito** and was not
subject to civilian control. For some time senior Japanese military had
been seeking an "incident" to gain full control over Manchuria. On
18 September 1931, during night maneuvers near **Mukden**, the Japanese military claimed they had been attacked by Chinese troops.
Seizing upon this "incident," the Japanese army occupied all of Manchuria, renamed it **Manchuko**, and established **Puyi**, the last Chinese
emperor, as their puppet head of state.

Well aware that China's Nationalist government, led by **Chiang
Kai-shek**, was not strong enough to reclaim Manchuria, the Japanese
military eagerly sought another "incident" to extend Japanese influence into north China. On 7 July 1937, Japanese troops stationed in
Beijing conducted night maneuvers west of the city near the Marco
Polo Bridge. Mistakenly, the Japanese commander thought the Chinese army had captured one of his soldiers and ordered an attack on
a nearby Chinese garrison.

The Marco Polo Bridge incident marked the opening of eight years
of brutal warfare between China and Japan. From the beginning of
the conflict the Japanese military targeted Chinese civilians for special
treatment. Japanese aircraft bombed and strafed Chinese cities. By
late November Japanese troops had captured **Beijing** and **Shanghai**
and were besieging **Nanking**. On 13 December 1937, Japanese
forces captured Nanking and initiated a horrifying policy of massacre,
rape, and genocide resulting in the death of more than 350,000 ci-

vilians. By 1945 more than 1.3 million Chinese soldiers had died in the Sino-Japanese War and approximately 3 million Chinese civilians had been killed.

Suggestions for Term Papers

1. Emperor Hirohito (1926–1989) chose the word *Showa* or "bright peace" at the time of his enthronement as the name of his reign. Investigate the life of Emperor Hirohito and assess *Showa* as a descriptor for his reign.
2. Read Puyi's autobiography (see Suggested Sources) as part of a review of the Japanese takeover of Manchuria. What role did he play as the Japanese puppet ruler of Manchuria?
3. Examine the photographs in Shi Young and James Yin's *The Rape of Nanking: An Undeniable History in Photographs* (see Suggested Sources) and write a paper focusing on the experiences of Chinese women during the Japanese occupation of the city.
4. Iris Chang titles her book *The Rape of Nanking: The Forgotten Holocaust of World War II* (see Suggested Sources). Write a paper on why the Japanese rape of Nanking was "forgotten."
5. Evaluate the importance of the Sino-Japanese War in Japan's decision to attack the United States at Pearl Harbor on 7 December 1941.
6. To what extent did the participation of the Chinese Communist Party in the war against Japan contribute to its victory in 1949 over the Chinese Nationalists?

Research Suggestions

In addition to the boldfaced items, look under the entries for "Mao Zedong and the Long March, 1934–1935" (#25), "Kita Ikki and Ultranationalism in Japan, 1936–1937" (#27), "The Holocaust, 1941–1945" (#34), and "The Victory of the Chinese Communist Party, 1949" (#46). Search under **Battle of Nomonhan, Panay Incident**, and **Pearl Harbor**.

SUGGESTED SOURCES

Primary Sources

Chang, Jung. *Wild Swans: Three Daughters of China*. New York: Anchor Books, 1991. The third chapter of this memoir focuses on the Japanese occupation of Manchuria.

Letcher, John S. *Good-bye to Old Peking: The Wartime Letters of U.S. Marine Captain John Seymour Letcher, 1937–1939*. Edited by Roger B. Jeans and Katie Letcher Lyle. Athens: Ohio University Press, 1998. Captain Letcher commanded the Marine Guard at the U.S. Embassy at the outbreak of the Sino-Japanese war. Good insights into daily life.

Puyi, Henry. *The Last Manchu: The Autobiography of Henry Puyi, Last Emperor of China*. Edited by Paul Kramer. Translated by Kuo Ying Paul Tsai. New York: Putnam, 1967. A good insight into Japanese occupation policies in Manchuria.

Rabe, John. *The Good Man of Nanking: The Diaries of John Rabe*. Translated by John E. Woods. New York: Knopf, 1998. John Rabe was a German businessman in Nanking who is credited with saving thousands of Chinese from slaughter. His diaries are a damning record of the genocide.

Secondary Sources

Chang, Iris. *The Rape of Nanking: The Forgotten Holocaust of World War II*. New York: Basic Books, 1997. The most recent and accessible account of the tragedy. Chang also examines why China and the United States have not pressed Japan for a complete accounting of why Japan treated China so harshly.

Duus, Peter, et al. *The Japanese Wartime Empire, 1931–1945*. Princeton: Princeton University Press, 1996. Based on a Stanford University conference, this collection has fresh interpretations of Japan's occupation policy in China.

Ineaga, Saburo. *The Pacific War: 1931–1941*. Translated by Frank Baldwin. New York: Pantheon Books, 1978. Written by a leading Japanese scholar who shows how Japanese misconceptions of China led to unwarranted, brutal policies of occupation.

Iriye, Akira. "Japanese Aggression and China's International Position, 1931–1949." In *Cambridge History of China* 13, part 2. Edited by John K. Fairbank and Denis Twitchett, 492–540. Cambridge: Cambridge University Press, 1978. Within a brief compass this gives a good overview of the plight of China during this period.

Wilson, Dick. *When Tigers Fight: The Story of the Sino-Japanese War, 1937–*

1945. New York: Viking Press, 1982. A crisp account of the war that emphasizes the racial character of Japanese aggression.

Young, Shi, and James Yin. *The Rape of Nanking: An Undeniable History in Photographs.* 2nd ed. Chicago: Innovative Publishing Group, 1997. A shocking collection of photographs documenting the assault on Nanking.

29. THE SPANISH CIVIL WAR, 1936–1939

The 1936 election of a **Popular Front** government (a coalition of democrats, socialists, and the revolutionary left) in Spain produced a turn to violence on the part of those who opposed the republic and its government. Spaniards divided between supporters of the new Popular Front government on the one hand and those who called themselves the **Nationalists** (drawn from the army, the Catholic Church, large landowners, and Spanish Fascists) on the other.

The Nationalists began the **Spanish Civil War** on 18 July 1936 with a revolt by Spanish army troops in **Spanish Morocco**. With transport planes from **Fascist Italy, General Francisco Franco**, the leader of the Nationalist forces, brought the troops to Spain. Aid from Fascist Italy and **Nazi Germany** was crucial to the Spanish Nationalist cause. The Spanish Republic received help from the **Soviet Union, Mexico**, and the volunteers who made up the **International Brigades**. The British and the French sponsored the **Non-Intervention Agreement**, which all the European powers signed but only Britain and France actually abided by.

The Spanish Civil War gave permission, as it were, to thousands of Spanish **anarchists** and **syndicalists** to act on radical demands. The revolutionary left among the Spanish Republicans wanted to use the emergency to advance revolution in the form of industrial and agricultural collectives and decentralized administration. Officials from the **Communist International (Comintern)** worked to maintain a broad coalition of republicans, socialists, and communists and to keep the focus on winning the war. Behind the Comintern, of course, stood the Soviet Union, in this period supporting the idea of **collective security** against fascism. Aid furnished by the Soviet Union served to counter the assistance given the Nationalists by Fascist Italy and Nazi Germany, but at the same time hostility to radical tendencies doomed the revolutionary aspects of the Republican effort in the civil war.

The Spanish Civil War provoked tremendous controversy. Supporters of the Spanish Republic regarded the civil war as a contest between democracy and fascism. Writers such as **Ernest Hemingway**, and **André Malraux** and artists such as **Pablo Picasso** supported the Spanish Republic. Supporters of the Spanish Nationalists regarded their cause as a crusade against godless communism.

In the end, the response of the great powers made the difference. The Nationalist victory ended any thought of revolution or even reform in Spain for the next three decades.

Suggestions for Term Papers

1. A Popular Front government was elected in France as well as Spain in 1936. Compare the leading personalities and the histories of the two Popular Front governments. In particular, comment on why the French Popular Front government initially came to the aid of the Spanish Republic, then turned to the idea of a Non-Intervention Agreement. Begin with Eugen Weber, *The Hollow Years* (see Suggested Sources).

2. What kind of career did General Francisco Franco have before the Spanish Civil War? Why was he chosen to lead the Spanish Nationalist forces?

3. Investigate the history of anarchism in Spain during the Spanish Civil War and before. How might one account for the popularity of anarchism in Spain in the 1930s?

4. A large number of writers and artists rallied to the cause of the Spanish Republicans. Trace the activities of one or more and read or view some of the works inspired by the Spanish Civil War.

5. Examine the roles played in the Spanish Civil War by the Communist International (Comintern) and the Soviet Union. In particular, pay close attention to connections between the Comintern and the Soviet Union.

6. The Spanish Nationalists received essential aid from Fascist Italy and Nazi Germany. Also, the Falange, generally considered a fascist organization, played a large role in Spanish Nationalist politics. To what extent might one consider the Nationalists and General Franco to be fascists?

Research Suggestions

In addition to the boldfaced items, look under the entries for "The Nazi 'Seizure of Power' in 1933" (#24), "Kita Ikki and Ultranationalism in Japan, 1936–1937" (#27), and "The Nazi-Soviet Pact, 1939" (#32). Search under **Manuel Azana, *GUERNICA*, Federico Garcia Lorca, Barcelona**, and **Madrid**.

SUGGESTED SOURCES

Primary Sources

Orwell, George. *Homage to Catalonia*. London: Gollanz, 1938. Orwell's finest book. An account of his experiences in the International Brigades.

The Spanish Earth [Videotape]. 60 minutes, bw. A 1937 documentary film by Joris Ivens, with participation by Hemingway, John Dos Passos, Orson Welles, and Lillian Hellman, among others.

Secondary Sources

Bolloten, Burnett. *The Spanish Revolution*. Chapel Hill: University of North Carolina Press, 1979. A devastating attack on communist involvement in the war. Originally published as *The Grand Camouflage*.

Brenan, Gerald. *The Spanish Labyrinth*. Cambridge: Cambridge University Press, 1943. A classic examination of Spain that places the Spanish Civil War in broad historical context.

Carr, Raymond. *The Civil War in Spain*. London: Weidenfeld and Nicolson, 1986. Perceptive and insightful. Published earlier under the title *The Spanish Tragedy* (1977).

Cattell, David T. *Communism and the Spanish Civil War*. Berkeley: University of California Press, 1955. An older but still useful study of this crucial topic.

Ellwood, Sheelagh. *Franco*. London: Longwood, 1994. A brief but solid biography of the Spanish leader.

Hemingway, Ernest. *The Fifth Column: And Four Stories of the Spanish Civil War*. New York: Scribner, 1969. Hemingway's play about the battle for Madrid.

———. *For Whom the Bell Tolls*. New York: Scribner, 1940. One of Hemingway's best known novels, the romantic account of the experiences of Robert Jordan, an American volunteer in the Spanish Civil War.

Historical Dictionary of the Spanish Civil War, 1936–1939. Edited by James W. Cortada. Westport, Conn.: Greenwood Press, 1982. A useful reference work.

Large, David Clay. *Between Two Fires: Europe's Path in the 1930s.* New York: W. W. Norton, 1991. Contains a very readable and informative chapter on the bombing of Guernica in 1937, one of the most controversial episodes of the Spanish Civil War.

Malraux, André. *Man's Hope.* New York: Random House, 1938. An important fictional treatment of the Spanish Civil War by a committed supporter of the Spanish Republic.

Payne, Stanley G. *The Spanish Revolution.* New York: W. W. Norton, 1970. Excellent on the revolutionary left before and during the Spanish Civil War.

Preston, Paul. *The Spanish Civil War, 1936–1939.* Chicago: Dorsey Press, 1986. An excellent introduction.

Stansky, Peter, and William Abraham. *Journey to the Frontier: Two Roads to the Spanish Civil War.* Boston: Little, Brown, 1966. An account of two talented and privileged British students, Julian Bell and John Cornford, who went to Spain to defend the republic. Both died in the war.

Thomas, Hugh. *The Spanish Civil War.* New York: Harper and Row, 1961. Very long and most readable. A classic account.

Weber, Eugen. *The Hollow Years: France in the 1930s.* New York: W. W. Norton, 1994. A highly readable account by as leading historian of France.

World Wide Web

"Spanish Civil War: The Posters of the Spanish Revolution." *http://burn.ucsd.edu.scwtable.htm.* An introduction and twenty-five posters from the Spanish Civil War.

30. THE MUNICH AGREEMENT, 1938

The **Munich Agreement** was the most important in a series of events leading to World War II. Before Munich, **Adolf Hitler**, the leader of **Nazi Germany**, moved Germany back into the ranks of major powers through several bold moves. In 1935 Germany announced its intention to rearm. The following year the German army moved into the **Rhineland**, a part of Germany that had been demilitarized by the **Versailles Treaty** (following World War I) and the **Locarno Agreements** (1925).

Early in 1938 Germany annexed Austria. Then Hitler turned to Czechoslovakia and the **Sudetenland** issue. This concerned an area of Czechoslovakia whose population was primarily German. Although

Czechoslovakia treated its minorities well, many Sudeten Germans complained about discrimination. Hitler encouraged **Konrad Henlein**, the leader of a Sudenten German party sympathetic to Nazi goals, to make demands Czech leaders could not meet.

Neville Chamberlain, the British prime minister, sought ways to negotiate a settlement between Germany and Czechoslovakia. Chamberlain believed that Germany had legitimate grievances stemming from the Versailles Treaty and that Hitler should be encouraged to settle these through negotiation. When it looked in mid-September 1938 like war was likely, Chamberlain flew to Hitler's mountain retreat at **Berchtesgaden** to meet Hitler. He acceded to Hitler's demand for separation of the Sudetenland from Czechoslovakia. When he met Hitler again, however, Hitler had new, unacceptable terms. Now the separation of the Sudetenland had to take place within three days, and German troops had to enter the area immediately.

At the last minute, **Benito Mussolini**, the leader of Fascist Italy, proposed a conference in Munich that would involve Germany, Britain, France and Italy. Hitler accepted the proposal. Czechoslovakia was not invited. Neither was the Soviet Union. The participants agreed to transfer the Sudetenland to Germany, and, in turn, Hitler guaranteed the integrity of Czechoslovakia.

The Munich Agreement managed to delay war about a year. It became a synonym for **appeasement**, which came to mean a foolish attempt of weak men to satisfy the insatiable demands of dictators.

Suggestions for Term Papers

1. Hitler seemed determined to use force to gain the Sudetenland. Survey Nazi foreign policy and military preparations between 1936 and 1938 and determine to what extent Hitler's tactics and strategy were changing in this period.

2. What did Neville Chamberlain hope to accomplish with what is now termed appeasement?

3. Investigate the history of Czechoslovakia in the interwar period and assess its successes and failures as a new state by 1938.

4. Some historians believe it would have been better to challenge Hitler in 1938, rather than in 1939, after he attacked Poland. Review the evidence in support of this opinion and write an essay on why you believe or do not believe war should have come in 1938.

5. France had an obligation under a treaty with Czechoslovakia to come to its aid in case of attack. Why did France decide to follow the British lead and force Czechoslovakia to give in on the Sudetenland issue?

6. Why did Mussolini suggest the Munich Conference, and what role did he play there?

Research Suggestions

In addition to the boldfaced items, look under the entries for "The Spanish Civil War, 1936–1939" (#29), "*Kristallnacht* ('The Night of Broken Glass'), 1938" (#31), and "The Nazi-Soviet Pact, 1939" (#32). Search under **Stanley Baldwin, Anthony Eden, Edouard Daladier,** and **The Franco-Soviet Pact**.

SUGGESTED SOURCES

Primary Sources

Churchill, Winston S. *The Gathering Storm*. Boston: Houghton Mifflin, 1948. Churchill's classic account of the coming of World War II.

Documents on British Foreign Policy, 1919–1939. Third Series, Vol. 1, *1938*; Vol. 2, *1938*, and Vol. 3, *1938–1939*. London: His Majesty's Stationery Office, 1949, 1950. Helpful in reconstructing the development of British policy.

Documents on German Foreign Policy, 1918–1945, from the Archives of the German Foreign Ministry. Series D (1937–1945), Vol. 2, *Germany and Czechoslovakia, 1937–1938*. Washington, D.C.: Government Printing Office, 1949. How the German Foreign Ministry saw events in 1938.

Hitler, Adolf. *The Speeches of Adolf Hitler, April 1922–August 1939*. 2 vols. Edited by Norman H. Baynes. London: Oxford University Press, 1942. Useful background material.

Secondary Sources

Adamthwaite, Anthony P. *France and the Coming of the Second World War, 1936–1939*. London: Frank Cass, 1977. An important book on the French involvement in Munich and other events leading up to World War II.

Bullock, Alan. *Hitler and Stalin: Parallel Lives*. New York: Random House, 1993. A good review of this period with useful comparisons between Hitler and Stalin.

Charmley, John. *Chamberlain and the Lost Peace*. Chicago: I. R. Dee, 1990. A defense of Chamberlain's efforts to secure a negotiated settlement.

Eubank, Keith. *Munich*. Norman: University of Oklahoma Press, 1963. An older but still useful study.

Gilbert, Martin, and Richard Gott. *The Appeasers*. London: Weidenfeld and Nicolson, 1963. An excellent introduction to the controversy.

Kaiser, David E. *Economic Diplomacy and the Origins of the Second World War: Germany, Britain, France, and Eastern Europe, 1930–1939*. Princeton: Princeton University Press, 1980. An important study of the economic context of diplomacy.

Large, David Clay. *Between Two Fires: Europe's Path in the 1930s*. New York: W. W. Norton, 1991. Contains a chapter on the Munich Conference. An excellent book to consult first.

Mommsen, Wolfgang J., and Lothar Kettenacker. *The Fascist Challenge and the Policy of Appeasement, 1937–1940*. Boston: G. Allen and Unwin, 1983. An excellent collection of chapters on aspects of the issue of appeasement.

Murray, Williamson. *The Change in the European Balance of Power, 1938–1939: The Path to Ruin*. Princeton: Princeton University Press, 1984. An assessment of the military context within which diplomatic discussions took place.

Taylor, A.J.P. *The Origins of the Second World War*. London: Hamish Hamilton, 1961. A controversial and entertaining book. Taylor asserts that Hitler was just another German statesman. Well worth reading but should be matched by a more conventional account.

Taylor, Telford. *Munich: The Price of Peace*. New York: Random House, 1979. A comprehensive account that asserts that the Western powers should have tried to stop Hitler in 1938.

Weber, Eugen. *The Hollow Years: France in the 1930s*. New York: W. W. Norton, 1994. A readable history of France in the 1930s. Helpful in providing context for the French role in the Munich Conference.

Weinberg, Gerald L. *The Foreign Policy of Hitler's Germany: Starting World War II, 1937–1939*. Atlantic Highlands, N.J.: Humanities Press, 1994. The best discussion available of Hitler's intentions.

World Wide Web

"History of the United Kingdom—Primary Documents." *http//library.byu. ed/~rdh/eurdocs/uk.html*. Links to the Munich Pact and Neville Chamberlain's "Peace for Our Time" speech. Part of the large and very useful "EuroDocs: Primary Historical Documents from Western Europe" Web site.

31. *KRISTALLNACHT* ("THE NIGHT OF BROKEN GLASS"), 1938

Between 1933 and 1938, German Jews were subject to increasing persecution, mostly of a quasi-legal nature. Legislation, in particular the **Nuremberg Laws** of 1935, excluded Jews from the Civil Service, which included the teaching profession; deprived them of German citizenship; and made marriages and sexual relations with non-Jews illegal. The object of the laws, regulations, and informal practices appeared to be to force German Jews to leave the country. Many countries, including the United States, refused to do anything to make it easier for Jews to immigrate.

In 1938 a new and harsher phase in the persecution of German Jews began, starting with "The Night of Broken Glass" or Kristallnacht, 9–10 November. It was called "The Night of Broken Glass" because of all the plate glass windows broken in Jewish shops by members of the Nazi party and the **S.A.** (Stormtroopers, the paramilitary auxilliary of the Nazi Party). The excuse for these attacks was the report that a German diplomat had been killed by **Hershl Grynszpan**, a seventeeen-year-old Polish Jewish student, to protest the deportation of his parents. In actuality, **Josef Goebbels**, Hitler's minister of propaganda, coordinated a campaign that encouraged S.A. and party members to rape, murder, and pillage.

In a coordinated effort that night all over Germany, synagogues and Jewish institutions were burned down. Thousands of Jewish businesses were destroyed. Nearly a hundred Jews were killed. Many others were beaten or tortured.

In the aftermath, German Jews were subjected to new restrictions, which denied them access to public places such as beaches and movie theaters and expelled their children from German schools. While Jews were compensated for damages if they had insurance, the government confiscated their compensation and fined them an additional billion marks. Furthermore, a comprehensive decree excluded Jews from virtually all areas of economic life.

In a speech to the Reichstag on 30 January 1939, Hitler threatened German and other European Jews: If the Jewish international financiers succeed in involving the nations in another war, the result will not be world Bolshevism and therefore a victory for Judaism; it will be the destruction [*Vernichtung*] of the Jews in Europe."

Suggestions for Term Papers

1. Investigate the framing of the Nuremberg Laws, in particular the attempts to define who was a Jew. Use this material as the basis for an essay discussing why Nazi Germany would begin the persecution of the Jews through legislation.

2. Some historians believe the eugenics movement of the 1920s and 1930s inadvertently prepared the way for Nazi anti-Semitism by attempts to establish a scientific basis for racial theories. Do a report on the eugenics movement in Germany and its connections to Nazi anti-Semitism and racial theories. Use Detlev Peukert's essay in *Nazism and German Society, 1933–1945* (see Suggested Sources) as a starting point.

3. It has been suggested that the Jim Crow laws of the American South furnished a model for Nazi Germany to follow. Determine the extent to which this was true and reflect on the similarities and differences between the persecution of Jews in Germany and segregation in the American South in the 1930s.

4. Read eyewitness accounts of Kristallnacht and write a story or a television show dramatizing an aspect of that event. Use as starting points *State, Economy and Society, 1933–1939* and Alison Owings, *Frauen* (see Suggested Sources).

5. Following its annexation to Germany, techniques developed in Austria to compel its Jewish population to emigrate were introduced into Germany. Review the Austrian situation and assess the importance of extending practices used there to Germany itself.

6. Reinhard Heydrich was centrally involved in the persecution of Jews after Kristallnacht—report on his career before and after Kristallnacht. Begin with Joachim Fest, *The Face of the Third Reich*.

Research Suggestions

In addition to the boldfaced items, look under the entries for "The Nazi 'Seizure of Power' in 1933" (#24) and "The Holocaust, 1941–1945" (#34). Search under **Adolf Eichmann, Reinhard Heydrich,**

Heinrich Himmler, Hermann Göring, eugenics, Social Darwinism, and euthanasia.

SUGGESTED SOURCES

Primary Sources

Sax, Benjamin, and Dieter Kuntz, eds. *Inside Hitler's Germany: A Documentary History of Life in the Third Reich.* Lexington, Mass.: D. C. Heath, 1992. Chapter 13 includes documents on anti-Semitism, including some on Kristallnacht.

Noakes J., and G. Pridham, eds. *Nazism, 1919–1945.* Vol. 2, *State, Economy and Society, 1933–1939.* Exeter, U.K.: University of Exeter Press, 1994. Chapter 23 contains a number of documents on anti-Semitism between 1933 and 1939, including several on Kristallnacht.

Secondary Sources

Bullock, Alan. *Hitler and Stalin: Parallel Lives.* New York: Knopf, 1992. Although Bullock's earlier work, *Hitler: A Study in Tyranny* (1964) is more detailed, the dual biography reflects recent scholarship.

Dawidowicz, Lucy S. *The War Against the Jews, 1933–1945.* New York: Bantam Books, 1986. First published in 1975. One of the best histories of the Holocaust. A good place to begin a study of Kristallnacht.

Fest, Joachim C. *The Face of the Third Reich: Portraits of the Nazi Leadership.* New York: Pantheon Books, 1970. Excellent biographical sketches of most of the Nazi leaders.

Fischer, Klaus P. *Nazi Germany: A New History.* New York: Continuum, 1995. An excellent recent survey.

Fisher, David, and Anthony Read. *Kristallnacht: The Nazi Night of Terror.* New York: Viking Penguin, 1989. Highly readable. A good introduction.

Friedlander, Saul. *Nazi Germany and the Jews.* Vol. 1, *The Years of Persecution, 1933–1939.* New York: HarperCollins, 1997. The first volume of what will undoubtedly become a standard work on the Holocaust.

Gellately, Robert. *The Gestapo and German Society: Enforcing Racial Policy, 1933–1945.* New York: Oxford University Press, 1990. A good introduction to a key institution in the attempts to define and enforce Nazi racial ideas.

Hilberg, Raul. *The Destruction of the European Jews.* Rev. ed. New York: Holmes and Meier, 1985. First published in 1961. A massive history of the Holocaust, probably the best single book on the subject.

Owings, Alison. *Frauen: German Women Recall the Third Reich*. New Brunswick: Rutgers University Press, 1994. Interviews with a wide variety of German women who recall their experiences in the Third Reich.

Peukert, Detlev. "The Genesis of the 'Final Solution' from the Spirit of Science," in David F. Crew, ed. *Nazism and German Society, 1933– 1945*. London: Routledge, 1994. A fascinating article on the connection between science and Nazi racial policies.

———. *Inside Nazi Germany: Conformity, Opposition, and Racism in Everyday Life*. New Haven: Yale University Press, 1987. Gives an idea of what daily life was like in Nazi Germany.

32. THE NAZI-SOVIET PACT, 1939

In the mid-1930s, the Soviet Union strongly supported the idea of **collective security** against fascist aggression. **Maxim Litvinov**, the Soviet foreign minister, arranged treaties with France and Czechoslovakia. He also sought to make the **League of Nations** a more effective organization. The **Munich Agreement** (see entry #30), represented a severe defeat for his policy.

Early in 1939, **V. V. Molotov, Josif Stalin**'s close associate, replaced Litvinov. Over the next several months, the Soviet Union hinted that it desired better relations with Germany. At the same time, it continued to negotiate with Great Britain and France. Also that year, **Adolf Hitler** completed the destruction of Czechoslovakia and put pressure on Poland to cede the free city of **Danzig** (which contained a mixed population of Poles and Germans) to Germany. Great Britain and France responded by guaranteeing support to Poland.

Hitler was determined to use the Danzig issue to force a war with Poland. He apparently did not believe Britain and France would actually defend Poland. He did, however, want to avoid a two-front war, which meant securing the neutrality of the Soviet Union. The Soviet Union also feared a two-front war, in its case one with Japan and Germany.

In August, while negotiations involving the Soviet Union, Britain, and France continued in Moscow, Stalin suddenly agreed to allow **Joachim von Ribbentrop**, the Nazi foreign minister, to come to Moscow. Ribbentrop, who had tried vainly to secure an appointment, quickly agreed. At the talks, Molotov, Stalin, and Ribbentrop drafted a **Non-Aggression Treaty** between Germany and the Soviet Union. In addition to agreeing not to attack one another, the two countries agreed that, if one country became involved in a war with a third country, the other would not aid the third country. The two countries also agreed to a **secret protocol** calling for the Soviet Union to enter a war against Poland should one break out and also dividing eastern and central Europe into spheres of influence.

Stalin, who believed Britain and France might be planning to turn Nazi Germany against the Soviet Union, signed the treaty despite the complete about-face it represented. Many communists outside the Soviet Union found it difficult to understand why Stalin would make such a cynical deal, but most accepted it as necessary. Hitler, now reassured, went ahead with the invasion of Poland on 1 September 1939.

Suggestions for Term Papers

1. Investigate the career of Maxim Litvinov and his interest in collective security. How sincere was his support of collective security?

2. How had Joachim von Ribbentrop become foreign minister in Germany, and what had he accomplished up to the point of negotiating the Nazi-Soviet Pact?

3. Review the efforts of the British and French to negotiate cooperation with the Soviet Union in the Polish question. Why did the negotiations fail?

4. Survey the history of Poland between the wars and assess its successes and failures in this period. See Richard M. Watt, *Bitter Glory: Poland Its Fate, 1918–1939* (see Suggested Sources).

5. Follow the efforts of Germany and the Soviet Union to work out the details of the secret protocol over the two years between the signing of the pact and the German invasion of the Soviet Union.

6. Stalin has been criticized not so much for signing the Nazi-Soviet Pact as for ignoring signs that Hitler intended to discard it and invade the Soviet Union. Examine the period during which the pact was in force and evaluate Stalin's handling of the situation.

Research Suggestions

In addition to the boldfaced items, look under the entries for "The Spanish Civil War, 1936–1939" (#29), "The Munich Agreement, 1938" (#30), and "The Battle of Stalingrad, 1942–1943" (#33). Search under **Baltic States (Estonia, Latvia, Lithuania), Bessarabia, Finland, Sitzkrieg ("Phoney War"),** and **Operation Barbarossa.**

SUGGESTED SOURCES

Primary Sources

Documents on German Foreign Policy, 1918–1945, from the Archives of the German Foreign Ministry. Series D (1937–1945), Vol. 6, *The Last Months of Peace, March–August 1939;* Vol. 7, *The Last Days of Peace, August 9–September 3, 1939.* Washington, D.C.: Government Printing Office, 1956. The German Foreign Ministry's view of 1939 and the coming of war.

Nazi-Soviet Relations, 1939–1941: Documents from the Archives of the German Foreign Office. Washington, D.C.: Government Printing Office, 1948. Captured German documents which offer a rich source for the study of the Nazi-Soviet Pact.

Hitler, Adolf. *The Speeches of Adolf Hitler, April 1922–August 1939.* 2 vols. Edited by Norman H. Baynes. London: Oxford University Press, 1942. Useful background material.

Secondary Sources

Adamthwaite, Anthony P. *France and the Coming of the Second World War, 1936–1939.* London: Frank Cass, 1977. An important book on the French involvement in events leading to World War II.

Bullock, Alan. *Hitler and Stalin: Parallel Lives.* New York: Random House, 1993. A good review of the developments leading up to the Nazi-Soviet Pact.

Haslam, Jonathan. *The Soviet Union and the Search for Collective Security, 1933–1939.* New York: St. Martin's Press, 1984. Places the Nazi-Soviet Pact in the larger context of Soviet efforts in the 1930s to create dependable security arrangements.

Murray, Williamson. *The Change in the European Balance of Power, 1938–1939: The Path to Ruin.* Princeton: Princeton University Press, 1984. An assessment of the military context within which diplomatic discussions took place.

Read, Anthony, and David Fisher. *The Deadly Embrace: Hitler, Stalin, and the Nazi-Soviet Pact, 1939–1941*. New York: W. W. Norton, 1988. A highly readable narrative.

Roberts, Geoffrey K. *The Unholy Alliance: Stalin's Pact with Hitler*. Bloomington: Indiana University Press, 1989. A recent, well-informed study.

Scott, William Evans. *Alliance Against Hitler: The Origins of the Franco-Soviet Pact*. Durham, N.C.: Duke University Press, 1962. A careful study of efforts by the French and Russians to establish an alliance in the mid-1930s.

Tucker, Robert C. *Stalin in Power: The Revolution from Above, 1928–1941*. New York: W. W. Norton, 1990. The second of a projected three-volume biography of Stalin. An outstanding study.

Watt, Richard M. *Bitter Glory: Poland Its Fate, 1918–1939*. New York: Simon and Schuster, 1979. A highly readable account.

Weinberg, Gerald L. *The Foreign Policy of Hitler's Germany: Starting World War II, 1937–1939*. Atlantic Highlands, N.J.: Humanities Press, 1994. The best discussion available of Hitler's intentions.

World Wide Web

"Treaty of Nonaggression between Germany and the Union of Soviet Socialist Republics." *http://www.yale.edu/lawweb/avalon/nazsov/nonagres.htm*. Part of "The Avalon Project at the Yale Law School." The secret protocol to the Nazi-Soviet Pact is the next document on the Web site.

33. THE BATTLE OF STALINGRAD, 1942–1943

Stalingrad (now **Volgograd**) was an industrial city on the Volga River. It became the site of a ferocious battle between German and Soviet forces in World War II and marked a downturn in the military fortunes of **Adolf Hitler** and Nazi Germany.

The battle for Stalingrad grew out of a German campaign in June 1942 for the oil resources of the Caucasus region. The **Sixth German Army** was ordered to take Stalingrad to block Russian efforts to intervene in the Caucasus campaign. Both sides soon came to see Stalingrad as the place where the main battle in the south would be fought.

The German attack, led by **General Friedrich Paulus**, came in August. Soviet troops in Stalingrad were led by **General Vasily Chuikov**. with **General Georgii Zhukov** in overall charge of Soviet forces. Hitler, especially, and **Josif Stalin** followed the campaign closely and often participated in the planning.

The German forces were at first overwhelmingly successful, pushing the Russian forces almost into the **Volga River**. By the end of September the Germans controlled most of Stalingrad, which was an oddly shaped city strung out along twenty miles

General Zhukov devised a plan in September for a wide encirclement of the German forces. While the battle raged in Stalingrad, street by street, building by building, and, finally, room by room, Zhukov assembled troops to the north and south of Stalingrad.

The Russian counterattack began on 19 November 1942. On 23 November the Russian forces met at Kalach on the Don River west of Stalingrad. This was **Operation Uranus**. Its success left the Germans, their Romanian, Austrian, and Italian allies, and the so-called Hiwis (Russian and Ukrainian volunteers) encircled in what was called the **Kessel** or cauldron.

Hitler refused to let Paulus attempt to break out, and efforts to supply the troops by air failed. By January conditions within the Kessel were unbearable. Soldiers slowly starved to death or froze. After sending the Germans an ultimatum to surrender, the Russian forces launched a final attack on 10 January 1943. At the end of the month the German headquarters was overrun.

Stalingrad was a staggering defeat for the German army. Hundreds of thousands of troops were killed. A great deal of equipment that could not be easily replaced was destroyed. Germany continued to fight for two more years, but the Soviet Union now had the upper hand in the east. After the British and American forces landed at Normandy in 1944, defeat was only a matter of time.

Suggestions for Term Papers

1. Investigate the personal reasons Stalin had for wanting to maintain Soviet control of Stalingrad.
2. Hitler had not been particularly interested in the conquest of Stalingrad originally, yet it eventually became an obsession with him. Write a research paper on his obsession with Stalingrad and the consequences of this for the German war effort.

3. Stalingrad was only one of the several desperate situations the Soviet Union contended with in 1942. Place it in the context of events of that year by discussing the major campaigns and issues of that time.

4. Review some of the descriptions of combat in Stalingrad and write a short story that describes a day in the life of a Soviet or German enlisted man.

5. Georgii Zhukov was the Soviet Union's great military hero from World War II, easily the equivalent of Dwight Eisenhower or Douglas MacArthur. Study his wartime and postwar career and compare it with either Eisenhower's or MacArthur's.

6. What happened to Stalingrad (later Volgograd) after the war? Read about the reconstruction of the city and efforts to commemorate the Battle of Stalingrad.

Research Suggestions

In addition to boldfaced terms, look under the entries for "The Holocaust, 1941–1945" (#34) and "The Yalta Conference, 1945" (#36). Search under **Hermann Göring, Vasily Grossman, Nikita Khrushchev, NKVD** (Soviet security police), **Operation Barbarossa**, and *Stavka* **(Soviet Supreme General Staff)**.

SUGGESTED SOURCES

Primary Sources

Battle for Stalingrad: The 1943 Soviet General Staff Study. Edited by Louis Rotundo. Washington, D.C.: Pergamon-Brassey's International Defence, 1989. The Soviet military's view of what happened and why.

Chuikov, V. I. *The Battle for Stalingrad.* New York: Holt, Rinehart and Winston, 1964. The memoirs of the Soviet commander in Stalingrad.

Werth, Alexander. *The Year of Stalingrad: A Historical Record and a Study of Russian Mentality, Methods and Policies.* New York: Knopf, 1947. An excellent account by a perceptive and well-informed British journalist of Russian background.

Zhukov, Georgii K. *Marshal Zhukov's Greatest Battles.* New York: Harper and Row, 1969. Includes Zhukov's account of his great triumph in the Battle of Stalingrad.

Secondary Sources

Beevor, Anthony. *Stalingrad: The Fateful Siege, 1942–1943.* New York: Viking Penguin, 1998. The best single book on Stalingrad, based on archival material and extensive interviews with Russian and German survivors.

Erickson, John. *The Road to Stalingrad: Stalin's War with Germany.* Boulder: Westview Press, 1984. A fine history of the war on the Eastern Front. The last two chapters cover the Battle of Stalingrad through Operation Uranus.

Görlitz, Walter. *Paulus and Stalingrad: A Life of Field-Marshal Friedrich Paulus.* London: Methuen Press, 1963. A biography of the main German commander by a German military historian.

Grossman, Vasily. *Life and Fate.* New York: Harper and Row, 1985. A major twentieth-century novel on Stalingrad by a journalist who spent many years after the war studying the battle.

Jukes, Geoffrey. *Hitler's Stalingrad Decisions.* Berkeley: University of California Press, 1985. A study of Hitler's disastrous intervention in the Battle of Stalingrad.

Ryback, Timothy W. "Stalingrad: Letters from the Dead," *The New Yorker*, 1 February 1993. Letters from German soldiers describing conditions at Stalingrad.

Stalingrad. Directed by Joseph Vilsmaier, 1996. 105 minutes, subtitles. A highly praised film by the director of *Das Boot.*

Webster, Donovan. *Aftermath: The Remnants of War.* New York: Pantheon Books, 1996. Chapter 2, "Ghosts," is an unusual look at Stalingrad, focusing on the efforts to identify and bury the many thousands of dead left unburied for decades after the battle.

34. THE HOLOCAUST, 1941–1945

The **Holocaust** (or **Shoah**, the Hebrew word for the event) was the deliberate effort by **Adolf Hitler** and other Nazis during **World War II** to annihilate all the Jews of Europe. **Anti-Semitism** had always been an important part of the Nazi ideology, but only in the course of the war did the Nazis come to believe they could carry out a policy of **genocide**.

In 1939 and 1940 the Holocaust began to take shape, first in the brutal treatment of Poles, both gentile and Jewish, and, second, in the so-called **euthanasia** (mercy killings) effort in Germany that targeted the mentally ill and the physically handicapped. The euthanasia effort was temporarily suspended because of protests, but it had already provided the Nazis with experience in selecting particular groups, collecting them at convenient points, systematically murdering them, and efficiently disposing of the bodies.

With the decision to invade the Soviet Union, the Holocaust as such began. Task forces, the **Einsatzgruppen**, accompanied the German army in search of communist officials and Jews. The army and other non-Nazi groups often participated enthusiastically in the slaughter of Russian Jews and Slavs.

In 1941 the decision was made to construct death camps, concentration camps with facilities for the killing of large numbers of people in ways that were systematic, routine, and highly bureaucratic. **Heinrich Himmler** oversaw the entire process, but **Reinhard Heydrich**, a high-ranking official in the **SS** (**Schutzstaffel**, originally Hitler's bodyguards), was given the task of implementing the **"Final Solution"** to the **"Jewish Question."** The **Wannsee Conference**, which met in January 1942 in a Berlin suburb, dealt with coordination of tasks necessary to the Holocaust.

The process of genocide involved, first, systematic efforts to identify the Jewish inhabitants of the European countries occupied by the Nazis and to isolate them from the rest of the population. The Warsaw ghetto was one such attempt. After that, Jews were rounded up and shipped in cattle cars across Europe to the death camps. At the camps, the old, the very young, and women with young children were sent immediately to the **gas chambers**, where they were killed and their bodies destroyed in **crematoria**. Those who were selected for work details faced appalling conditions that led in most cases to death.

Some Jews tried to survive by going into hiding or by seeking help in reaching neutral countries. The diary of **Anne Frank** records the efforts of the Frank family to hide from the Nazis in Amsterdam.

At the end of the war the world was stunned to learn of the enormity of the horror of the Holocaust. Between 5 and 6 million Jews were killed by the Nazis. Other groups singled out were the **Roma** and **Sinti** (gypsies), **homosexuals**, and members of the **Jehovah's Witnesses**. Millions of Poles, Russians, and Ukrainians also were murdered in the course of the war, but not in the same concerted and systematic way as the Jewish people.

Suggestions for Term Papers

1. The so-called euthanasia (mercy killing) campaign that targeted the mentally ill and physically handicapped in Germany between 1939 and 1941 foreshadowed the Holocaust. Discuss what happened in this campaign and the ways in which it contributed to methods used in the Holocaust.

2. Heinrich Himmler is probably the single individual most responsible for the actual course the Holocaust took. Study his career in the late 1930s and the 1940s and discuss the extent to which he shaped the experience of the Holocaust.

3. Read several survivors' accounts of their experiences and write a paper that discusses factors that might account for surviving an experience like the Holocaust.

4. Review the history of the Warsaw Ghetto Uprising in 1943 and write a research paper about the difficulties involved in the decision to stage an armed uprising against enormous odds.

5. As a group project, do one or more oral histories with Holocaust survivors or children of Holocaust survivors. In addition to asking about experiences during the Holocaust, you may want to talk with survivors about their lives after the Holocaust.

6. Since the publication of Daniel Goldhagen's *Hitler's Willing Executioners*, historians have tended to follow either Goldhagen's view that most Germans by the 1930s were deeply anti-Semitic and eager to help the Nazis with the Holocaust or the views of Christopher Browning, who holds that ordinary people may decide to do terrible things for many different reasons. Read Goldhagen and Browning and write a paper presenting your ideas about the motivations of the perpetrators in the Holocaust.

Research Suggestions

In addition to the boldfaced items, look under the entries for "*Kristallnacht* ('The Night of Broken Glass'), 1938" (#31), "The Battle of Stalingrad, 1942–1943" (#33), "D-Day, 1944" (#35), and "The Yalta Conference, 1945"(#36). Search under **Heinrich Himmler, Adolf Eichmann, Rudolf Hoess, Auschwitz, Belzec, Birkenau, Chelmno, Majdanek, Sobibor, Treblinka, Zyklon B, Judenraete (Jewish Councils), Genocide, Elie Wiesel,** and **Pope Pius XII.**

SUGGESTED SOURCES

Primary Sources

The Chronicle of the Lodz Ghetto, 1941–1944. Edited by Lucjan Dobroszycki. New Haven: Yale University Press, 1984. Documents from one of the main ghettos in Poland that provide a picture of the terrible conditions endured by the inhabitants.

Frank, Anne. *The Diary of a Young Girl. The Definitive Edition.* New York: Viking, 1997. While there are still a few pages not included, this new translation includes portions of the diary not printed in the original edition.

Hillesum, Etty. *An Interrupted Life: The Diaries, 1941–1943* and *Letters from Westerbork.* New York: Henry Holt, 1996. Etty also lived in Amsterdam, but was in her twenties in the period covered by the diaries. Just as interesting as Anne Frank but on a different level.

Levi, Primo. *Survival in Auschwitz: The Nazi Assault on Humanity.* New York: Simon and Schuster, 1996. Originally published in English as *If This Is a Man.* An important memoir.

Shoah. Directed by Claude Lanzmann, 1985. Five videotapes, 570 minutes. Distributed by New Yorker Films. Text of the film is available in *Shoah: An Oral History of the Holocaust* (New York: Pantheon Books, 1985). A long but often moving and powerful documentary.

Wiesel, Elie. *Night.* New York: Bantam Books, 1986. Twenty-fifth anniversary edition. A brief but very powerful portrait of a young man's descent into the hell of Auschwitz.

Secondary Sources

Bartov, Omer. *Hitler's Army: Soldiers, Nazis and the War in the Third Reich.* New York: Oxford University Press, 1991. A revisionist history that argues that the German army was heavily implicated in some aspects of the Holocaust.

Bauer, Yehuda. *A History of the Holocaust.* New York: Franklin Watts, 1982. A dependable and comprehensive discussion of the Holocaust.

Berenbaum, Michael. *The World Must Know: The History of the Holocaust as Told in the United States Holocaust Memorial Museum.* Boston: Little, Brown, 1993. A very effective presentation of the Holocaust.

Breitman, Richard. *The Architect of Genocide: Himmler and the Final Solution.* New York: Knopf, 1991. An excellent study of the man in charge of the Holocaust.

Browning, Christopher. *Ordinary Men: Reserve Police Battalion 101 and the*

Final Solution in Poland. New York: HarperCollins, 1992. An important book that concludes that even "ordinary men" are capable of great cruelty in certain circumstances.

Epstein, Eric Joseph, and Philip Rosen, eds. *Dictionary of the Holocaust: Biography, Geography, and Terminology.* Westport, Conn.: Greenwood Press, 1997. An excellent reference book.

Fischel, Jack R. *The Holocaust.* Westport, Conn.: Greenwood Press, 1998. A convenient source of a great deal of information on the Holocaust.

Goldhagen, Daniel. *Hitler's Willing Executioners: Ordinary Germans and the Holocaust.* New York: Knopf, 1996. An important book. It contains a wealth of information about the Holocaust, but its perspective on anti-Semitism in Germany before World War II is highly controversial.

Hilberg, Raul. *Perpetrators, Victims, Bystanders: The Jewish Catastrophe, 1933–1945.* New York: HarperCollins, 1992. A most helpful series of essays by one of the leading experts on the Holocaust.

Historical Atlas of the Holocaust. New York: Macmillan, 1996. Compiled under the auspices of the United States Holocaust Memorial Museum. Consists of a computer laser optical disk plus a guide.

The Holocaust: In Memory of Millions. Video, 92 minutes, 1994. Narrated by Walter Cronkite and produced by the Holocaust Memorial Museum in Washington, D.C., this is a gripping introduction to the Holocaust.

Langer, Lawrence L. *Preempting the Holocaust.* New Haven: Yale University Press, 1998. An important critical study of versions of the Holocaust that appear to dilute its powerful message.

Marrus, Michael R. *The Holocaust in History.* Hanover, N.H.: University Press of New England, 1987. A superb introduction to the topic.

Schindler's List. Directed by Stephen Spielberg, 1994. 2 videocassettes, 197 minutes. Distributed by MCA Universal Home Video. A powerful presentation of the true story of a deeply flawed man who, in many ways because of his flaws, was able to save the lives of scores of Jews.

Wyman, David S. *The Abandonment of the Jews: America and the Holocaust, 1941–1945.* New York: The New Press, 1998. First published in 1984. An indictment of the failure of the United States to do more to stop the Holocaust.

Yahil, Leni. *The Holocaust: Fate of the European Jews.* Oxford: Oxford University Press, 1991. An excellent, comprehensive study of the Holocaust.

World Wide Web

"United States Holocaust Memorial Museum." *http://www.ushmm.org.* A
valuable Web site with a searchable "Museum Collections and Archives" section and links to other sites.

35. D-DAY, 1944

The most important question of the war for the **Allies** (Britain, the
Soviet Union, and the United States) concerned the opening of a
second front, a Western Front to match the Eastern Front that had
existed since the summer of 1941 between Nazi Germany and the
Soviet Union. The campaign in Italy in 1943 was not adequate, in
the opinion of the Soviets, and so **Overlord**, a massive cross-Channel
invasion of Europe was planned for 1944. It was an impressive logistical feat to assemble the men, supplies, ships, and aircraft needed
for the invasion. The Allies also carried out an elaborate and successful
deception to convince Nazi Germany that the landing would take
place in the Pas de Calais area instead of in Normandy.

On the night of 5–6 June, after delays because of bad weather,
General Dwight D. Eisenhower, Supreme Commander of the Expeditionary Force, gave the go-ahead for the invasion. It began with
British and U.S. airborne troops parachuting into France. Early on
the morning of 6 June, British, Canadian, and American troops came
ashore on beaches code named **Gold, Juno, Sword, Utah**, and
Omaha. Initial losses were heavy, and at Omaha Beach American
forces met especially fierce resistance. Nevertheless, by the end of the
day the Allies had gained control of the beaches.

The question then became whether the Allies could reinforce the
initial assault before the Germans could concentrate enough troops
to drive the Allies back into the sea or contain them within a small
area. The Germans lost the "battle of the build-up" for several reasons. **Field Marshal Erwin Rommel**, the "Desert Fox" of North
Africa, who had been brought in to improve the **"Atlantic Wall,"**
was away on leave when the invasion began. The Germans continued
to believe that the main invasion would be in the Pas de Calais area
and kept back troops and tanks badly needed in the Normandy sector.
Hitler tried to manage the defense from his headquarters.

Nevertheless, the German forces made good use of the bocage, hedgerows so impenetrable that ordinary tanks could not get through. Air superiority was a key factor in the ability of the Allies to wear the German forces down. By the first part of August, Allied forces had broken out in open country. By 24 August, Free French forces had entered **Paris**.

Although the war continued for eight more months, the cross-Channel invasion was a success. Nazi Germany was now caught between the gigantic pincers formed by the Soviet forces in the east and the Allied forces in the west. Defeat was only a matter of time.

Suggestions for Term Papers

1. The Soviets pressed the Americans and British from 1942 on to establish a second front in Europe. Review the history of the diplomacy associated with the second front, especially the Teheran Conference.

2. Investigate the conditions of life in Britain before the launching of the invasion. In particular, examine the reception of American soldiers by the British.

3. Read some of the oral histories provided by those who came ashore on D-Day and write a short story or play based on the experiences of ordinary soldiers.

4. Review the efforts by Field Marshal Erwin Rommel to strengthen the "Atlantic Wall." What difference would it have made to the German defensive efforts if Rommel had been present 6 June 1944?

5. What role did General Charles de Gaulle and the Free French play in the campaign?

6. Evaluate Field Marshal Bernard "Monty" Montgomery's role in the planning and conduct of Overlord (see Suggested Sources).

Research Suggestions

In addition to the boldfaced items, look under the entries for "The Battle of Stalingrad, 1942–1943" (#33) and "The Yalta Conference, 1945" (#36). Search under **Field Marshal Bernard "Monty" Montgomery, General George Patton, General George C. Marshall, General Charles de Gaulle,** and the **Teheran Conference.**

SUGGESTED SOURCES

Primary Sources

Allied Forces. Supreme Headquarters. *Report by the Supreme Commander to the Combined Chiefs of Staff on the Operations in Europe of the Allied Expeditionary Force, 6 June 1944 to 8 May 1945.* Washington, D.C.: Government Printing Office, 1946. General Eisenhower's report on D-Day and subsequent efforts to defeat Nazi Germany.

Voices of D-Day. Edited by Ronald J. Drez. Baton Rouge: Louisiana State University Press, 1994. Oral histories of participants in D-Day from the Eisenhower Center for American Studies at the University of New Orleans.

Secondary Sources

Ambrose, Stephen E. *D-Day, June 6, 1944: The Climactic Battle of World War II.* New York: Simon and Schuster, 1994. The best single book on D-Day, based on 1,400 oral histories.

D-Day Remembered [video]. 1994, 53 minutes. Distributed by Direct Cinema Limited. Part of the highly regarded American Experience series and based on oral histories contributed by veterans of the campaign.

D'Este, Carlo. *Decision in Normandy.* 1983. Reprint, New York: Dutton, 1994. A careful study by a prominent American military historian.

Hastings, Max. *OVERLORD: D-Day and the Battle for Normandy.* New York: Simon and Schuster, 1984 (reissued in 1993). An excellent account that compares the performances of the American and German armies.

Keegan, John. *Six Armies in Normandy: From D-Day to the Liberation of Paris: June 6th–August 25th, 1944.* New York: Viking Press, 1982. A unique and valuable approach, the book follows the fortunes of the American, Canadian, Scottish, English, German, and Polish armies in northern France in the summer of 1944.

Mitcham, Samuel W., Jr. *The Desert Fox in Normandy: Rommel's Defense of Fortress Europe.* New York: Praeger, 1997. A look at D-Day from the German perspective. Mitcham is somewhat uncritical of Rommel.

Normandy: The Great Crusade. CD-ROM. Bethesda: Discovery Channel CD-ROM, 1994. Based on the documentary film.

Ryan, Cornelius. *The Longest Day.* 1959. New York: Simon and Schuster, 1994. Until the appearance of Stephen Ambrose's book, the best-known history of the invasion. Source for the motion picture *The Longest Day.*

Saving Private Ryan. Directed by Steven Spielberg, 1998. A searing depiction of D-Day.

The Simon and Schuster D-Day Encyclopedia: A Multimedia Exploration! CD-ROM. Hatboro, PA: Context Systems, 1994. The print version of the encyclopedia expanded by video and audio material.

Weinberg, Gerald L. *A World at Arms: A Global History of World War II.* Cambridge: Cambridge University Press, 1994. The best one-volume account of the war available.

Wilt, Alan F. *The Atlantic Wall: Hitler's Defenses in the West, 1941–1944.* Ames: Iowa State University Press, 1975. The best account of this important effort by the German military.

World Wide Web

"D Day." *http://www.pbs.org/wgbh/pages/amex/dday.* The transcript of the documentary *D-Day Remembered* and other interesting features.

Encyclopedia Britannica Web site on D-Day. *http://normandy.eb.com.* Comprehensive information including maps and bibliography.

"Stephen Ambrose on 'Booknotes.'" *http://www.booknotes.org/transcripts/10005.htm.* A transcript of Ambrose's comments on *D-Day, June 6, 1944: The Climactic Battle of World War II.*

36. THE YALTA CONFERENCE, 1945

The **Yalta Conference** in February was the first of two major meetings of the **Big Three** (Great Britain, the United States, and the Soviet Union) in 1945. It is sometimes viewed as the conference at which **President Franklin Roosevelt** made too many concessions to **Josif Stalin**, the Soviet leader, and did not maintain a united front with **Winston Churchill**, the British prime minister.

Four major issues dominated the conference. First was the status of Poland. The Soviet Union had installed a Polish government. The other Allies wanted free elections and some members of the Polish government-in-exile brought into the government. Stalin promised to grant these requests.

The Soviet Union also pushed for drastic changes in its borders with Poland in order to take in former Polish territory it claimed. Poland would be compensated with German territory to the west. The presence of the **Red Army** in Poland and the rest of eastern Europe was an important fact of life. The Allies agreed to the boundary changes but referred them to a final determination by a peace conference. They also agreed to a **Declaration on Liberated Europe** calling for self-determination and free elections.

The second issue was the German Question. The decision to occupy Germany and divide it into zones had already been taken. Britain and the United States believed France should also have an occupation zone. The Soviet Union agreed but insisted the French zone should come from the British and American zones. There was also agreement to demilitarize and de-Nazify Germany.

The reparations issue caused many difficulties. The Soviet Union proposed that Germany pay $20 billion, half going to them. The British and Americans, thinking back to the experience after World War I, were reluctant. The matter was turned over to the foreign ministers to be worked out later.

A third major issue involved bringing the Soviet Union into the war against Japan. It was thought the Pacific war might last until 1947. The Soviet Union agreed to enter that war two to three months after the end of the war in Europe. In return, Stalin wanted several concessions from China. Since China was not represented at Yalta, the United States undertook to secure its agreement.

A final major item concerned the **United Nations**. The United States, eager to avoid the problems that dogged the **League of Nations**, got the Soviets to agree that permanent members could veto any resolution of the **Security Council**, the main organ of the UN. Additionally, the Soviets agreed to have a total of three votes in the main representative body, the **General Assembly**, instead of one vote for each of the republics making up the USSR. Finally, Britain and the United States agreed to repatriate Soviet citizens, against their wishes if necessary. This created a tragic situation for many individuals for whom repatriation was virtually a death sentence.

Much was decided before Yalta and only confirmed there. Also, the rapid progress of the Red Army created situations where there was no possibility of negotiation. However, the Allies sincerely believed in continued cooperation. By July, when the Allies met in **Potsdam**, it became clear that the alliance was frayed.

Suggestions for Term Papers

1. The Americans and the British met before the conference at Yalta on the island of Malta. Investigate this meeting and discuss the extent to which the Americans and British developed a common

strategy for dealing with the Soviet Union before flying to the Yalta conference.

2. Evaluate Winston Churchill's role in the Yalta Conference. What were his main concerns and to what extent was he able to obtain them? Use the biography by Martin Gilbert as a starting point (see Suggested Sources).

3. Stalin clearly wanted a free hand in Poland and pointed out that Britain did what it wanted in Greece, and the United States in Italy. Study the differing situations and decide whether this was a fair comparison.

4. Several plans were proposed for Germany after the war, some of them quite harsh. Review these plans and discuss the feasibility of alternatives to the decisions made at Yalta.

5. Write a biographical sketch of one of Roosevelt's key advisors. Either his secretary of state, Edward R. Stettinius, or the chief of staff, General George C. Marshall, would be good choices. Use James M. Burns, *Roosevelt: The Soldier of Freedom, 1940–1945*, as a starting point (see Suggested Sources).

6. How did the American military view prospects for the war against Japan? Was the effort to involve the Soviet Union in the war in the Pacific a good idea?

Research Suggestions

In addition to the boldfaced items, look under the entries for "The Establishment of the United Nations, 1945" (#38) and "The Marshall Plan (The European Recovery Act), 1948–1951" (#44). Search under **George Marshall, Vyacheslav Molotov, Anthony Eden, Edward Stettinius, Teheran Conference** (1943), and **Dumbarton Oaks Meeting** (1944).

SUGGESTED SOURCES

Primary Sources

Stettinius, Edward R. *Roosevelt and the Russians: The Yalta Conference.* Westport, Conn.: Greenwood Press, 1970. Stettinius, Roosevelt's secretary of state at Yalta, presents an insider's account.

Tehran-Yalta-Potsdam: The Soviet Protocols. Edited by Robert Beitzell. Gulf Breeze, Fla.: Academic International Press, 1970. The Soviet version of Yalta and the two other major meetings of the Big Three.

U.S. Department of State. *Foreign Relations of the United States, Diplomatic Papers: The Conferences of Malta and Yalta.* Washington, D.C.: Government Printing Office, 1955. Reprint, Westport, Conn.: Greenwood Press, 1976. The official record.

Secondary Sources

Burns, James M. *Roosevelt: The Soldier of Freedom, 1940–1945.* New York: Harcourt Brace Jovanovich, 1970. A standard biography of Roosevelt.

Clemens, Diane Shaver. *Yalta.* New York: Oxford University Press, 1970. An excellent discussion of the Yalta Conference.

Elliott, Mark. *Pawns of Yalta: Soviet Refugees and America's Role in Their Reparation.* Urbana: University of Illinois Press, 1982. A useful book on the highly controversial repatriation of Soviet citizens.

Gardner, Lloyd C. *Spheres of Influence: The Great Powers Partition Europe, from Munich to Yalta.* Chicago: Ivan R. Dee, 1994. A solid survey of prewar and wartime diplomacy that places Yalta in context.

Gilbert, Martin. *Churchill: A Life.* New York: Holt, 1991. A comprehensive biography by a leading expert on Churchill.

Mastny, Vojtech. *Russia's Road to the Cold War: Diplomacy, Warfare, and the Politics of Communism, 1941–1945.* New York: Columbia University Press, 1979. The best book for ascertaining Soviet positions on events.

37. THE USE OF ATOMIC BOMBS IN WORLD WAR II, 1945

In the 1930s several physicists realized that the nuclear energy obtained from splitting an atom could be the basis for a powerful weapon. **Albert Einstein**, in a 1939 letter to **President Franklin Roosevelt**, warned that Nazi Germany might be the first to develop such a weapon.

In June 1942, Roosevelt approved a major program for the construction of an atomic bomb. This program, known as the **Manhattan Project**, involved an extraordinary level of cooperation among scientists, industrialists, military officials, and government leaders. Secret facilities were constructed at Oak Ridge, Tennessee; Hanford, Washington; and **Los Alamos, New Mexico**. The director of the project was **General Leslie R. Groves. Dr. J. Robert Oppenheimer** headed the laboratory that designed the bomb.

The project was a joint effort of the United States and Britain, but neither country saw any reason to inform their ally the Soviet Union about the effort. Nevertheless, the Soviet Union was well informed about the progress of the project through its network of spies in Britain and the United States. In the meantime, Germany, lacking the resources, and optimistic about advances in other weapons programs, dropped out of the race.

The war in Europe ended before the atomic bomb could be tested. The war against Japan, however, looked to be far from over in July 1945 when President Harry S Truman received word that the bomb had been successfully tested. The decision to drop it in warfare was based primarily on the experience of the American military in **Okinawa**, where fierce Japanese resistance had resulted in 75,000 American casualties. It was feared that the invasion of the home islands of Japan, scheduled for the late fall, would produce large numbers of U.S. casualties, perhaps 200,000. There was the possibility that the use of atomic bombs would shock the Japanese into surrender.

On 6 August 1945 the *Enola Gay* dropped the first atomic bomb on **Hiroshima**. A second bomb was dropped a few days later on **Nagasaki**. On 15 August, **Emperor Hirohito**, in an unprecedented radio broadcast, announced Japan's surrender. Controversy continues concerning the role played by the bombs in Japan's surrender. Even more important, the use of atomic weapons in 1945 opened a new era in human history. It contributed to the long Cold War and to the arms race that was one of its major features.

Suggestions for Term Papers

1. Report on what was known about the atom in the 1930s and speculation then about uses for atomic energy. Use Richard Rhodes, *The Making of the Atomic Bomb* as a starting point (see Suggested Sources).

2. The Manhattan Project was a mammoth undertaking involving an

unprecedented coordination of personnel, resources, and money. What factors made it possible for the United States to complete it successfully?

3. Leo Szilard was the most prominent of the scientists who wanted to block the use of the atomic bomb. Investigate his life by reading his autobiography (see Suggested Sources) and discuss why he opposed the use of atomic weapons.

4. Trace the process by which the decision was reached in 1945 to use atomic weapons, and determine the extent of President Truman's contribution to the process.

5. Compare accounts by survivors in Hiroshima and Nagasaki. Do common themes emerge, or is each survivor's story unique?

6. Investigate Soviet espionage in connection with Anglo-American efforts to develop the atomic bomb. Determine how much Soviet espionage contributed to their efforts to build atomic weapons.

Research Suggestions

In addition to the boldfaced items, look under the entry for "The Establishment of the United Nations, 1945" (#38). Search under **Werner Heisenberg, Klaus Fuchs, Leo Szilard, Lavrenty Beria**, and **"Trinity."**

SUGGESTED SOURCES

Primary Sources

Hachiya, Michihiko. *Hiroshima Diary: The Journal of a Japanese Physician, August 6–September 30, 1945*. Chapel Hill: University of North Carolina Press, 1955. A fascinating eyewitness account.

Jones, Vincent C. *Manhattan: The Army and the Atomic Bomb*. Washington, D.C.: Government Printing Office, 1985. The official history of the project.

Stimson, Henry L. "The Decision to Use the Atomic Bomb," *Harper's Magazine* vol. 194, no. 1161 (February 1947): 97–107. Stimson, secretary of war in 1945, attempted to justify the use of the atomic bomb by pointing to the large number of casualties that were avoided. The figures used in the article are far larger than the estimates in 1945.

Secondary Sources

Alperowitz, Gar. *Atomic Diplomacy: Hiroshima and Potsdam*. Rev. ed. New York: Simon and Schuster, 1985. Alperowitz is the leading exponent of "atomic diplomacy," the idea that Truman, in attempting to use atomic weapons to gain an advantage over the Soviet Union, did much to set off the Cold War.

Bernstein, Barton J. "The Atomic Bombing Reconsidered," *Foreign Affairs* 74, no. 1 (January-February 1995): 135–52. A careful review of the controversy by a moderate revisionist.

The Day after Trinity: J. Robert Oppenheimer and the Atomic Bomb. New York: Voyager, 1995. A CD-ROM based on Jon Else's 1980 documentary. It also includes a selection of documents and biographies of many of those involved in the Manhattan Project.

Feis, Herbert. *The Atomic Bomb and the End of World War II*. Princeton: Princeton University Press, 1966. An important study by a strong supporter of the decision to drop the atomic bomb.

Hersey, John. *Hiroshima*. New York: Knopf, 1946. A classic work of journalism that originally appeared in the *New Yorker*, it tells the story of several victims of the first atomic bomb.

Holloway, David. *Stalin and the Bomb*. New Haven: Yale University Press, 1994. The extraordinary story of how the Soviet Union became a nuclear power.

Lifton, Robert Jay. *Death in Life: Survivors of Hiroshima*. Chapel Hill: University of North Carolina Press, 1991. First published in 1968. An influential book on the problems of those who survived the dropping of the first atomic bomb.

Rhodes, Richard. *The Making of the Atomic Bomb*. New York: Simon and Schuster, 1986. A long but very readable account of the Manhattan Project.

Sherwin, Martin J. *A World Destroyed: Hiroshima and the Origins of the Arms Race*. New York: Vintage Books, 1987. Probably the best single book on the use of the atomic bombs. The 1987 edition contains twenty-three documents from the period.

Szilard, Leo. *Leo Szilard: His Version of the Facts. Selected Recollections and Correspondence*. Cambridge, Mass.: MIT Press, 1978. Vol. 2 of *The Collected Works of Leo Szilard* (1972). Szilrad helped to develop the atomic bomb, but then became convinced it would be a mistake to use it.

Walker, J. Samuel. *Prompt and Utter Destruction: Truman and the Use of Atomic Bombs Against Japan*. Chapel Hill: University of North Carolina Press, 1997. A thorough discussion by one of the leading students of Truman's decision.

Walker, Mark. *German National Socialism and the Quest for Nuclear Power, 1939–1949*. Cambridge, Mass.: Harvard University Press, 1989. Why Nazi Germany did not develop an atomic bomb.

38. THE ESTABLISHMENT OF THE UNITED NATIONS, 1945

Inspired by the universal vision of the **League of Nations** and promoted by **President Franklin D. Roosevelt** and **Prime Minister Winston S. Churchill** of Great Britain, the idea of a **United Nations** grew out of discussions among the **Allied Powers** during **World War II**. The first expression of the idea of a United Nations appeared in the **Atlantic Charter** of 1941. In addition to pledging the destruction of Nazi tyranny, the charter announced that Roosevelt's **Four Freedoms**—freedom of speech, freedom of religion, freedom from fear, and freedom from want—would be the basis of a postwar new world order. In January 1942, at the **Washington Conference**, President Roosevelt for the first time used the words United Nations to identify the twenty-six nations pledged to defeat Germany, Italy, and Japan.

Although keenly interested in advancing military cooperation among the **"Big Three"** allied powers of Great Britain, the Soviet Union, and the United States, Roosevelt did not invest much time in the organizational or political structure of the United Nations until 1944. At the **Dumbarton Oaks Conference**, held outside of Washington in 1944, Great Britain, China, the Soviet Union, and the United States established the general organization of the United Nations. The final draft of the UN Charter was completed on 26 June 1945.

Representatives of fifty nations signed this charter, which went into effect on 24 October 1945. The principal organs of the UN are a **General Assembly**, a **Security Council**, an **Economic and Social Council**, a **Trusteeship**, an **International Court of Justice**, and a **Secretariat**. Although virtually all countries have membership in the General Assembly, China, France, Great Britain, Russia, and the United States are the five permanent members of the Security Council and exercise a preponderance of influence in military and security issues. A veto by one of the five permanent members can halt a Security Council action or resolution.

Suggestions for Term Papers

1. Most Americans seem to support U.S. membership in the UN, but a significant number of Americans are opposed to UN membership. Write a paper recommending or opposing continued U.S. membership in the UN based on an investigation of the UN's history.

2. Although President Roosevelt played an important role in establishing the UN, Eleanor Roosevelt was a delegate to the UN and drafted its statement on human rights in 1948. Do a research project on Mrs. Roosevelt's work in the UN, particularly on her work in promoting human rights (see Suggested Sources).

3. Many observers argue today that the five permanent members of the Security Council (Great Britain, the People's Republic of China, France, Russia, and the United States) should no longer have veto power in the Security Council, but that smaller, less powerful countries should have the same power. Evaluate the merits of this position and write an essay defending or refuting this suggestion (see Suggested Sources).

4. Some jurists argue that the International Court of Justice should be able to prosecute all leaders of governments, even the president of the United States, if they have been charged with crimes against humanity by the International Court. Assess the evidence in support of and against this argument and write an essay expressing your reasoned opinion.

5. The United Nations peacekeeping mission in the former Yugoslavia has been a source of considerable controversy. Taking into account what the peacekeeping mission was intended to do and the circumstances in which it had to work, do a case study of the effectiveness of this peacekeeping mission.

6. Trygve Lie, Dag Hammarskjöld, U Thant, Kurt Waldheim, and Kofi Annan are among the better-known secretaries-general of the UN. Write a research paper evaluating the tenure as secretary-general of one of the above men (see Suggested Sources).

Research Suggestions

In addition to the boldfaced items, look under the entries for "The Korean War, 1950–1953" (#48), "The Six-Day War, 1967" (#66),

"The Dissolution of Yugoslavia in the 1990s" (#93), and "Genocide in Rwanda, 1994" (#95). Search under **human rights** and **crimes against humanity**.

SUGGESTED SOURCES

Primary Sources

Black, Allida, ed. *Courage in a Dangerous World: The Political Writings of Eleanor Roosevelt.* New York: Columbia University Press, 1999. Affords a good understanding of Eleanor Roosevelt's role in supporting the ideals of the UN.

Churchill, Winston S. *The Second World War.* 6 vols. Boston: Houghton Mifflin, 1948–1953. A lucid memoir showing how Churchill supported the idea of a United Nations.

Cordier, Andrew Wellington, ed. *Public Papers of the Secretaries-General of the United Nations.* New York: Columbia University Press, 1969. The first volume has the papers of Trygve Lie, the UN's first secretary-general. Volume 2 has the papers of Dag Hammarskjöld, the UN's second secretary-general.

Lie, Trygve. *In the Cause of the Peace: Seven Years with the United Nations.* New York: Macmillan, 1954. A good glimpse into launching the UN.

Roosevelt, Eleanor. *Autobiography.* New York: Harper, 1961. A candid account of her unflagging idealism.

Secondary Sources

Burns, James MacGregor. *Roosevelt: The Soldier of Freedom.* New York: Harcourt Brace Jovanovich, 1970. The best study of FDR's approach to war and politics. Excellent bibliography and index.

Havel, Václav. "Kosovo and the End of the Nation-State." *New York Review of Books* 46 (10 June 1999): 4–6. The president of the Czech Republic argues that the UN Security Council should reflect a "multipolar world," and that the UN, not the nation-state, should shape international relations in the twenty-first century.

Iriye, Akira. *Cultural Internationalism and World Order.* Baltimore: Johns Hopkins University Press, 1997. A well-reasoned estimate of how the UN can advance peace in the twenty-first century.

Roberts, Adam. "Towards a World Community? The United Nations and International Law." In *The Oxford History of the Twentieth Century.* Edited by Michael Howard and Wm. Roger Louis. New York: Oxford University Press, 1999. A reliable summary of the UN's first fifty years and a useful bibliography.

39. THE INVENTION OF THE COMPUTER, 1944–1946

In the 1930s mathematical calculations were still done mostly by hand or with the help of a simple machine such as the adding machine. Analog calculating machines also existed for special purposes. Essentially physical models of the problem under investigation, they approached the problem through analogy (hence the term "analog"). One example might be the **AC (Alternating Current) Network Calculator** used to help design electrical power networks.

The **Harvard Mark I**, developed by **IBM (International Business Machines)** between 1937 and 1943 on the basis of specifications provided by **Howard Aiken**, marked an advance from analog calculating machines toward the modern computer. As an electromechanical device, however, it was very slow. Its main importance lay in the fact that it was the first fully automatic calculating machine.

About the same time the Harvard Mark I was introduced, work was starting at the Moore School of Electrical Engineering at the University of Pennsylvania on the **ENIAC (Electronic Numerical Integrator and Computer)**. **John W. Mauchly**, associated with the Moore School, developed the ENIAC to speed calculations needed for artillery being developed in **World War II**. Most of the engineering was the work of **J. Presper Eckert**, a young electrical engineer. Another important figure was **John von Neumann**, an eminent mathematician, who became familiar with the ENIAC project and helped develop the concept of the **stored-program computer**. The basis for modern computer design, this called for the instructions and data to be kept separate from the part of the computer that would process the data.

The ENIAC, only put into service in November 1945, came too late to contribute to the war effort. One thousand times as fast as the Harvard Mark I, its debut made clear that the future of the computer would be electronic rather than electromechanical. A few years later, in 1949, scientists at the University of Manchester in Great Britain successfully developed a working model of the stored-program concept. Computers developed rapidly in the 1950s and by the end of the decade were used extensively in business, government work, and research.

Suggestions for Term Papers

1. Charles Babbage is a good example of an inventor whose ideas ran well ahead of the technology of his times. Investigate his career and write a paper connecting his ideas to the development of the first computers (see Suggested Sources).
2. Howard Aiken's work was financed by IBM, a firm that became synonymous with computers for a time. Do a research project on IBM's involvement with computers in the 1940s and the 1950s.
3. John V. Atanasoff and his student Clifford Berry are a part of the great tradition of independent innovators who never receive their fair share of the fame and wealth associated with their work. Compare their experiences with those of Philo Farnsworth and his associates (see entry #26) or Rosalind Franklin (see entry #49).
4. Use the ENIAC project as a case study of how war may help bring about breakthroughs in areas of science and technology. Comment on the advantages and disadvantages of working under wartime conditions.
5. J. Presper Eckert and John Mauchly failed to make a commercial success of their work. Write a paper on the problems they faced in attempting to market the computer.
6. The early days of computers featured success stories in which scientists with quite limited resources made important breakthroughs. Do a research project on the work of Maurice Wilkes with the first stored-program computer (see Suggested Sources).

Research Suggestions

In addition to the boldfaced items, look under the entries for "General Broadcasting of Television in Britain, 1936" (#26), "The Use of Atomic Bombs in World War II, 1945" (#37), and "The Internet in the 1990s" (#99). Search under **Charles Babbage, Adele Goldstein, Grace Hopper, Ada Lovelace, Alan Turing,** and **Maurice Wilkes**.

SUGGESTED SOURCES

Primary Sources

Bernard, I. Cohen, Gregory W. Welch, and Robert Campbell. *Makin' Numbers: Howard Aiken and the Computer.* Cambridge, Mass.: MIT Press, 1999. Reminiscences of working with Aiken as well as reprints of his technical papers from the days of the Harvard Mark I.

Wilkes, Maurice. *Memoirs of a Computer Pioneer.* Cambridge, Mass.: MIT Press, 1985. Wilkes was the creator of the EDSAC, the first practical stored-program computer.

Secondary Sources

Aspray, William. *Computing before Computers.* Ames: Iowa State University Press, 1990. A good background source.

————. *John von Neumann and the Origins of Modern Computing.* Cambridge, Mass.: MIT Press, 1990. The best book on von Neumann, one of the most significant contributors to the early development of the computer.

Ceruzzi, Paul E. *Reckoners: The Prehistory of the Digital Computer, from Relays to the Stored Program Concept, 1935–1945.* Westport, Conn.: Greenwood Press, 1983. A good overview.

Cohen, I. Bernard. *Howard Aiken: Portrait of a Computer Pioneer.* Cambridge, Mass.: MIT Press, 1999. The best biography of Aiken.

Goldstine, Herman H. *The Computer: From Pascal to von Neumann.* Princeton: Princeton University Press, 1972. A good overview.

McCartney, Scott. *ENIAC: The Triumphs and Tragedies of the World's First Computer.* New York: Walker and Co., 1999. A thorough study of the development of the ENIAC. McCartney also examines the problems Mauchly and Eckert faced in marketing their invention.

Mollendorf, Clark R. *Atanasoff: Forgotten Father of the Computer.* Ames: Iowa State University Press, 1988. The fascinating story of John V. Atanasoff, whose early electronic computer may have contributed to the development of the ENIAC.

Zachary, G. Pascal. *Endless Frontier: Vannevar Bush, Engineer of the American Century.* Cambridge, Mass.: MIT Press, 1999. Bush, Roosevelt's science advisor in World War II, figured prominently in early work on the computer. An excellent biography.

40. JUAN PERÓN AND ARGENTINE POLITICS, 1946–1955

Juan Perón (1895–1974), the most popular leader in Argentina's history, was born into a middle-class family. He graduated from the national military academy and made good progress as an army officer. Posted to Italy in the 1930s, he was quite impressed with **fascism** and especially with **Benito Mussolini**'s fascist economic policies. In 1943, back in Argentina, he joined a group of disgruntled army officers who seized power in a coup d'état. Initially Perón served as under-secretary of labor and welfare; later he became vice president and minister of war. In 1946 Perón was elected president, winning 54 percent of the vote. He immediately threw his support to the large labor unions and the urban workers. Perón insisted he was the new champion of the workers and encouraged them to strike for better wages and working conditions. This policy was immensely popular with the poorest Argentineans (the *descamisados*, or the shirtless ones).

Perón's political philosophy, which he called **Justicialism**, was an amalgam of beliefs quite similar to fascism. Like the European fascists, Perón favored the military, promised a more equitable distribution of wealth, and urged national unity. Perón pledged to abolish civil strife, promote social justice, and ensure that the children would be the only privileged members of Argentinean society. Perón had little regard for civil liberties. He used the military and the labor unions to stifle political opposition. Perón's greatest political asset was his second wife, **Eva Duarte de Perón**. Affectionately known as **Evita**, she had superb political instincts. Evita quickly became the most popular woman in Argentina because of her well-publicized charitable work among the poor.

Perón's policies were popular enough to ensure that he was reelected president in 1951, winning 67 percent of the vote. In 1952, however, tragedy struck. Evita Perón, at thirty-three, died of cancer. Bereft of his best advisor and faced with deepening economic problems, Perón attacked the Roman Catholic Church, initiated an authoritative style of rule, and failed to root out corruption in his government. **Perónism**, though still popular with the *descamisados*, was increasingly distrusted by the military. In September 1955, the

military forced Perón into exile and attempted to purge his supporters. The appeal of Perónism, however, did not die, and in 1972 Juan
Perón returned to Argentina. He won the presidential elections of
1973 and, along with his third wife, Isabel, whom he named vice
president, appeared destined to recapture his old popularity. Ten
months after his election on 1 July 1974, Juan Perón died. **Isabel
Perón** succeeded him, but she was unable to overcome severe economic problems and was forced out of power by the military in
l976.

Perón's political legacy is mixed. His authoritative style of rule assisted the military in governing Argentina in the 1980s. But his social
legislation was popular enough to ensure that **Carlos Saúl Menem**,
a Perónist, was elected president of Argentina in 1988 and reelected
in 1995.

Suggestions for Term Papers

1. After reading Perón's statement of Justicialism (see Suggested
   Sources), write a paper explaining his economic policies.
2. What exactly was Perón's appeal? Why was Argentina in the 1940s
   ripe for a leader like Perón?
3. Who are the *descamisados?* Write a comparative study of their role
   in Perónist politics and in present-day politics.
4. How can one account for Evita's popularity? Investigate her life
   and write a biographical sketch that focuses on reasons for her
   popularity in Argentina.
5. Investigate the circumstances that led the military to force Isabel
   Perón from power in 1976.
6. Compare and contrast the nature of the Perónist party of Carlos
   Saúl Menem with that of its founder. In what ways is the party
   different today? Why is this?

Research Suggestions

In addition to the boldfaced items, look under the entries for "The
Nazi 'Seizure of Power' in 1933" (#24), "The Guatemalan Coup,
1954" (#50), and "The Overthrow of Salvador Allende in Chile,
1973" (#76). Search under **fascism**.

SUGGESTED SOURCES

Primary Sources

Perón, Eva. *My Mission in Life*. Translated by Ethel Cherry. New York: Vantage Press, 1953. A powerful reminder of how important Eva was to her husband's appeal.

Perón, Juan Domingo. *Perón Expounds His Doctrine*. Buenos Aires, 1948. New York: AMS Press, 1973. Accessible selections of Perón's speeches and writings.

———. *Perónist Doctrine*. Buenos Aires: Perónist Party, 1952. This contains the twenty truths of Justicialism.

Secondary Sources

Barager, Joseph R., ed. *Why Perón Came to Power: The Background to Peronism in Argentina*. New York: Knopf, 1968. This provides differing perspectives on Perón's appeal during the 1940s.

Barnes, John. *Evita, First Lady: A Biography of Eva Perón*. New York: Grove Press, 1996. A brief but readable introduction to Evita.

Blanksten, George. *Perón's Argentina*. Chicago: University of Chicago Press, 1953. Despite its age this is a good introduction to the initial Perón era (1946–1955).

Crassweller, Robert D. *Perón and the Enigmas of Argentina*. New York: W. W. Norton, 1987. A useful study that situates Perón and his policies in the context of Argentine history.

Di Tella, Guido. *Argentina under Perón, 1973–76: The Nation's Experience with a Labour-Based Government*. New York: St. Martin's Press, 1983. A careful examination of the appeal of Perón among the *descamisados*.

Dujovne Ortiz, Alicia. *Eva Perón*. Translated by Shawn Fields. New York: St. Martin's Press, 1996. A readable translation of a standard biography.

McGuire, James W. *Peronism Without Perón: Unions, Parties, and Democracy in Argentina*. Stanford: Stanford University Press, 1997. The most complete study of Perón's political legacy.

Page, Joseph A. *Perón*. New York: Random House, 1983. This remains the best English-language biography.

Taylor, J. M. *Eva Perón: The Myths of a Woman*. Chicago: University of Chicago Press, 1979. This study shows the enduring appeal of Evita in and beyond Argentina.

Turner, Frederick C., and José Enrique Miguens, eds. *Juan Perón and the Reshaping of Argentina*. Pittsburgh: University of Pittsburgh Press, 1983. A useful set of essays examining Perón's influence on Argentina.

41. HO CHI MINH AND THE VIETNAMESE WAR AGAINST THE FRENCH, 1946–1954

Ho Chi Minh (1890–1969), the leader of Vietnam's struggle for independence from France, was born in central Vietnam. Refusing to submit to the French colonial authorities that had ruled his country for half a century, Ho left Vietnam as a ship's cabin boy in 1911. By 1918 he was living in Paris and had changed his name to **Nguyen Ai Quoc (Nguyen the Patriot)**. In 1920 he joined the **French Communist Party** and by 1924 he was undertaking advanced revolutionary training in Moscow. His movements for the remainder of the 1920s are uncertain, but in 1925 he surfaced in Canton; in 1930 in Hong Kong he founded the **Indochinese Communist Party**.

In the spring of 1940, after more than three decades of exile, Ho finally returned to Vietnam, where in May 1941 he founded the **League for the Independence of Vietnam (Viet Minh)**. Although small in number, the Viet Minh caught the attention of U.S. officials, who used them to conduct military operations against the Japanese in northern Vietnam. In 1945 Ho, with limited U.S. assistance, led his Viet Minh in the liberation of Vietnam from the Japanese.

Unable to block the return of the French colonial administration to Vietnam, Ho began a bitter eight-year guerrilla war against France, the **First Indochina War (1946–1954)**. Drawing upon centuries of Vietnamese resistance to foreign invaders, Ho warned the French, "You can kill ten of my men for every one I kill of yours. But even at those odds you will lose and I will win." True to his word, Ho and his field commander, **General Vo Nguyen Giap**, wore down the French and in May 1954 at the Battle of **Dien Bien Phu** forced the French army to surrender. The Viet Minh lost at least 200,000 soldiers in this war. France lists 34,798 names of its dead on its **Vietnam War Memorial**. The **1954 Geneva Agreements** ending the war provided for (1) a temporary division of Vietnam into two parts at the 17th parallel; (2) general elections to be held no later than 1956; (3) creation of the states of Laos and Cambodia; and (4) the end of the French empire in Indochina.

Enigmatic, slight of build, and unprepossessing in appearance, Ho was consistently undervalued and misread by his adversaries. He was both a ruthless communist and a fervent Vietnamese nationalist. Not only did he defeat the French, but he presided over the military and political system that would defeat the United States in the **Second Indochina War (1957–1975)**.

Suggestions for Term Papers

1. In 1945 Ho Chi Minh asked the United States to assist him in preventing the French from returning to Vietnam and to make all of Indochina an American protectorate. Why did the Truman administration reject this request? Should the United States have listened more closely to Ho?

2. Although a communist, Ho was also a Vietnamese nationalist. Discuss the importance of nationalism in shaping his politics.

3. Investigate the military strategy of General Vo Nguyen Giap, the man who defeated both France and the United States. Why was General Giap so successful?

4. What factors caused the French to lose the Battle of Dien Bien Phu?

5. Although Ho spent several years in China and welcomed Chinese assistance in his struggle against France and the United States, he did not trust China. Why was this? To what extent can this be explained by the historical relationship between China and Vietnam?

6. Evaluate the results of the 1954 Geneva Conference and determine the extent to which Ho obtained what he believed Vietnam had won on the battlefield. What shaped the decisions reached on Vietnam at the conference?

Research Suggestions

In addition to the boldfaced items, look under the entries for "The 1968 Tet Offensive" (#68) and "Pol Pot and the Cambodian Incursion, 1970–1978" (#72). Search under **Geneva Conference (1954)**.

SUGGESTED SOURCES

Primary Sources

Fall, Bernard B., ed. *Ho Chi Minh on Revolution: Selected Writings, 1920–1966.* New York: Praeger, 1967. The most accessible edited collection of Ho's writings.

Ho Chi Minh. *Ho Chi Minh: Selected Writings, 1920–1969.* Hanoi: Foreign Languages Publishing House, 1973. The authoritative Vietnamese edition of Ho's major works.

Woddis, Jack., ed. *Ho Chi Minh: Selected Articles and Speeches, 1920–1967.* New York: International Publishers, 1970. Another useful edition of Ho Chi Minh's important writings.

Secondary sources

Clayton, Anthony. *The Wars of French Decolonization.* New York: Longman, 1994. A reliable treatment from the French point of view.

Fall, Bernard. *Hell in a Very Small Place: The Siege of Dien Bien Phu.* Philadelphia: J. B. Lippincott, 1966. A classic analysis of why Ho beat France.

———. *Street Without Joy: Insurgency in Indochina, 1946–1963.* Harrisburg, Pa.: Stackpole Books, 1961. One of the best books on the Vietnam War.

Halberstam, David. *Ho.* New York: Random House, 1971. A brief, sympathetic introduction.

Lacouture, Jean. *Ho Chi Minh: A Political Biography.* Translated by Peter Wiles. New York: Random House, 1968. Despite its age this remains the best biography of Ho in English.

Marr, David G. *Vietnam 1945: The Quest for Power.* Berkeley: University of California Press, 1995. The third volume of the most authoritative analysis of Ho's struggle for power.

Patti, Archimedes L.A. *Why Vietnam? Prelude to America's Albatross.* Berkeley: University of California Press, 1980. An engaging discussion by an American officer who worked closely with Ho and the Viet Minh during the war against Japan.

Pike, Douglas Eugene. *History of Vietnamese Communism, 1925–1976.* Stanford: Hoover Institution Press, 1978. A concise introduction to Ho's role as a party leader.

Vietnam: A Television History. Part I: "Roots of a War (1945–1953)." Originally broadcast on PBS, 4 October 1983. The first episode of a distinguished documentary series.

World Wide Web

"The American Experience: Vietnam Online." *http://www.pbs.org/wgbh/amex/vietnam*. Although this Web site is largely devoted to the U.S. involvement in Vietnam, it does contain transcripts for each segment of *Vietnam: A Television History*.

42. THE INDEPENDENCE OF INDIA AND PAKISTAN, 1947

As the largest and most populous colony in the British Empire, India assured Britain a huge market for its manufactured goods, access to key raw materials, and a strategic position in southwest Asia. Not surprisingly, Britain resisted the repeated demands of the **Indian National Congress** for independence. Led by **Mohandas Gandhi**, who was ably assisted by **Jawaharlal Nehru**, the Hindu-dominated Congress increasingly challenged British rule in India. During the 1920s and 1930s Gandhi preached *Satyagraha* ("holding fast to the truth") and asked Indians to adopt a policy of nonviolence and noncompliance with British rule. Gandhi's protest movement gained worldwide notoriety in 1930 when he led a boycott of the British salt monopoly (see entry #20).

In 1935 Britain gave India greater local autonomy and seemed to be preparing it for self-governance. However, with the outbreak of **World War II** in 1939 and the Japanese attack on Pearl Harbor and Hong Kong in 1941, Britain refused to grant India any further autonomy. Gandhi objected to this and demanded that Britain "quit India" immediately.

Although immensely popular among Hindus, Gandhi did not speak for Muslim India. When World War II ended in 1945 the spokesman for Muslim India was **Muhammad Ali Jinnah**, leader of the **Muslim League**. Jinnah supported Gandhi's efforts to gain independence but insisted that Muslims could never live securely in a Hindu-dominated India. Muslims, insisted Jinnah, must have their own independent state of Pakistan. Jinnah's concerns seemed validated when tensions between Muslim and Hindu exploded in several days of bloody rioting in **Calcutta** in August 1946. In February 1947 British **Prime Minister Clement Attlee** announced that Britain would leave India by June 1948 and sent **Lord Louis Mountbatten** to oversee independence. Mounbatten advanced the date of independence to midnight, 14 August 1947, when India would be partitioned into two states, India and Pakistan (the latter made up of two large provinces separated by more than 1,000 miles of Indian territory). Nehru would be prime minister of India, and Jinnah would be governor general of Pakistan. Throughout the summer of 1947 millions of Hindus and **Sikhs** (a religion combining elements of Hindu and Muslim beliefs) migrated from Pakistan to India, and millions of Muslims left India for Pakistan. More than 500,000 people were killed in the disorders and sectarian violence that accompanied independence.

Independence has not brought peace. The deep antagonisms between India and Pakistan have resulted in several border clashes and three armed conflicts, in 1947–1948, 1965, and 1971, which resulted in **East Pakistan** gaining independence from **West Pakistan** and taking the name **Bangladesh**. In 1998 both India and Pakistan tested nuclear weapons and threatened to use them in the 1999 summer firefights over Kashmir.

Suggestions for Term Papers

1. Investigate Gandhi's concept of *Satyagraha*. How important were the non-Indian influences in shaping his views on nonviolence?

2. What role did Jawaharlal Nehru play in securing independence for India?

3. Why did Muhammad Ali Jinnah demand a separate state of Pakistan? Examine the relations between Muslims and Hindus in colonial India in the 1930s and 1940s.

4. Why has the governance of the province of Kashmir been such a delicate problem for the two countries?

5. Evaluate Lord Mountbatten's handling of the British exit from India in the summer of 1947. To what extent were the British responsible for the bloodshed that accompanied independence?

6. Why have India and Pakistan been such adversaries since gaining independence? What is the current state of the relationship?

Research Suggestions

In addition to the boldfaced items, look under the entry for "Gandhi's Salt March, 1930" (#20). Search under **Amritsar, Benazir**

Bhutto, Zulfikar Ali Bhutto, Indira Gandhi, and **Edwina Mountbatten (Lady Mountbatten)**.

SUGGESTED SOURCES

Primary Sources

De Bary, William, et al., eds. *Sources of Indian Tradition*. New York: Columbia University Press, 1958. Part six has key documents for 1947.

Gandhi, Mahatma. *Mahatma Gandhi: Selected Political Writings*. Dennis Dalton, ed. Indianapolis: Hackett Publishing, 1996. A fine collection of Gandhi's writings prefaced by a helpful introduction to Gandhi's thought.

Norman, Dorothy, ed. *Nehru, the First Sixty Years*. 2 vols. New York: John Day, 1965. Principal writings and speeches of Nehru. The second volume is focused on independence.

Secondary Sources

Ahmed, Akbar S. *Jinnah, Pakistan and Islamic Identity: The Search for Saladin*. London: Routledge, 1997. The most complete study available.

Brown, Judith M. *Nehru*. New York: Longman, 1999. A short, lucid biography with a good bibliographical essay.

Collins, Larry and Dominique Lapierre. *Freedom at Midnight*. New York: Simon and Schuster, 1975. A popular, well-written account of the summer of 1947.

Gilmartin, David. "Partition, Pakistan, and South Asian History: In Search of a Narrative." *Journal of Asian Studies* 57 (1998): 1068–95. Good for an understanding of Muslim views on partition; contains as well an extensive bibliographical discussion of relations between the two countries.

Jalal, Ayesha. *The Sole Spokesman: Jinnah, the Muslim League, and the Demand for Pakistan*. Cambridge: Cambridge University Press, 1985. The most readable study of Jinnah.

Menon, Ritu, and Kamla Bhasin. *Borders and Boundaries: Women in India's Partition*. Berkeley: University of California Press, 1998. Most of the victims of the 1947 violence were women. This is a solid examination of their plight.

Mosley, Leonard. *The Last Days of the British Raj*. New York: Harcourt, Brace and World, 1962. A graphic account of the summer of 1947.

Read, Anthony, and David Fisher. *The Proudest Day: India's Long Road to Independence*. New York: W. W. Norton, 1997. The best study available on British rule in India.

Van der Veer, Peter. *Religious Nationalism: Hindus and Muslims in India.* Berkeley: University of California Press, 1994. This study extends beyond the independence issue and provides perspective on the deep-seated religious rivalries between Hindu and Muslim.

Wolpert, Stanley. *A New History of India.* 6th ed. New York: Oxford University Press, 2000. A standard history of India that gives ample coverage of the independence issue.

43. THE ESTABLISHMENT OF THE STATE OF ISRAEL, 1948

In 1947 **Great Britain** announced it was giving up its **mandate** to administer **Palestine** and requested that the **United Nations (UN)** devise a plan to bring peace to Palestine. On 29 November 1947 the UN General Assembly decreed that Palestine would be partitioned into Arab and Jewish states. On 14 May 1948, one day before the British mandate for governing Palestine expired, **David Ben-Gurion**, Israel's first prime minister, proclaimed the birth of the state of Israel. This announcement pitted 600,000 Jews against more than 1 million **Arab Muslims** and 149,000 **Arab Christians** residing in Palestine. Immediately the states of **Syria, Transjordan, Iraq, Lebanon**, and **Egypt** sent 18,000 Arab soldiers into Palestine to annihilate the new state of Israel. Initially, the Arab armies did well enough so that on 11 June the UN secured a four-week cease-fire. The cease-fire did not hold and by October 1948 the Arab armies were in full retreat. By January 1949 Israeli forces controlled 77 percent of Palestine and had signed armistices (but no peace treaties) with each Arab state. Israel did not control the **Gaza strip** and parts of the **West Bank** of the **Jordan River**. But it did control **West Jerusalem** and the key port of **Eilat** on the **Gulf of Aqaba**, thereby assuring access to the Red Sea.

Israel's **Proclamation of Independence** (1948) explains that the establishment of an Israeli state was necessary because (1) the land of Israel was the birthplace of the Jewish people; (2) the **Balfour Declaration** of 1917 and the subsequent British mandate acknowledged the right of Israel to exist; (3) Hitler's **Holocaust** proved anew that only an independent Israel could safeguard the Jewish people from annihilation; and (4) the **UN Resolution of 29 November 1947** called for the establishment of an independent Jewish State in Palestine.

Although these justifications received widespread support in Europe and in the United States, Arab countries, and particularly Palestinians who fled Israel, have argued that the price of an Israeli state has been the denial of a homeland for the Palestinian people. In the course of the 1948 war more than 700,000 Palestinians sought refuge in other Arab lands. Between 1948 and 1999 there have been five major conflicts between Israel and its Arab neighbors and more than fifty years of bloody guerrilla warfare between Palestinians and Israelis.

Suggestions for Term Papers

1. Examine the debates on Palestine in the United Nations in 1947–1948 and write an analysis of why the UN plan for partition of Palestine failed.

2. Read the State of Israel "Proclamation of Independence" (see Suggested Sources) and write a paper analyzing and commenting on the historical, political, and religious arguments put forth in the document.

3. Investigate the strategy and tactics of the Israeli army in 1948 and evaluate its role in the establishment of the state of Israel.

4. What factors might explain why 700,000 Palestinians left their homes in 1948?

5. What role did the United States play in the establishment of Israel in 1948?

6. Use the State of Israel "Proclamation of Independence" (1948); the "Palestinian Declaration of Independence" (1988); and the "Wye River Memorandum" (1998), signed between Israel and the Palestinian Authority (see Suggested Sources) as the basis for a paper analyzing Israeli-Palestinian relations over the years.

Research Suggestions

In addition to the boldfaced items, look under the entries for "The British Mandate of Palestine, 1922" (#13), "The Holocaust, 1941–1945" (#34), "Gamal Abdel Nasser and the Suez Crisis, 1956" (#52), and "The Six-Day War, 1967" (#66). Search under **Mena-**

chem **Begin, Count Folke Bernadotte, Exodus, Haganah, Irgun,** and the **Stern Gang.**

SUGGESTED SOURCES

Primary Sources

Ben-Gurion, David. *Memoirs: David Ben-Gurion.* New York: World, 1970. Reflections on the struggle for independence by Israel's first prime minister.

Dayan, Moshe. *Story of My Life.* London: Sphere Books, 1978. Important memoirs by one of the most accomplished Israeli soldiers of the fighting in 1948, 1956, and 1967.

Laqueur, Walter, and Barry Rubin, eds. *The Israel-Arab Reader: A Documentary History of the Middle East Conflict.* New York: Penguin Books, 1984. The most accessible collection of documents, including the State of Israel "Proclamation of Independence" (1948).

Palestinian National Council. "Palestinian Declaration of Independence." *Journal of Palestine Studies* 18 (Winter 1989): 213–16. The key document for the dream of an independent Palestinian state.

Weizmann, Chaim. *Trial and Error: The Autobiography of Chaim Weizmann.* New York: Harper, 1949. Autobiography of the first president of Israel.

"The Wye River Memorandum and Related Documents." *Journal of Palestine Studies* 28 (Winter 1999): 135–46. The most recent effort by the United States to engage Israelis and Palestinians in a durable peace process.

Secondary Sources

Collins, Larry, and Dominique Lapierre. *O Jerusalem!* New York: Simon and Schuster, 1972. A popular, well-written account of the summer of 1948.

Luttwak, Edward, and Dan Horowitz. *The Israeli Army.* New York: Harper and Row, 1975. A solid study with a good bibliography.

Ovendale, Ritchie. *The Origins of the Arab-Israeli Wars.* 2nd ed. New York: Longman, 1992. The best short introduction to the fighting in 1948.

Reinharz, Jehuda. *Chaim Weizmann: The Making of a Statesman.* New York: Oxford University Press, 1993. A useful biography of one of the founding fathers of Israel.

Sachar, Howard M. *A History of Israel from the Rise of Zionism to Our Time.* New York: Knopf, 1979. A standard history with good coverage of the birth of Israel.

Troen, S. Ilan, and Noah Lucas, eds. *Israel: The First Decade of Independence.* Albany: State University of New York Press, 1995. A good overview of all aspects of Israeli life.

World Wide Web

"Department of History Map Library." *http://www.dean.usma.edu/history/dhistorymaps//MapsHome.htm.* Click on "Atlases" for United States Military Academy (West Point) maps for 1948.

44. THE MARSHALL PLAN (THE EUROPEAN RECOVERY ACT), 1948–1951

The winter of 1946–1947 in Europe was one of the coldest in recorded history. The economy had not recovered from **World War II**, and many observers believed that Europe was near collapse. U.S. **Secretary of State George Marshall**, frustrated after fruitless meetings with the Russian, British, and French foreign ministers in Moscow in March and April, asked for a private meeting with **Josif Stalin**. That meeting convinced Marshall that the Russians believed doing nothing would work to their advantage.

In May 1947, Marshall charged **George F. Kennan**, head of the Policy Planning Staff in the State Department, to make recommendations on the European situation. Kennan's report stressed that Europeans should draw up the plans for recovery. Also, American economic aid should be available to all Europe. Finally, the rehabilitation of the German economy would be a vital part of any plan.

Marshall presented the American offer to help in a speech at Harvard University in June. He advocated economic measures to meet economic and social problems, declaring, "Our policy is directed not against any country or doctrine but against hunger, poverty, desperation and chaos."

Ernest Bevin, the British foreign secretary, heard a news report on the speech and responded almost immediately. A conference was held in July in Paris, attended not only by west European countries but also by the Soviet Union, Poland, and Czechoslovakia. **Vyacheslav Molotov**, the Soviet foreign minister, suspicious of U.S. intentions to begin with, heard from his intelligence service that the **Marshall**

Plan was an American plot. He left the conference bitter and angry. Later, Poland and Czechoslovakia were prevented from participating by the Soviet Union.

The European proposal to the United States originally called for $28 billion. Later it was reduced to $19 billion. In the end, the United States provided about $13 billion. Marshall was instrumental in getting Congress to approve the plan in 1948. He was also helped by **Arthur Vandenberg**, a prominent Republican senator who had been won over to the idea.

The Marshall Plan emphasized mutual aid and joint programming by the Europeans. Most of the money supplied by the plan was actually spent in the United States to purchase food and raw material. This allowed rapid economic growth without causing undue hardship for Europeans. With the help of the plan, Europeans reduced inflation, increased productivity, and increased exports. The plan ended officially in December 1951. Experience with the Marshall Plan led to the decision to create the **European Coal and Steel Community**. The plan also reinforced the division between east and west in Europe. It is generally considered the most successful foreign aid program ever undertaken by the United States.

Suggestions for Term Papers

1. Using biographies of Marshall, Kennan's *Memoirs*, and other sources, trace the development of the idea of the Marshall Plan in the spring of 1947.

2. The Marshall Plan has been considered by some to be an economic counterpart to the Truman Doctrine (1947), which committed the United States to "support free peoples who are resisting attempted subjugation by armed minorities or by outside pressures." Compare these two major developments and come to a conclusion as to whether the Marshall Plan might be better seen as part of the Cold War or as an element in the economic recovery of Europe from World War II.

3. George C. Marshall played a crucial role in selling the plan to Congress. Review accounts of Marshall's testimony before Congress and his cross-country tour of the United States and determine why he was able to persuade a Congress that had planned to cut spending to agree to the European Recovery Act.

4. Select one of the countries that received Marshall Plan aid and investigate how that aid was used. Did the aid have any impact beyond the area of the national economy?

5. The Council for Mutual Economic Assistance (Comecon) was founded in 1949 as the Soviet Union's answer to the Marshall Plan. Imagine that you are a State Department official required to brief members of the new John F. Kennedy administration on the history and accomplishments of Comecon from its founding to the present (1961).

6. Various people suggested in the early 1990s that a Marshall Plan for eastern Europe was in order. Compare the situation in eastern Europe in 1991 with that of western Europe in 1948 and determine whether a new Marshall Plan for the nineties would have had the same prospects for success as the old plan.

Research Suggestions

In addition to the boldfaced items, look under the entries for "The Yalta Conference, 1945" (#36), "The Berlin Blockade and Airlift, 1948–1949" (#45), and "The Founding of the European Economic Community, 1957"(#55). Search under **Truman Doctrine, Jean Monnet**, and **Council for Mutual Economic Assistance (Comecon)**.

SUGGESTED SOURCES

Primary Sources

Kennan, George F. *Memoirs 1925–1950.* New York: Pantheon, 1967. Kennan devotes a chapter to his part in the origins of the Marshall Plan.

Marshall, George C. "Against Hunger, Poverty, Desperation, and Chaos." The text of Marshall's speech is in the special issue of *Foreign Affairs,* 76, no. 3 (May/June 1997).

Secondary Sources

Gimbel, John. *The Origins of the Marshall Plan.* Stanford: Stanford University Press, 1976. An authoritative discussion of the factors that led the United States to undertake an unprecedented program of foreign aid.

Hogan, Michael J. *The Marshall Plan: America, Britain, and the Reconstruction of Western Europe.* New York: Cambridge University Press, 1987. A comprehensive and thorough treatment of the Marshall Plan.

Leffler, Melvyn P. "The United States and the Strategic Dimensions of the Marshall Plan." *Diplomatic History* 12 (Summer 1988), 277–306. An important article on the Marshall Plan and the Cold War.

Maddox, Robert James. "Lifeline to a Sinking Continent," *American Heritage* 48, no. 4 (July-August 1997), 90–93. A well-written introduction to the topic.

Maier, Charles S., and Günter Bischof, eds. *The Marshall Plan and Germany*. New York: Berg, 1991. Articles on the crucial role played by West Germany in the Marshall Plan.

"Marshall Plan." In *The Cold War, 1945–1991*, Vol. 3, *Resources: Chronology, History, Concepts, Events, Organizations, Bibliography, Archives*. Edited by Benjamin Frankel. Detroit: Gale Research, Inc., 1992. A useful sketch of the Marshall Plan with cross-references to related articles in this three-volume encyclopedia. A good place to start.

The Marshall Plan: Against All Odds. Directed by Ira H. Klugerman. Produced by the Educational Film Center, 1997. An interesting, well-informed documentary on the Marshall Plan.

"The Marshall Plan and Its Legacy." *Foreign Affairs* 76, no. 3 (May/June 1997). A most useful collection of articles and reflections on the fiftieth anniversary of Marshall's Harvard speech.

Zubok, Vladislav, and Constantine Pleshakov *Inside the Kremlin's Cold War: From Stalin to Khrushchev*. Cambridge, Mass: Harvard University Press, 1996. The best source of information presently available on Soviet ideas about the Marshall Plan and related Cold War topics.

World Wide Web

"Marshall Plan, 1947–1952." *http://www.cnn.com/SPECIALS/cold.war/episodes/03*. Based on CNN's *Cold War* documentary series, the Web site includes background, documents, a transcript of the program, and other features.

45. THE BERLIN BLOCKADE AND AIRLIFT, 1948–1949

On 24 June 1948, the Soviet authorities closed all rail, road, and water routes from western Germany to West Berlin, which was located deep within East Germany. The Soviet Union blockaded Berlin primarily to protest plans by the United States, Britain, and France to establish a West German state. The **currency reform of 21 June 1948**, which called for the introduction of a new deutsche mark, formed the specific catalyst for the blockade. The Soviet Union not only hoped to block the formation of a West German state but also believed it might force the other Allies out of Berlin.

The U.S. military governor of Germany, **General Lucius D. Clay**, suggested the use of an armed convoy to challenge the blockade. Other advisors of **President Harry Truman** convinced him not to try the plan. Instead President Truman approved the idea of supplying the city by air. On 26 June the United States began **Operation Vittles**, an airlift meant to supply the more than 2 million inhabitants of Berlin and the Allied personnel stationed there. Britain began a similar effort shortly thereafter.

The airlift, one of the great logistical feats of the century, began as a "cowboy operation," lacking in organization and coordination. It quickly became clear that good intentions were not enough. **Major General William H. Tunner**, beginning on 1 August 1948, brought much-needed order and planning to the effort. The amount of goods delivered increased dramatically. American and British airmen flew more than a quarter of a million flights to **Tempelhof Airport** in the American sector and **Gatow Airport** in the British sector. During the airlift **Tegel Airport** was constructed in the French sector and brought into use. At least seventy-eight Americans, British, and Germans died in connection with the airlift.

In December 1948 the Soviet Union hinted it was ready to negotiate an end to the impasse. Agreement was reach in May 1949, with the blockade ending formally at one minute past midnight on 12 May. As a precautionary measure, Operation Vittles continued until 30 September 1949.

The willingness of the more than 2 million Berliners in the western zones to endure considerable hardship contributed enormously to the success of the Allied resistance. Their courage became a source of pride to Germans everywhere. The experience also led to a very different relationship between Germans and Americans.

The blockade and airlift form a crucial event in the Cold War. Western Europe and the United States took heart from the successful resistance to Soviet pressures and established a formal military alliance, the **North Atlantic Treaty Organization (NATO)**. West Berlin remained an outpost of democracy over the next forty years.

Suggestions for Term Papers

1. Behind the Berlin Blockade lay differing U.S. and Soviet ideas about how Berlin and the rest of Occupied Germany should be treated. Investigate Soviet occupation policies and comment on the major objectives of those policies (see Suggested Sources).

2. One result of the Berlin Blockade and Airlift was a change in American opinions of Germans. Read the coverage of the Berlin Airlift in contemporary American newspapers and trace the development of this change in opinion.

3. Ernst Reuter, mayor of Berlin during the blockade, contributed in an important way to the determination of Berliners to resist Soviet pressures. Write a profile of Reuter that might be used as a three-minute segment on a radio broadcast covering the blockade and airlift. Begin with *From Shadow to Substance, 1945–1963* (see Suggested Sources).

4. Imagine that you are a German boy or girl living in Berlin. Write a story or play that reflects your experiences during the blockade.

5. The Berlin Blockade and Airlift is an integral part of events leading to the formation of the Federal Republic of Germany (West Germany). Follow the process by which West Germany took form in 1948 and 1949 and determine why the United States decided to promote the formation of a new German state. Begin with *From Shadow to Substance, 1945–1963* (see Suggested Sources).

6. The German Democratic Republic (East Germany) appeared a few months after the formation of the Federal Republic of Germany. Examine Soviet policies in 1948 and 1949 with regard to their occupation zone and determine why they decided to form the Democratic Republic of Germany.

Research Suggestions

In addition to the boldfaced items, look under the entries for "The Yalta Conference, 1945" (#36), "The Marshall Plan (The European Recovery Act), 1948–1951" (#44), and "The Berlin Wall, 1961" (#59). Search under **Secretary of State George C. Marshall, Josif Stalin, V. V. Molotov, Ernst Reuter, Walter Ulbricht,** and **West Berlin**.

SUGGESTED SOURCES

Primary Sources

Clay, Lucius D. *Decision in Germany.* Garden City, N.Y.: Doubleday, 1950. General Clay's memoirs of his service as military governor of Germany, with chapters on the Blockade and the airlift.

U.S. Department of State. Office of Public Affairs. *Germany, 1947–1949: The Story in Documents.* A selection of important documents related to the Berlin Blockade and Airlift.

Secondary Sources

Bark, Dennis L., and David B. Gress. *From Shadow to Substance, 1945–1963.* Oxford: Blackwell, 1989. Vol. 1 of *A History of West Germany.* A solid and comprehensive discussion of the emergence and development of West Germany.

"The Berlin Airlift and the City's Future" [commemorative section]. *Foreign Affairs 77*, no. 4 (July/August 1998): pp. 147–94. A helpful collection of articles.

Eisenberg, Carolyn. *Drawing the Line: The American Decision to Divide Germany, 1944–1949.* Cambridge: Cambridge University Press, 1996. A provocative study of U.S. policy with regard to Germany.

Gimbel, John. *The American Occupation of Germany: Politics and the Military, 1945–1949.* Stanford: Stanford University Press, 1968. The best study of the American occupation of Germany.

Haydock, Michael D. *City under Siege: The Berlin Blockade and Airlift, 1948–49.* Dulles, Va.: Brassey's, 1999. A recent and dependable history of the two events.

Parrish, Thomas. *Berlin in the Balance, 1945–1949: The Blockade, the Airlift, the First Major Battle of the Cold War.* Reading, Mass.: Addison Wesley Longman, 1998. Useful for setting the blockade and airlift in historical context.

Public Broadcasting System. *The Berlin Airlift.* 1998, 60 minutes. Distributed by Unapix/Miramar. A fascinating account of the Berlin Airlift featuring contemporary footage and interviews with some of the participants.

Shlaim, Avi. *The United States and the Berlin Blockade, 1948–49.* Berkeley: University of California Press, 1983. The leading study of the Berlin Blockade.

Smith, Jean Edward. *Lucius Clay: An American Life.* New York: Henry Holt, 1992. The major biography of General Clay.

World Wide Web

"Berlin, 1948–1949." *http://www.cnn.com/SPECIALS/cold.war/episodes/ 04.* Based on CNN's *Cold War* documentary series, the Web site includes background, documents, a transcript of the program, and other features.

"The Berlin Airlift." *http://www.whistlestop.org/study-collections/berlin___ airlift/large/berlin__airlift.htm.* A superb Web site. Filled with documents and photographs.

46. THE VICTORY OF THE CHINESE COMMUNIST PARTY, 1949

On 1 October 1949, **Mao Zedong**, chairman of the **Chinese Communist Party (CCP)**, stood on the reviewing stand of the Gate of Heavenly Peace in Beijing and proclaimed the birth of the **People's Republic of China**. The victory of Mao Zedong's CCP over **President Chiang Kai-shek's Guomindang** (Nationalist) army was a stunning and unexpected event. Fourteen years earlier, in 1935, Mao Zedong and his small band of communists had retreated to the caves of **Yenan** in **Shaanxi** province in remote north-central China to escape certain annihilation by Chiang Kai-shek's forces.

Safe in the caves of Yenan, Mao Zedong developed what he called **"Yenan-style Communism,"** a form of communism focusing on the plight of the Chinese peasants rather than the concerns of the industrial workers in the sprawling coastal cities. Had it not been for the Japanese invasion of China in July 1937, Mao Zedong's CCP would have remained a marginal political force, with virtually no prospect for extending its influence beyond Shaanxi province. But late in 1937 Mao Zedong and Chiang Kai-shek, bitter enemies, put aside their enmities and agreed to fight the Japanese invader. Although Chiang Kai-shek had a much larger army, it was inefficient and corrupt, and had a reputation for abusing and exploiting Chinese peasants. Mao Zedong's army, though smaller in size, was well disciplined, and because of its reputation for treating the peasants with respect, enjoyed widespread support in rural China. By 1945 Mao Zedong had nearly 1 million men in his army. When Japan surrendered in August 1945, Mao had established control over Manchuria, and with Soviet help he began attacking

Guomindang troops in northern China. In January 1946 **Secretary of State George C. Marshall** went to China and tried to persuade Mao to end hostilities. Mao asked for American help in coming to power but refused to stop fighting. Starting in 1947 Mao's forces gradually extended their control south from Manchuria so that by the summer of 1949 Chiang Kai-shek's government had abandoned mainland China to seek refuge on the island of **Taiwan.**

Mao Zedong's victory in 1949 marked a dramatic expansion of the ever-widening **Cold War** between communism and democracy in Asia. The United States viewed both the Korean War (1950–1953) and the war in Indochina (1946–1954) in a different light because of the existence of the People's Republic of China. Policy makers in the West assumed that these wars were part of the world communist movement's efforts to promote the expansion of communism throughout Asia.

Suggestions for Term Papers

1. Do a research project on Mao Zedong's stay in Yenan and write a paper on his "Yenan-style Communism." In particular, discuss the ways in which his approach to communism differed from that of Soviet leaders.

2. Educated as a teacher, Mao proved to be a surprisingly successful military leader. Investigate his ideas on military strategy and write a paper on his military leadership during the Chinese Civil War of 1946–1949 (see Suggested Sources).

3. After 1949 most Americans were convinced that China and the Soviet Union were close allies and Mao and Stalin close comrades. Write a paper that examines whether this was the case and more generally assesses the relationship between Mao and Stalin.

4. General George C. Marshall of the United States used his prestige and experience to attempt to end the Chinese Civil War. Why did his mission fail? Was he or other American officials active in the Far East somehow responsible for "losing" China to the Communists? Begin with *Marshall's Mission to China* (see Suggested Sources).

5. After losing to Mao Zedong in 1949, Generalissimo Chiang Kai-shek moved his Nationalist government to Taiwan, where he continued to receive U.S. support. Examine the relationship between

the United States and Chiang after 1949. Use Nancy Tucker, *Taiwan, Hong Kong, and the United States* (see Suggested Sources).

6. After the Chinese Communist victory in 1949, the United States refused to recognize the People's Republic of China (PRC) until 1972. Evaluate the policy of nonrecognition of the PRC between 1949 and 1972 in terms of its advantages and disadvantages. Begin with *Sentimental Imperialists* (see Suggested Sources).

Research Suggestions

In addition to the boldfaced items, look under the entries for "The May 4th Movement in China, 1919" (#12), "Mao Zedong's 'Report on an Investigation of the Peasant Movement in Hunan, March, 1927'" (#17), "Mao Zedong and the Long March 1934–1935" (#25), "The Rape of Nanking, 1937" (#28), "The Sino-Soviet Split, 1959–1969" (#60), and "The Chinese Economy at the End of the Twentieth Century" (#100). Search under **Zhou Enlai** and **Josif Stalin**.

SUGGESTED SOURCES

Primary Sources

Hinton, William. *Fashen: A Documentary of Revolution in a Chinese Village.* New York: Monthly Review Press, 1966. A classic account of the civil war on the village level.

Mao Tse-tung. *Selected Military Writings of Mao Tse-tung.* Peking: Foreign Languages Press, 1966. The starting point for understanding his strategic thinking.

———. *Selected Works of Mao Tse-tung.* 5 vols. Peking: Foreign Languages Press, 1965. The fifth volume of this series is focused on the civil war.

Selden, Mark. *The People's Republic of China: A Documentary History of Revolutionary Change.* New York: Monthly Review Press, 1979. A very useful collection of documents on all aspects of the civil war.

U.S. Department of State. *United States Relations with China, with Special Reference to the Period 1944–1949.* Washington, D.C., 1949. Reprint, Stanford: Stanford University Press, 1967. A convenient collection of key U.S. policy documents on the civil war.

Van Slyke, Lyman, ed. *Marshall's Mission to China: December 1945–January 1947: Report and Appended Documents.* Arlington, VA: University Publications of America, 1976. Documents on General Marshall's mission to China with helpful introductory and editorial comments.

Secondary Sources

Chasin, Lionel. *The Communist Conquest of China: A History of the Civil War, 1945–1949*. Translated by Timothy Osato and Louis Gelas. Cambridge, Mass.: Harvard University Press, 1965. Despite its age, this remains a solid account of the period.

Fairbank, John King. *The Great Chinese Revolution, 1800–1985*. New York: Harper and Row, 1986. A good summary of the civil war that puts the CCP's victory in the context of China's revolutionary tradition.

Spence, Jonathan D. *The Gate of Heavenly Peace: The Chinese and Their Revolution, 1895–1980*. New York: Viking, 1981. A brilliant analysis that is written in an engaging style.

Terrill, Ross. *A Biography: Mao*. New York: Harper and Row, 1980. His chapters on Mao's leadership during this period underscore Mao's capacity for dealing well with adversity.

Thompson, James C., Peter W. Stanley, and John Curtis Perry. *Sentimental Imperialists: The American Experience in East Asia*. New York: Harper and Row, 1981. Chapters sixteen and twenty are good discussions of American policy vis-à-vis China.

Tucker, Nancy B. *Taiwan, Hong Kong, and the United States, 1945–1992: Uncertain Friendships*. New York: Twayne Publishers, 1994. A good overview of U.S. policy toward Taiwan.

47. THE JAPANESE ECONOMIC MIRACLE IN THE 1950s

In 1945 Japan was a defeated country with its economy in shambles. Yet, in less than four decades it emerged as the second most powerful economy in the world. This Japanese economic miracle is due in part to the deeply rooted symbiotic relationship between government and business, which the **Meiji Reforms** (Meiji means period of "Enlightened Rule") of the 1870s had accelerated. The Meiji committed Japan to become "a rich but strong state." Democratic Japanese governments in the 1950s continued this tradition by relying upon the **Ministry of International Trade and Industry (MITI)**, a small but powerful group of government bureaucrats, to plan the Japanese economy. MITI encouraged an export-driven economy, one that would be built on an entirely new industrial base and would be committed to exporting high quality automobiles, electronics, and manufactured goods to world markets. Japanese businessmen proved to be particularly skilled in combing Western manufacturing and managerial techniques with the Japanese work ethic. **W. E. Deming**'s ideas on "quality circles," discussion groups of management and workers, focused on improving productivity and quality first tried in America in the 1930s, were brought to Japan in the 1960s with stunning success.

Japanese governments encouraged the growth of large conglomerates or *keiretsu*. The huge **Mitsui** *keiretsu* is a conglomerate of more than a dozen companies including **Toshiba Electric, Toyota** automobiles, and the Mitsui Bank. To protect Japanese industry from foreign competition, the government developed elaborate import licensing procedures for foreign products. These procedures, along with a system of tariffs, guaranteed that there would be little foreign competition in Japanese markets. Japanese workers, renowned for their tenacious work ethic and frugal lifestyle, contributed to this economic miracle with double-digit rates of personal saving and willingness to accept modest wages and long hours.

As a result of these policies Japan was able to accrue huge yearly trade surpluses with its trading partners. By 1986 Japan's per capita gross national product was $17,000, thereby surpassing the United States, which averaged $16,000 per capita. By 1992 the United States had become the world's largest debtor nation, while Japan had become the world's largest creditor. By 1997, however, the Japanese economic miracle had paled considerably. Japanese banks had overextended themselves underwriting a number of questionable loans, and in 1998 several Japanese banks and investment firms collapsed. An economic recession in **South Korea, China, Russia, Thailand**, and Latin America severely affected Japan's exports. In 1999, for the first time since World War II, large numbers of Japanese workers were unemployed.

Suggestions for Term Papers

1. Write a paper examining what Japanese students study in their secondary schools (see Suggested Sources), how they are admitted to college, and how Japanese education helped Japan to become an economic power.

2. Gather information on a *keiretsu* and write a paper assessing its strengths and weaknesses.

3. John Dower (see Suggested Sources) writes that American occupation policies in Japan after World War II were an undervalued part of Japan's economic miracle. Agree or disagree, stating your reasons for your position on this issue.

4. Investigate W. Edward Deming's ideas on management (see Suggested Sources) and write a paper on how his ideas influenced the growth of Japan's economy.

5. The Ministry of International Trade and Industry (MITI) has been called the "brain trust" of Japan. Write a paper on MITI's role in the Japanese economic miracle and decide whether its reputation is justified.

6. Large industrial trade unions have not had much influence in Japan. In a paper on industrial relations between management and workers in Japan since the war, comment on the factors that might explain the lack of influence that trade unions have had.

Research Suggestions

In addition to the boldfaced items, look under the entries for "The Asian Economic Meltdown at the End of the 1990s" (#97) and "The Chinese Economy at the End of the Twentieth Century" (#100).

SUGGESTED SOURCES

Primary Sources

"The Second Maekawa Report." In *Japan, Exploring New Paths*, edited by Jon K.T. Choy, 14–18. Washington, D.C.: Japan Institute, 1988. These were sweeping recommendations made to bring Japan's economy into harmony with the world's economy. It provides a good insight into Japanese economic thinking in the 1980s.

Secondary Sources

Aguayo, Rafael. *Dr. Deming: The American Who Taught the Japanese about Quality*. New York: Simon and Schuster, 1991. A good summary of W. Edward Deming's influence on Japan.

Cutts, Robert L. *An Empire of Schools: Japan's Universities and the Molding of a National Power*. Armonk, N.Y.: M. E. Sharpe, 1997. A solid explanation of how Japanese universities shape economic and public policy.

Dower, John W. *Embracing Defeat: Japan in the Wake of World War II.*

New York: W. W. Norton, 1999. A very useful discussion of American occupation policies and the response of Japanese to them.

Johnson, Chalmers A. *Japan: Who Governs? The Rise of the Developmental State*. New York: W. W. Norton, 1995. One of the best explanations of how Japanese bureaucrats have combined developmental economics with free market capitalism.

————. *MITI and the Japanese Miracle: The Growth of Industrial Policy, 1925–1975*. Stanford: Stanford University Press, 1983. The classic examination of how the Ministry of International Trade and Industry planned Japan's economic miracle.

Katz, Joshua D., and Tilly C. Friedman-Lichtschein, eds. *Japan's New World Role*. Boulder: Westview Press, 1985. A concise exposition of the connections between Japan's economic power and its international responsibilities.

Katz, Richard. *Japan, the System that Soured: The Rise and Fall of the Japanese Economic Miracle*. Armonk, N.Y.: M. E. Sharpe, 1998. A journalist's careful account of when and how the Japanese miracle faded.

Vogel, Ezra F. *Japan as Number One: Lessons for America*. Cambridge, Mass.: Harvard University Press, 1979. A succinct analysis of what Americans can learn from Japan.

Wolferen, Karel Van. *The Enigma of Japanese Power: People and Politics in a Stateless Nation*. New York: Knopf, 1989. A Dutch journalist's insightful explanation why Japanese bureaucrats, not the politicians, plan and run Japan's economy.

World Wide Web

"The CIA Factbook, 1999." *http://www.odci.gov./cia/publications/factbook/index.html*. This Central Intelligence Agency site is updated yearly.

48. THE KOREAN WAR, 1950–1953

After defeating Japan in August, 1945, the United States and the Soviet Union divided Korea, a country Japan had occupied since 1910, at the 38th parallel. The Soviets selected **Kim Il-Sung** to rule the **Democratic People's Republic of Korea** north of the 38th parallel. The United States chose **Syngman Rhee** to govern the **Republic of Korea** south of this line.

On 25 June 1950, 90,000 North Korean troops invaded South Korea and within one week had captured the capital, **Seoul**. The **United Nations Security Council** condemned North Korea's aggression. **President Harry Truman** announced that the United

States, along with sixteen other nations, was undertaking a "police action" to rescue South Korea.

After sending an American relief force to **Pusan, General Douglas MacArthur** counterattacked behind North Korean lines at **Inchon**. The Inchon landing caught the North Koreans by surprise. By October UN forces had crossed the 38th parallel. As the United Nations forces neared the **Yalu River**, the boundary between North Korea and China, China issued warnings. Then, on 26 November 1950, Chinese troops crossed the Yalu River. American forces retreated, but they did not break.

President Truman refused to give General MacArthur permission to bomb industrial and military targets in China. MacArthur launched a public relations campaign to gain support for widening the war. On 11 April 1951, Truman removed MacArthur from command and appointed **General Matthew Ridgway** to take his place.

After two more years of bitter fighting a truce was signed at **Panmunjom**. This truce again divided Korea at the 38th parallel, provided for an exchange of prisoners, and created a **demilitarized zone (DMZ)** separating the two Koreas, but it did not lead to a comprehensive peace treaty.

The Korean War resulted in nearly 4 million casualties, most of whom were civilians. American forces suffered 142,000 casualties, including 54,000 deaths. Several lessons were drawn from the war. First, President Truman considered it a "police action" and did not seek a formal declaration of war from Congress; successive administrations used this precedent in prosecuting the **Vietnam War**. Second, the President's newly established **National Security Council (NSC)** argued that the Soviet Union and the People's Republic of China would continue to challenge the United States and recommended a dramatic increase in American defense spending. Third, American policy planners noted that although U.S. forces did not win in Korea, they did not lose, and that therefore the United States should use its forces where necessary to stop the spread of communism.

Suggestions for Term Papers

1. Read some of the soldiers' oral histories of the Korean War (see Suggested Sources) and write a paper that draws on these recollections.

2. Interview a Korean War veteran about his experiences.

3. Explore President Truman's decision to fire General MacArthur and write a paper that assesses whether the decision was correct.

4. In what ways might the Korean War have influenced the United States' decision to aid France in Indochina in the early 1950s?

5. On 27 July 1995, President Clinton dedicated the Korean War Memorial in Washington, D.C. Write a paper discussing the reasons why it took the United States forty-two years to build the memorial.

6. Investigate the role of the Soviet Union and the People's Republic of China in encouraging North Korea to begin the Korean War.

Research Suggestions

In addition to the boldfaced items, look under the entries for "Ho Chi Minh and the Vietnamese War against the French, 1946–1954" (#41), "The Berlin Blockade and Airlift, 1948–1949" (#45), and "The Victory of the Chinese Communist Party, 1949" (#46). Search under **Cold War, Mao Zedong,** and **Josif Stalin.**

SUGGESTED SOURCES

Primary sources

Berry, Henry. *Hey, Mac, Where Ya Been? Living Memories of the U.S. Marines in the Korean War.* New York: St. Martin's Press, 1988. Personal recollections of U.S. Marines on all aspects of the war.

Horwitz, Dorothy G., ed. *We Will Not Be Strangers: Korean War Letters between a M.A.S.H. Surgeon and His Wife.* Urbana: University of Illinois Press, 1997. A poignant set of letters that captures the loneliness of the war.

Kaufman, Burton I. *The Korean Conflict.* Westport, Conn.: Greenwood Press, 1999. A good overview for students, with accompanying biographical profiles and primary documents.

Knox, Donald. *The Korean War: An Oral History.* 2 vols. San Diego: Harcourt Brace Jovanovich, 1985–1988. One of the most comprehensive oral histories of the war.

Russ, Martin. *Last Parallel.* New York: Farrar, Straus and Giroux, 1999. One of the very best combat memoirs to come out of Korea.

Tomedi, Rudy. *No Bugles, No Drums: An Oral History of the Korean War.* New York: Wiley, 1993. A first-rate personal narrative of the grim realities of combat.

Secondary Sources

Brune, Lester H. *The Korean War: Handbook of the Literature and Research.* Westport, Conn.: Greenwood Press, 1996. A useful guide to all aspects of the war.

Cumings, Bruce. *The Origins of the Korean War.* 2 vols. Princeton: Princeton University Press, 1981–1990. A thorough and quite critical study of American conduct of the war.

Foot, Rosemary. *The Wrong War: American Policy and the Dimensions of the Korean Conflict, 1950–1953.* Ithaca: Cornell University Press, 1985. A solid study that shows how Cold War perceptions shaped the decision to go to war in Korea.

Goncharov, S., J. W. Lewis, and Xue Litai. *Uncertain Partners: Stalin, Mao, and the Korean War.* Stanford: Stanford University Press, 1993. A fascinating discussion of how Kim Il-Sung played Mao off against Stalin to gain backing for his attack on South Korea.

Matray, James I. *Historical Dictionary of the Korean War.* Westport, Conn.: Greenwood Press, 1991. A comprehensive overview of all aspects of the war with good bibliographic leads.

————. *The Uncivil War: Korea, 1945–1953.* Armonk, N.Y.: M. E. Sharpe, 1999. A fresh interpretation that brings together the latest research on the war.

Russ, Martin. *Breakout: The Chosin Reservoir Campaign: Korea 1950.* New York: Fromm International Publishing, 1999. A gripping firsthand account how 12,000 U.S. Marines battled 60,000 Chinese in a desperate battle in sub-zero temperatures.

World Wide Web

"Cold War International History Project." *http://cwihp.si.edu/default.htm.* Useful studies and good documentation for all aspects of the Korean War.

"Korea, 1949–1953." *http://www.cnn.com/SPECIALS/cold.war/episodes/05.* Based on CNN's *Cold War* documentary series, the Web site includes background, documents, a transcript of the program, and other features.

"The National Security Archive." *http://www.gwu.edu/~nsarchiv.* The National Security Archive, an independent, nongovernmental institution, makes available documents from the Cold War period. Many documents having to do with the Korean War are located on its Web site.

49. THE DISCOVERY OF THE DOUBLE HELICAL STRUCTURE OF DNA, 1953

In the early 1950s one of the major scientific questions concerned the structure of **DNA (deoxyribonucleic acid)**. DNA molecules, present in the chromosomes of all plant and animal cells, were thought to contain instructions for passing on hereditary characteristics and for the functions of cells. Learning more about their structure would be a scientific breakthrough of immense significance.

The breakthrough came in 1953 as a result of the efforts of two somewhat unorthodox scientific investigators, **Francis Crick** and **James Watson**. Crick was a British biophysicist working at the Cavendish Laboratory at Cambridge University. In 1951 he met and became friends with James Watson, a former Quiz Kid on the radio who received a Ph.D. in genetics from Indiana University at age twenty-two. The two were supposed to be working on other projects, but kept coming back to the idea that a model of the structure of the DNA molecule was the key to several important questions.

In the early 1950s the investigator closest to the secret of the structure of DNA was **Rosalind Franklin**, a brilliant physical chemist who had been working on X-ray crystallography methods in Paris. In 1951 she joined a research unit at King's College, London. Unfortunately, she and a member of the research unit who had been working on X-ray diffraction of DNA, **Maurice Wilkins**, got off to a bad start and never worked together effectively.

It was a lecture by Franklin in 1951 that sent Watson and Crick off to build their first model of DNA. Watson had heard the lecture but had not taken notes. Franklin later viewed the model and subjected it to a devastating critique. Crick and Watson were actually banned from working on DNA afterwards by the head of the Cavendish Laboratory.

In America, **Linus Pauling**, a physical chemist who had constructed the first satisfactory model of a protein molecule, came very close to determining the structure of DNA in a paper he published in January 1953. Watson obtained a copy of the paper and knew that Pauling might soon be the first to publish a paper on the structure of DNA. Watson was aided by Wilkins, who showed him one of Franklin's X-ray photographs, without her knowledge or consent. Watson also obtained data presented by Franklin to a departmental seminar.

Crick realized that Franklin's data suggested an **antiparallel double helix structure** (a slightly twisted ladder the rungs of which are composed of pairs of nitrogen-containing nucleotides, which allows half of the molecule to serve as a template for the construction of the other half).

Crick and Watson published a paper in the British journal *Nature* on 18 March 1953. Only the day before, Franklin had drafted a paper that spelled out most of the structure, but priority of publication was what counted. In 1962 Watson, Crick, and Wilkins received the Nobel Prize in Physiology or Medicine. Franklin had died of cancer in 1958. Had she lived, she undoubtedly would have shared in the Nobel Prize she had inadvertently done so much to make possible.

Suggestions for Term Papers

1. Write a paper on what was known in the early 1950s about genes.
2. Compare the account of the discovery of the structure of DNA presented by James Watson in *The Double Helix* with that of Crick and of historians.
3. Investigate the life of Rosalind Franklin, a key figure in the search for the structure of DNA, and write a paper on her as scientist and as woman.
4. Follow James Watson's career after he and Crick discovered the structure of DNA. To what extent has his career fulfilled the extraordinary promise that he showed in his early twenties?
5. Develop a time line that traces the developments coming after Crick and Watson discovered the structure of DNA. Use the cloning of Dolly the sheep in 1997 as a cutoff point. Books by Lee M. Silver and by Necia Grant Cooper will be useful (see Suggested Sources).

Research Suggestions

In addition to the boldfaced items, look under the entries for "The 'Green Revolution' in Agriculture in the 1960s" (#61), "First 'Test-

Tube' Baby Born, 1978" (#79), and "Dolly the Sheep Cloned, 1997" (#96). Search under **Recombinant DNA, DNA Sequencing, Human Genome Project**, and **Cloning**.

SUGGESTED SOURCES

Primary Sources

Crick, Francis. *Of Molecules and Men*. Seattle: University of Washington Press. 1966. A discussion of some of the implications of the revolution in molecular biology.
———. *What Mad Pursuit: A Personal View of Scientific Discovery*. New York: Basic Books. 1988. Crick's account of the work he and James Watson carried out.
Watson, James. *The Double Helix: A Personal Account of the Discovery of the Structure of DNA*. New York: Athenaeum, 1968. Also published as a Norton Critical Edition in 1980. One of the best known twentieth-century accounts of scientific discovery.

Secondary Sources

Cooper, Necia Grant, ed. *The Human Genome Project: Deciphering the Blueprint of Heredity*. Mill Valley, Ca.: University Science Books, 1994. Useful overviews of progress in genetic research since Crick and Watson.
Gribbin, John. *In Search of the Double Helix: Quantum Physics and Life*. New York: McGraw-Hill. 1985. An excellent introduction.
Judson, Horace Freeland. *The Eighth Day of Creation: The Makers of the Revolution in Biology*. Expanded ed. Plainview, N.Y.: Cold Spring Harbor Laboratory Press, 1996. A good discussion of the discovery of the structure of DNA.
Licking, Ellen F. "Double-Teaming the Double Helix." *U.S. News & World Report*, 17 August 1998, 72–73. An excellent overview.
Sayre, Ann. *Rosalind Franklin and DNA*. New York: W. W. Norton, 1975. Dr. Franklin's work was vital to the success of Crick and Watson. Unfortunately, her death from cancer in 1958 meant she did not share the Nobel Prize with them.
Silver, Lee M. *Remaking Eden: How Genetic Engineering and Cloning Will Transform the American Family*. New York: Avon, 1998. This edition contains an afterword. Silver, a molecular biologist at Princeton, provides a popular and solid discussion of genetics and gene manipulation.

50. THE GUATEMALAN COUP, 1954

For over a century, Guatemalan dictators, supported by the army, the **Roman Catholic Church**, American businesses, and a small land-owning oligarchy, ruled the country. In 1944 **Juan José Arévalo**, a non-Marxist socialist, was elected president and promised a policy of land reform and progressive social legislation as enacted in a new constitution in 1945. Although Arévalo had widespread support among the peasantry, he immediately won the enmity of the land-owners and American companies, especially the powerful **United Fruit Company (UFC)**.

In 1951 **Jacobo Arbenz Guzman** succeeded Arévalo as president. Arbenz had close ties with the Guatemalan military and was expected to scrap his predecessor's social policy, but he did not. He continued to implement social legislation, worked closely with labor unions, and in 1953 announced a new agrarian reform law. The new law provided for the expropriation of 234,000 acres of uncultivated land from UFC. Arbenz offered to pay UFC $1 million for the land, but the company insisted upon $16 million. Arbenz refused. He pointed out that UFC owned 42 percent of all Guatemala, controlled all of the country's railroads, and owned the largest electrical generating stations.

UFC cried foul. In a well-orchestrated **public relations campaign**, UFC insisted that communists had infiltrated Arbenz's government, that he was "soft" on communism, and that only American intervention could prevent Guatemala from falling to communism. Caught in the grip of the Cold War, the Eisenhower administration was quite sympathetic to UFC's argument. **President Eisenhower**'s personal secretary was married to the UFC's chief public relations officer. Before becoming Eisenhower's secretary of state, **John Foster Dulles** worked for the New York law firm that represented UFC. **Allen Dulles**, brother of the secretary of state and director of the **Central Intelligence Agency** (CIA), had been a member of UFC's board of trustees.

Allen Dulles was quite confident his CIA could remove Arbenz from power. He chose **Colonel Carlos Castilo Armas**, an American-educated officer, to lead a coup and spent about $7 million to train a ragtag army of 200 soldiers. Following orders from his American advisors, on 18 June 1954 Armas launched his coup from a UFC plantation in Honduras. The Guatemalan military refused to support Arbenz, and on 27 June he resigned. Armas, escorted by U.S. Ambassador **John Peurifoy**, entered the capital and took control. Armas returned all lands to UFC and set about executing hundreds of peasants and labor leaders. Although the Eisenhower administration claimed the 1954 coup prevented a communist Guatemala, there is no evidence for this. As a result of the 1954 coup Guatemala has endured more than four decades of brutal military rule during which more than 100,000 Guatemalans have been killed.

Suggestions for Term Papers

1. How was it possible for a business like the United Fruit Company (UFC) to wield as much power as it did in Guatemala? Investigate the growth of the UFC and write a paper analyzing its influence on twentieth-century Guatemala.

2. In the two decades prior to the 1954 coup the United States prided itself on being a "good neighbor" in its relations with Central America. What was the Good Neighbor Policy and why was it eventually discarded?

3. Secretary of State John Foster Dulles was convinced that communism was such a threat to Guatemala that President Arbenz should be replaced. Evaluate the extent of a threat of communism in Guatemala in the early 1950s.

4. Allen Dulles, director of the CIA, was very confident his agency could execute the coup quickly and professionally. Assess the role of the CIA in Guatemala and write a paper commenting on its planning and execution of the 1954 coup.

5. Do a research project on the role played by Edward L. Bernays, the public relations expert hired by the UFC to improve its "image" and to raise fears about communism in Guatemala. To what extent was he successful, and why (see Suggested Sources)?

6. Evaluate the role played by John Peurifoy, United States ambassador to Guatemala, in the coup.

Research Suggestions

In addition to the boldfaced items, look under the entries for "Fidel Castro and the Cuban Revolution, 1959" (#57), "The Overthrow of Salvador Allende in Chile, 1973" (#76), and "The Sandinistas and the Contras in Nicaragua, 1981–1989" (#88). Search under **Cold War, human rights**, and **liberation theology**.

SUGGESTED SOURCES

Primary Sources

Hunt, E. Howard. *Undercover: Memoirs of an American Secret Agent.* New York: Putnam, 1974. Although Hunt gained more notoriety for his Watergate caper, this is a revealing look at his CIA role in Guatemala.

Secondary Sources

Cullather, Nick. *Secret History: The CIA's Classified Account of Its Operations in Guatemala, 1952–1954.* Stanford: Stanford University Press, 1999. Makes use of the declassified secret internal history of the CIA's activities in Guatemala in the 1950s.

Immerman, Richard. *The CIA in Guatemala: The Foreign Policy of Intervention.* Austin: University of Texas Press, 1982. Based on a large number of interviews with CIA operatives, this is the best study of the CIA's role.

——, ed. *John Foster Dulles and the Diplomacy of the Cold War.* Princeton: Princeton University Press, 1990. Good introduction and a penetrating chapter on Latin American communism.

Lafeber, Walter. *Inevitable Revolutions: The United States in Central America.* 2nd ed. New York: W. W. Norton, 1993. A reliable study by a premier diplomatic historian.

Rabe, Stephen. "The Clues Didn't Check Out: Commentary on the CIA and Castillo Armas." *Diplomatic History* 14 (1990): 87–95. An update of the historiography of the CIA's role in the coup.

Schlesinger, Stephen, and Stephen Kinzer. *Bitter Fruit: The Untold Story of the American Coup in Guatemala.* New York: Doubleday, 1982. The single best study, it remains the most incisive analysis of the coup.

Tye, Larry. *The Father of Spin: Edward L. Bernays and the Birth of Public Relations.* New York: Crown, 1998. Revealing portrait of how the image of the communist threat was used by the CIA.

World Wide Web

"The National Security Archive." *http://www/gwu.edu/~nsarchiv.* Abundant documentation on the coup may be found at this Web site.

51. KHRUSHCHEV'S "SECRET SPEECH" AT THE TWENTIETH PARTY CONGRESS, 1956

On 24 February 1956, in a secret address to the Twentieth Congress of the Soviet Communist Party, **Nikita Khrushchev**, secretary of the Communist Party, stunned his audience by exposing the crimes of **Josif Stalin**. Stalin ruled the Soviet Union from 1929 until his death in 1953. Although he did not invent the police state, Stalin systematically used police and terror to destroy all opposition to his rule within the Soviet Union. Perhaps the single most grotesque example of Stalin's policy was his **starvation famine** of the **Ukraine**, resulting in the deaths of 5 million Ukrainian peasants. Stalin's drive to consolidate power in the Soviet Union and to establish his brutal dictatorship resulted in the deaths of more than 10 million people.

Although Khrushchev did not describe Stalin's crimes in detail, his speech was the first official, public admission that Stalin had perpetrated an immense reign of terror against his own people and that he had indeed slaughtered millions of Soviet citizens. In his speech, Khrushchev not only condemned Stalin's dictatorship, which he euphemistically called **"the cult of the individual,"** but also suggested that members of the all-important **Politburo** of the Communist Party's **Central Committee** failed to check the excesses of Stalin's dictatorship. To prevent any further abuses Khrushchev called for the eradication of "the cult of the individual," a return to the Leninist principles of service to the workers, and a collective leadership within the Communist Party, "characterized by the wide practice of criticism and self criticism."

Khrushchev's speech accelerated his own consolidation of power within the Soviet Union and resulted in the removal of old guard Stalinists from the government. Millions of political prisoners in the Soviet Union were released. Khrushchev's speech, however, inadvertently raised the hope of reform and a loosening of Soviet control in eastern Europe. **Wladyslaw Gomulka** came to power in **Poland** in the summer of 1956, where he initiated modest reforms, but only after pledging loyalty to the Soviet Union. **Imre Nagy**, who came to power in Hungary in October 1956, refused to obey Khrushchev, and as a result Soviet tanks crushed the **Hungarian Revolution**, killing 3,000 Hungarians. Khrushchev's speech announced a thaw in the **Cold War** and his intention to seek better relations with the United States. It was not well received in China. **Mao Zedong**, China's communist leader, did not approve of Khrushchev's policy of **peaceful coexistence** and considered Khrushchev's attack on Stalin an attack on his own Stalinist style of leadership. Khrushchev's attack on Stalin signaled the opening round of a serious rift in **Sino-Soviet relations**, one that would result in a complete break between the two countries by 1960.

Suggestions for Term Papers

1. Investigate the crimes of Josif Stalin and write a paper explaining why Khrushchev would condemn Stalin for promoting "the cult of the individual."

2. Read Khrushchev's speech and compare it to Mikhail Gorbachev's 6 February 1990 speech (see Suggested Sources) asking the Communist Party to give up its role as the only political party in the Soviet Union. Based on these two speeches, how would you compare these two Soviet leaders?

3. Write a paper on Khrushchev's policy of "peaceful coexistence" with the West in which you evaluate the reception of the policy by the West.

4. Known for his rough, earthy humor, Khrushchev always drew a big audience when he visited America. Do a research project on his diplomatic style and special brand of humor during his American visits.

5. Investigate Khrushchev's role in repressing the Hungarian uprising of November 1956. To what extent does he bear responsibility for the decision to crush the Hungarians?

6. Despite Khrushchev's attack on Stalin, there are many in Russia today who still revere Stalin. Write a paper on the current ideas of Russians about Stalin.

Research Suggestions

In addition to the boldfaced items, look under the entries for "The 1917 Russian Revolution" (#10), "Stalin's First Five-Year Plan, 1928–1932 (#23), "The Hungarian Revolution, 1956" (#53), "The Sino-Soviet Split, 1959–1969" (#60), and "The Breakup of the Soviet Union, 1991" (#91). Search under **Leonid Brezhnev** and **Alexis Kosygin**.

SUGGESTED SOURCES

Primary Sources

Gorbachev, Mikhail. "Address to the Communist Party." *New York Times*, 6 February 1990, A16.

Khrushchev, Nikita S. "Address to the Twentieth Party Congress." *Congressional Record, 84th Congress, 2nd Session* (Washington, D. C.: Government Printing Office, 1956), CII, 9389–403. This is the full text of the speech and the best starting point for research.

———. *Khrushchev Remembers.* Translated and edited by Strobe Talbott. Boston: Little, Brown, 1970. A well-edited collection of Khrushchev's memoirs and speeches.

Secondary Sources

Burnt by the Sun [videorecording]. Culver City, Calif.: Columbia TriStar Home Video, 1995. The best film on how ordinary Russians endured the crimes of Stalin.

Conquest, Robert. *The Great Terror: A Reassessment.* New York: Oxford University Press, 1990. The most accessible treatment of Stalin's part in the Purges.

———. *Stalin: Breaker of Nations.* New York: Viking, 1991. A solid biography of Stalin by a premier Soviet scholar.

Dallin, Alexander, ed. *The Khrushchev and Brezhnev Years.* New York: Garland, 1992. A good collection of articles examining Khrushchev's political strategies.

Khrushchev, Sergei. *Khrushchev on Khrushchev: An Inside Account of the Man and His Era.* Edited and translated by William Taubman. Boston: Little, Brown, 1990. Written by his son, who is now an American citizen, these are candid reflections on Khrushchev's failures and achievements.

Richter, James G. *Khrushchev's Double Bind: International Pressures and Domestic Coalition Politics.* Baltimore: Johns Hopkins University Press, 1994. A careful analysis of Khrushchev's political career.

Zubok, V. M., and Constantine Pleshakov. *Inside the Kremlin's Cold War: From Stalin to Khrushchev.* Cambridge, Mass.: Harvard University Press, 1996. The best account of how Khrushchev's attack on Stalin assisted his rise to power.

World Wide Web

"The National Security Archive." *http://www.gwu.edu/~nsarchiv.* Key documents for the Khrushchev period.

52. GAMAL ABDEL NASSER AND THE SUEZ CRISIS, 1956

In 1952 a small group of disaffected Egyptian army officers led a coup against the corrupt **King Farouk**. For two years **General Mohammad Naguib** seemingly was in control, but in 1954 Gamal Abdel Nasser (1918–1970) emerged as the new leader of Egypt's 22 million people. Tall, handsome, and politically astute, Nasser committed Egypt to a policy of economic modernization and complete independence from Great Britain. In 1955 he signed an agreement with Great Britain stipulating that by June 1956 Britain would withdraw all its troops from Egypt and turn over control of the **Suez Canal**, an important lifeline of British and European shipping, to a private company.

Nasser soon emerged as the spokesman not only for Egypt but also for young Arab modernizers throughout the Middle East. His writings and speeches suggested that Nasser was the only Arab leader capable of challenging Israel.

Two key elements of Nasser's modernization plans were the expansion of the military and the building of the huge **Aswan Dam** on the upper Nile. After failing to get sufficient Western equipment for his military, Nasser worked out an arrangement whereby **Egyptian cotton** would be traded for armaments from **Czechoslovakia** and the **Soviet Union**. Such an arrangement underscored Nasser's determination to free Egypt from military dependence on the West and, at the same time, demonstrate his independent, **nonaligned policy** in the emerging **Cold War**. Despite his new friendship with the Soviet Union, Nasser expected Great Britain and the United States to assist him in the Aswan project. He was shocked in July 1956 when, the two countries, concerned that Nasser was too friendly with the Soviet Union, withdrew funding for Aswan.

Nasser retaliated by nationalizing the Suez Canal Company. **Prime Minister Anthony Eden** had little difficulty convincing France and Israel to join with Britain in attacking Egypt and seizing the canal. On 29 October 1956 Israeli tanks cut across the **Sinai Peninsula** and in less than five days defeated all Egyptian forces east of Suez. On 5 November British and French forces occupied the Egyptian city of **Port Said** and were poised to seize the Suez Canal. The **United Nations (UN)** condemned the attack on Egypt and, at the behest of the United States and the Soviet Union, a cease-fire was accepted on 6 November 1956. **UN peacekeepers** were dispatched to oversee the withdrawal of foreign forces from Egyptian territory.

Nasser emerged from the Suez crisis much stronger than before. He demonstrated to the world that he could stand up to Great Britain, France, and Israel and that he was the most potent leader in the Arab world. The Soviet Union immediately replenished his arsenal and assured Nasser they would provide full assistance in completing the Aswan Dam.

Suggestions for Term Papers

1. Great Britain operated the Suez Canal for more than seven decades. Determine whether Nasser was justified in seizing the canal in 1956 and provide evidence for your position.

2. Nasser ruled Egypt from 1954 to 1970. Assess the impact of his period in power.

3. Investigate the Aswan Dam project and evaluate its role in the modernization of Egypt.

4. The United States opposed Britain, France, and Israel's action against Nasser in 1956. Comment on why the United States did this and on the consequences of its actions.

5. Write a paper analyzing the role of the Israeli military in the 1956 Suez crisis.

6. After 1956 Nasser drew closer to the Soviet Union in order to obtain economic and military assistance. What impact did this have on the balance of power in the Middle East?

Research Suggestions

In addition to the boldfaced items, look under the entries for "The Establishment of the State of Israel, 1948" (#43), "The Hungarian Revolution, 1956" (#53), and "The Six-Day War, 1967" (#66). Search under **David Ben-Gurion, John Foster Dulles, Moshe Dayan**, and **Guy Mollet**.

SUGGESTED SOURCES

Primary Sources

Dayan, Moshe. *Diary of the Sinai Campaign*. New York: Harper and Row, 1966. A personal account of the fighting by one of Israel's military leaders.

Eden, Anthony. *Full Circle: The Memoirs of Anthony Eden*. Boston: Houghton Mifflin, 1960. The final chapter in these memoirs gives a good account of Britain's policy.

Laqueur, Walter, and Barry Rubin, eds. *The Israel-Arab Reader: A Documentary History of the Middle East Conflict*. New York: Penguin Books, 1984. Document 32 is a speech by Nasser on Zionism and Israel.

Nasser, Gamal Abdel. *Egypt's Liberation: The Philosophy of the Revolution*. Washington, D.C.: Public Affairs Press, 1955. A succinct outline of Nasser's dream of leading the Islamic world.

Sadat, Anwar el-. *Revolt on the Nile*. New York: John Day, 1957. A personal account of Nasser's seizure of power by Nasser's successor. Nasser wrote the foreword to this book.

Secondary Sources

Beattie, Kirk J. *Egypt During the Nasser Years: Ideology, Politics and Civil Society*. Boulder: Westview Press, 1994. Excellent analysis of Nasser's political strategy.

Kyle, Keith. *Suez*. New York: St. Martin's Press, 1991. A good starting point for understanding the international reaction to the crisis.

Louis, Wm. Roger. "Dulles, Suez and the British." In *John Foster Dulles and the Diplomacy of the Cold War*, edited by Richard H. Immerman. Princeton: Princeton University Press, 1990. A clear statement of U.S. policy during the crisis.

Love, Kennett. *Suez—The Twice-Fought War: A History*. New York: McGraw-Hill, 1969. A comprehensive military history of all the belligerents.

Nutting, Anthony. *Nasser.* New York: E. P. Dutton, 1972. The most complete biography in English.

Ovendale, Ritchie. *The Origins of the Arab-Israeli Wars.* 2nd ed. New York: Longman, 1992. A crisp account of the fighting in 1956.

Thomas, Hugh. *Suez.* New York: Harper and Row, 1967. A well-written account complete with maps and a good bibliography.

Woodward, Peter, *Nasser.* London: Longman, 1992. A good overview of Nasser's career.

World Wide Web

"Department of History Map Library." *http://www.dean.usma.edu/history /dhistorymaps//MapsHome.htm* Click on "Atlases" for United States Military Academy (West Point) maps related to the military campaign.

53. THE HUNGARIAN REVOLUTION, 1956

Soviet Premier **Nikita Khrushchev**'s secret speech to the Twentieth Party Congress in February 1956 stunned the communist world by revealing the crimes of **Josif Stalin** and denouncing Stalin's autocratic rule. After learning of Khrushchev's speech, dissidents throughout Europe began to agitate for change. Communists in Poland and Hungary were heartened to learn that Khrushchev had endorsed the view that "the ways of socialist development vary in different countries and conditions."

In April 1956, Communist Poland's leaders granted political amnesty to 20,000 political prisoners. Later that same month thousands of Polish coal miners went on strike. Khrushchev did not intervene, and he permitted the Polish Communist Party to install **Wladyslaw Gomulka** as premier. Gomulka was a loyal communist who proposed a moderate policy of improving conditions in the mines and relaxing some state controls, but he kept very close military ties to the Soviet Union.

Emboldened by the Polish example, Hungarian reformers, particularly students, increased their demands for political reform in Hungary. On 23 October 1956, thousands of students took to the streets of **Budapest** demanding reform. The first target of the student demonstrators was a forty-foot bronze statue of Stalin, which they pulled down, dismembered, and painted with graffiti. When the students attempted to take over a radio station, the government ordered the **Hungarian army** into Budapest. Although a few shots were fired, the army quickly went over to the side of the demonstrators. The government of **Erno Gero** was paralyzed. To salvage the situation, the Russian advisors in Budapest selected **Imre Nagy** as premier, expecting him to imitate Gomulka's cautious reform policies.

Although a communist, Nagy proved to be an independent-minded reformer. He released from prison **József Cardinal Mindszenty**, the Roman Catholic leader of Hungary. Mindszenty, who had been serving a life sentence for political crimes, called for the immediate dismantling of the communist dictatorship in Hungary. Nagy refused to discipline Mindszenty and announced that his communist government would welcome opposition parties. Thousands of cheering Hungarians took to the streets of Budapest to celebrate. On 30 October, Nagy declared Hungary a multiparty state, and the next day he announced Hungary's withdrawal from the Soviet Union's military alliance, the **Warsaw Pact**. Seemingly the Russians agreed with these dramatic changes. But on 4 November 1956, Soviet troops along with 2,500 tanks rolled into Budapest and opened fire in the crowded streets. At least 3,000 Hungarians were killed and more than 200,000 Hungarians fled their country. Imre Nagy was arrested and eventually executed. Cardinal Mindszenty sought sanctuary in the U.S. Embassy and remained there until 1971. The Russians installed **Janos Kadar**, a tough Hungarian communist, who launched a campaign of political repression that signaled to the world that Khrushchev could be just as brutal as Stalin in repressing dissent.

Suggestions for Term Papers

1. Investigate the role of Imre Nagy in the revolution and try to determine why he was executed.
2. Before and after the revolt József Cardinal Mindszenty was the Hungarian symbol of resistance to communism. Discuss his popularity and the reasons why he symbolized anti-communism to many people.
3. In a research paper on the decision by the Soviet Union to intervene in Hungary, write about the reasons for Soviet intervention and the military tactics they used.

4. After reading György Konrád's novel *The Case Worker* (see Suggested Sources), write a paper on its portrait of life in communist Hungary.

5. Discuss how the Eisenhower administration reacted to the Soviet suppression of the Hungarian Revolution and assess the reasons for the approach it took.

6. Set up a panel discussion on the connections between the Hungarian Revolution and the Suez Canal Crisis.

Research Suggestions

In addition to the boldfaced items, look under the entries for "Khrushchev's 'Secret Speech' at the Twentieth Party Congress, 1956" (#51) and "Gamal Abdel Nasser and the Suez Crisis, 1956" (#52). Search under **Cold War** and **John Foster Dulles**.

SUGGESTED SOURCES

Primary Sources

Beke, László. *A Student's Diary: Budapest, October 16–November 1, 1956.* Translated by Leon Kossar and Ralph M. Zoltan. New York: Viking Press, 1957. A short, accessible eyewitness account by a student participant.

Haraszti-Taylor, Eva, ed. *The Hungarian Revolution of 1956: A Collection of Documents from the British Foreign Office.* Nottingham: Astra, 1995. Candid views of British observers of the street violence.

Lasky, Melvin J., ed. *The Hungarian Revolution: A White Book. The Story of the October Uprising as Recorded in Documents, Dispatches, Eye-Witness Accounts, and World-Wide Reactions.* New York: Praeger, 1957. An accessible collection of eyewitness accounts.

Lomax, Bill. *Hungarian Workers' Councils in 1956.* Translated by Bill Lomax and Julian Schöpflin. New York: Columbia University Press, 1990. A powerful expression of the idealism and realities of the uprising.

Mindszenty, József. *Memoirs: József Cardinal Mindszenty.* Translated by Richard and Clara Winston. New York: Macmillan, 1974. A poignant set of reflections by the spiritual leader of Hungary.

Nagy, Imre. *On Communism: In Defense of the New Course.* New York: Praeger, 1957. A succinct explanation of Nagy's appeal.

Secondary Sources

Barber, Noël. *Seven Days of Freedom: The Hungarian Uprising 1956.* New York: Stein and Day, 1974. A reliable introduction to the revolt.

Fehér, Ferenc. *Hungary 1956 Revisited: The Message of a Revolution, a Quarter of a Century After*. Boston: Allen and Unwin, 1983. A personal retrospective that captures the idealism of the revolt.

Gadney, Reg. *Cry Hungary! Uprising 1956*. New York: Atheneum, 1986. A brief introduction to the revolt.

Granville, Johanna C. *In the Line of Fire: The Soviet Crackdown on Hungary, 1956–1958*. Pittsburgh: Center for Russian and East European Studies, 1998. A crisp summary of recent scholarship.

Király, Béla K., and Paul Jónás, eds. *The Hungarian Revolution of 1956 in Retrospect*. New York: Columbia University Press, 1978. A fine collection of articles including one on Nagy's trial.

Konrád, György. *The Case Worker*. Translated by Paul Aston. New York: Harcourt Brace Jovanovich, 1974. This novel captures the oppressive atmosphere of Hungary in the 1950s.

Radványi, János. *The Secret Trial of Imre Nagy*. Westport, Conn.: Praeger, 1994. An insight into the brutality of the communist system.

World Wide Web

"The National Security Archive." *http://www.gwu.edu/~nsarchiv/*. Good links to Soviet decisions on Hungary.

54. KWAME NKRUMAH AND THE INDEPENDENCE OF GHANA, 1957

Kwame Nkrumah was the first black African to lead a country to independence in the twentieth century. Born in the British colony of the **Gold Coast**, Nkrumah (1909–1972) received his early education in Catholic schools. He later graduated from **Lincoln University** and did additional work at the **University of Pennsylvania**. Although Nkrumah studied Karl Marx, he was more impressed with the African American writer **Marcus Garvey**, especially Garvey's ideas on **Black Power**. He also developed friendships with the African American leader **W.E.B. Du Bois** and the brilliant Caribbean writer **C.L.R. James**. In 1945 he moved to Britain and attended the **London School of Economics**, acquiring a wide reputation for his **Pan-African** ideas on African unity.

In 1947 Nkrumah returned home and became secretary-general of the **United Gold Coast Convention (UGCC)**. His political activities landed him in jail for a year. In 1949 he founded the **Convention**

People's Party (CPP). Like **Gandhi** and **Congress** in India, the CPP refused to cooperate with the British and adopted a **"positive action"** policy of strikes and civil disobedience. In 1951 Nkrumah was elected to the legislative assembly, and in 1952 became prime minister. He demanded complete independence. In March 1957 Ghana became the first British colony to win independence.

Nkrumah quickly consolidated his power. In 1958 he announced the **Preventive Detention Act**, ensuring arrest for anyone declared a security risk. Starting in 1959 he began to remove his opponents from the national assembly. In 1960 he was elected president and in 1962 named president for life. Firmly in control of Ghana, Nkrumah now sought to realize his dream of leading all of Africa. This idea found its fullest expression in his **"Statement of African Unity,"** which proposed that the entire continent of Africa should form one nation, much like the United States, and that Nkrumah should be its leader. His ideas on African unity received a great deal of support from other African states. Despite this, Nkrumah lost control of Ghana. On 24 February 1966, while he was out of the country, disaffected army officers seized power and refused to permit Nkrumah to return. He spent the last six years of his life in exile, writing and dreaming of a return to power.

Nkrumah's legacy is mixed. He was an inspirational and effective leader against British colonial rule. Many African leaders imitated his style of leadership and his policy of **nonalignment** in the **Cold War**. In power, however, he was authoritative and egotistical, and did not find a way to placate his political opponents. His dream of African unity underscored the great economic and political potential of Africa, but his proposal that the United States be the model failed to take into account the immense variety of African cultural and political traditions.

Suggestions for Term Papers

1. Investigate Nkrumah's "African American connection." To what extent did the ideas of Marcus Garvey, W.E.B. Du Bois, or C.L.R. James (see Suggested Sources) influence his thinking?

2. After reading Nkrumah's autobiography (see Suggested Sources) write a paper explaining his political philosophy.

3. Read Nkrumah's *I Speak of Freedom* (see Suggested Sources) and write a paper on his vision for Africa.

4. Compare and contrast Nkrumah's methods with those of Nelson Mandela and the African National Congress (ANC) in South Africa in the 1950s and 1960s.

5. In a paper focused on the events leading to the coup of 1966, explain why Nkrumah was overthrown.

6. How do Ghanaians view Nkrumah today? Analyze his legacy in contemporary Ghana.

Research Suggestions

In addition to the boldfaced items, look under the entries for "Mustafa Kemal Atatürk and the Founding of the Republic of Turkey, 1923" (#15), "Gandhi's Salt March, 1930" (#20), "Apartheid in South Africa from the 1950s to the 1970s" (#58), and "Civil War in Nigeria (Biafra), 1967–1970" (#67). Search under **Organization of African Unity**.

SUGGESTED SOURCES

Primary Sources

Nkrumah, Kwame. *Africa Must Unite*. New York: International Publishers, 1970. The fullest statement of his vision for Africa.

———. *Consciencism: Philosophy and Ideology for De-colonization*. New York: Monthly Review Press, 1970. Short but profound statement of his political philosophy.

———. *Dark Days in Ghana*. New York: International Publishers, 1968. An assessment of the 1966 coup and how it affected Ghana.

———. *Ghana: The Autobiography of Kwame Nkrumah*. New York: International Publishers, 1971. The starting point for an understanding of his achievements.

———. *I Speak of Freedom: A Statement of African Ideology*. New York: Praeger, 1962. A very readable introduction to his thought and his views of Africa in the world. The preface contains his "Statement of African Unity."

———. *Selected Speeches: Kwame Nkrumah*. 5 vols. Compiled by Samuel Obeng. Accra, Ghana: Afram Publications, 1997. A five-volume set of speeches expressing Nkrumah's political and social vision.

Secondary Sources

Amissah, G. McLean. *Picture Story of Kwame Nkrumah and Ghana.* Cape Coast: Germain Publications, 1993. Captures the dramatic appeal of Nkrumah and his home.

Birmingham, David. *Kwame Nkrumah: The Father of African Nationalism.* Athens: Ohio University Press, 1998. A clearly written analysis of his importance for contemporary Africa.

Davidson, Basil. *Black Star: A View of the Life and Times of Kwame Nkrumah.* New York: Praeger, 1973. A short, balanced biography.

James, C.L.R. *Nkrumah and the Ghana Revolution.* London: Allison and Busby, 1977. A readable, important study by a Caribbean writer who knew Nkrumah.

Owusu-Ansah, David, and Daniel Miles McFarland. *Historical Dictionary of Ghana.* 2nd ed. Metuchen, N.J.: Scarecrow Press, 1995. A most helpful starting point for understanding Ghana and Nkrumah.

Shillington, Kevin. *Ghana and the Rawlings Factor.* New York: St. Martin's Press, 1992. Examines the long-term implications of the military's involvement in Ghanaian politics.

55. THE FOUNDING OF THE EUROPEAN ECONOMIC COMMUNITY, 1957

The **European Economic Community (EEC),** the largest free trade zone in the world, traces its beginnings to the late 1940s. In 1947 **Winston Churchill** (Great Britain), **Léon Blum** (France), **Paul-Henri Spaak** (Belgium), and **Alcide de Gasperi** (Italy) met and proposed both a European economic union and the formation of a European parliament. That same year, the American-funded **Marshall Plan (European Recovery Act)** insisted that an **Organization for European Economic Cooperation (OEEC)** be established to oversee the rebuilding of Europe. Quickly regional European free trade zones were established. Belgium, the Netherlands, and Luxembourg formed the **Benelux Economic Union** (1948). This was followed by the **Franco-Italian Customs Union** (1950) and the **Scandinavian Customs Union** (1950).

In 1950 **Robert Schuman,** the French foreign minister, announced plans for a coal and steel community which would include France, West Germany, the Benelux countries, and eventually Italy.

In 1951 the **European Coal and Steel Community (ECSC)** came into being, and **Jean Monnet**, a French economic planner, was named its president. Under Monnet's leadership the ECSC promoted a climate of economic integration by coordinating agricultural policies, regulating investments, and sponsoring greater economic cooperation throughout Europe. On 25 March 1957, the six members of the ECSC signed the **Treaty of Rome**, which committed all members to create a common trade zone, the European Economic Community (EEC), better known as the **Common Market**, which would be free of all tariffs within twelve years.

In 1967 the EEC became known as the **European Community (EC)** when previously separate agencies joined the EEC. In 1973 Great Britain, Ireland, and Denmark joined the European Economic Community. Greece joined in 1981, Portugal and Spain became members in 1986, and the former East Germany was included in 1990 (by virtue of unification with West Germany). Since 1993 the EC has been known as the **European Union (EU)**. Austria, Finland, and Sweden became members in 1995.

The EU, a free trade zone inhabited by more than 300 million people, has overcome many obstacles in harmonizing tariffs, transportation, travel, and immigration policies among its member nations. It has also worked toward greater European political cooperation, particularly through the **Council of Europe** in Strasbourg, France, and fiscal cooperation with the launching in 1999 of the European single currency, the **euro**.

Suggestions for Term Papers

1. Investigate the ideas of Jean Monnet and write a paper analyzing his influence in the shaping of the European Economic Community.

2. As a group research project, have each student pick a member country of the European Union and present a report on that country's involvement with the EU during the period of its membership.

3. Organize a debate on the following topic: Does the success of the EU mean the end of the individual sovereign state in Europe?

4. The EU has pledged to underwrite the rebuilding of the former Yugoslavia. Evaluate its success to date in fulfilling this pledge.

5. Although western European countries constitute the majority of

the EU, there is interest in having eastern European countries join as well. What would be the impact if Russia joined?

6. Despite the fact that 300 million Europeans live and trade in the EU, Europeans are reluctant to assume full responsibility for defense, and expect the United States to shoulder most of that burden. Draft a policy statement recommending the U.S. position on this matter in the future.

Research Suggestions

In addition to the boldfaced items, look under the entries for "The Japanese Economic Miracle in the 1950s" (#47), "Gamal Abdel Nasser and the Suez Crisis, 1956" (#52), and "The Hungarian Revolution, 1956" (#53). Search under **free trade, GATT,** and **NAFTA**.

SUGGESTED SOURCES

Primary Sources

Bliss, Howard, comp. *The Political Development of the European Community: A Documentary Collection*. Waltham, Mass.: Blaisdell, 1969. The best collection of English language documents available for the important first decade.

Monnet, Jean. *Memoirs*. Translated by Richard Mayne. Garden City, N.Y.: Doubleday, 1978. The memoirs underscore Monnet's singular importance in launching the Common Market.

Schuman, Robert. *French Policy Towards Germany Since the War*. Translated by Kathleen Parnell. London: Oxford University Press, 1954. A good insight into why France and Germany worked so well in the EEC.

Secondary Sources

Brinkley, Douglas, and Clifford P. Hackett. *Jean Monnet: The Path to European Unity*. New York: St. Martin's Press, 1991. A clear exposition of Monnet's role in nurturing the dream of European unity.

Cameron, Rondo. *A Concise Economic History of the World: From Paleolithic Times to the Present*. 3rd ed. New York: Oxford University Press, 1997. Places the EU in a global context.

Duchêne, François. *Jean Monnet: The First Statesman of Interdependence*. New York: W. W. Norton, 1994. A good biographical introduction to Monnet.

Duina, Francesco G. *Harmonizing Europe: Nation States Within The Common Market*. Albany: State University of New York Press, 1999. A crisp introduction to law, ecology, and labor in the EU.

Harrison, D. M. *The Organization of Europe: Developing a Continental Market Order.* New York: Routledge, 1995. A clear explanation of the EU's organization.

Landes, David S. *The Unbound Prometheus: Technological Change and Industrial Development in Western Europe from 1750 to the Present.* Cambridge: Cambridge University Press, 1969. Chapter 7 gives a good summary of the founding of the EEC.

Urwin, Derek W. *The Community of Europe: A History of European Integration since 1945.* 2nd ed. New York: Longman, 1995. An excellent introduction.

Vaubel, Roland. *The Centralisation of Western Europe: The Common Market, Political Integration, and Democracy.* London: Institute of Economic Affairs, 1995. A good overview of how the EU works.

Wells, Sherrill B. *Jean Monnet: Visionary and Architect of European Union: A Brief Biography and Documents.* Boston: Bedford Books, forthcoming. The most up-to-date treatment; also contains key documents on the EEC.

56. FRANCE AND THE ALGERIAN REVOLUTION, 1954–1962

Determined to teach the **Dey of Algiers** a lesson for striking the French consul with his fly whisk, 30,000 French soldiers captured the city of Algiers in July 1830. By 1848 France had conquered all of **Algeria**. Initially, French administrators spoke of "assimilating" **Berber, Muslim**, and **Jewish Algerians** and educating them to become French citizens. Assimilation, however, proved too difficult and was soon replaced by a rigid colonial administration. By 1954, 1 million Europeans (called *pieds noirs* for their black shoes) controlled 9 million Algerians.

Many Algerians had long dreamt of independence from France, but it was not until 1954 that this idea appeared likely. On 1 November 1954, the **Algerian Front de Libération Nationale (FLN)** declared war on France. For the next eight years the ill-equipped Algerian guerrillas fought a brutal war against the well-equipped and very determined French military.

On 13 May 1958, a group of *pieds noirs* seized power in Algiers and demanded that **General Charles de Gaulle** be appointed prime minister of France. Largely because of their demands, de Gaulle was named prime minister and soon became president of the new Fifth French Republic. Although he gave the impression of supporting the *pieds noirs*, de Gaulle was convinced that Algeria must be independent. In a series of bold political maneuvers he opened negotiations with the FLN to end the war.

On 8 April 1962, France granted Algeria full independence and recognized **Ahmed Ben Bella**, of the FLN, as president of Algeria. The Algerian revolution left a bitter legacy for both sides. The French army lost more than 17,000 soldiers. Nearly 1 million *pieds noirs* left Algeria in 1962 and immigrated to France. Disaffected elements in the French army **(Secret Army Organization)** branded de Gaulle a traitor and repeatedly attempted to assassinate him. Algeria suffered 1 million military and civilian deaths in the war. Despite its economic promise, Algeria has not been able to staunch the flow of emigrants or to find the political stability the FLN revolution promised.

Suggestions for Term Papers

1. View the film *Battle of Algiers* (see Suggested Sources) and write a paper analyzing the tactics the French army used in Algeria.
2. Examine the ways in which "Barricades Week" of January 1960 in Algiers threatened to bring civil war to France.
3. Many officers in the French army felt betrayed by de Gaulle's Algerian settlement and formed a secret society to assassinate him. Write a paper on the O.A.S. (*Organisation armée secrète* or Secret Army Organization) and its effort to assassinate de Gaulle.
4. The writer Albert Camus, born in Algeria, thought it should remain French. Read his essays (see Suggested Sources) and write a paper on his views on Algerian independence.
5. After reading Frantz Fanon's arguments for Algerian independence (see Suggested Sources), assess his ideas about colonialism.
6. Despite the fact that Algeria and France were once enemies, hundreds of thousands of Algerians now reside in France. How has this largely Muslim Algerian community been received in France? Write a paper examining the problems of Algerian immigrants living in contemporary France.

Research Suggestions

In addition to the boldfaced items, look under the entries for "Ho Chi Minh and the Vietnamese War Against the French, 1946–1954" (#41) and "May 1968 in France" (#69). Search under **Houari Boumedienne, Albert Camus, Jacques Soustelle, French Fourth Republic, French Fifth Republic**, and **Islamic Salvation Front**.

SUGGESTED SOURCES

Primary Sources

Camus, Albert. *Resistance, Rebellion, and Death.* Translated by Justin O'Brien. New York: Knopf, 1961. The essays on Algeria present the *pieds noirs* side of independence.

De Gaulle, Charles. *Memoirs of Hope: Renewal and Endeavor.* Translated by Terence Kilmartin. New York: Simon and Schuster, 1971. A powerful set of reflections on how Algeria's war for independence afforded de Gaulle the chance to remake France.

Fanon, Frantz. *The Wretched of the Earth.* Translated by Constance Farrington. New York: Grove Press, 1968. A forceful argument for an independent Algeria.

Maier, Charles S., and Dan S. White, eds. *The Thirteenth of May: The Advent of de Gaulle's Republic.* New York: Oxford University Press, 1968. The most accessible collection of French documents in English. Contains excerpts from French and Algerian newspapers and the final peace accords.

Servan-Schreiber, Jean-Jacques. *Lieutenant in Algeria.* Translated by Ronald Matthews. London: Hutchinson, 1958. The author, who became the editor of the French weekly *L'Express*, records the grim duty of draftees in this brutal war.

Secondary Sources

Battle of Algiers [videorecording]. Directed by Gillo Pontecorvo. Stella Productions, 1966. Subtitled in English. A film that is faithful to the history of the war. It is particularly good in showing the importance of Algerian women in the struggle.

Clayton, Anthony. *The Wars of French Decolonization.* New York: Longman, 1994. His section of Algeria is the most up to date, brief introduction to the war.

Dine, Philip D. *Images of the Algerian War: French Fiction and Film, 1954–1992.* New York: Oxford University Press, 1994. A solid analysis of how the Algerian war has been documented in French film and literature.

Horne, Alistair. *A Savage War of Peace: Algeria, 1954–1962.* New York: Viking, 1978. The best single-volume study in English. It has good photographs of the participants.

Hutchinson, Martha Crenshaw. *Revolutionary Terrorism: The FLN in Algeria, 1954–1962.* Stanford: Hoover Institution Press, 1978. A good explanation of the organization of the FLN and its use of terror.

Ruedy, John. *Modern Algeria: The Origins and Development of a Nation.* Bloomington: Indiana University Press, 1992. Chapter 6 is a good overview of the war.

Schalk, David L. *War and the Ivory Tower: Algeria and Vietnam.* New York: Oxford University Press, 1991. Helpful for its focus on the peace and protest movements in France during the Algerian War.

57. FIDEL CASTRO AND THE CUBAN REVOLUTION, 1959

Fidel Castro (1927–   ), the leader of the most successful social revolution in Latin American history, was born into a wealthy landowning family. While a student at the **University of Havana**, Castro took an active interest in radical politics. He joined a group of dissidents who dreamed of overthrowing **Fulgencio Batista**, who had seized power in a coup d'état in 1952 (he had been in and out of power since the 1930s). An ally of the United States who received large amounts of American aid, Batista presided over a corrupt dictatorship that favored the large landowners and exploited the peasants.

On 26 July 1953, Castro led a small band of Cuban revolutionaries in a raid on an army barracks near **Santiago**, Cuba. The attack, though a failure, was significant in three respects. First, it gave identity to Castro's nationalist-inspired revolutionary movement, henceforth known as the **26th July Movement**. Second, in melodramatic oratory, Castro conducted his own trial defense, ending with the impassioned words "History will absolve me." This speech was later printed and distributed throughout Cuba, winning Castro widespread support. Third, after serving a prison term of nineteen months Castro visited Mexico, where in 1955 he met **Ernesto Ché Guevara**, who became his second in command and the most celebrated martyr of the Cuban Revolution.

In 1956 Castro, his brother **Raúl**, and Ché Guevara secretly returned to Cuba, where the 26th July Movement began a guerrilla insurgency against Batista. By 1958 Castro's 3,000 guerrillas, along with other Cuban revolutionaries, had seized control of large parts of Cuba. Unable to stop Castro or to convince the United States to support him, Batista fled to Miami on 1 January 1959. Upon taking power in February 1959, Castro disbanded the Cuban parliament and instituted the **Fundamental Law of the Republic**, which gave full power to Castro, who served as prime minister and first secretary of the Communist Party. Castro then launched a program of **land reform**, redistribution of wealth, comprehensive, free public education, and **universal public health**. To help pay for his social revolution, Castro began to expropriate American companies such as **Coca-Cola, Sears, Texaco**, and **Standard Oil**. Castro argued that longtime American exploitation of Cuba justified his expropriation of American property. Initially, the **Eisenhower administration** used an economic embargo, causing Castro to seek aid from the Soviet Union. Later the Eisenhower administration severed diplomatic relations with Castro, and the **Kennedy administration** supported the failed invasion of the **Bay of Pigs** by Cuban exiles, in 1961.

Suggestions for Term Papers

1. How was Cuba ruled before Castro came to power? Write a paper examining Cuba under Fulgencio Batista between 1952 and 1959.

2. Who was Ernesto Ché Guevara? Why did he become one of the most celebrated revolutionaries of the 1960s?

3. Investigate the attempted invasion of Cuba by Cuban exiles at the Bay of Pigs in 1961. Why did it fail? To what extent did the failure of the operation influence the Kennedy administration's Cuban policy?

4. Many Cubans point to Castro's achievements in education and health care. Do a research project on what has been accomplished in education and health care and what remains to be done.

5. Many Cubans fleeing Cuba in 1959 and in following years settled in Florida. Examine the political and economic influence of these Cuban Americans. Use *The Cuban Americans* as a starting point (see Suggested Sources).

6. For nearly forty years, the United States has refused to trade with Cuba. Assess this policy in terms of what it has and has not accomplished. Begin with *The Cuban Americans* (see Suggested Sources).

Research Suggestions

In addition to the boldfaced items, look under the entries for "The Guatemalan Coup, 1954 (#50), "The Cuban Missile Crisis, 1962" (#64), "The Overthrow of Salvador Allende in Chile, 1973" (#76), and "The Sandinistas and the Contras in Nicaragua, 1981–1989" (#88). Search under **Platt Amendment, Cold War, Trade Embargo**, and **Helms-Burton Act**.

SUGGESTED SOURCES

Primary Sources

Castro, Fidel. *Che: A Memoir.* Edited by David Deutschmann. New York: Talman Co., 1994. An insight into the close comradeship between the two men.
———. *Cuba: At the Crossroads.* New York: Ocean Press, 1996. An explanation of Cuba's economic problems.
———. *Fidel Castro Speeches.* Edited by Michael Taber. New York: Pathfinder Press, 1981. Three volumes of Castro's speeches.
———. *My Early Years.* Edited by Deborah Shnookal and Pedro Álvarez Tabío. New York: Ocean Press, 1998. Recollections of his early life.
———. *Revolutionary Struggle, 1947–1958.* Edited by Rolando E. Bonachea and Nelson P. Valdés. Cambridge, Mass: MIT Press, 1972. A good starting point for Castro's early thinking.

Secondary Sources

Balfour, Sebastian. *Castro.* 2nd ed. London: Longman, 1995. A brief introduction to Castro's years in power.
Draper, Theodore. *Castro's Revolution: Myths and Realities.* New York: Praeger, 1962. An important early analysis of the Cuban Revolution.
Gonzales-Pando, Miguel. *The Cuban Americans.* Westport, Conn.: Greenwood Press, 1998. Good overview of the political power of Cuban exiles and Cuban-Americans, particularly in Florida. Helpful listing of immigration population statistics in the appendices.
Leonard, Thomas M. *Castro and the Cuban Revolution.* Westport, Conn.: Greenwood Press, 1999. A good source of information for students, with accompanying biographical profiles and primary documents.

Liss, Sheldon B. *Fidel! Castro's Political and Social Thought.* Boulder: West-view Press, 1994. A solid explanation of Castro's thought.

Lockwood, Lee. *Castro's Cuba, Cuba's Fidel.* Boulder: Westview Press, 1990. A review of three decades of Castro's rule.

Perez, Louis. A. *Cuba: Between Reform and Revolution.* New York: Oxford University Press, 1995. A comprehensive examination of Castro's revolution.

Pérez-Stable, Marifeli. *The Cuban Revolution: Origins, Course, and Legacy.* New York: Oxford University Press, 1993. Highlights the political and economic factors that made Cuba susceptible to revolution.

Quirk, Robert E. *Fidel Castro.* New York: W. W. Norton, 1993. A detailed scholarly study of Castro's rule.

Ruiz, Ramon E. *Cuba: The Making of a Revolution.* New York: W. W. Norton, 1968. An important study of the causes of the revolution.

Thomas, Hugh. *Cuba: The Pursuit of Freedom.* New York: Harper and Row, 1971. Dense but well-written history of Cuba before as well as under Castro.

———. *The Cuban Revolution, Twenty-five Years Later.* Boulder: Westview Press, 1984. A helpful retrospective appraisal.

World Wide Web

"The World Factbook, 1999." *http://www.odci.gov/cia/publications/ factbook/index.html.*. This Central Intelligence Agency site is updated yearly.

"The National Security Archive." *http://www.gwu.edu/~nsarchiv.* Places the Cuban Revolution in the Cold War context.

58. APARTHEID IN SOUTH AFRICA FROM THE 1950s to the 1970s

Segregation of whites and blacks in South Africa before the 1950s was largely a matter of custom. After the **National Party** victory in the 1948 elections, the government established the **apartheid** system, which provided segregation with an elaborate legal basis. The National Party was the party of the **Afrikaners**, descendants of Dutch, German, and French settlers.

In the 1950s a series of laws forced nonwhites to move to shanty towns (townships), created the so-called homelands (**Bantustans**), and abolished the **Natives Representative Council**, the only official countrywide institution for blacks. The police gained enormous power through a series of legislative acts. The **Suppression of Communism Act** in 1950 was part of the official explanation of the necessity of apartheid.

The **African National Congress (ANC)**, founded in 1912, attempted to defend the rights of blacks and other nonwhites in South Africa. The **Freedom Charter** of 1955 emphasized the importance of a nonracial democracy for all South Africans. A turning point came in March 1960, when police fired on a crowd of demonstrators at **Sharpeville** and killed about seventy. The next month the ANC and other anti-apartheid organizations were banned. It became apparent that peaceful demonstrations, such as those advocated by American civil rights leaders, would not work.

By the end of the 1960s the system of apartheid seemed unchallengeable. **Nelson Mandela** was imprisoned along with other African National Congress leaders on **Robben Island**. The ANC was banned in South Africa; those leaders not in jail had gone into exile. The armed wing of the ANC, **Spear of the Nation** (Umkhonto we Sizwe), was sending people into South Africa to carry out terrorist activities, but most were caught before they could accomplish much.

The situation began to change in the 1970s. The **Black Consciousness (BC) movement** emerged in the mid-1970s in **Soweto (Southwest Township)**. Its most prominent representative was **Steve Biko**, a medical student, who formed the exclusively black **South African Students Organisation (SASO)**. Biko, only twenty-four in 1970, was a charismatic leader who encouraged blacks to think not about reform but about transformation of the South African system. Biko was arrested and then killed by the police in 1977, but his message had already taken hold.

In the meantime, beginning in 1976 students in Soweto began a protest against educational policies that emphasized **Afrikaans** (the language of the Afrikaners, similar to Dutch). The slogan was "No education before liberation." Hundreds were killed in the demonstrations. As it turned out, this was the beginning of the end of apartheid, but it would take another decade to accomplish this.

Suggestions for Term Papers

1. Compare the civil rights movement in the United States in the 1950s and 1960s with the civil rights movement in South Africa in the same period.

2. Trace the early career of Nelson Mandela from his work in the ANC Youth League down to 1964, when he was sentenced to life imprisonment.

3. Investigate the ideas underlying the apartheid system, particularly the idea that each race must have the possibility of developing separately.

4. Review the legislation of the 1950s that established apartheid and write a paper on the way in which the system was constructed.

5. *Cry Freedom* is an American film that tells the story of Steve Biko mostly through the experiences of Donald Wood, a South African journalist who knew and wrote about Biko. View the film and discuss why the director approaches Biko's life indirectly through Wood's life and whether this approach is effective.

6. Read *A Sport of Nature* (see Suggested Sources) and comment on the way it presents the history of South Africa in this period.

Research Suggestions

In addition to the boldfaced items, look under the entry for "Nelson Mandela and the End of Apartheid in South Africa, 1989–1994" (#92). Search under **Oliver Tambo, Walter Sisulu, Pan-Africanist Congress, Defiance Campaign, Mixed Marriages Act** (1949), **Group Areas Act** (1950), **Population Registration Act** (1950), and **Hendrik Verwoerd.**

SUGGESTED SOURCES

Primary Sources

Biko, Steve. *I Write What I Like*. Chicago: LPC/In Book, 1996. A collection of writings by the foremost leader of the Black Consciousness movement.

Mandela, Nelson. *Long Walk to Freedom: The Autobiography of Nelson Mandela*. Boston: Little, Brown, 1994. Mandela's own story of how he triumphed over apartheid.

Ramphele, Mamphela. *Across Boundaries: The Journey of a South African Woman Leader*. New York: Feminist Press, 1997. The autobiography of Ramphele, a leading South African activist and scholar, and a close friend of Biko's.

Secondary Sources

Cry Freedom. Directed by Richard Attenborough, 1987. Distributed by MCA Home Video. 157 minutes. A film about a South African journalist, Donald Woods, who knew and wrote about Steve Biko. Woods later had to leave South Africa because of his support for Biko.

Fredrickson, George M. *Black Liberation: A Comparative History of Black Ideologies in the United States and South Africa*. New York: Oxford University Press, 1995. A fascinating discussion of black liberation movements in the two countries.

———. *White Supremacy: A Comparative Study in American and South African History*. New York: Oxford University Press, 1981. A very fine overview of ideas about white superiority.

Gordimer, Nadine. *A Sport of Nature*. New York: Viking Penguin, 1987. An interesting, well-written novel about a white South African woman who becomes involved with the ANC.

Marx, Anthony W. *Making Race and Nation: A Comparison of the United States, South Africa, and Brazil*. New York: Cambridge University Press, 1998. A fascinating comparative study that brings out the many similarities between the United States and South Africa.

Sampson, Anthony. *Nelson Mandela: The Authorized Biography*. New York: Knopf, 1999. The best biography of Mandela available.

Thompson, Leonard. *A History of South Africa*. New Haven: Yale University Press, 1990. An excellent introduction to South African history. A good place to begin.

———. *The Political Mythology of Apartheid*. New Haven: Yale University Press, 1985. An excellent study of the ideas behind the system of apartheid.

Woods, Donald. *Biko*. New York: Henry Holt, 1991. A detailed biography of Biko by a South African journalist who knew him well.

59. THE BERLIN WALL, 1961

The Berlin Wall, a major symbol of the Cold War for twenty-eight years, divided West Berlin, which the West viewed as an outpost of democracy, from East Berlin, which the Soviet bloc saw as the showcase for communism. In a sense, the Wall was an admission by the **German Democratic Republic** (GDR) that communism could not compete successfully with democracy.

Between 1949 and 1961, several million Germans fled the GDR. Even after the border between the GDR and the **Federal Republic of Germany** (FRG) was closed, Berlin remained open and East Germans could use it as an escape route. In November 1958, **Soviet**

Premier Nikita Khrushchev began the **Berlin Crisis** by demanding that the Western powers leave Berlin. He threatened to turn over control of Berlin to the GDR if the Western powers did not leave within six months.

The United States called Khrushchev's bluff, but the question of Berlin continued to be a crucial issue in the Cold War. In the summer of 1961 the crisis flared up again. In part, it was based on Khrushchev's appraisal of **President John F. Kennedy**. The two had met in Vienna in April for a summit conference. Khrushchev had decided Kennedy was weak.

Behind the question of Berlin was the larger issue of the viability of the GDR. It was losing skilled and well-educated people daily. **Walter Ulbricht**, the most powerful figure in the GDR, convinced the Soviets to allow construction of the Wall. The person actually in charge of the construction was **Erich Honecker**, the man who later replaced Ulbricht.

The operation was carried out with great secrecy. Troops, equipment, and workers were concentrated in East Berlin, but no one knew for what purpose. In the early morning hours of 13 August 1961, construction began. Within hours West Berlin was sealed off by barbed wire.

American reaction was muted. The Wall did not threaten American rights in Berlin as such. Kennedy responded with a few gestures, among them sending **Vice President Lyndon B. Johnson** to Berlin. A more serious crisis came a few months later, in October, when a U.S. diplomat was not allowed to cross into East Berlin. **General Lucius C. Clay**, who had returned to Berlin to command the U.S. forces there, sent tanks to **Checkpoint Charlie**, one of the main crossing points between West Berlin and East Berlin, to test Soviet resolve. The Soviets also sent tanks, but late in October they withdrew. The Wall remained, but the Allies maintained right of access to East Berlin.

Over the next two decades, the Wall became an elaborate structure that featured concrete walls, barbed wire fences, and death strips of cleared ground. East Germans were often amazingly resourceful, but the Wall soon became virtually impregnable. With little possibility of leaving, people in the GDR tried to make the best of the situation. For a few years the system appeared remarkably successful. When the Wall fell on 9 November 1989, however, it revealed a deeply flawed system.

Suggestions for Term Papers

1. Write a comparative history of West Germany and East Germany in the 1950s. Why might citizens of East Germany be tempted to move to the West?

2. Assuming that you have access to film footage showing life in East and West Berlin before the Berlin Wall and also footage portraying the initial construction of the Wall, draft a script for a television documentary on the building of the Wall.

3. Determine why Nikita Khrushchev and other Soviet leaders were so concerned in the late 1950s with the division of Berlin and why they thought the Berlin Wall offered a solution.

4. A large part of President John F. Kennedy's reputation rests on the speech he gave in 1963 in Berlin. Review the way he handled the Berlin Crisis and draw conclusions as to whether he was correct in not directly challenging the construction of the Berlin Wall.

5. Investigate the evolution of the Berlin Wall Construct a layout to scale that shows the most important features of what might be considered a representative section of the Wall.

6. Read about living with the Berlin Wall, particularly in the book edited by the Merritts and the novel by Schneider, and discuss the problems involved in living either in West or in East Berlin.

Research Suggestions

In addition to the boldfaced items, look under the entries for "The Yalta Conference, 1945" (#36), "The Berlin Blockade and Airlift, 1948–1949" (#45), and "German Reunification, 1989–1990" (#90). Search under **Cold War, Willy Brandt, Ostpolitik, East Berlin, West Berlin, East Germany, West Germany, North Atlantic Treaty Organization (NATO)**, and **Warsaw Treaty Organization (WTO)**.

SUGGESTED SOURCES

Primary Sources

Brandt, Willy. *People and Politics.* Boston: Little, Brown, 1978. Brandt was mayor of West Berlin at the time the Berlin Wall was constructed.

The Flights from the Soviet Zone and the Sealing-Off Measures of the Com-munist Regime of 13th August 1961 in Berlin. Bonn/Berlin: Federal Ministry for All-German Questions, 1962. The official West German comment on the construction of the Wall.

Honecker, Erich. *From My Life.* Oxford: Pergamon Press, 1980. The memoirs of the person in charge of the construction of the Berlin Wall.

Secondary Sources

Beschloss, Michael R. *The Crisis Years: Kennedy and Khrushchev, 1960–63.* New York: Edward Burlingame Books, 1991. A good overview by a knowledgeable historian.

Cate, Curtis. *The Ides of August: The Berlin Wall Crisis—1961.* New York: M. Evans, 1978. A careful study of the Berlin Wall Crisis.

Gelb, Norman. *The Berlin Wall: Kennedy, Khrushchev, and a Showdown in the Heart of Europe.* New York: Dorset Press, 1990. A dependable and readable popular account.

Merritt Richard L., and Anna J. Merritt, eds. *Living with the Wall: West Berlin, 1961–1985.* Durham, N.C.: Duke University Press, 1985. Nonfiction accounts of life with the Wall.

Schneider, Peter. *The Wall Jumper.* New York: Pantheon, 1983. A fictional look at the surreal nature of the Berlin Wall.

Slusser, Robert M. *The Berlin Crisis of 1961.* Baltimore: Johns Hopkins University Press, 1973. A careful discussion of the crisis.

Tusa, Ann. *The Last Division: Berlin and the Wall.* Reading, Mass.: Addison-Wesley, 1997. A recent account.

Wyden, Peter. *Wall: The Inside Story of Divided Berlin.* New York: Simon and Schuster, 1989. A panoramic popular history of the Berlin Wall that covers almost every aspect over the twenty-eight years of its existence.

World Wide Web

"The Wall, 1958–1963." *http://www.cnn.com/SPECIALS/cold.war/episodes/09.* Based on CNN's *Cold War* documentary series, the Web site includes background, documents, a transcript of the program, and other features.

60. THE SINO-SOVIET SPLIT, 1959–1969

Mao Zedong's Communist Party victory in the Chinese Civil War in 1949 seemingly affirmed the monolithic face of communism. Behind this monolithic face, however, the Sino-Soviet relationship was laced with tension. Soviet leaders **V. I. Lenin** and **Josif Stalin** had both considered Mao Zedong a thickheaded peasant, and neither had ever given him their full support. Mao Zedong knew this, and with good reason never fully trusted his Soviet allies.

In 1958 Mao had launched his **"Great Leap Forward,"** a bootstrap economic policy aimed at collectivizing agriculture and increasing iron and steel production. Initial indicators suggested that Mao's policies were successful, but by 1959 it was clear that the Great Leap Forward was a disaster, and increased Russian technical assistance and economic aid were desperately needed to keep China's economy moving forward.

In addition to economic assistance, Mao Zedong needed Soviet military technology, especially missiles and nuclear weapons. He was severely disappointed when **Soviet Premier Nikita Khrushchev** not only refused to give China atomic weapons but also announced he was committed to a policy of **"peaceful coexistence"** with the West. Increasingly it seemed that Khrushchev saw China as a liability; he frequently joked about Mao Zedong's economic failures and repeatedly made fun of his peasant appearance. In 1960 Khrushchev recalled 12,000 Russian technicians working in China and summarily canceled hundreds of Sino-Soviet economic projects. Mao Zedong was furious. By 1964 the Sino-Soviet split was so deep that Mao declared that Russia, not the United States, was China's worst enemy. This observation was verified in 1969 when Chinese and Soviet troops clashed along the **Ussuri River** in northern **Manchuria**.

The Sino-Soviet split weakened both leaders. Coming at the same time as the **Cuban Missile Crisis**, the split was used by Khrushchev's critics within the Soviet Central Committee to oust him from power in 1964. The split also ensured that Mao Zedong could not hide the dismal failures of his economic policies and prompted him to launch the **Great Proletarian Cultural Revolution**. By illustrating that communism did not have a monolithic face and that Russian and Chinese national interests were more important than ideological unity, the Sino-Soviet split assisted in improving East-West relations and contributed to ending the **Cold War**. The United States took full advantage of the split. In 1972 **President Richard Nixon** and Mao Zedong signed a joint communiqué normalizing relations between China and the United States.

Suggestions for Term Papers

1. Investigate Mao's "Great Leap Forward" and write a paper analyzing the economic, political, and demographic consequences of this venture.

2. Although publicly Mao expressed friendship for the Soviet Union, he never fully trusted his Russian allies. Write a paper explaining why Mao distrusted the Russians.

3. Between 1946 and 1960 the Soviet Union gave huge amounts of aid to China, but Premier Nikita Khrushchev abruptly halted this aid in the summer of 1960 and ordered the Russian advisors to leave China. Write a paper on Khrushchev's reasons for doing this.

4. Examine the 1969 border clashes between Chinese and Russian troops and analyze their effects on Sino-Soviet relations.

5. In what ways did the Sino-Soviet split influence President Richard Nixon's decision to recognize Mao as China's legitimate leader?

6. Assess the effect of the dissolution of the Soviet Union on relations between China and the states that were once part of the Soviet Union.

Research Suggestions

In addition to the boldfaced items, look under the entries for "Mao Zedong and the Long March, 1934–1935" (#25), "The Victory of the Chinese Communist Party, 1949" (#46), "Khrushchev's 'Secret Speech' at the Twentieth Party Congress, 1956" (#51), and "The Chinese Economy at the End of the Twentieth Century" (#100). Search under **Zhou Enlai** and **Henry Kissinger**.

SUGGESTED SOURCES

Primary Sources

Khrushchev, Nikita. *Khrushchev Remembers.* Translated and edited by Strobe Talbott. Boston: Little, Brown, 1970. A well-edited collection of Khrushchev's memoirs and speeches that gives Khrushchev's position on the split.

Kissinger, Henry. *White House Years.* Boston: Little, Brown, 1979. An insightful explanation of the American decision to recognize China.

Mao Tse-tung. *Selected Works of Mao Tse-tung.* 5 vols. Peking: Foreign Languages Press, 1965. The fifth volume of this series gives perspective on the split.

Nixon, Richard M. *RN: The Memoirs of Richard Nixon.* New York: Grosset and Dunlap, 1978. President Nixon gives a candid appraisal of Mao and U.S. policy.

Selden, Mark. *The People's Republic of China: A Documentary History of Revolutionary Change.* New York: Monthly Review Press, 1979. A most useful collection of documents providing a good perspective on the split.

Secondary Sources

Brzezinski, Zbigniew. *The Grand Failure: The Birth and Death of Communism in the Twentieth Century.* New York: Scribner, 1989. This former national security adviser's analysis of the split shows its importance for the twentieth century.

Khrushchev, Sergei. *Khrushchev on Khrushchev: An Inside Account of the Man and His Era.* Edited and translated by William Taubman. Boston: Little, Brown, 1990. Written by his son, who became an American citizen, these are candid reflections on Khrushchev's achievements.

Riasanovsky, Nicholas. *A History of Russia.* 6th ed. New York: Oxford University Press, 1999. A solid treatment of the split with a good bibliography. This is a good starting point for the Russian perspective.

Spence, Jonathan. *The Search for Modern China.* New York: W. W. Norton, 1990. His explanation of the split, along with his critical bibliography, is an excellent starting point for the Chinese perspective.

Terrill, Ross. *A Biography: Mao.* New York: Harper and Row, 1980. A fast-paced, well written biography by a premier student of modern China.

Whiting, Allen. "The Sino-Soviet Split." In *Cambridge History of China,* vol. 14, part 1. Cambridge: Cambridge University Press, 1987. The most accessible short scholarly assessment of the split.

World Wide Web

"The National Security Archive." *http://www.gwu.edu/~nsarchiv.* Contains good documentary links on the split.

61. THE "GREEN REVOLUTION" IN AGRICULTURE IN THE 1960s

In 1970 **Norman Borlaug** (1918–   ), a plant breeder who had spent most of his life in developing countries, was awarded the Nobel Peace Prize. He was the person most responsible for the so-called **Green Revolution**, a series of agricultural techniques which greatly increased crop yield. The Green Revolution played a key role in the postwar expansion of global food production that for decades outran increases in population.

Growing up in the Midwest, Borlaug was familiar with the **Dust Bowl** phenomenon of the 1930s (severe dust storms and top soil loss caused by drought and poor farming practices). He decided that it was not caused by using technological farming methods but rather by failure to use these methods. High-yield farming methods appeared to help prevent the spread of the Dust Bowl. Borlaug wanted to spread these techniques to other countries.

A chance to do this came in 1943 when the **Rockefeller Foundation** established a program in Mexico to help poor farmers. Borlaug became the director of the wheat program at the **Cooperative Mexican Agricultural Program**. His major accomplishment was the perfection of dwarf spring wheat. The idea was to develop a short plant that would expend less energy on the inedible column sections and more on growing grain. Dwarf spring wheat did, however, require fertilizer and irrigation.

In 1962 Borlaug, working out of the **International Maize and Wheat Center**, an outgrowth of the original program, worked to spread the concept of high-yield agriculture to India and Pakistan. Despite a variety of difficulties, including war between India and Pakistan, Borlaug planted a crop of dwarf wheat. Yields were 70 percent higher than crops of wheat had been in previous years and the next harvest even better. By 1968 Pakistan was self-sufficient in wheat production. In the 1970s and 1980s food production in both Pakistan and India increased faster than the rate of population growth. Similar developments in the cultivation of rice at the **International Rice Research Institute** in the Philippines, established in 1962 on the model of the Mexican program, led to significant increases in the production of that crop.

The Green Revolution has also had critics. High-yield techniques require the use of artificial fertilizers, insecticides, pesticides, and irrigation. Borlaug and most other agronomists now stress the use of "integrated pest management" in place of insecticides and pesticides. Nonetheless, the techniques cost more than many farmers can afford and favor a commercial approach to agriculture. It also appears that limits are being reached in terms of the use of fertilizer and irrigation. The application of fertilizer, for example, does not increase yield beyond a certain point. It also may not be possible to sustain irrigation levels much longer because water tables are being depleted faster than they can recharge. A major question mark at this point is what genetic engineering might contribute to food production in the future.

Questions for Term Papers

1. What led the Rockefeller Foundation to set up a program in Mexico in 1943? Write a report on what the foundation hoped to accomplish.

2. What techniques did Borlaug use in the 1940s and 1950s to develop the dwarf spring wheat that proved to be so successful?

3. One of the most important developments in agriculture since World War II has been the expansion in the use of artificial fertilizer. Discuss changing ideas about the use of fertilizer and present statistics on the expansion of its use and its contribution to expanded yield in one region of the world.

4. The expanded use of irrigation in agriculture has been another major reason for the increases in food production over the last forty years. As in #3, discuss changing ideas about irrigation and present relevant statistics for one region of the world.

5. Investigate the role of commercial agriculture in one country or region. To what extent has commercial agriculture contributed to food insecurity, i.e., problems people have obtaining inexpensive, locally-grown food supplies, by encouraging farmers to grow cash crops?

6. Oxfam International is an organization working in Africa and other parts of the world to introduce many of the ideas associated with Norman Borlaug. Do a report on a region of the world in

which Oxfam is active and evaluate the effectiveness of projects it sponsors. Begin with the Oxfam Web site (see Suggested Sources).

Research Suggestions

In addition to the boldfaced items, look under the entries for "The 1992 Earth Summit in Rio" (#94), "Dolly the Sheep Cloned, 1997" (#96), and "The Chinese Economy at the End of the Twentieth Century" (#100). Search under **M. S. Swaminathan, Frances Moore Lappé, Food First, Oxfam, Catholic Relief Services, Jimmy Carter,** and **Ryoichi Sasakawa**.

SUGGESTED SOURCES

Primary sources

Future Global Food Production. [videorecording]. McKean, Penn: Idea Channel, 1993. Norman Borlaug talks about feeding the world in the future.

Secondary Sources

Brown, Lester R. "Feeding Nine Billion." In Lester R. Brown, Christopher Flavin, and Hilary French, eds., *State of the World 1999.* New York: W. W. Norton, 1999. The latest thinking about the question of food security. Brown is critical of many of the ideas associated with the Green Revolution.

————. *Tough Choices: Facing the Challenge of Food Scarcity.* New York: W. W. Norton, 1996. A good introduction to the question of food security.

Easterbrook, Gregg. "Forgotten Benefactor of Humanity." *Atlantic Monthly* 279, no. 1 (January 1997): 75–82. Also available on-line at *http://www.theatlantic/issues/97jan.* Biographical sketch of Norman Borlaug.

Lappé, Frances Moore. *World Hunger: Twelve Myths,* 2nd ed. New York: Grove Press, 1998. First published in 1977 as *World Hunger: Ten Myths.* Lappé suggest political and social rather than technological solutions for world hunger.

Postel, Sandra. *Pillar of Sand: Can the Irrigation Miracle Last?* New York: W. W. Norton, 1999. Postel is a leading expert on the question of water supplies for the future.

World Wide Web

Borlaug, Norman. "The Green Revolution: Peace and Humanity." *http: //www.theatlantic.com/issues/97jan/borlaugh/speech.htm.* Borlaug's 1970 Nobel Prize acceptance speech.

Easterbrook, Greg. "Forgotten Benefactor of Humanity." *http://www. theatlantic.com/issues/97jan/borlaug/borlaug.htm.* The on-line version of Easterbrook's article.

"Oxfam International." *http://www.oxfam.org.* Contains the 1998 annual report and many other useful features.

62. YURI GAGARIN, THE FIRST MAN IN SPACE, 1961

Yuri Alekseyevich Gagarin (1934–1968), the first person in space, played a major part in the Soviet Union's remarkable accomplishments in space technology in the late 1950s and 1960s. Although the United States was the first country to land men on the moon, the Soviet Union held the lead in space exploration for most of the 1960s.

Gagarin grew up on a collective farm and graduated from trade school in 1951. His interest in flying led him to enter the Soviet air force cadet school from which he graduated in 1957, the same year the Soviet Union launched *Sputnik* (**Fellow Traveler**), the first satellite in space. As a young and promising pilot, Gagarin joined the Soviet space program and was selected as the first **cosmonaut**. In 1961 he completed a single orbit around the earth aboard the spacecraft *Vostok 1.*

When Gagarin landed safely back in the Soviet Union, he instantly became everyone's hero, not just in the USSR but all over the world. It was, of course, something that had never been done before. He was awarded the Order of Lenin and made a Hero of the Soviet Union and Pilot Cosmonaut of the Soviet Union. It was very much like the 1930s in the Soviet Union when record-setting pilots distracted the masses from the hardships of the Five-Year Plans.

Gagarin never went into space again; instead he became a trainer of other cosmonauts. Tragically, his life was cut short in 1968 when he and another pilot crashed on a routine training flight.

The Soviet space program continued under the leadership of *Sergei Pavlovich Korolev* (1907–1966). Korolev directed the design, testing, construction, and launching of the **Vostok, Voskhod,** and **Soyuz** manned spacecraft. While Gagarin became the man of the hour after his successful flight, Korolev, in accordance with Soviet policy, worked in anonymity. His role in the Soviet space program was revealed only after his death.

In the 1960s the Soviet space program was the first to send a woman into space and the first to send up a flight during which a man floated free in space. In the 1970s the Soviet space program experimented mostly with the construction and maintenance of space stations and in 1986 sent up the **Mir** space station.

Suggestions for Term Papers

1. Both the Soviet and the U.S. space programs depended initially on German rocket technology developed during World War II. Investigate the influence of German technology and German scientists on the two space programs.

2. Trace Gagarin's career after his space flight. Why did he make such a good symbol for the Soviet space program and for Soviet science more generally?

3. Korolev was the central figure in the Soviet space program. Review his contributions to the program in the 1950s and 1960s.

4. It was a great disappointment to Korolev that he was not able to land a cosmonaut on the moon. What obstacles, scientific and political, prevented him from accomplishing this.

5. Compare the Soviet and U.S. space programs in the 1960s. Was one more successful than the other? State reasons for your position.

6. What goals did the Soviet Union set for its space program when it began the construction of space stations in the 1970s and 1980s? To what extent did it fulfill those goals? Provide evidence for your position.

Research Suggestions

In addition to the boldfaced items, look under the entries for "Khrushchev's 'Secret Speech' at the Twentieth Party Congress,

1956" (#51), "Chernobyl, 1986" (#86), and "The Breakup of the Soviet Union, 1991" (#91). Search under **Valentina Tereshkova, Aleksey Leonov**, and **Semipalatinsk** (Soviet space facilities).

SUGGESTED SOURCES

Primary Sources

Gagarin, Yuri A., and V. I. Lebedev. *Survival in Space.* New York: Praeger, 1969. Also published as *Psychology and Space.* Gagarin on his record-breaking flight.

Lothian, Antonella. *Valentina: First Woman in Space: Conversations with A. Lothian.* Edinburgh: Pentland Press, 1993. Valentina Tereshkova talks about being the first woman in space.

Secondary Sources

Baker, David. *Conquest: A History of Space Achievements from Science Fiction to the Shuttle.* Salem, N.H.: Salem House, 1984. A good introduction.

Clark, Phillip. *The Soviet Manned Space Program: An Illustrated History of the Men, the Missions, and the Spacecraft.* New York: Orion Books, 1988. A good discussion of the Soviet program.

Harford, James. *Korolev: How One Man Masterminded the Soviet Drive to Beat America to the Moon.* New York: John Wiley and Sons, 1997. Makes use of Russian sources. The best biography in English of this important figure.

Hooper, Gordon R. *The Soviet Cosmonaut Team: A Comprehensive Guide to the Men and Women of the Soviet Manned Space Programme.* 2 vols. 2nd rev. ed. Lowestoft, Suffolk, England: GRH Publications, 1990. An exhaustive reference source.

Logsdon, John M., and Alain Dupas. "Was the Race to the Moon Real?" *Scientific American* 270, no. 6 (June 1994), 36–40. An interesting discussion of the "space race" in the 1960s.

McDougall, Walter A. *The Heavens and the Earth: A Political History of the Space Age.* New York: Basic Books, 1985. An excellent history of the exploration of space.

Newkirk, Dennis. *Almanac of Soviet Manned Space Flight.* Houston: Gulf Publishing, 1990. A good reference source.

Secret Soviet Moon Mission [videorecording]. 60 minutes. Distributed by PBS Home Video, 1999. Covers the career of Sergei Pavlovich Korolev and focuses in particular on his efforts to land a Soviet cosmonaut on the moon.

World Wide Web

"A Giant Leap for Mankind: Russia Was First." *http://www.pathfinder. com/Life/space/giantleap/sec1/sec1.html.* This Web site contains articles and pictures from coverage by *Life* magazine of major events in space exploration. A fascinating site.

"Space Race." *http://www.nasm.edu/galleries/gal/114.* A comprehensive discussion of U.S. and Soviet competition in space.

"Sputnik, 1949–1961." *http://www.cnn.com/SPECIALS/cold.war/episodes/ 08.* Based on CNN's *Cold War* documentary series, the Web site includes background, documents, a transcript of the program, and other features.

63. VATICAN II, 1962–1965

"We must shake off the imperial dust that has accumulated on the throne of St. Peter since Constantine," announced **Pope John XXIII** on 25 July 1959. Such an announcement by the jovial, rotund former papal diplomat caught the **Vatican** bureaucrats (**curia**) by surprise. By inviting more than 3,000 bishops, theologians and scholars to attend an ecumenical (world) council in **St. Peter's Basilica**, Pope John initiated the most profound changes in the **Roman Catholic Church** in four centuries. Unlike every other ecumenical council, there was no heresy, no threat to Church leadership, and no sign of revolution on the horizon. Not surprisingly, Pope John faced stiff resistance from within his curia. One member of the curia bluntly told him, "It is absolutely impossible to open the Council in 1963." "Fine," replied a smiling Pope John, "we'll open it in 1962!"

Presiding over the opening session on 11 October 1962, Pope John announced that the aim of the council was to promote peace and unity, to heal the divisions between all churches, and to bring the Catholic Church fully into the modern world. He outflanked his opponents in the curia by ensuring that non-Italian theologians such as **Leo-Josef Cardinal Suenens** (Belgium), **Yves Congar** (France), **Karl Rahner** (Germany), and **John Courtney Murray** (United States) would have considerable influence in drafting key council documents. In addition he endorsed progressive voices for reform within the council and welcomed new democratic structures within council procedure.

Three years after opening the council, Pope John died and was replaced by Milan's Cardinal Montini, who took the name **Pope Paul VI**. A respected scholar familiar with Vatican politics, Pope Paul presided over the final three sessions of the council and continued to press for reform. When the council finally completed its work on 7 December 1968, sixty-five major documents, ranging from "The Constitution on the Sacred Liturgy" to "Pastoral Constitution on the Church in the Modern World," had been approved.

From the very opening of the council, non-Catholic observers from other Christian churches were its special guests. In writing all of the documents, serious attention was given to ensure respect, healing, and reconciliation between the major Christian churches. In a dramatic gesture of reconciliation between East and West, Pope Paul and **Ecumenical Patriarch Athenagoras I of Constantinople** publicly embraced each other and rescinded the degrees of excommunication that had separated Roman Catholic and **Orthodox Christians** since the year 1054. Ecumenical reconciliation was not limited to relations between Christian churches. For the first time the Roman Catholic Church admitted it had much to learn from non-Christian religions and that it "rejects nothing that is true and holy" in **Hinduism, Buddhism, Judaism**, or **Islam**. Because of the special historical and spiritual affinity between Catholics and Jews, an entire document was focused on Catholic-Jewish relations. The council decreed that Jews were not responsible for the death of Christ and urged Catholic universities to establish centers of Jewish studies to promote deeper scholarly understanding between Christians and Jews.

The most durable results of Vatican II were (1) the recognition that the Church is a **sacrament**, not an institution or organization; (2) the use of national vernacular languages, not Latin, as the preferred language for the celebration of the **Mass** and all other liturgies; (3) strong statements on religious liberty and ecumenical dialogue; and (4) affirmation of the importance of the laity in assuming positions of leadership within the Church.

Suggestions for Term Papers

1. Do a research project on the humor of Pope John XXIII and write an essay on how he used laughter to lead the Church.

2. Read selections from the Second Ecumenical Council's statements on ecumenism and write a paper tracing how ecumenism has affected Catholicism's relations with another faith tradition.

3. Interview some older Catholics and ask them to compare their impressions of Catholicism before and after Vatican II.

4. How did Vatican II affect Catholic women? Read the council's statements on the laity and write an essay focused on the role of women in contemporary Catholicism.

5. Many believe Pope John XXIII will be declared a saint early in the twenty-first century. Investigate the way the Vatican declares beatification and write a paper assessing Pope John XXIII's prospects.

6. Investigate the career of Pope Paul VI after the end of Vatican II.

Research Suggestions

In addition to the boldfaced items, look under the entry for "John Paul II's First Twenty Years as Pope, 1978–1999" (#98). Search under **Vatican I, papacy, College of Cardinals**, and **encyclical**.

SUGGESTED SOURCES

Primary Sources

Flannery, Austin, ed. *Vatican Council II: The Conciliar and Post Conciliar Documents.* Northport, N.Y.: Costello Publications, 1975. A well edited collection of all the council's documents.

Miller, John H., ed. *Vatican II: An Interfaith Appraisal.* Notre Dame, Ind.: University of Notre Dame Press, 1966. Many of the participants who attended the council, such as Congar and Rahner, took part in this appraisal.

Secondary Sources

Fesquet, Henri, ed. *Wit and Wisdom of Good Pope John.* Translated by Salvator Attanasio. New York: P. J. Kenedy, 1964. A marvelous collection of John XXIII's quick wit, laughter, and charm.

Glazier, Michael, and Monika K. Helwig, eds. *The Modern Catholic Encyclopedia.* Collegeville, MN: Liturgical Press, 1994. A good starting point for all issues dealing with Vatican II.

Hebblethwaite, Peter. *John XXIII, Pope of the Council.* London: Chapman, 1985. A reliable biography by a respected Vatican scholar.

Schillebeeckx, Eduard. *The Real Achievement of Vatican II.* Translated by H.J.J. Vaughan. New York: Sheed and Ward, 1967. An insightful commentary by one of the most influential theologians of the council.

World Wide Web

"Catholic Information Center on Internet." *http://catholic.net*. Search under "Vatican Council" for documents and interpretation of Vatican II.

64. THE CUBAN MISSILE CRISIS, 1962

In October 1962, the United States and the Soviet Union came close to nuclear war. The problem began with Soviet attempts to place nuclear missiles in Cuba.

Soviet leader **Nikita S. Khrushchev** made the decision to place the missiles in Cuba. He acted in part to defend the Cuban Revolution. Although **President Fidel Castro** successfully defeated the U.S.-sponsored invasion of Cuba by Cuban exiles in 1961, Khrushchev considered direct American intervention a possibility. He also hoped to reduce the overwhelming American strategic nuclear balance.

After the **Bay of Pigs** fiasco (the failed invasion of Cuba in 1961 by Cuban exiles with CIA support), the disappointing **Vienna Summit** (at which Khrushchev thought he saw in **President John F. Kennedy** a weak man), and the decision not to challenge the construction of the **Berlin Wall**, President Kennedy was under considerable political pressure from Republican critics. The discovery of missile launch sites under construction in Cuba was a challenge he and the government had to meet.

Kennedy met with the Executive Committee (ExComm) of the **National Security Council** after the discovery of the launch sites. This group included **Secretary of State Dean Rusk, Secretary of Defense Robert McNamara, Attorney General Robert Kennedy,** and **National Security Advisor McGeorge Bundy,** among others. An initial consensus called for an air strike to take out the missile sites, airfields, and aircraft. It was also suggested that an invasion of the island would be necessary. Kennedy worried that the Soviet response might lead to nuclear war. Military leaders favored the air strike–invasion combination, and sooner rather than later.

Kennedy, in consultation with his brother Robert, favored the idea of blockade (quarantine) plus surveillance and diplomacy. He announced this in a speech televised nationally on 22 October 1962.

Khrushchev sent two letters in response to the American announcement of quarantine. The first, probably a personal reply, was emotional and conciliatory. The second, possibly a joint production of the Soviet leadership, took a tougher line. The United States chose to respond to the first and ignore the second.

The world waited tensely to see what would happen when Soviet ships reached the American quarantine line. Before this happened, however, they were ordered to return to the Soviet Union. The Soviet Union agreed to withdraw its missiles, planes, and most of the troops sent to Cuba in return for a guarantee by the United States that it would not invade the island. The United States secretly indicated that it would remove missiles, which were in any case obsolete, from Turkey.

The United States and the Soviet Union realized how close they had come to nuclear conflict, and each side made efforts to manage the Cold War better in the future. Nonetheless, the Cold War did not end until the collapse of the Soviet Union in 1991.

Suggestions for Term Papers

1. The origins of the Cuban Missile Crisis go back to 1961 and earlier. Investigate relations between the United States and Cuba before October 1962.

2. Follow the views and activities of one or more of the members of ExComm, President Kennedy's advisors during the crisis, and try to determine reasons for their views and activities.

3. Investigate Khrushchev's decision to place nuclear missiles in Cuba and to do this secretly.

4. By reviewing newspapers and newsmagazines from the period, trace the development of public opinion about the crisis in the period between President Kennedy's speech on 22 October and Khrushchev's message on 28 October effectively ending the crisis. Or conduct interviews and write an oral history of people's memories of the period.

5. The Cuban role in the Cuban Missile Crisis is generally overlooked. Write about the crisis from the Cuban point of view to the extent permitted by the sources available.

6. The Cuban Missile Crisis did not end neatly with Khrushchev's message of 28 October. Examine the negotiations and discussions that took place in November as the two countries tried to agree on terms and also tried to get Cuba to conform to those terms.

Research Suggestions

In addition to boldfaced items, look under the entries for "The Guatemalan Coup, 1954" (#50), "Fidel Castro and the Cuban Revolution, 1959" (#57), and "The Berlin Wall, 1961" (#59). Search under **Operation Mongoose, Andrei A. Gromyko, John A. McCone, John A. Scali, Theodore C. Sorensen, Adlai E. Stevenson,** and **General Maxwell D. Taylor.**

SUGGESTED SOURCES

Primary Sources

Chang, Laurence, and Peter Kornbluh, eds. *The Cuban Missile Crisis, 1962: A National Security Archive Documents Reader.* New York: The New Press, 1992. An excellent selection of documents together with an extensive chronology and other helpful material.

Kennedy, Robert. *Thirteen Days: A Memoir of the Cuban Missile Crisis.* New York: W. W. Norton, 1969. An influential portrait of the crisis by one of the most important participants.

May, Ernest R., and Philip D. Zelikow, eds. *The Kennedy Tapes: Inside the White House During the Cuban Missile Crisis.* Cambridge, Mass.: Belknap Press of Harvard University Press, 1997. A fascinating look at the crisis as it appeared to those at the very highest levels of government.

Secondary Sources

Beschloss, Michael R. *The Crisis Years: Kennedy and Khrushchev, 1960–1963.* New York: Edward Burlingame Books, 1991. A highly readable, solid study of the period.

Blight, James G., Bruce J. Allyn, and David A. Welch. *Cuba on the Brink: Castro, the Missile Crisis, and the Soviet Crisis.* New York: Pantheon Books, 1993. Blight organized a number of scholarly conferences that produced new evidence on the crisis. This book covers material from the Havana conference, the last in the series.

Blight, James G., and David A. Welch. *On the Brink: Americans and Soviets Reexamine the Cuban Missile Crisis*. New York: Hill and Wang, 1989. The first of several books presenting new evidence on the crisis drawn from scholarly conferences.

Divine, Robert A. "Alive and Well: The Continuing Cuban Missile Crisis Controversy." *Diplomatic History* 18 (Fall 1994), 551–560. Excellent survey of the historiography of the crisis by one of the leading historians of American diplomacy.

Fursenko, Aleksandr, and Timothy Naftali. *One Hell of a Gamble: Khrushchev, Kennedy and Castro, 1958–1964.* New York: W. W. Norton, 1998. Based to a large extent on Soviet archival sources. One of the best books on the Soviet side of the crisis.

Gaddis, John Lewis. *We Now Know: Rethinking Cold War History.* Oxford: Clarendon Press, 1997. Chapter 9 offers a thoughtful review of scholarship on several major issues connected with the crisis.

Garthoff, Raymond L. *Reflections on the Cuban Missile Crisis*. Rev. ed. Washington, D.C.: Brookings Institution, 1989. An important book by a participant who is also a leading scholar of U.S.-Soviet relations.

Lebow, Richard Ned, and Janice Gross Stein. *We All Lost the Cold War.* Princeton: Princeton University Press, 1994. The Cuban Missile Crisis is one of two case studies in an extended discussion of the realities of crisis management in international affairs.

Moser, Don. "The Time of the Angel: The U-2, Cuba, and the CIA." *American Heritage*, 28 (October 1977), 4–15. A useful introduction.

World Wide Web

"Cold War International History Project." *http://cwihp.si.edu/default.htm.* This Web site provides documents and excellent scholarship on the Cold War.

"Cuba, 1959–1962." *http://www.cnn.com/SPECIALS/cold.war/episodes/10.* Based on CNN's *Cold War* documentary series, the Web site includes background, documents, a transcript of the program, and other features.

"The Cuban Missile Crisis, 1962." *http://www.gwu.edu/~nsarchiv/nsa/ cub_mis_cri/cub_mis_cri.html.* This site, part of the large National Security Archive Web site, provides an introduction, chronology, glossary, and photographs on the Cuban Missile Crisis.

65. THE BEATLES, 1964

Between 1962 and 1971 the **Beatles** were the most popular rock band in the world. They changed popular music and entertainment in general in several important ways. In 1964 they came to the United States to perform on *The Ed Sullivan Show* and unleashed what became known as **"Beatlemania."**

The Beatles came from **Liverpool** and working-class backgrounds. **Paul McCartney** (1942–   ) and **John Lennon** (1940–1980) began playing together in 1956. **George Harrison** (1943–   ) joined in 1957. **Ringo Starr** (originally Richard Starkey, 1940–   ) replaced one of the original members of the band in 1962. That same year another member of the band, **Stu Sutcliff**, died of cancer.

The Beatles played clubs in Liverpool and Hamburg for several years before becoming popular. **Brian Epstein**, who began to manage them in 1962, had a great deal to do with their success. Under his influence, the Beatles became a more polished act, started dressing more fashionably, and began wearing their hair longer than was then customary.

In 1962 and 1963 several Lennon-McCartney songs, among them **"Love Me Do," "Please, Please Me," "She Loves You,"** and **"I Want to Hold Your Hand,"** became hits in England. In 1964 "She Loves You" and "I Want to Hold Your Hand" became hits in America.

The Beatles stopped performing in public in 1966. By then they had moved from an enthusiastic blend of early rock and roll and rhythm and blues to experiments with musical forms and social commentary. In 1967 they produced *Sgt. Pepper's Lonely Hearts Club Band*, an album that broke new ground in that it was seen as a unified production and not merely a collection of songs. The Beatles made a number of other popular albums in the late 1960s, including their last one, *Abbey Road* (1969). The two films made by the Beatles, *A Hard Day's Night* (1964) and *Help!* (1965), were well received.

The group broke up in 1971, in part because of the pressures of the enormous popularity it enjoyed but also because of diverging individual interests. Paul McCartney was probably the most successful of the four in the post-Beatles period with his band **Wings** and a career of recording and composing. John Lennon, a political activist in the 1970s, remained popular as a musician. George Harrison had some success as a musician and film producer but became best known for organizing a concert to raise money for famine relief in Bangladesh. Ringo Starr appeared in several movies and continued to perform and record. Rumors that the Beatles would reunite persisted, even after Lennon was shot and killed by a deranged fan in New York City in 1980.

The Beatles, in the short time they were together, helped to explode the conventions that governed the writing of popular songs, which meant songs could not only be entertaining but also commentaries on social problems and political issues. Additionally, they played a vital role in the creation of a new youth culture that swept the United States and many other parts of the world in the 1960s and 1970s. More than any other musical group in the twentieth century, they changed the face of popular culture.

Suggestions for Term Papers

1. Trace the development of the Beatles from the point where Lennon and McCartney began playing together to 1962, when Brian Epstein became their manager and Ringo Starr was recruited as the drummer.

2. Investigate the Beatles' tour of America in 1964. Suggest reasons why they were so enormously popular.

3. Lennon and McCartney are often seen as one of the greatest songwriting teams of this century. Compare them with one or more famous songwriting teams in terms not only of popularity but also of contributions to popular music.

4. Watch *A Hard Day's Night* (see Suggested Sources) and examine the critical response to it. Do you agree with the generally favorable reception of the critics? Provide evidence for the position you take.

5. Yoko Ono, Lennon's second wife, has often been blamed for the breakup of the Beatles. After reviewing the Beatles' financial affairs, artistic differences, and personal relations, determine what caused the breakup. Provide reasons for the position you take.

6. The Rolling Stones are generally considered the other great musical group of the 1960s. Compare the music they produced in

this period with that of the Beatles. Which group was more influential? Defend your decision.

Research Suggestions

Search under the **Rolling Stones, the Who, Bob Dylan, Yoko Ono, Linda McCartney, George Martin**, and **Rock Music**.

SUGGESTED SOURCES

Primary Sources

The Beatles Anthology. 8 videocassettes. 10 hours, 28 minutes. Turner Home Entertainment, 1996. The 1995 ABC network production, *The Beatles Anthology*, an enormous collection of songs, interviews, and other material.

The Compleat Beatles. Distributed by MGM/UA Home Video, 1983. Videodisc, 119 minutes. A useful compilation.

Epstein, Brian, and Martin Lewis. *A Cellarful of Noise: The Autobiography of the Man Who Made the Beatles, with a New Companion Narrative.* New York: Pocket Books, 1998. First published in 1964. Epstein did as much as anyone to make the Beatles an extraordinary success in the 1960s.

A Hard Day's Night. Distributed by Voyager Co., 1993. CD-ROM. A treasure trove for fans of the movie.

Lennon, John. *Lennon Remembers: The "Rolling Stone" Interviews.* New York: Popular Library, 1971. Lennon on the Beatles just as they were breaking up.

———. *The Writings of John Lennon.* New York: Simon and Schuster, 1981. Lennon's collected works. Slight but witty. Introduction by Paul McCartney.

Neises, Charles, ed. *The Beatles Reader: A Selection of Contemporary Views, News, and Reviews of the Beatles in Their Heyday.* Ann Arbor: Popular Culture, Ink., 1991. A useful anthology.

Secondary Sources

Davies, Hunter. *The Beatles.* 2nd rev. ed. New York: W. W. Norton, 1996. An excellent biography.

Everett, Walter. *The Beatles as Musicians: Revolver Through the Anthology.* New York: Oxford University Press, 1999. An important study of the development of the Beatles as musicians.

Hertsgaard, Mark. *A Day in the Life: The Music and Artistry of the Beatles.* New York: Delacorte Press, 1995. One of the best biographies available.

Knight, Judson. *Abbey Road to Zapple Records: A Beatles Encyclopedia.* Dallas: Taylor, 1999. A very useful reference book.

Kozinn, Allan. *The Beatles.* New York: Chronicle Books, 1995. Kozinn takes the Beatles seriously as important composers.

MacDonald, Ian. *Revolution in the Head: The Beatles' Records and the Sixties.* 2nd ed. London: Fourth Estate, 1997. Places the Beatles in the context of their era.

McKean, William. *The Beatles: A Bio-Bibliography.* New York: Greenwood Press, 1989. A versatile reference source.

Miller, James. *Flowers in the Dustbin: The Rise of Rock and Roll, 1947–1977.* New York: Simon and Schuster, 1999. Miller, a well-known rock critic, devotes five chapters to the Beatles. Thoughtful comments and comprehensive coverage.

Norman, Philip. *Shout! The Beatles in Their Generation.* 2nd ed. New York: Simon and Schuster, 1996. Perhaps the best biography of the Beatles.

World Wide Web

"Abbeyrd's Beatles Page." *http://www.best.com/~abbeyrd* An excellent source of Beatles information. Good links to other sites.

"The Internet Beatles Album." *http://www.getback.org/bmain.html.* Another excellent Web site on the Beatles.

66. THE SIX-DAY WAR, 1967

Throughout the 1960s there were deep, unresolved tensions among **Israel, Syria, Egypt, Jordan**, and the **Palestinian Liberation Organization (PLO)**, an organization founded in 1964 to free Palestine from Israeli control. **United Nations (UN) peacekeepers**, assigned to the **Sinai Peninsula** after the **1956 Suez Crisis**, had kept Egyptian and Israeli forces apart, but there were frequent border clashes and guerrilla attacks among Israeli, Arab, and PLO forces.

These tensions came to flash point on 16 May 1967, when **President Nasser** of Egypt ordered the UN peacekeepers out of the Sinai. On 22 May Nasser announced that the **Gulf of Aqaba**, Israel's access to the Red Sea, was closed to Israeli ships. Israel's prime minister, **Levi Eshkol**, protested the closure and sought U.S., British, and UN assistance in guaranteeing Israeli ships the right of free passage throughout the Gulf of Aqaba.

Israel, a country of 2.5 million people, had long committed itself to a strong, modern military and a preemptive offensive strategy against its enemies. On 1 June 1967, Eshkol named **General Moshe Dayan**, an offensive-minded strategist, as minister of war. On 5 June Israeli jets, in a series of lethal air strikes, destroyed the Egyptian, Jordanian, and Syrian air forces. Within two days Israel gained full air superiority. By 11 June 1967, Israel had occupied the **Golan Heights**, the **West Bank territories** of the **Jordan River, East Jerusalem**, and the **Sinai**. A UN-sponsored cease-fire halted the fighting on 11 June 1967.

As a result of the Six-Day War, Israel sustained 1,000 casualties, inflicted more than 25,000 casualties on its enemies, increased the size of its territory by one-third, and added 1.5 million Palestinians to its population. **UN Resolution 242**, of November 1967, provided for the withdrawal of Israeli forces from some of the territories occupied in the Six-Day War and recognized the right of all states in the region to exist. But neither the Six-Day War nor UN Resolution 242 brought peace to the region. By occupying the Golan Heights, Israel improved its border defenses with Syria, but Israel's occupation of the **Gaza Strip**, East Jerusalem, and the West Bank territories aggravated relations between Israel and its neighbors. **PLO commando** attacks against Israeli targets dramatically increased after the war, and Israel security forces reacted by engaging in acts of bloody reprisal against Palestinians. Eventually Egypt and Israel entered into negotiations to resolve their differences, but it was not until 1979 that **Prime Minister Menachem Begin** of Israel and **President Anwar Sadat** of Egypt signed a peace treaty ending the Six-Day War. In 1994 **Prime Minister Yitzak Rabin** of Israel and **King Hussein** of Jordan finally signed a peace treaty.

Suggestions for Term Papers

1. Analyze the strategy and tactics of General Moshe Dayan and the Israeli military command in their planning for the Six-Day War.
2. Examine the role of the Israeli air force in the Six-Day War. Why were the Israeli pilots so successful?
3. Evaluate the role of the United Nations in the war. How effective has UN Resolution 242 (see Suggested Sources) been in reducing tensions in the region?
4. What was the reaction of the United States to the Six-Day War?

5. How did the Egyptian military respond to the defeats of the Six-Day War?

6. Investigate the role of President Jimmy Carter (see Suggested Sources) in persuading Prime Minister Menachem Begin of Israel and President Anwar Sadat of Egypt to sign a peace treaty in 1979.

Research Suggestions

In addition to the boldfaced items, look under the entries for "The British Mandate of Palestine, 1922" (#13), "The Establishment of the State of Israel, 1948" (#43), "Gamal Abdel Nasser and the Suez Crisis, 1956" (#52), and "Terrorism in the 1970s" (#78). Search under **Yasir Arafat, Abba Eban**, and **President Jimmy Carter**.

SUGGESTED SOURCES

Primary sources

Carter, Jimmy. *Keeping Faith: Memoirs of a President*. New York: Bantam Books, 1982. Useful insights into the Camp David agreements signed between Egypt and Israel in 1979.

Dayan, Moshe. *Story of My Life*. New York: Morrow, 1976. Israel's war minister explains how Israel won the war.

Laqueur, Walter, and Barry Rubin, eds. *The Israel-Arab Reader: A Documentary History of the Middle East Conflict*. New York: Penguin Books, 1984. The most accessible collection of documents, including key UN documents and Arab views of the war.

Nasser, Gamal Abdel. *Egypt's Liberation: The Philosophy of the Revolution*. Washington, D.C.: Public Affairs Press, 1955. A succinct outline of Nasser's dream of leading the Islamic world.

Rabin, Yitzhak. *The Rabin Memoirs*. Translated by Dov Goldstein. Berkeley: University of California Press, 1996. Chapter 6 focuses on the Six-Day War.

Secondary Sources

Luttwak, Edward, and Dan Horowitz. *The Israeli Army*. New York: Harper and Row, 1975. A solid study with a good bibliography.

O'Balance, Edgar. *The Third Arab-Israeli War*. Hamden, Conn.: Archon Books, 1972. A reliable military history of the Six-Day War.

Ovendale, Ritchie. *The Origins of the Arab-Israeli Wars*. 2nd ed. New York: Longman, 1992. Short chapter on the war with clear maps of the territories occupied in 1967.

Reiser, Stewart. *The Israeli Arms Industry: Foreign Policy, Arms Transfers, and Military Doctrine of a Small State.* New York: Holmes and Meier, 1989. A good survey of Israeli weapons.

Sachar, Howard M. *A History of Israel: From the Rise of Zionism to Our Time.* New York: Knopf, 1979. A standard history with good coverage on the 1967 war.

Stoessinger, John G. *Why Nations Go to War.* 7th ed. New York: St. Martin's Press, 1998. A lucid discussion of the war framed within the half-century of Arab-Israeli conflict.

World Wide Web

"Department of History Map Library." *http://www.dean.usma.edu/history/ dhistorymaps//MapsHome.htm.* Click on "Atlases" for United States Military Academy (West Point) maps of the fighting on all fronts.

67. CIVIL WAR IN NIGERIA (BIAFRA), 1967–1970

When **Nigeria** gained its independence from Great Britain in 1960, it was a rich country of great promise. It had a population of nearly 50 million people, a workable federal constitution, and an experienced class of civil servants. Beneath the surface, though, Nigeria was a country of regional strife and ethnic tension, particularly among the **Hausa, Yoruba, Fulani**, and **Ibo** peoples. Nigeria's federal government ruled over more than 200 tribes speaking dozens of languages. Tensions came to flashpoint in 1966 when a group of Ibo army officers staged a coup resulting in the death of **Sir Abubakar Tafawa Balewa**, the federal prime minister. Although the coup failed, it triggered a year of violence, plunging Nigeria into political chaos.

Two strong military leaders emerged. In July 1966, **Colonel Yakubu Gowon**, a professional soldier, became Nigeria's head of state. Gowon, a member of the **Angas** tribe, had strong support in northern and western Nigeria. He was opposed by **Colonel Emeka Ojukwu**, an Ibo and military governor of eastern Nigeria. Neither leader was able to stop the violence, especially the political assassinations. Ojukwu repeatedly insisted that Gowon was targeting Ibos for extermination and that only an independent Ibo state in eastern Nigeria—**Biafra**—could prevent the genocide of his people. Others insisted that the discovery of oil in the Ibo region was the real motivating factor in Biafra's call to separate.

On 30 May 1967, Ojukwu declared the independence of Biafra and its 13 million people. Gowon refused to recognize secessionist Biafra and ordered his federal army to attack the rebels. Both armies were poorly trained and ill equipped. Gradually, however, Gowon's federal army grew to 100,000 and benefited from weapons and supplies from **Great Britain** and the **Soviet Union**. Ojukwu's Biafran force, made up of very young soldiers, received some clandestine support from **France** and diplomatic recognition from four African countries, but little else. Both armies welcomed foreign mercenary soldiers, though the more celebrated mercenaries, such as the German ex-Foreign Legionnaire **Rolf Steiner**, fought with the Biafrans against the British-backed federal troops.

Lasting from 1967 to 1970, the Nigerian Civil War was a savage and bloody struggle that quickly turned into a starvation famine. Unable to defeat the ragtag Biafran army, Gowon's federal army cut off the food supply to Biafra. Thousands of Biafrans, especially children, died from starvation. By 1969 the grim spectacle of a starving Biafra appeared daily in the world press. The international community sent food to Biafra but did nothing to stop the killing. Ojukwu refused to surrender but did agree to a peace on 12 January 1970 before seeking exile in the **Ivory Coast**. Surprisingly, Gowon granted amnesty to all who had fought for Biafra. This magnanimous gesture, however, could not alter the fact that the Nigerian Civil War killed 600,000 people, cost $2 billion, and has left a legacy of political instability, lawlessness, and corruption that still plagues Nigeria today.

Suggestions for Term Papers

1. Who are the Ibo people? Do a research project on their history and write a paper on their significance for Nigeria.

2. The distinguished Nigerian writer Chinua Achebe worked for the Biafran Ministry of Information and served in the Biafran diplomatic corps. Read his *Christmas in Biafra and Other Poems* (see Suggested Sources) and write a paper commenting on his poetry.

3. Flora Nwapa, Nigeria's leading female writer, has written *Never Again* (see Suggested Sources), a novel about the struggles of

Biafran women caught up in the fighting. Use this and other sources for a paper on the role of women in the civil war.

4. Investigate the Biafran army in the civil war and write a paper evaluating its strategy and tactics.

5. Select an American newsmagazine such as *Time* or *Newsweek* and write a paper assessing its coverage of Biafra during 1969.

6. How important were the European mercenaries in the civil war? Read Chapter 12, "The Hired Guns," in *The Brothers' War* (see Suggested Sources) and write a paper on the role of mercenaries in the civil war.

Research Suggestions

In addition to the boldfaced items, look under the entries for "Kwame Nkrumah and the Independence of Ghana, 1957" (#54), "Apartheid in South Africa from the 1950s to the 1970s" (#58), and "Genocide in Rwanda, 1994" (#95). Search under **genocide** and **human rights**.

SUGGESTED SOURCES

Primary Sources

Kirk-Green, A.H.M. *Crisis and Conflict in Nigeria: A Documentary Sourcebook, 1966–1970.* 2 vols. Oxford: Oxford University Press, 1971. A very accessible collection of wide-ranging documents on the war.

Ojukwu, C. Odumegwu. *Biafra: Selected Speeches and Random Thoughts.* New York: Harper and Row, 1969. A good view of the Biafran leader's views on the struggle.

Saro-Wiwa, Ken. *A Month and a Day: A Detention Diary.* New York: Penguin Books, 1995. A poignant reflection on the war and a call for protection of minority rights.

Secondary Sources

Achebe, Chinua. *Christmas in Biafra and Other Poems.* Garden City, N.Y.: Doubleday, 1973. A poignant evocation of Biafra at war.

Clarke, John Digby. *Yakubu Gowon: Faith in a United Nigeria.* Totowa, N.J.: F. Cass, 1987. A short biography of the Nigerian leader.

Falola, Toyin. *The History of Nigeria.* Westport, Conn.: Greenwood Press, 1999. Useful for placing the civil war in historical context.

Meredith, Martin. *The First Dance of Freedom: Black Africa in the Postwar*

Era. New York: Harper and Row, 1984. His chapter on Nigeria's civil war is a good overview of the struggle.

Niven, Rex. *The War of Nigerian Unity, 1967–1970.* Totowa, N.J.: Rowman and Littlefield, 1971. A short account, with maps, that provides political context to the civil war.

Nwapa, Flora. *Never Again.* Trenton, NJ.: Africa World Press, 1992. A novel that examines the effects of war on Biafran women.

St. Jorre, John de. *The Brothers' War: Biafra and Nigeria.* Boston: Houghton Mifflin, 1972. Despite its age, this is the best starting point for the military history of the war.

Word Wide Web

"Association of Concerned Africa Scholars (ACAS) Alerts & Related Material on Ken Saro-Wiwa & Nigeria." *http://www.prairienet.org/acas/siro.html.* Good links for all aspects of contemporary Nigeria.

68. THE 1968 TET OFFENSIVE

American confidence in winning the **Vietnam War** (1957–1975) in late 1967 was quite high. In November **General William C. Westmoreland**, the commander of American forces in Vietnam, told the nation he believed U.S. forces could begin withdrawing from Vietnam in 1969. American troop strength was then approaching 500,000 men. **President Lyndon Johnson** and **Secretary of Defense Robert S. McNamara** had repeatedly characterized the Vietnam War with the optimistic phrase "There is light at the end of the tunnel."

American optimism did not deter the leaders of Communist North Vietnam, **President Ho Chi Minh** and his chief military advisor **General Vo Nguyen Giap**. On 30 January 1968 the **North Vietnamese Army (NVA)** and their South Vietnamese allies in the **National Liberation Front (FLN or Viet Cong)** launched a military offensive against the U.S. Marine base at **Khe Sanh** to coincide with the Vietnamese lunar New Year celebrations of Tet. The NVA also infiltrated 80,000 NVA and Viet Cong soldiers into South Vietnam's cities during the traditional Tet New Year's truce.

Despite meticulous planning, the NVA launched the Tet offensive prematurely in six northern provinces of South Vietnam. By 31 January 1968, South Vietnamese and American military were well aware that a widespread, well-coordinated offensive was under way. Emblematic of the fighting was the firefight, shown on U.S. television, between Viet Cong and U.S. Marines inside the American Embassy compound in Saigon. By the end of April 1968, the Tet offensive had been broken. The American and South Vietnamese forces, although surprised by the attack, had taken back all the territory they had lost initially and had inflicted heavy casualties on the NVA and especially the Viet Cong. The NVA and Viet Cong had sustained 45,000 casualties, while the South Vietnamese and American casualties were less than 4,000.

The dramatic television images, especially scenes from the United States embassy compound in Saigon, the fighting in Hue, and, above all, the execution of a captured Viet Cong by a South Vietnamese official on a Saigon street, shocked Americans. Many were also perturbed to see how unrealistic General Westmoreland's optimistic assessment of the situation in South Vietnam was. Paradoxically, many perceived the failed Tet offensive as a military victory for the communists. Neither President Johnson nor General Westmoreland could disabuse Americans of this perception. It remains one of the great ironies of the Vietnam War that the Tet offensive, a clear military defeat for the NVA and Viet Cong, nevertheless became a great communist propaganda victory, one that energized the American antiwar effort and ultimately convinced President Johnson not to seek reelection. Despite its failure, the Tet offensive was the decisive battle of the **Second Indochina War,** for it convinced the American public that the Vietnam War was unwinnable.

Suggestions for Term Papers

1. Do a research project on the Battle of Khe Sanh. Why, after holding Khe Sanh for months at great expense, were the Marines ordered to evacuate the battlefield?

2. View episodes 6 and 7 of the film series *Vietnam, 1945–1975: The Ten Thousand Day War* (see Suggested Sources) and write a commentary on how the American media portrayed the Tet offensive.

3. Drawing on General Westmoreland's account of Tet and essays in Gilbert and Head's *The Tet Offensive* (see Suggested Sources), write a paper evaluating the American military's response to the Tet offensive. Determine why an American military victory was perceived by the general public as a defeat.

4. Beginning in February 1968, read *Time, Newsweek*, and other magazines and newspapers and write a paper discussing their reporting of the Tet offensive.

5. What was Tet's impact on the American antiwar movement, especially during the period between the March on the Pentagon in the fall of 1967 and the October and November 1969 moratoriums, when millions of middle-class Americans participated in antiwar protests?

6. Investigate the career of General Vo Nguyen Giap, the man who planned the Tet offensive, and write a paper on his leadership during the war against the United States.

Research Suggestions

In addition to the boldfaced items, look under the entries for "Ho Chi Minh and the Vietnamese War Against the French, 1946–1954" (#41) and "Pol Pot and the Cambodian Incursion, 1970–1978" (#72). Search under **Geneva Conference** (1954), **Vietnam War**, and **Ellsworth Bunker**.

SUGGESTED SOURCES

Primary Sources

United States. Pacific Command. *Report on the War in Vietnam, as of 30 June 1968: Index. Section I: Report on Air and Naval Campaigns Against North Vietnam and Pacific Command-wide Support of the War, June 1964–July 1968, by U.S.G. Sharp, USN, Commander in Chief Pacific. Section II: Report on Operations in South Vietnam, January 1964–June 1968.* Washington, D.C.: Government Printing Office, 1969. Commonly referred to as the "Sharp Report," this also contains General Westmoreland's reflections on Tet.

Vietnam, 1945–1975: The Ten Thousand Day War [videorecording]. Los Angeles: Embassy Home Entertainment, 1985. Episodes 6 and 7 document Tet and its effects on American public opinion.

Westmoreland, William C. *A Soldier Reports.* Garden City, N.Y.: Doubleday, 1976. This memoir contains the American commander's account of how the Tet offensive was broken.

Secondary Sources

Braestrup, Peter. *Big Story: How the American Press and Television Reported and Interpreted the Crisis of Tet 1968 in Vietnam and Washington.*

2 vols. New Haven: Yale University Press, 1977. An incisive, detailed account of efforts by the media to report theVietnam War. Braestrup accuses the media of inaccurate and biased reporting.

Gilbert, Marc Jason, and William Head, eds. *The Tet Offensive*. Westport, Conn.: Praeger, 1996. A balanced collection of fourteen essays examining the importance of Tet in the full context of the Vietnam War.

McMaster, H. R. *Dereliction of Duty: Lyndon Johnson, Robert McNamara, the Joint Chiefs of Staff, and the Lies that Led to Vietnam*. New York: HarperCollins, 1997. Written by a U.S. Army officer, this is a candid appraisal of the muddled thinking that led to Tet.

Oberdorfer, Don. *Tet!* Garden City, N.Y.: Doubleday, 1971. A reliable narrative of the offensive.

Wirtz, James J. *The Tet Offensive: Intelligence Failure in War*. Ithaca: Cornell University Press, 1991. The authoritative study of the intelligence breakdown in the American military command.

World Wide Web

"The National Security Archive." *http://www/gwu.edu/~nsarchiv*. Good documentation on the entire Vietnam War.

"Department of History Map Library." *http://www.dean.usma.edu/history/dhistorymaps//MapsHome.htm*. Click on "Atlases" for United States Military Academy (West Point) maps of the Vietnam War.

"Vietnam, 1954–1968." *http://www.cnn.com/SPECIALS/cold.war/episodes/11*. Based on CNN's *Cold War* documentary series, the Web site includes background, documents, a transcript of the program, and other features.

69. MAY 1968 IN FRANCE

"France is bored," proclaimed an editorial in *Le Monde* for 15 March 1968. Six weeks later, on 3 May, student demonstrations at the University of Paris shattered this malaise. Fully aware of the effectiveness of the American **anti-Vietnam War protests**, French students, many of whom were frustrated with overcrowding in the universities and fearful about future employment, took to the streets of the Latin Quarter demanding university reforms.

Flamboyant leaders such as **Daniel Cohn-Bendit**, a.k.a. "Dany the Red," taunted riot police and used Marxist rhetoric to energize the demonstrators. Soon disgruntled workers, many of whom worked a forty-eight-hour week in government-run automobile factories, joined the student rioters. By 14 May, 700,000 workers had joined in the student demonstrations, and on 20 May, 7 million French workers throughout France went on strike demanding a shorter work week and better pay.

Initially, the government of **President Charles de Gaulle** and **Prime Minister Georges Pompidou** ignored the rioters. De Gaulle was in Romania while riots paralyzed Paris. After a hasty return, he went on television and gave a limp, uninspiring speech. Shaken and confused, de Gaulle secretly flew to Baden, Germany, on 29 May. There he met with the commander of French forces in Germany. Although it remains unclear what transpired in Baden, appearances suggest that de Gaulle was preparing to use troops against the rioters.

Back in Paris, de Gaulle blamed the **communists** for the riots, refused to make concessions, asked his supporters (and the police) to reclaim the streets, dissolved Parliament, and called elections for 23 June.

De Gaulle's Gaullist Party won a large majority in the elections and seemingly an endorsement of his handling of the "May events." One month later, however, de Gaulle replaced Pompidou as prime minister with **Maurice Courve de Murville** and hinted he would propose a national referendum early in 1969. Despite warnings from his advisors that a referendum would be political suicide, de Gaulle offered a poorly worded referendum proposing reform in regional governance and restructuring the French Senate. On 27 April 1969, 53 percent of French voters rejected the referendum, and de Gaulle immediately resigned.

The events of May 1968 ended the decade-long presidency of Charles de Gaulle, who died seventeen months after leaving office. May 1968 also rekindled briefly the dream of a student-worker alliance. Perhaps the most durable effects of May 1968 were the election of Georges Pompidou as the new president of France and the recognition that French universities needed reform.

Suggestions for Term Papers

1. When President de Gaulle met with General Massu, commander of the French army in Germany, he gave the impression that he

was not above using troops against the protesters. Investigate the use of the military against protesters in recent history and write a paper about the dangers such actions entail.

2. Daniel Cohn-Bendit, a.k.a. "Dany the Red," was probably the most celebrated student leader of May 1968. What was the basis for his appeal? What kind of program did he offer?

3. Write a one-act play in which a French automobile worker and a student from the University of Paris meet during the events of May 1968. What would be some common concerns uniting the two? Use John Ardagh as a starting point (see Suggested Sources).

4. Write a paper contrasting the support of the French students by the French labor unions with the hostility to American students protesting the Vietnam War by American labor unions. How would you explain the differing attitudes?

5. Investigate Charles de Gaulle's role in the events of May 1968. Why was he in the end so effective in rallying France to his leadership?

6. Consider the proposition that France, despite a long revolutionary tradition, needs and admires strong leaders such as Napoleon and de Gaulle. Base your essay in part on an examination of the constitution of the Fifth Republic, especially the powers given the president. Use also books by Charles Cogan and Jean Lacouture (see Suggested Sources).

Research Suggestions

In addition to the boldfaced items, look under the entry for "France and the Algerian Revolution, 1954–1962" (#56). Search under **student revolt, French Fifth Republic, Gaullists, educational reform, François Mitterrand,** and **trade union movement.**

SUGGESTED SOURCES

Primary Sources

Bourges, Hervé. *The French Student Revolt: The Leaders Speak: Daniel Cohn-Bendit and Others.* Translated by B. R. Brewster. New York: Hill and Wang, 1968. Good first-person accounts of what the leaders of May 1968 attempted to achieve.

Cohn-Bendit, Daniel, and Gabriel Cohn-Bendit. *Obsolete Communism: The*

Left-Wing Alternative. New York: McGraw-Hill, 1968. Stridently Marxist in tone, this book suggests why the French political left has had such difficulty making allies.

Secondary Sources

Ardagh, John. *The New French Revolution.* New York: Harper and Row, 1969. A readable account of France in the 1960s with material on French labor relations.

Caute, David. *The Year of the Barricades: A Journey Through 1968.* New York: Harper and Row, 1988. Contains two chapters on France. Also useful for placing France in the context of events around the world.

Cogan, Charles. *Charles de Gaulle: A Brief Biography with Documents.* Boston: Bedford Books, 1996. A crisp outline of events with good bibliographical leads.

Hoffmann, Stanley. *Decline or Renewal: France since the 1930s.* New York: Viking, 1974. Hoffmann's chapter on the May confrontation shows how far out of touch de Gaulle and his government had become by 1968.

Lacouture, Jean. *De Gaulle: The Ruler, 1945–1970.* Translated by Allan Sheridan. New York: W. W. Norton, 1992. The best English-language treatment of de Gaulle's vacillation in Paris and strange behavior in Baden.

Marwick, Arthur. *The Sixties: Cultural Revolution in Britain, France, Italy, and the United States, c. 1958–c. 1974.* Oxford: Oxford University Press, 1998. A detailed and useful analysis by a prominent British historian.

Seale, Patrick, and Maureen McConville. *Red Flag/Black Flag: French Revolution, 1968.* New York: Putnam, 1968. Although written and published a few months after the May riots, this remains the most accessible treatment of May 1968 in English.

Wylie, Laurence William, et al., eds. *France: The Events of May–June 1968: A Critical Bibliography.* Pittsburgh: Council for European Studies, 1973. Based largely on French sources, this has the major contemporary accounts of the riots.

70. THE PRAGUE SPRING, 1968

In spring 1968, **Czechoslovakia**, hitherto one of the most loyal Soviet satellites in eastern Europe and a member of the **Warsaw Treaty Organization** (WTO), began experimenting with reforms designed to bring into being **"socialism with a human face."** Although the

Prague Spring was crushed by the August invasion of troops from the WTO, it left a legacy that was revived in the revolutions in eastern and central Europe in 1989.

By the mid-1960s, Czechoslovakia was ripe for reform. Reformers in the **Czechoslovak Communist Party** called for political change and for new economic policies in place of the disastrous emphasis on heavy industry. The 1967 Writers' Congress also featured demands for political reforms.

Antonin Novotny was replaced in January 1968 as first secretary of the Czech Communist Party by **Alexander Dubcek**. Dubcek represented the moderate reform element in the party and, as a Slovak, he also spoke for Slovak interests (Slovaks had long complained that the party had neglected Slovakia). Reforms began cautiously with an end to censorship. The announcement of an **"Action Program"** came in April. It called for concentration on consumer goods production and for the expansion of political freedom. Plans for more extensive reforms, which were to be presented at the **Fourteenth Party Congress**, called for a more pluralistic but still one-party system.

The pace of events quickened. Quasi-political clubs appeared and the Social Democratic Party was revived. A radical declaration, **"2,000 Words,"** appeared in June. By then, support for reform came not only from students and intellectuals but also from the working class.

Conservative elements in the Czechoslovak Communist Party began to wonder if the party could maintain its political monopoly. The WTO also grew nervous. In particular, the Soviet Union, Poland, and the German Democratic Republic wanted an end to the Czech experiment. Czech leaders met with their counterparts from the WTO in July and in August. Dubcek believed both times he had successfully convinced the WTO that the Czechoslovak Communist Party had the situation under control.

On the night of 20–21 August, WTO troops and tanks crossed into Czechoslovakia in **Operation Danube**. Within a week, the invasion force numbered about 500,000 men and more than 6,000 tanks. The Czechs followed a policy of nonviolent protest, which slowed but did not stop the invasion. Dubcek and other leaders were arrested and taken to Moscow. They were allowed to return only because other Czech leaders would not cooperate until they came back. Over the next few years the "normalization" of Czechoslovakia took place under **Gustav Husak**, who replaced Dubcek in April 1969. Some half million members of the Czech Communist Party were thrown out of the party and, in most cases, lost their jobs. People who had been officials or doctors now worked as janitors, construction workers, and window washers.

For the Czech people, invasion and "normalization" of the country meant a repressive government and two decades of economic decline. Outside Czechoslovakia, some viewed the Prague Spring as a lost opportunity for communism to show it could reform itself. Others criticized the assertion of **Leonid Brezhnev**, head of the **Communist Party of the Soviet Union**, that the USSR had an obligation to intervene in Czechoslovakia to preserve socialism. Criticism of the **"Brezhnev Doctrine,"** however, did not prevent the United States and the USSR from continuing the development of **détente** over the next few years.

Suggestions for Term Papers

1. Investigate Alexander Dubcek's life and his role in 1968. Write an essay on how Dubcek viewed the reform movement and what he hoped to accomplish for Czechoslovakia in the Prague Spring.

2. Read "2,000 Words." Assume that you are a high-ranking official in the Czechoslovak Communist Party and that you must decide whether the declaration performs a useful function in the reform movement or whether it is politically unwise. Provide a justification for your decision.

3. Why would Poland and the German Democratic Republic be nervous about the Prague Spring? Base your answer on an examination of the history of one or the other country in the 1960s.

4. Follow the course of events in Czechoslovakia in 1968 in at least two newspapers or periodicals such as the *New York Times* or *Newsweek*. Compare the kind of coverage provided by each of your sources in terms of the amount of space devoted to articles, the placement of articles, and editorial comment, whether explicit or implicit.

5. Czech films from the mid-1960s were highly praised and often very popular. View one or more and write a review discussing the film(s) on their own merits and as documents of the times.

6. Russian soliders believed they had entered Czechoslovakia in August, 1968, to help preserve socialism in the country. Czechs, of course, saw it differently. After reading about these different perspectives, write a one-act play in which a young Russian tank commander climbs out of his tank to ask directions and is confronted by an angry Czech woman about his age.

Research Suggestions

In addition to the boldfaced items, look under the entries for "The Hungarian Revolution, 1956" (#53), "The Cuban Missile Crisis, 1962" (#64), and "Solidarity in Poland, 1980–1990" (#82). Search under **Warsaw Treaty Organization, Jan Palach, Ota Sik, Slovakia**, and **Ludvik Svoboda**.

SUGGESTED SOURCES

Primary Sources

Dubcek, Alexander, with Jiri Hochman. *Hope Dies Last: The Autobiography of Alexander Dubcek*. New York: Kodansha International, 1993. The year 1968 as seen by the political leader at the center of the Prague Spring.

Pelikan, Jiri, ed. *The Secret Vysocany Congress: Proceedings and Documents of the Communist Party of Czechoslovakia, 22 August 1968*. London: Allen Lane, 1971. Documents from the Fourteenth Party Congress held in secret as the invasion of WTO forces was taking place.

Remington, Robin Alison, ed. *Winter in Prague: Documents on Czechoslovak Communism in Crisis*. Cambridge, Mass.: MIT Press, 1969. Documents from 1968.

Secondary Sources

Golan, Galia. *The Czechoslovak Reform Movement: Communism in Crisis, 1962–1968*. Cambridge: Cambridge University Press, 1971. One of the best studies available of events leading up to the Prague Spring.

———. *Reform Rule in Czechoslovakia: The Dubcek Era, 1968–1969*. Cambridge: Cambridge University Press, 1973. An essential book on the Prague Spring.

Kundera, Milan. *The Unbearable Lightness of Being*. New York: Harper and Row, 1984. A brilliant novel that, among many other things, explores aspects of 1968.

Kusin, Vladimir. *The Intellectual Origins of the Prague Spring: The Development of Reformist Ideas in Czechoslovakia, 1956–1967*. Cambridge:

Cambridge University Press, 1971. An excellent source for tracing the roots of the reform movement.

Rothschild, Joseph. *Return to Diversity: A Political History of East Central Europe since World War II.* 2nd ed. New York: Oxford University Press, 1993. The best book with which to begin.

Shawcross, William. *Dubcek: Dubcek and Czechoslovakia, 1918–1990.* London: Weidenfeld and Nicolson, 1991. A recent study of Dubcek and Czech politics by a biographer of Dubcek.

Skilling, H. Gordon. *Czechoslovakia's Interrupted Revolution.* Princeton: Princeton University Press, 1976. An older but nonetheless valuable study.

Valenta, Jiri. *Soviet Intervention in Czechoslovakia, 1968: Anatomy of a Decision.* Rev. ed. Baltimore: Johns Hopkins University Press, 1991. A useful effort to explain the Soviet decision to invade.

Williams, Kieran. *The Prague Spring and Its Aftermath: Czechoslovak Politics, 1968–1970.* Cambridge: Cambridge University Press, 1997. An analysis of the reform movement and its suppression by the Soviet Union using archival sources available since the events of 1989.

World Wide Web

"Cold War International History Project." *http://cwihp.si.edu/default.htm.* This major Web site for the study of the Cold War contains both documents and articles on the Prague Spring.

"Red Spring, 1960s." *http://www.cnn.com/SPECIALS/cold.war/episodes/14.* Based on CNN's *Cold War* documentary series, this Web site has many interesting and useful features.

71. NORTHERN IRELAND AND "THE TROUBLES," 1969–1998

For more than four hundred years, the bitter tensions between the oppressed Irish Catholic majority and the dominant English Protestant ruling minority in Ireland frequently erupted in grim scenes of bloody, sectarian violence (commonly called "The Troubles"). In 1912, while the British Parliament was seriously considering greater autonomy for Ireland (**Home Rule**), the powerful **Ulster Unionist Party**, representing the Protestant majority of the six northern counties of Ireland, declared its unalterable opposition to Home Rule.

During Easter week 1916, the Irish nationalist party **Sinn Fein**

("We ourselves") led a bloody, weeklong rebellion in Dublin protesting British rule, culminating in the Declaration of a Provisional Government for an Irish Republic. The **Easter Rising** was brutally suppressed, but the political agitation, violence, and fighting among Irish Republicans, Ulster Unionists, and the British troops continued until a truce was signed on 6 December 1921 recognizing the twenty-six counties of southern Ireland as the Irish Free State. In 1937 the Irish Free State changed its name to **Eire**, or the **Republic of Ireland**.

The six counties of Northern Ireland (Ulster) withdrew from this Irish Free State and have remained part of the **United Kingdom**. Unfortunately these political arrangements did not end the violence. The outlawed **Irish Republican Army** (IRA) has advanced its goal of unifying the two Irelands by attacking British military units in Northern Ireland and by terror-bombings throughout the United Kingdom. Although there were sporadic attacks in the 1950s and 1960s, 1969 marked the beginning of a sustained campaign that lasted until 1998. So, too, the political authorities of Northern Ireland have a well-established record of denying the Catholic minority of Northern Ireland civic and economic rights and have used brutality and torture in interrogating IRA suspects and their supporters.

In 1969, following riots in **Derry** and **Belfast**, the British army was deployed in force throughout all of Northern Ireland. In the next thirty years more than 3,500 people were killed in the sectarian violence. At the root of the violence are two groups with differing views of Northern Ireland: **Unionists**, who are largely Protestant, and wish to remain part of the United Kingdom; and **Nationalists**, who are largely Catholic, and wish to affiliate with the Irish Republic. The most promising moment for cessation of the troubles came on 22 May 1998, when both Irelands approved the **Good Friday Accords** of 10 April, brokered by former U.S. Senator **George Mitchell**. Key elements of the accords are (1) a new 108-seat legislature ensuring that Catholics have a real voice in governance; (2) a cross-border ministerial council linking northern and southern Ireland; (3) changes in Ireland's constitution renouncing the Irish Republic's claim upon the six northern counties; and (4) a commitment by all parties to disarm and to turn away from violence. British Prime Minister **Tony Blair**, Irish Prime Minister **Bertie Ahern**, and **David Trimble**, head of the Ulster Unionist Party, signed the accords. **Gerry Adams**, head of Sinn Fein, did not sign but pledged his support.

Suggestions for Term Papers

1. What happened during the Dublin Easter Rising of 1916? Why is this event important in Irish history?

2. What was the strategy of the Irish Republican Army (IRA) during the 1970s and 1980s? How effective was it?

3. What was the strategy of the British army in Northern Ireland during the 1970s and 1980s? How effective was it?

4. Evaluate the role of former U.S. Senator George Mitchell in brokering the Good Friday Accords of 1998 (see Suggested Sources).

5. Write a paper analyzing the impact of the Good Friday Accords on Northern Ireland (see Suggested Sources).

6. Investigate the parts played by Great Britain and the Irish Republic in helping the people of Northern Ireland resolve "The Troubles." Should or could they have done more?

Research Suggestions

In addition to the boldfaced items, look under the entries for "Terrorism in the 1970s" (#78) and "Margaret Thatcher and the Conservative Revolution in Britain, 1979–1990" (#81). Search under **Long Kesh, Orange Lodges, Ian Paisley**, and **Bobby Sands**.

SUGGESTED SOURCES

Primary Sources

Amnesty International, UK. *Killings by Security Forces in Northern Ireland*. London: Amnesty International, 1990. First-person accounts of the difficulty of using the military in counterinsurgency operations against civilians.

Mitchell, George J. *Making Peace*. New York: Knopf, 1999. Valuable personal reflections by the chief U.S. negotiator who assisted in the diplomacy of the Good Friday Accords.

Thatcher, Margaret. *The Downing Street Years*. London: HarperCollins, 1993. Prime Minister Thatcher's candid admission of how difficult "The Troubles" were for her government.

Secondary Sources

Aughey, Arthur, and Duncan Morrow, eds. *Northern Ireland Politics*. New York: Longman, 1996. An excellent overview of political and administrative issues. The appendices have a good bibliography and a helpful chronology.

Bartlett, Thomas, and Keith Jeffrey, eds. *A Military History of Ireland*. Cambridge: Cambridge University Press, 1996. The chapters on "The Troubles" provide a succinct analysis of their human costs.

Bell, J. Bowyer. *IRA Tactics and Targets*. Dublin: Poolberg, 1990. An incisive examination by the IRA's leading historian.

Bruce, Steve. *The Red Hand: Protestant Paramilitaries in Northern Ireland*. Oxford: Oxford University Press, 1992. A useful summary of Irish Protestant military organizations.

Hart, Peter. *The I.R.A. and Its Enemies: Violence and Community in Cork, 1916–1923*. Oxford: Oxford University Press, 1998. A poignant case study of the early troubles, along with an extensive bibliography.

Kennedy-Pipe, Caroline. *The Origins of the Present Troubles in Northern Ireland*. New York: Longman, 1997. The best starting point for understanding the issues.

Ruane, Joseph, and Jennifer Todd, eds. *The Dynamics of Conflict in Northern Ireland: Power, Conflict and Emancipation*. Cambridge: Cambridge University Press, 1996. A solid analysis of the economic, military, and cultural dimensions of the conflict.

World Wide Web

"Northern Ireland Assembly: The Agreement." *http://www.ni-assembly. gov.uk/agreement.htm*. The full text of the 1998 agreement with links to other aspects of "The Troubles."

72. POL POT AND THE CAMBODIAN INCURSION, 1970–1979

Pol Pot (1925?–1998), one of the most brutal killers of the twentieth century, was born in French-ruled Cambodia. He joined the Cambodian Communist Party in 1946 and was a frequent critic of Cambodia's president, **Norodom Sihanouk**. In 1963 Pol Pot took refuge in the jungles of northwest Cambodia, where he and his **Khmer Rouge** guerrillas fought against the Cambodian government. With the entry in 1957 of the United States into the **Second Indochina War** in neighboring Vietnam, however, the Khmer Rouge guerrillas became more active. Though officially neutral in the Vietnam conflict, Norodom Sihanouk permitted North Vietnam to supply the **Viet**

Cong (National Liberation Front or NLF) via the **Ho Chi Minh Trail**.

Throughout the 1960s the United States urged Sihanouk to be more aggressive in policing his borders. In 1969 the Nixon administration ordered sustained, heavy bombing of NLF targets in Cambodia. In March 1970, in a carefully planned coup, the United States assisted **Lon Nol**, former defense minister and premier of Cambodia, in ousting Norodom Sihanouk from power. On 30 April 1970, President Nixon announced that U.S. forces were invading Cambodia to destroy North Vietnamese and NLF targets and thereby shorten the war in Vietnam. This Cambodian incursion, though lasting only two months, had two immediate effects. First, the American antiwar movement exploded: student demonstrations at **Kent State** University resulted in four deaths, and two students were killed at **Jackson State** University. A second consequence of the incursion was the dramatic growth of the Khmer Rouge insurgency. Lon Nol was increasingly portrayed in Cambodia as an American puppet and a close ally of Cambodia's traditional enemy, Vietnam. Quickly Pol Pot's insurgency grew strong enough so that by 1975 his Khmer Rouge captured the city of **Phnom Penh** and began the systematic killing of Cambodians deemed "enemies of the people." Between 1975 and 1979 over 1 million Cambodians, out of a population of 7 million, were executed in the Khmer Rouge killing fields by Pol Pot's forces. This genocide, one of the most horrific of the twentieth century, could not have come about without the American incursion. Ironically, Pol Pot's genocide ended in 1979 when Vietnam invaded Cambodia and forced Pol Pot again to seek refuge deep in the jungles of northwestern Cambodia, where he remained until his death in April 1998.

Suggestions for Term Papers

1. Some scholars see the Cambodian incursion as an example of the influence of President Nixon's national security adviser (later Secretary of State), Dr. Henry Kissinger. Write a paper on the part played by Kissinger in this decision.

2. View *The Killing Fields* (see Suggested Sources) and compare its portrayal of the Cambodian genocide with "The Dith Pran Holocaust Awareness Project" (see Suggested Sources).

3. Should the United States have intervened to stop Pol Pot from practicing genocide in Cambodia? Review the evidence on the response of the United States to events in Cambodia and take a position. Provide reasons for your position.

4. Shortly before he died, Pol Pot gave one of his rare interviews. Read Nate Thayer's "Day of Reckoning" (see Suggested Sources) and compare Pol Pot's reflections on his governance of Cambodia with the documentation contained in "The Yale Cambodian Genocide Project" (see Suggested Sources).

5. Compare and contrast Pol Pot's genocide with the Holocaust and/or genocide in Rwanda. (See entries #34 and #95.)

6. Investigate the events at Kent State and Jackson State universities in 1970. Write a paper comparing them and analyzing why the events at Kent State received far more attention than those at Jackson State. Begin with *Campus Wars* by Kenneth J. Heineman (see Suggested Sources).

Research Suggestions

In addition to the boldfaced items, look under the entries for "The Holocaust, 1941–1945" (#34), "Ho Chi Minh and the Vietnamese War Against the French, 1946–1954" (#41), "The 1968 Tet Offensive" (#68), "The Dissolution of Yugoslavia in the 1990s" (#93), and "Genocide in Rwanda, 1994" (#95). Search under **Geneva Conference** (1954), **Vietnam War, Henry Kissinger**, and **Richard Nixon**.

SUGGESTED SOURCES

Primary Sources

Pran, Dith, Ben Kiernan, and Kim DePaul. *Children of Cambodia's Killing Fields: Memoirs by Survivors.* New Haven: Yale University Press, 1997. Graphic eyewitness accounts by the children who survived the Khmer Rouge genocide.

Thayer, Nate. "Day of Reckoning." *Far Eastern Economic Review* 60, no. 44 (30 October 1997): 14–23. The last interview given by Pol Pot is a chilling insight into his genocide.

Secondary Sources

Chandler, David P. *The Tragedy of Cambodian History: Politics, War, and Revolution since 1945.* New Haven: Yale University Press, 1991. A reliable starting point for understanding modern Cambodia.

Heineman, Kenneth J. *Campus Wars: The Peace Movement of American State Universities in the Vietnam Era.* New York: New York University Press, 1993. The starting point for research on campus protests. Good bibliographical leads on the Kent State and Jackson State protests.

Kiernan, Ben. *The Pol Pot Regime: Race, Power, and Genocide in Cambodia under the Khmer Rouge, 1975–79.* New Haven: Yale University Press, 1996. Ben Kiernan, who founded the Yale Cambodian Genocide Project, is a leading authority on Pol Pot's genocide.

The Killing Fields [videorecording]. Burbank, Calif.: Warner Home Video, 1985. A vivid account of Dith Pran's harrowing experiences in the killing fields of Cambodia. Based on the book by Sydney Schanberg (see below).

Schanberg, Sydney. *The Death and Life of Dith Pran.* New York: Viking, 1985. Schanberg's powerful report of how his friend and translator Dith Pran survived in the Cambodian killing fields.

Shawcross, William. *Sideshow: Kissinger, Nixon and the Destruction of Cambodia.* New York: Simon and Schuster, 1979. A highly critical account of the Cambodian incursion.

World Wide Web

"Department of History Map Library." *http://www.dean.usma.edu/history/dhistorymaps//MapsHome.htm.* Click on "Atlases" for United States Military Academy (West Point) maps of the war in Cambodia.

"The Dith Pran Holocaust Awareness Project." *http://www.dithpran.org/goal.htm.* Contains a range of material on Cambodia's killing fields.

"The National Security Archive." *http://www.gwu.edu/~nsarchiv.* Documentation on Cambodia.

"The Yale Cambodian Genocide Project." *http://www.yale.edu/cgp.* Founded by Ben Kiernan, this is the most extensive and accessible collection of primary sources available.

73. THE GREAT PROLETARIAN CULTURAL REVOLUTION IN CHINA, 1966–1976

To consolidate his power, **Mao Zedong**, chairman of the **Chinese Communist Party** (CCP), initiated in 1966 a series of reforms that launched the **Great Proletarian Cultural Revolution**, an event that shook the very foundations of China between 1966 and 1976. In addition, Mao tightened his grip on the CCP by pushing aside his designated successor, **Liu Shaoqi**. This indicated that **Lin Biao**, head of the **People's Liberation Army** (PLA), was now second in command. Lin used the PLA to support the Cultural Revolution. He also proved his loyalty to Mao by publishing *Quotations from Chairman Mao*, a collection of Mao's aphorisms and sayings. This **"little red book"** became the bible of the Cultural Revolution.

Lin Biao urged teenagers to organize **Red Guard units** and become the vanguard of Mao's revolution. The Red Guards were ordered to attack the **"four olds"** (old customs, old habits, old culture, and old thinking). By 1967 Red Guard units had achieved striking success, particularly in the cities, where they both verbally and physically attacked "capitalist roaders," that is, enemies of Mao in the CCP, in the schools and universities, and in the government bureaucracies, driving millions from the cities into the countryside. Soon 16 million people had been forced to seek "reeducation" as laborers in rural China. Holding high their "little red books" and chanting quotations from Mao Zedong, the Red Guards attacked all symbols of authority, even units of the PLA.

Taking full advantage of the chaos and upheaval, Mao Zedong purged the CCP and for three years used the Red Guards to attack real or imagined enemies. But by 1969 the revolution was out of control. It had spread too far and destroyed too much. Urged on by his third wife, **Jiang Qing**, Mao moved to oust Lin Biao, who died in a failed coup against Mao in 1971. By this date, however, more than 100 million Chinese had been affected; perhaps 1 million had died from the violence and starvation accompanying the rampages of the Red Guards. Only Mao Zedong's death in 1976 finally ended the Cultural Revolution.

For China the years 1966–1976 were truly a lost decade. Its economy was in shambles, its 800 million people had suffered immense hardships, and an entire generation of children had missed secondary and university education. Not until 1978, when **Deng Xiaoping** finally overcame the opposition of Jiang Qing and the **"Gang of Four,"** who ruled China after Mao's death, was China able to begin to recover from the Cultural Revolution.

Suggestions for Term Papers

1. Read selections from *Quotations from Chairman Mao* (see Suggested Sources) and write a one-act play featuring dialogue between a member of the Red Guards and a history teacher.

2. Why did Mao Zedong ask teenagers and not their elders to form the Red Guards? What was the role of the Red Guards in the Cultural Revolution?

3. During the early years of the Cultural Revolution, Lin Biao was one of the most powerful men in China. By 1971, however, he was in disgrace and was reported to have died trying to flee China. Assess his role in the Cultural Revolution.

4. The Cultural Revolution relied heavily on propaganda to energize China, especially the Red Guards. Analyze parts of *Quotations from Chairman Mao* and estimate their propaganda value for the Cultural Revolution.

5. Jiang Qing, Mao's third wife, was the most powerful woman in China during the Cultural Revolution. How did she come to wield such power and influence during this period?

6. Deng Xiaoping, once a close ally of Mao, was attacked and stripped of power during the Cultural Revolution. Investigate the means he used to survive the chaos of the Cultural Revolution and his highly important contributions to recovery in the post–Cultural Revolution period.

Research Suggestions

In addition to the boldfaced items, look under the entries for "Mao Zedong and the Long March, 1934–1935" (#25), "The Victory of the Chinese Communist Party, 1949" (#46), "The Sino-Soviet Split, 1959–1969" (#60), and "The Chinese Economy at the End of the Twentieth Century" (#100).

SUGGESTED SOURCES

Primary Sources

Chen, Jerome. *Mao Papers, Anthology and Bibliography*. New York: Oxford University Press, 1970. A solid collection of Mao's thoughts on the Cultural Revolution.

Gao, Yuan. *Born Red: A Chronicle of the Cultural Revolution.* Stanford: Stanford University Press, 1987. A readable account of the chaos inflicted on China.

Liang Heng and Judith Shapiro. *Son of the Revolution.* New York: Vintage Books, 1983. A graphic "I was there" account of the chaos during this period.

Mao Tse-tung. *Quotations from Chairman Mao Tse-tung.* Edited by Stuart R. Schram. New York: Praeger, 1967. This is the starting point for understanding Mao's influence in this episode.

Secondary Sources

Chang, Jung. *Wild Swans: Three Daughters of China.* New York: Anchor Books, 1991. Her chapter entitled "Father Is Close, Mother Is Close but Neither Is as Close as Chairman Mao" suggests the nightmare the Cultural Revolution was for Chinese children.

Fairbank, John King. *The Great Chinese Revolution, 1800–1985.* New York: Harper and Row, 1986. A concise, readable summary based on a lifetime's study of China.

Jin, Qui. *The Culture of Power: The Lin Biao Incident in the Cultural Revolution.* Stanford: Stanford University Press, 1999. The most authoritative study of the mystery surrounding Lin Biao.

MacFarquhar, Roderick. *The Origins of the Cultural Revolution.* 2 vols. New York: Columbia University Press, 1974–1983. The best scholarly treatment to date.

Spence, Jonathan D. *The Search for Modern China.* New York: W. W. Norton, 1990. His chapter on the episode and his critical bibliography remain the best starting point.

White, Lynn. *Policies of Chaos: The Organizational Causes of Violence in China's Cultural Revolution.* Princeton: Princeton University Press, 1989. Good bibliographical leads for all aspects of the Cultural Revolution.

Witke, Roxane. *Comrade Chiang Ch'ing.* Boston: Little, Brown, 1977. Flattering but accessible biography of Jiang Qing (Chiang Ch'ing).

Yang, Benjamin. *Deng: A Political Biography.* Armonk, N.Y.: M. E. Sharpe, 1998. A reliable study of this reformer.

World Wide Web

"The National Security Archive." *http://www.gwu.edu/~nsarchiv.* Good links to Cold War perspectives on the Cultural Revolution.

74. SALT I AGREEMENT, 1972

The breakthrough **Strategic Arms Limitation Talks (SALT)**, signed in 1972 by the **United States** and the **Soviet Union**, marked a new chapter in the **Cold War** and a foreign policy triumph for **President Richard Nixon**.

Shortly after taking office in 1969, Richard Nixon announced a policy of **détente** or improving relations with America's principal Cold War rivals, the **People's Republic of China** and the Soviet Union. In February 1972 Nixon went to China, shook the hand of **Chairman Mao Zedong**, and told Mao that America would welcome China's help in ending the **Vietnam War**. Nixon's trip to China caught everyone by surprise, especially the Soviet Union. In 1969 simmering tensions between China and the Soviet Union had erupted in a series of firefights between Soviet and Chinese troops at the Soviet-Chinese border along the **Ussuri River**. Soviet leader **Leonid Brezhnev** was very eager to have Nixon visit Moscow and sign a SALT agreement.

Nixon was eager to go to Moscow for three reasons. First, he wanted to take advantage of the **Sino-Soviet split** and increase American trade with the Soviet Union. Second, he wanted a foreign policy triumph to bolster his position in the forthcoming **1972 presidential elections**. Third, a SALT agreement would improve relations with the Soviet Union and afford Nixon an opening to seek Soviet assistance in ending the Vietnam War.

For some time prior to the Moscow meeting, U.S. and Soviet negotiators had been working on an arms limitation agreement. When President Nixon and his national security adviser, **Henry Kissinger**, arrived in Moscow, most of the preliminary negotiations had been concluded. On 22 May 1972, Nixon and Brezhnev signed four very detailed, technical agreements covering a wide range of weapon systems. The agreement limited the Soviet Union to 1,410 **land-based offensive missiles** and 950 **submarine-based missiles**. The United States was limited to 1,000 land-based missiles and 710 submarine-based missiles. Both sides also agreed not to deploy a comprehensive antiballistic system, and each party pledged to seek ways to avoid confrontation and advance **peaceful coexistence**. Although severely criticized for giving away too much in the SALT treaties, Nixon insisted that SALT was a strategic victory for the United States. The United States Senate agreed by approving the SALT treaties by a vote of 88 to 2.

Suggestions for Term Papers

1. How important was the SALT agreement in relaxing tensions between the Soviet Union and the United States in the 1970s? What kind of impact did it have on the Cold War?
2. Compare and contrast Leonid Brezhnev and Richard Nixon as negotiators and statesmen.
3. In his memoirs President Nixon insists that Henry Kissinger played a secondary role in the SALT negotiations. Investigate Kissinger's role in the SALT negotiations and assess Nixon's claim.
4. Should the United States have agreed not to deploy a comprehensive antiballistic missile system as part of the SALT agreement? Provide reasons for your position.
5. President Nixon insisted that the SALT agreement would result in better trade relations between the United States and the Soviet Union. Did this turn out to be the case? Explain your reasoning.
6. How important was the SALT agreement in President Nixon's 1972 presidential campaign?

Research Suggestions

In addition to the boldfaced items, look under the entries for "The Sino-Soviet Split, 1959–1969" (#60), "The 1968 Tet Offensive" (#68), and "The Great Proletarian Cultural Revolution in China, 1966–1976" (#73). Search under **Warsaw Pact** and **NATO**.

SUGGESTED SOURCES

Primary Sources

Brezhnev, Leonid. *Memoirs.* Translated by Penny Dole. Oxford: Pergamon Press, 1982. A thin collection of Brezhnev's candid views on his role in world affairs.

———. *Peace, Détente, Cooperation.* New York: Consultants Bureau, 1981. Brezhnev on how SALT could lessen Cold War tensions.

Kissinger, Henry. *White House Years.* Boston: Little, Brown, 1979. Insightful comments by Nixon's national security adviser and later secretary of state on the nuts and bolts of SALT negotiations.

Nixon, Richard M. *RN: The Memoirs of Richard Nixon.* New York: Grosset and Dunlap, 1978. A readable and candid account of why President Nixon worked so hard to get a SALT treaty.

Smith, Gerard. *Doubletalk: The Untold Story of SALT.* Garden City, N.Y.: Doubleday, 1981. A damning view by the chief American delegate of the duplicity and mischievous quality of Nixon's SALT diplomacy.

Secondary Sources

Ambrose, Stephen A. *Nixon: The Triumph of a Politician, 1962–1972.* New York: Simon and Schuster, 1989. Well-researched account that underscores the pragmatic side of Nixon's SALT diplomacy.

Anderson, Richard. *Public Politics in an Authoritarian State: Making Foreign Policy During the Brezhnev Years.* Ithaca: Cornell University Press, 1993. A good overview of how Brezhnev approached the SALT talks.

Blum, John Morton. *Years of Discord: American Politics and Society, 1961–1974.* New York: W. W. Norton, 1991. Especially strong on the domestic considerations of SALT.

Edmonds, Robin. *Soviet Foreign Policy: The Brezhnev Years.* New York: Oxford University Press, 1983. A useful introduction to Brezhnev's foreign policy.

Gaddis, John Lewis. *Strategies of Containment: A Critical Appraisal of Postwar American National Security Policy.* New York: Oxford University Press, 1982. Helpful for placing SALT in the context of Cold War security issues.

Hoff-Wilson, Joan. *Nixon Reconsidered.* New York: Basic Books, 1994. A lucid and authoritative treatment of Nixon's thinking on SALT.

Lefeber, Walter. *The American Age: United States Foreign Policy at Home and Abroad since 1750.* New York: W. W. Norton, 1994. A colorfully written diplomatic history complete with political cartoons and an extensive bibliography.

Patterson, James T. *Grand Expectations: The United States, 1945–1974.* New York: Oxford University Press, 1996. A solid appraisal with an excellent bibliography.

75. OPEC AND THE OIL PRICE SHOCK, 1973

Prompted by **Standard Oil of New Jersey**'s decision to reduce oil prices, **Abdullah Tariki, Saudi Arabia**'s director of oil and mining affairs, and **Juan Pablo Pérez Alfonzo, Venezuela**'s minister of mines and hydrocarbons, met on 9 September 1960 to found the **Organization of Petroleum Exporting Countries (OPEC)**. OPEC's goal was to coordinate oil policies, levels of production, and market prices, thereby giving the oil exporting countries some leverage against companies such as Standard Oil. Eventually seventeen other oil-producing countries, including **Iran, Iraq**, and **Kuwait**, joined OPEC.

For its first decade OPEC exerted little influence. By 1963 both Tariki and Alfonzo had resigned and **Ahmed Zaki Yamani**, Saudi Arabia's new oil minister, became OPEC's chief spokesman. In 1967 when **Israel** attacked **Egypt, Jordan**, and **Syria**, OPEC's **oil embargo** directed at the **United States, Great Britain**, and **western Europe** had little effect. This was not the case in October 1973, when Egypt attacked Israel. Now OPEC's oil embargo, aimed at the industrialized world, accompanied by severe cuts in oil production and a series of price hikes, immediately affected world oil supply. Western Europe, Japan, and the United States all ran short of oil. In December 1973, OPEC raised the price of its oil from $5.12 to $11.65 a barrel and announced further cuts in production.

For the first time since World War II Americans waited in long lines at gas stations. The **Nixon administration** urged electrical generating stations to shift from oil to coal, and for the first time Americans spoke of an **"energy crisis."** The economies of Europe and Japan began to slow down, and the threat of a worldwide recession affected world financial markets. Books such as E. F. Schumacher's *Small Is Beautiful* (1973), a plea for a simpler life, became huge bestsellers. Slowly the effect of the oil shock and the power of OPEC began to diminish. Despite Yamani's leadership OPEC members were unable to agree on common price and production levels.

In March 1975, **King Faisal** of Saudi Arabia was assassinated by one of his nephews. Later that year a band of terrorists shot their way into OPEC's Vienna offices, kidnapped Yamani, and flew him to Algiers before releasing him. Fearful that the terrorists might have been sponsored by Arab governments who resented his role in OPEC, Yamani sought better relations with the United States and resisted moves within OPEC to raise oil prices. But by 1980 a barrel of OPEC oil cost $30.00, a price that most industrialized nations could still afford in large part because the price shocks of 1973 had underscored the need for energy conservation and the value of a comprehensive national energy policy.

Suggestions for Term Papers

1. How did President Nixon and his administration deal with the oil price shock of 1973? How did American consumers react to this crisis?

2. Why would Schumacher's *Small Is Beautiful* (see Suggested Sources) become such a popular book in the 1970s? Evaluate its arguments and provide reasons for your position.

3. During the 1970s and 1980s Ahmed Zaki Yamani, Saudi Arabia's oil minister and OPEC's spokesman, was regarded as one of the most powerful men in the world (see Suggested Sources). Investigate the sources of his power and decide whether he was as powerful as the press portrayed him as being.

4. Spurred by the prospect of diminished petroleum sources, some automobile companies have begun to manufacture cars powered by alternative fuels. How successful has this been? What is the present status of alternative fuels?

5. President Carter, as a result of the oil price shock, began to develop a national energy policy. What reasons did President Reagan give for not continuing the policy?

6. All industrial nations except for the United States have a comprehensive energy policy. Organize a debate on whether the United States should have a national energy policy or not.

Research Suggestions

In addition to the boldfaced items, look under the entries for "The Six-Day War, 1967" (#66), "Terrorism in the 1970s" (#78), "Chernobyl, 1986" (#86), and "The 1992 Earth Summit in Rio" (#94). Search under **energy crisis** and **Desert Storm**.

SUGGESTED SOURCES

Primary Sources

OPEC: Official Resolutions and Press Releases, 1960–1990. Vienna: Organization of Petroleum Exporting Countries, 1990. A good starting point for OPEC's policies.

OPEC Series. Vienna: OPEC, 1989– . First published in 1989, this is an annual report of OPEC policy papers.

Secondary Sources

Amuzegar, Jahangir. *Managing the Oil Wealth: OPEC's Windfalls and Pitfalls.* London: I. B. Tauris, 1999. Highlights the unpredictable character of OPEC's history.

Evans, John. *OPEC: Its Member States and the World Energy Market.* Detroit: Gale Research, 1986. Scholarly profiles of OPEC countries and their economic impact.

Feldman, David Lewis. *The Energy Crisis: Unresolved Issues and Enduring Legacies.* Baltimore: Johns Hopkins University Press, 1996. A useful examination of the effects of the energy crisis on America.

Fink, Gary M., and Hugh Davis Graham, eds. *The Carter Presidency: Policy Choices in the Post-New Deal Era.* Lawrence: University of Kansas Press, 1998. Thomas J. Sugrue's essay is a helpful examination of the Carter energy policy.

Ghanem, Shukri Mohammed. *OPEC: The Rise and Fall of an Exclusive Club.* London: Routledge and Kegan Paul, 1986. A brief history of OPEC.

Karl, Terry Lynn. *The Paradox of Plenty: Oil Booms and Petro-States.* Berkeley: University of California Press, 1997. A good look at OPEC in the 1990s.

Robinson, Jeffrey. *Yamani: The Inside Story.* New York: Atlantic Monthly Press, 1989. A reliable biography of OPEC's most authoritative leader.

Salman, Khalik. *A Macroeconomics Model and Stabilisation Policies of the OPEC Countries: With Special Reference to the Iraqi Economy.* Aldershot, England: Ashgate, 1999. An examination of OPEC's economic policies in the 1990s.

Schumacher, Ernst Friedrich. *Small Is Beautiful: Economics as If People Mattered.* New York: Harper and Row, 1973. A powerful argument that consumption does not bring happiness.

Skeet, Ian. *OPEC: Twenty-Five Years of Prices and Politics.* Cambridge: Cambridge University Press, 1988. An accessible history of OPEC's worldwide influence.

Terzian, Pierre. *OPEC: The Inside Story.* Translated by Michael Pallis. London: Zed, 1985. An explanation of how OPEC sets policy.

Tugwell, Franklin. *The Energy Crisis and the American Political Economy: Politics and Markets in the Management of Natural Resources.* Stanford: Stanford University Press, 1988. A comprehensive study of how the energy crisis has shaped American trade policy.

Yergin, Daniel. *The Prize: The Epic Quest for Oil, Money, and Power.* New York: Touchstone, 1993. Solid chapters on OPEC and an excellent bibliography.

76. THE OVERTHROW OF SALVADOR ALLENDE IN CHILE, 1973

Trained as a physician, **Salvador Allende** (1908–1973) was one of the founders of Chile's **Socialist Party**. As the leader of the leftist coalition **Popular Action Front**, Allende failed to win the presidential elections of 1958 and 1964. In the election of 1970, however, Allende won a thin 36 percent plurality. This was enough to ensure that he would become the first Marxist president of Chile. Allende's agenda included an aggressive policy of land reform, nationalization of large foreign companies, including the American-owned **Anaconda Copper Mining Company**, raising workers' wages, and freezing prices.

In 1972, however, three problems emerged. First, a fall in world copper prices severely weakened Chile's economy. Second, many business leaders, large landowners, and the media attacked Allende's policies in the press, on the radio, and in the Congress. Many of his conservative critics began to look to the military for new political leadership. Third, Allende's takeover of American-owned companies operating in Chile angered the Nixon administration. **President Richard Nixon** and his national security adviser, **Henry Kissinger**, refused to accept the fact that Chile could elect a Marxist president. Kissinger publicly stated, "I don't see why we have to let a country go Marxist just because its people are irresponsible."

Initially resorting to economic measures, the Nixon administration wanted to bring down Allende and blocked international loans earmarked for Chile. Nixon also authorized the **Central Intelligence Agency (CIA)** to spend $10 million to "destabilize" the Allende government. The CIA gave more than $8 million to Allende's political opponents, strengthened ties with the Chilean military, and subsidized a national truck drivers' strike as well as an employers' lock-out of workers.

By 1973 Chile's economy was in shambles. The Nixon Administration's destabilization policies had undermined Chile's economy and weakened Allende's control. Inflation was running at 150 percent; a series of strikes, lock-outs and poor harvests had increased unemployment and disrupted government services. Yet, despite these problems, in the March 1973 elections Allende's party won 43 percent of the vote. To placate conservatives in the military, Allende appointed **General Augusto Pinochet** as chief of staff. Pinochet warned Allende that unless he changed his economic policies the military would seize power. Allende refused to change course. On 11 September 1973, Pinochet ordered an attack on the presidential palace in Santiago. Allende was in the palace and died in the attack. It remains unclear if he was murdered or committed suicide.

Pinochet, who ruled Chile as dictator from 1973 to 1990, immediately instituted a free-market economic policy. He also began a vigorous crackdown on Allende's supporters, journalists, and virtually all opposition groups at home and abroad. Pinochet's National Intelligence Directorate or **DINA** embarked on a policy of terror and repression that resulted in the death or dissappearance of more that 4,000 people. One blatant example was the car bombing by security forces that killed **Orlando Letellier**, Allende's foreign minister, in September 1976, in Washington, D.C.

Suggestions for Term Papers

1. Investigate the holdings of the Anaconda Copper Mining Company in Chile in the 1970s and Allende's reasons for nationalizing the company.

2. Why did the Nixon administration decide to take an anti-Allende position? Evaluate its reasons for doing this.

3. In a research project on General Pinochet's coup in 1973 and the death of Allende, pay particular attention to the role played by the CIA.

4. The Pinochet regime was criticized for its record of human rights violations. Among the most blatant was the car bombing that killed Orlando Letellier and an American associate in Washington, D.C. Do a research project on the involvement of DINA in this act and the U. S. government's official response. Was the response appropriate? Provide reasons for the position you take.

5. After reviewing the evidence in the case of the disappearance of Charles Horman, an American journalist, while covering the aftermath of Pinochet's coup, write an essay discussing what you think happened and why it happened. Defend the position you

take. Use Thomas Hauser's book as a starting point (see Suggested Sources).

6. Some scholars argue that Pinochet's human rights abuses must be balanced against his economic record. After reviewing Pinochet's economic policies and the performance of the Chilean economy during his time as dictator (see Suggested Sources), write a paper commenting on the impact of his economic policies.

Research Suggestions

In addition to the boldfaced items, look under the entries for "The Guatemalan Coup, 1954" (#50) and "Fidel Castro and the Cuban Revolution, 1959" (#57). Search under **Isabel Allende, Ariel Dorfmann**, and **human rights**.

SUGGESTED SOURCES

Primary Sources

Allende, Salvador. *Chile's Road to Socialism.* Translated by J. Darling. Baltimore: Penguin Books 1973. Allende's explanation of his policies.

Debray, Régis. *The Chilean Revolution: Conversations with Allende.* New York: Pantheon Books, 1972. Candid revelations by Allende on how he wanted to bring socialism to Chile.

Report of the Chilean National Commission on Truth and Reconciliation. 2 vols. Translated by Phillip E. Berryman. Notre Dame, Ind.: University of Notre Press, 1993. A chilling collection of accounts verifying Pinochet's extensive human rights abuses.

United States Congress. House Committee on Foreign Affairs. Subcommittee on Inter-American Affairs. *United States and Chile During the Allende Years, 1970–1973.* Washington: Government Printing Office, 1975. Wide-ranging testimony of the implications of the Nixon administration's policies.

Secondary Sources

Davis, Nathaniel. *The Last Two Years of Salvador Allende.* Ithaca: Cornell University Press, 1985. Provides a good understanding of Allende's economic and political problems.

De Vylder, Stefan. *Allende's Chile: The Political Economy of the Rise and Fall of the Unidad Popular.* Cambridge: Cambridge University Press, 1974. Focuses on the economic conditions that brought Allende to power.

Falcoff, Mark. *Modern Chile, 1970–1989: A Critical History.* New Brunswick, N.J.: Transaction, 1989. A good introduction to Allende's place in Chilean history.

Hauser, Thomas. *The Execution of Charles Horman: An American Sacrifice.* New York: Harcourt Brace Jovanovich, 1978. This case of an American journalist, who was probably executed in Chile for his reporting on the Pinochet regime, prompted his father to sue Secretary of State Henry Kissinger and formed the basis for the 1982 Costa-Gavras film *Missing.*

Ramos, Joseph R. *Neoconservative Economics in the Southern Cone of Latin America, 1973–1983.* Baltimore: Johns Hopkins University Press, 1986. Strong on showing how Pinochet's economic policies were part of a trend throughout South America.

Rojas, Róbinson. *The Murder of Allende and the End of the Chilean Way to Socialism.* Translated by Andrée Conrad. New York: Harper and Row, 1976. A critical account of U.S. policy in Chile.

Sigmund, Paul E. *The Overthrow of Allende and the Politics of Chile, 1964–1976.* Pittsburgh: University of Pittsburgh Press, 1977. Balanced and well written. A good starting point for understanding Allende's policies.

World Wide Web

"The National Security Archive." *http://www.gwu.edu/~nsarchiv.* Key United States government documents on Pinochet's coup.

77. THE HELSINKI ACCORDS, 1975

The **Helsinki Accords** or the **Helsinki Final Act** signed on 1 August 1975 concluded the first **Conference on Security and Cooperation in Europe (CSCE).** Thirty-five nations signed the document, including every country in Europe (except Albania) and the United States and Canada. It may be seen as the high point of **détente,** the efforts by countries involved in the **Cold War** to find areas of agreement and ways of lessening tension.

The members of the **Warsaw Treaty Organization,** the alliance dominated by the Soviet Union, had pressed for a conference on security issues since the 1960s. In 1973, after preparatory talks, foreign ministers met in Helsinki to begin negotiations. Between 1973 and 1975 committees met in Geneva to work out agreements in three areas or **"baskets."** The first basket concerned security interests and resulted in a declaration that the borders of each European nation were "inviolable." The principle of noninterference in the internal affairs of each nation was also recognized. Additionally, plans were made for **Confidence and Security Building Measures (CSBMs)**, which might involve, for example, exchanging military observers.

The second basket, the least controversial, called for cooperation in the areas of trade, technology, science, and the environment, and for cultural exchanges. Basket III, the most controversial, concerned human rights and the free exchange of ideas and people.

For the Soviet Union, the Helsinki Accords furnished an implicit recognition of the postwar settlement in eastern Europe and existing borders. The United States emphasized respect for human rights and the free flow of information. In follow-up meetings of the CSCE, the United States criticized the human rights records of the Soviet Union and its WTO allies. The Soviet Union complained that the United States was violating its pledge of nonintervention in internal affairs of sovereign nations.

After the revolutions in eastern Europe in 1989 and the unification of Germany in 1990, the CSCE summit in Paris that year declared a formal end to the Cold War in the **Charter of Paris for a New Europe**. In the 1990s the CSCE transformed itself into the **Organization for Security and Cooperation in Europe (OSCE)** with headquarters in Prague. While it has played an important role in European affairs in the 1990s, particularly in the area of human rights, it has lost ground in comparison with the central positions of the **North Atlantic Treaty Organization (NATO)** and the **European Union (EU)**.

Suggestions for Term Papers

1. Trace the development of détente in the 1970s up to the Helsinki Accords. Discuss the most important developments that led to the calling of the first Conference on Security and Cooperation in Europe.
2. Compare the motives of the Soviet Union and the United States in agreeing to the Helsinki Accords.
3. Investigate the activities of groups that formed in Czechoslovakia (Charter '77) or the Soviet Union (Helsinki Watch Group) to monitor their government's compliance with the Helsinki Accords.

4. Do a research project on the follow-up meeting of the CSCE at Madrid between 1980 and 1983. In particular, examine the use of the human rights issue by the United States.

5. Write a paper assessing the Charter of Paris for a New Europe (see Suggested Sources).

6. Evaluate the activities of the OSCE in the 1990s and its prospects in the twenty-first century.

Research Suggestions

In addition to the boldfaced items, look under the entries for the "SALT I Agreement, 1972" (#74), "Vaclav Havel and the 'Velvet Revolution,' 1989" (#89), "German Reunification, 1989–1990" (#90), and "The Breakup of the Soviet Union, 1991" (#91). Search under **Ostpolitik, Richard M. Nixon, Henry Kissinger, Andrei Sahkarov, Helsinki Watch Group, Vaclav Havel**, and **Charter '77**.

SUGGESTED SOURCES

Primary Sources

Dobrynin, Anatoly. *In Confidence: Moscow's Ambassador to America's Six Cold War Presidents.* New York: Times Books, 1995. A useful perspective from a participant who was thoroughly familiar with all the issues taken up in the Helsinki Accords.

Nixon, Richard M. *RN: The Memoirs of Richard Nixon.* New York: Grosset and Dunlap, 1978. Invaluable for establishing the political and diplomatic context within which the Helsinki Accords were negotiated.

Secondary Sources

Bundy, William. *A Tangled Web: The Making of Foreign Policy in the Nixon Presidency.* New York: Hill and Wang, 1998. A recent book by a Washington insider that is critical of U.S. foreign policy as practiced by Kissinger and Nixon.

Frankel, Benjamin, ed. *The Cold War, 1945–1991.* 3 vols. Detroit: Gale Research, 1992. A good reference source, particularly for biographies of people who participated in the Cold War.

Froman, Michael B. *The Development of the Idea of Détente: Coming to Terms.* New York: St. Martin's Press, 1991. A good introduction to the topic of détente.

Krieger, Joel, ed. *The Oxford Companion to Politics of the World.* New York: Oxford University Press, 1993. Brief but authoritative and up-to-date articles on various aspects of the Helsinki Accords and CSCE.

Mastny, Vojtech, ed. *Helsinki, Human Rights, and European Security.* Durham, N.C.: Duke University Press, 1986. A useful collection of essays on the most important aspects of the Helsinki Accords.

Ulam, Adam. *Dangerous Relations: The Soviet Union in World Politics, 1970–1982.* New York: Oxford University Press, 1983. An overview of Soviet activities in the international arena by a well-infomed and longtime observer.

Young, John W., ed. *The Longman Companion to Cold War and Détente, 1941–1991.* New York: Longman, 1993. A useful reference work.

World Wide Web

"Homepage of the OSCE [Organization for Security and Cooperation in Europe]." *http://www.osce.org.* A well-organized site with valuable links to CSCE and OSCE documents, including the Charter of Paris for a New Europe, 1990.

78. TERRORISM IN THE 1970s

Terrorism first appeared in the **French Revolution** when **Maximilien Robespierre** declared that "terror" must be used to rid France of its enemies. Robespierre's reign of terror was significant for linking political ideology with state-sponsored violence and insisting that terrorism was a patriotic duty.

Twentieth-century terrorism differs from that of the French Revolution in three respects. First, modern terrorists are relatively few in number. Most terrorist groups number less than three hundred; only a few can count more than five hundred members. Second, contemporary terrorists cannot exist without the media. **Skyjacking**, indiscriminate bombings of public buildings, and the slaughter of women and children are acts that capture a huge media audience, thereby giving a few terrorists the opportunity to instill disproportionate levels of fear in people. Third, identifying terrorists with precision is difficult. Terrorists insist that they are "freedom fighters" or "patriots" and that their enemies incorrectly label them "terrorists."

By the 1970s three distinct kinds of terrorist groups were active. First are **national liberation movements** that use terror against their opponents. The **Irish Republican Army (IRA)**, for example, committed to driving the British out of Ireland, did not shrink from bombing central London. Second are terrorists inspired by **religious**

fundamentalism that attack all emblems of secular culture. In 1979 **Iranian Revolutionary Guards** seized the **American Embassy in Teheran** and held fifty-two Americans hostage for fifteen months because Iran's political leadership labeled the United States "the Great Satan." State-sponsored terrorists striking at political enemies of the regime form a third category. **Libyan terrorists**, supported by their government, have been linked to attacks on French aircraft, the bombing of German nightclubs, and the bombing of **Pan Am Flight 103**, which exploded in 1988 over Lockerbie, Scotland, killing 259 people.

Democratic states that prize individual rights have proved to be more vulnerable to terrorist attacks than authoritarian states. However, **Israel, France**, and **Great Britain**, are three democratic countries that have developed effective procedures to combat terrorism.

Suggestions for Term Papers

1. The 1972 Olympic Games at Munich, Germany, were one of the first examples of how terrorists could capture the attention of the media. In what ways did the terrorists exploit media attention? How did this incident affect future Olympic Games?

2. In January 1976, Israeli anti-terrorist forces flew 2,000 miles to Entebbe, Uganda, to rescue hostages held by terrorists after an airline skyjacking. Investigate the planning and execution of this rescue mission.

3. For a group research project on the American hostages held by Iranian revolutionaries, pay particular attention to the initial seizure of the hostages and to the efforts by the Carter administration, diplomatic and otherwise, to free the hostages.

4. "Carlos the Jackal," born Ilich Ramierez Sanchez in Venezuela, killed more than eighty people over two decades. Review the evidence presented at his 1997 trial in Paris and evaluate the verdict.

5. Delta Force (U.S. military) and the FBI's Hostage Rescue Team (HRT) are two American counterterrorist units. Assess comparatively the effectiveness of the two units in combating terrorism.

6. Of all the counterterrorist units in the world, the elite British Special Air Service (SAS) is regarded as the best counterterrorist force in the world. Investigate the history, organization, training, and

operation of the SAS and write a paper assessing its strengths and weaknesses. Provide reasons for your assessment.

Research Suggestions

In addition to the boldfaced items, look under the entries for "Northern Ireland and 'The Troubles,' 1969–1998" (#71), "The Sandinistas and the Contras in Nicaragua, 1981–1989" (#88), "The Dissolution of Yugoslavia in the 1990s" (#93), and "Genocide in Rwanda, 1994" (#95). Search under **Shining Path, Osama Bin Laden**, and **Muammar Qadhafi**.

SUGGESTED SOURCES

Primary Sources

Patterns of Global Terrorism. Washington, D.C.: U.S. Department of State, 1983. State Department publication documenting terrorism throughout the world. This is updated annually.

Terrorism and Intelligence Operations: Hearing Before the Joint Economic Committee, Congress of the United States, May 20, 1998. Washington, D.C.: Government Printing Office, 1998. One of many major hearings before the U.S. Congress focusing on the economic and political dimensions of terrorist attacks in America.

Secondary Sources

Babkina, A. M. *Terrorism: An Annotated Bibliography*. Commack, N.Y.: Nova Science, 1998. Comprehensive and well organized.

Cameron, Gavin. *Nuclear Terrorism: A Threat Assessment for the Twenty-First Century*. Basingstoke: Macmillan, 1999. An overview of nuclear terrorism and its connections to political violence.

Chaliand, Gerard. *Terrorism: From Popular Struggle to Media Spectacle*. London: Saqi Books, 1985. The author has traveled throughout Africa, Latin America, and the Middle East to research this study. Good bibliography.

Cooley, John K. *Unholy Wars: Afghanistan, America and International Terrorism*. Sterling, Va.: Pluto Press, 1999. Explains America's concerns about Osama Bin Laden.

Falkenrath, Richard A., Robert D. Newman, and Bradley A. Thayer. *America's Achilles' Heel: Nuclear, Biological, and Chemical Terrorism and Covert Attack*. Cambridge, Mass.: MIT Press, 1998. An important reminder of how vulnerable the United States remains to nuclear terrorist attack.

Heymann, Philip B. *Terrorism and America: A Commonsense Strategy for a Democratic Society*. Cambridge, Mass.: MIT Press, 1998. Short and solid in its public policy recommendations.

Laqueur, Walter. *The Age of Terrorism*. Boston: Little, Brown, 1987. Wide-ranging coverage, especially good on developing nations.

———. *The New Terrorism: Fanaticism and the Arms of Mass Destruction*. New York: Oxford University Press, 1999. The best starting point; particularly good bibliography.

Laquer, Walter, and Yonah Alexander, eds. *The Terrorism Reader: A Historical Anthology*. New York: New American Library, 1987. A useful historical review of modern terrorism.

Tanter, Raymond. *Rogue Regimes: Terrorism and Proliferation*. New York: St. Martin's Press, 1998. The best introduction to state-sponsored terrorism.

79. FIRST "TEST-TUBE" BABY BORN, 1978

Louise Joy Brown, the first "test-tube" baby, was born on 25 July 1978 at Oldham Hospital in Oldham, England. At the time she was the first product of a radically new reproductive technique, **in vitro fertilization (ivf)**, pioneered by **Patrick C. Steptoe** (1913–1988), the senior obstetrician and gynecologist at Oldham Hospital, and **Robert Edwards** (1925–   ), a physiologist from Cambridge.

Edwards had been working independently on methods by which a human ovum (egg) might be fertilized outside the womb. After succeeding in doing this for the first time in 1968, he formed a partnership with Dr. Steptoe. Steptoe contributed, among other things, his experience with the **laparoscope**, a fiber-optic device that he had been using for minimally invasive abdominal surgery. He realized that he could use the laparoscope to siphon eggs from an infertile woman.

Edwards and Steptoe succeeded in fertilizing and implanting eggs in women who then became pregnant. All of the first pregnancies ended in miscarriages before ten weeks. Finally, the two decided to implant the embryo (technically, a blastocyst at this point) when it reached the eight-cell stage instead of waiting for one hundred cell divisions to occur.

The ivf protocol quickly became a source of moral, ethical, and religious controversy. The Catholic Church became a major opponent. In 1987 it issued a doctrinal statement opposing ivf for three reasons: (1) it opposed the destruction of human embryos not used for implantation; (2) it opposed ivf by a sperm donor who was not the husband of the woman attempting to become pregnant; and (3) it saw ivf as severing the essential connection between married sex and procreation, which the Church views as sacred.

Many other ethical, moral, and legal questions have been raised since the first test-tube baby was born. At first, the major problem concerned the use of **surrogate mothers**, women willing to carry a fertilized egg to term for a couple. Some surrogate mothers found it difficult to turn over the baby they gave birth to. Careful screening and counseling of potential surrogate mothers have helped with this problem. More recently, some problems have resulted from claims of ownership of **frozen sperm** and **frozen embryos**. Since the ivf protocol often results in multiple births, some observers have raised questions about the wisdom of its use. The major problem now, however, concerns the rapid development of genetic manipulation techniques and the possibility in the near future of using these techniques to create **designer children**.

In the period since the first test-tube baby was born, hundreds of thousands of children have been born through the use of one or another assisted reproduction techniques. These techniques are now available worldwide. They are likely to remain both popular and controversial for decades to come.

Suggestions for Term Papers

1. Investigate the decade between the formation of Edwards and Steptoe's partnership and the birth of Louise Brown. What were some of the obstacles that had to be overcome before a successful birth could occur?

2. Interview couples who have used ivf protocols to have children about their experiences.

3. Do a research project on the position of the Catholic Church on assisted reproduction (see Suggested Sources).

4. Review decisions in court cases involving surrogate mothers and write a paper outlining how you would rule in the cases.

5. Interview doctors who use ivf protocols about the latest developments in assisted reproduction.

6. Write a short story that speculates on the choices women and men in the year 2015 may have when they decide to have children.

Research Suggestions

In addition to the boldfaced items, look under the entries for "Dolly the Sheep Cloned, 1997" (#96) and "John Paul II's First Twenty Years as Pope, 1978–1999" (#98). Search under **Peter Singer, Jeremy Rifkin**, and *On the Value and Inviolability of Human Life* (*Evangelium Vitae*, papal encyclical, 25 March 1995).

SUGGESTED SOURCES

Primary Sources

Brown, Lesley. *Our Miracle Called Louise: A Parents' Story*. New York: Grosset and Dunlap, 1984. The story of the first test-tube baby from the perspective of the parents.

Edwards, R. G., and Patrick Steptoe. *A Matter of Life: The Story of a Medical Breakthrough*. New York: Morrow, 1980. The story of the first test-tube baby from the perspective of the doctors.

Secondary Sources

Charlesworth, M. J. *Bioethics in a Liberal Society*. New York: Cambridge University Press, 1993. A good overview of the ethical questions involved in ivf and other techniques.

Coughlan, Michael J. *The Vatican, the Law and the Human Embryo*. Basingstoke, England: Macmillan, 1990. A good introduction to the position taken by the Catholic Church.

Flynn, Eileen P. *Human Fertilization in Vitro: A Catholic Moral Perspective*. Lanham, Md.: University Press of America, 1984. A good discussion of the Catholic position.

Gosden, Roger. *Designing Babies: The Brave New World of Reproductive Technology*. New York: W. H. Freeman, 1999. Gosden, once an associate of Robert Edwards, presents, in nontechnical language, the latest information on reproductive technology.

Holmes, Helen Bequaert, ed. *Issues in—Reproductive Technology I: An Anthology*. New York: Garland Press, 1992. A convenient collection of articles on controversies associated with reproductive technology.

Marsh, Margaret, and Wanda Ronner. *The Empty Cradle: Infertility in America from Colonial Times to the Present*. Baltimore: Johns Hopkins University Press, 1996. The problem of infertility from a historical perspective.

Rifkin, Jeremy. *The Biotech Century: Harnessing the Gene and Remaking the World*. New York: Putnam Publishing Group, 1998. A warning about the dangers of biotechnology by an influential futurist.

Rosenberg, Helane S., and Yakov M. Epstein. *Getting Pregnant When You Thought You Couldn't: The Interactive Guide that Helps You Up the Odds*. New York: Warner, 1993. One of many guides to the array of possibilities currently available in reproductive technology.

Singer, Peter, ed. *Embryo Experimentation*. New York: Cambridge University Press, 1990. Best known as an animal rights advocate, Singer is also at the forefront of controversy about ivf and other medical techniques.

World Wide Web

"Catholic Information Center on Internet." *http://catholic.net*. Links to many Church documents including *On the Value and Inviolability of Human Life*, the papal encyclical from 1995.

"INCIID (International Council on Infertility Information Dissemination)." *http://www.inciid.org*. A convenient source for all kinds of information on infertility and assisted reproduction.

80. AYATOLLAH RUHOLLAH KHOMEINI AND THE IRANIAN REVOLUTION, 1979

Ruhollah Khomeini (1900?–1989) was born into a devout **Shiite Muslim** family in rural Iran. Trained as an Islamic scholar, he taught and wrote extensively on Islamic philosophy. By 1960 he had been awarded the title **Ayatollah**, or supreme Shiite religious scholar. He had also become the leading political spokesman of Iran's Shiite Muslim community. Because of his repeated criticism of **Shah Reza Pahlavi**, Iran's ruler, Khomeini was forced into exile in 1964.

Khomeini's criticism won greater Iranian popular support in the late 1970s, when the Shah's heavy-handed repression of political opposition sparked a series of protests in **Teheran**, the capital of Iran. In January 1978, Khomeini's supporters took to the streets of Teheran and clashed with police. Finally, on 16 January 1979, the Shah and his family fled Iran. On 1 February 1979, Khomeini returned to Teheran and was acclaimed as supreme religious leader of the Iranian Revolution.

Although Khomeini never formally held political office, he ruled Iran and presided over its Shiite Islamic-inspired revolution. Key elements of his revolution were investing power in the hands of Khomeini's **Islamic Republican Party** and his **Revolutionary Guards;** establishing a new legal system based on a strict Shiite interpretation of the **Koran** and the **Shariah** (Islamic law); repressing all opposition; forcing Iranian women to discard Western dress and wear traditional Muslim clothing; and exporting this new Shiite Islamic revolution to other Muslim countries.

When Islamic militants seized the U.S. Embassy in Teheran in November 1979 and kept **fifty-two Americans hostage** for fifteen months, Khomeini praised the militants for humiliating America, the "Great Satan." The hostage crisis added to Khomeini's stature in Iran, but it did not receive widespread support in neighboring Muslim countries. One of his neighbors, **President Saddam Hussein** of **Iraq**, increasingly viewed Khomeini's Shiite revolution as a threat. In September 1980 Iraq attacked Iran. Between 1980 and 1988, Iran and Iraq were locked in a bloody, fratricidal war that killed more than 300,000 Iranians. But even while fighting Iraq, Khomeini continued to act as the protector of Islamic orthodoxy throughout the world. After concluding the war with Iraq on 14 February 1989, Khomeini declared **Salman Rushdie**, a British citizen and author of *The Satanic Verses*, guilty of blasphemy for including a character parodying the life of Muhammad and for questioning the accuracy of the Koran. Khomeini offered a $6 million reward to any Muslim who would execute Rushdie.

Despite the huge losses in the long war with Iraq and the economic, political, and religious dislocations accompanying his revolution, Khomeini remained Iran's unquestioned and revered political leader until his death in 1989.

Suggestions for Term Papers

1. How did Khomeini use the beliefs of the Shiite Muslim religious tradition as the basis for his political revolution?

2. Should the Shah of Iran have stayed in his country in 1979, or was it better for Iran that he left? Provide reasons for your position.

3. Measured against other twentieth-century revolutions, how would you evaluate Khomeini's Iranian Revolution?

4. Assess the Carter administration's response to the seizure of the American Embassy and the taking of American hostages.

5. How effective was Khomeini as a leader in Iran's war against Iraq?

6. Read *The Satanic Verses* (see Suggested Sources) and write a paper discussing Khomeini's condemnation of Salman Rushdie for writing the book.

Research Suggestions

In addition to the boldfaced items, look under the entries for "Terrorism in the 1970s" (#78) and "The Iran-Iraq War, 1980–1988" (#85). Search under **Abu al-Hasan, Bani Sadr, Cyrus Vance,** and **Hostage Crisis**.

SUGGESTED SOURCES

Primary Sources

Algar, Hamid, ed. and trans. *Islam and Revolution: Writings and Declarations of Imam Khomeini*. Berkeley: Mizan Press, 1981. An accessible collection of Khomeini's writings from the exile period and the 1970s.

Harney, Desmond. *The Priest and the King: An Eyewitness Account of the Iranian Revolution*. London: British Academic Press, 1998. This is the daily diary of a British diplomat based in Teheran in 1979. Excellent coverage of the fall of the Shah and a useful bibliography.

Khomeini, Ruhollah. *Khomeini Speaks Revolution*. Translated by N. M. Shaikh. Karachi: International Islamic Publishers, 1981. Key statements of Khomeini on revolutionary government.

Shariati, Ali. *Reflections of Humanity: Two Views of Civilization and the Plight of Man*. Houston: Free Islamic Literatures Book Distribution Center, 1980. Dr. Shariati was the ideologue of Iran's Islamic revolution. His writings enjoyed enormous influence with Iranian intellectuals.

Secondary Sources

Bakhash, Shaul. *The Reign of the Ayatollahs: Iran and the Islamic Revolution*. New York: Basic Books, 1986. A concise explanation of Khomeini's revolutionary agenda.

Bill, James A. *The Eagle and the Lion: The Tragedy of American-Iranian*

Relations. New Haven: Yale University Press, 1988. A clear and comprehensive study based on firsthand research in Iran during the hostage crisis.

Milani, Mohsen M. *The Making of Iran's Islamic Revolution: From Monarchy to Islamic Republic.* 2nd ed. Boulder: Westview Press, 1994. Authoritative analysis of the causes of the revolution and Khomeini's consolidation of power.

Pipes, Daniel. *The Rushdie Affair: The Novel, the Ayatollah, and the West.* New York: Carol Publishing Group, 1990. A perceptive analysis of the connections between politics and censorship.

Ramazani, R. R. *Revolutionary Iran: Challenge and Response in the Middle East.* Baltimore: Johns Hopkins University Press, 1987. Written by the premier American scholar of Iran, this remains a standard interpretation.

Rushdie, Salman. *The Satanic Verses.* New York: Viking, 1989. Because of the many humorous references to Muslims and Islam, Khomeini considered this large, complicated novel blasphemous.

Schahgaldian, Nikola B. *The Iranian Military under the Islamic Republic.* Santa Monica: Rand Corp., 1987. A reliable survey complete with interviews with Iranian officers.

Sick, Gary. *All Fall Down: America's Tragic Encounter with Iran.* New York: Random House, 1985. A member of the Carter administration's view of America's failed policy.

Stoessinger, John G. *Why Nations Go to War.* 7th ed. New York: St. Martin's Press, 1998. Chapter 6 treats Iraq's war with Iran.

81. MARGARET THATCHER AND THE CONSERVATIVE REVOLUTION IN BRITAIN, 1979–1990

Margaret Thatcher (1925–   ), the longest serving British prime minister of the twentieth century, was born into a middle-class family, educated at **Oxford University** as a chemist, and elected as a **Conservative Member** of **Parliament** in 1959. As party leader she led the Conservatives to electoral victory in 1979, thereby becoming the first female prime minister in British history. For the next eleven years, she set about dismantling Britain's cradle-to-grave welfare state.

Her conservative revolution focused on three targets. First, she reduced inheritance and business tax rates. Second, she was determined to break the political and economic power of trade unions by supporting the secret ballot in union elections, limiting the length of strikes, and encouraging workers not to join unions. She made a special example of the **Coal Miners' Union** by closing unprofitable mines and cutting off government subsidies to miners. Third, she was determined to sell off government-owned industry and to privatize public housing. By 1987 more than ten state enterprises, including **British Airways, British Telecom**, and **Jaguar** automobiles, had been sold to private investors. By selling off large amounts of government housing, she widened the Conservative Party's support among new homeowners and encouraged workers, particularly in the depressed English Midlands, to move to the more prosperous South of England, where more jobs and better housing were available. Margaret Thatcher's conservative revolution made deep cuts in the welfare state, but, because of popular opposition, she was unable to bring radical change to education or the **National Health Service**.

In foreign affairs Thatcher was decisive and popular for sending thousands of troops to repel **Argentina**'s 1982 invasion of the **Falkland Islands**. She was, however, unable to find a solution to the sectarian violence in British-governed **Northern Ireland**. By 1990 Margaret Thatcher appeared to have lost touch with her electorate. Despite Britain's popular interest in Europe, she refused to join discussions aimed at a common European currency. Despite street riots and warnings from her advisors, she insisted on replacing the traditional graduated household tax with an unpopular standard-rate **"poll tax."** In November 1990 she resigned as party leader and six months later announced she would not seek reelection to the House of Commons. She did, however, ensure that **John Major**, her handpicked successor, replaced her as party leader and as Conservative prime minister. Although not entirely successful at privatizing all state services, Margaret Thatcher did break the power of the trade unions, thereby forcing the **Labour Party** to adopt a more moderate and centrist agenda, and she did demonstrate to the world that a female prime minister could govern Great Britain as well (or better) as any of her male contemporaries.

Suggestions for Term Papers

1. How successful was privatization for former state-owned companies in Great Britain? Investigate the economic fortunes of British

Airways, British Telecom, or Jaguar automobiles since they were privatized.

2. Some observers have argued that North Sea oil revenues paid for Margaret Thatcher's conservative revolution. Assess the importance of these revenues for funding the conservative revolution.

3. Discuss Margaret Thatcher's decision to break the Coal Miners' Union and evaluate her handling of the dispute.

4. Organize a debate on the Argentine attack on the Falkland (Malvinas) Islands and the British response.

5. Margaret Thatcher and President Ronald Reagan were very supportive of one another. How much in common did they have ideologically? Which was more successful in carrying out a conservative revolution?

6. Margaret Thatcher's conservative revolution failed to privatize the British National Health Service. What reasons can you suggest for this?

Research Suggestions

In addition to the boldfaced items, look under the entries for "The Suffrage Movement in Britain Before World War I, 1906–1914" (#6), "Northern Ireland and 'The Troubles,' 1969–1998" (#71), and "OPEC and the Oil Price Shock, 1973" (#75). Search under **British Labour Party, North Sea Oil,** and **Tony Blair.**

SUGGESTED SOURCES

Primary Sources

Thatcher, Margaret. *The Downing Street Years.* London: HarperCollins, 1993. The starting point for understanding her conservative revolution.
———. *In Defence of Freedom: Speeches on Britain's Relations with the World, 1976–1986.* Buffalo, N.Y.: Prometheus Books, 1987. A slim collection of speeches suggesting how close she and President Ronald Reagan were in their views.
———. *The Path to Power.* London: HarperCollins, 1995. Candid reflections on her rise to power and early years in politics.
———. *The Revival of Britain: Speeches on Home and European Affairs,*

1975–1988. Compiled by Alistair B. Cooke. London: Aurum, 1989. These convey the forthright appeal of Mrs. Thatcher's policies.

Secondary Sources

Cannadine, David. *History in Our Time.* New Haven: Yale University Press, 1998. Includes an excellent chapter on Margaret Thatcher and her politics.

Evans, Eric J. *Thatcher and Thatcherism.* New York: Routledge, 1997. A crisp introduction to her conservative revolution.

Kavanagh, Dennis. *The Reordering of British Politics: Politics after Thatcher.* New York: Oxford University Press, 1997. A balanced assessment of her influence through the 1990s.

Monaghan, David. *The Falklands War: Myth and Countermyth.* New York: St. Martin's Press, 1998. Questions the validity of Thatcher's Falkland strategy.

Pierson, Paul. *Dismantling the Welfare State? Reagan, Thatcher, and the Politics of Retrenchment.* New York: Cambridge University Press, 1996. Helpful in showing the ideological connections between the two conservative leaders.

Reitan, E. A. *Tory Radicalism: Margaret Thatcher, John Major, and the Transformation of Modern Britain, 1979–1997.* Lanham, Md.: Rowman and Littlefield, 1997. Places Mrs. Thatcher in the context of the conservative tradition.

Urban, G. R. *Diplomacy and Disillusion at the Court of Margaret Thatcher: An Insider's View.* New York: St. Martin's Press, 1996. A critical look at Mrs. Thatcher's revolution.

82. SOLIDARITY IN POLAND, 1980–1990

The trade union movement known as **Solidarity** first appeared in August 1980. It was a response to events of the 1970s, first the strikes protesting the increase in food prices in 1970 and then a similar set of events in 1976. In 1976 the intelligentsia offered assistance to the workers in the form of the **Workers' Defense Committee (KOR)**. The Catholic Church also offered help.

One other event before the beginnings of Solidarity in 1980 helped to prepare the way. In 1978 **Karol Cardinal Wojtyla** was elected to serve as **Pope John Paul II**. His pastoral visit to Poland in 1979 attracted enthusiastic crowds.

The 1980 strikes began in the **Lenin Shipyard** in Gdansk. From the beginning, the central figure was an electrician, **Lech Walesa**, who had already gained a reputation as an activist. Walesa excelled both in speaking to large groups and in negotiating. With the help of people from KOR, Walesa won a twenty-one-point agreement, the **Gdansk Agreement**, that allowed Solidarity to exist as an independent, self-governing trade union.

Over the next few months millions of workers around Poland joined Solidarity. It gained enormous power even though it was not formally part of the political system. The **Polish United Workers Party (PUWP)**, as the Polish Communist Party was known, found itself constantly on the defensive. There was some fear the Soviet Union would invade as it had in the case of Czechoslovakia in 1968. Finally, **General Wojciech Jaruzelski** declared martial law on 13 December 1981. He has claimed that this was necessary to forestall a Soviet invasion. The leaders of Solidarity were arrested and held without trial for varying lengths of time. Solidarity was forced to go underground, but it managed to preserve itself as an organization over the next several years. Walesa remained in the public eye. In 1983 he was awarded the Nobel Peace Prize.

By 1988 the Polish government under Jaruzelski had reached a dead end. The only recourse seemed to be discussions with Solidarity, which took place in the spring of 1989. The talks resulted in Solidarity again becoming a legal organization and participating in elections that summer. Solidarity was overwhelmingly successful in the elections. **Tadeusz Mazowiecki**, one of its members, became prime minister. Walesa was elected president the following year.

Walesa and Solidarity were better at being the opposition than governing. Walesa, especially, did not contribute that much to the difficult transition period to democracy and free enterprise. Nevertheless, both he and Solidarity had changed Polish history and had contributed to changes in the history of the Soviet bloc.

Suggestions for Term Papers

1. Edward Gierek replaced Wladyslaw Gomulka as first secretary of the Polish Communist Party in 1970 after the first strikes and set out to improve the standard of living. His failure to do this led to strikes in 1976 and again in 1980. Investigate his economic policies and write a report on what went wrong.

2. What did the Polish Catholic Church do in the 1970s to contribute to the success of Solidarity in 1980?

3. As a group project, do a presentation on the strikes, negotiations, and agreement of August 1980. One possibility might take the form of news reports and interviews.

4. There is some controversy about whether General Wojciech Jaruzelski had only a choice between a Soviet invasion and declaration of martial law (see Suggested Sources). Survey the evidence and draw your own conclusions as to the necessity of martial law.

5. Examine Lech Walesa's career from the late 1970s to the end of his term as president. What were his main contributions to Solidarity?

6. Survey the events of 1989 in Poland. How significant was Solidarity's willingness to participate in the talks, first, and then the elections, later? What dangers did it face in doing so?

Research Suggestions

In addition to the boldfaced items, look under the entries for "The Prague Spring, 1968" (#70) and "John Paul II's First Twenty Years as Pope, 1978–1999" (#98). Search under **Jacek Kuron, Adam Michnik, Edward Gierek, Stanislaw Kania, Warsaw Treaty Organization (WTO)**, and **Leonid Brezhnev**.

SUGGESTED SOURCES

Primary Sources

Michnik, Adam. *Letters from Prison and Other Essays*. Berkeley: University of California Press, 1985. Michnik was one of Solidarity's most important advisors from the intelligentsia.

Walesa, Lech. *The Struggle and the Triumph: An Autobiography*. New York: Arcade, 1992. Walesa's perspective on the heroic events of the 1980s.

Secondary Sources

Ascherson, Neal. *The Polish August: The Self-Limiting Revolution*. New York: Viking Press, 1982. An excellent introduction although now somewhat dated.

Boyes, Roger. *The Naked President: A Political Life of Lech Walesa*. London: Secker and Warburg, 1994. A good introduction to the central figure in Solidarity.

Garton Ash, Timothy. *The Magic Lantern: The Revolution of '89 Witnessed in Warsaw, Budapest, Berlin and Prague.* New York: Random House, 1990. Brilliant reporting from an observer who was often at the very center of events.

———. *The Polish Revolution.* New ed. London: Penguin, 1999. A well-informed study of Solidarity.

Man of Iron. Directed by Andrzej Wajda. MGM/UA Home Video. 140 minutes. Based on the strike in Gdansk in 1980. Filmed in 1981.

Rosenberg, Tina. *The Haunted Land: Facing Europe's Ghosts after Communism.* New York: Random House, 1995. Includes a long and fascinating section on Jaruzelski and whether the declaration of martial law was necessary.

Stokes, Gale, ed. *From Stalinism to Pluralism: A Documentary History of Eastern Europe since 1945.* 2nd ed. New York: Oxford University Press, 1996. A highly useful selection of documents that places 1989 in context.

Weschler, Lawrence. *Solidarity: Poland in the Season of Its Passion.* New York: Simon and Schuster, 1982. A very readable, solid account.

83. THE SPREAD OF AIDS IN THE 1980s

AIDS (acquired immunodeficiency syndrome), a term first used in 1982, is the last stage of a disorder of the immune system caused by **HIV (human immunodeficiency virus)**. During this stage, the immune system is no longer able to counter the malignancies and infections that lead to death.

The first cases identified in the United States as AIDS were in 1981 in Los Angeles. Since most of these cases were diagnosed in homosexual men or in intravenous drug users, many assumed that the disease was confined to homosexuals and drug addicts. Some concluded that it was God's punishment. In fact, 70 percent of the cases now reported worldwide originate through heterosexual intercourse.

HIV was isolated in 1983 by the **Institut Pasteur** in France. In 1985 serologic tests that could detect the virus appeared. That same year the first **International Conference on AIDS** took place in Atlanta.

For several years the medical community could do little in AIDS cases other than treat the infections and malignancies as they occurred in patients. Efforts to deal with AIDS focused on prevention by recommending sexual abstinence, monogamy, **"safe sex,"** and campaigns to stop drug addicts from sharing needles.

In 1987 **AZT (azidothymidine)** was approved by the Food and Drug Administration (FDA). This and other drugs were used in therapeutic procedures to slow the progress of AIDS. In 1991 the FDA approved another class of drugs, **reverse transcriptase inhibitors**, which worked in a different way to slow AIDS.

At the end of 1996 it was estimated that more than 8 million cases of AIDS worldwide had resulted in 6 million deaths. Another 23 million were infected with HIV. Two parts of the world have particularly high rates of infection. Sub-Saharan Africa accounts for more than 60 percent of the infections. In some countries nearly one-third of the inhabitants are infected. The other area is South and Southeast Asia, where about 20 percent of the global cases have been reported. The possibilities for economic and social disasters, including drastic depopulation, are especially high in **Zimbabwe, Botswana**, and **Namibia**.

The AIDS pandemic has brought out both the best and the worst in people. In France, for example, government health officials in 1985 decided to use tainted blood supplies until a French system for purifying blood became available later that year (in 1992 four health officials went on trial because of this decision; three were found guilty and one acquitted). On the positive side, numerous efforts have been made worldwide to memorialize victims of AIDS and to raise money for AIDS research. AIDS is a disease that has brought into focus countless moral, ethical, social, and legal issues. It will be a source of concern and controversy for decades to come.

Suggestions for Term Papers

1. Write a paper on the origins of HIV, particularly those theories that it jumped from simians to humans (see Suggested Sources).
2. Investigate the controversy surrounding the identification of HIV. Why did an American investigator try to claim credit for identifying HIV and discredit the claims of the Institut Pasteur?
3. Do a research project on the first International Conference on AIDS in Atlanta in 1985. What was known about AIDS and its treatment at that time?
4. In what ways has AIDS changed the lifestyles of homosexual men and women?

5. Many people have become HIV-positive because of blood transfusions. Write a paper about the efforts to make sure blood supplies were safe and untainted (see Suggested Sources) or about the experiences of those infected by tainted blood.

6. For a group research project, examine the efforts by several developed and developing countries to cope with AIDS, and make a comparative report on the findings.

Research Suggestions

In addition to the boldfaced items, look under the entries for "Alexander Fleming and the Discovery of Penicillin, 1928" (#18), "The Discovery of the Double Helical Structure of DNA, 1953" (#49), and "The 1992 Earth Summit in Rio" (#94). Search under **STD (sexually transmitted disease), Kaposi's sarcoma, T4 helper cells, AIDS Memorial Quilt, AmFAR (American Foundation for AIDS Research)**, and **Randy Shilts**.

SUGGESTED SOURCES

Primary Source

Feldman, Douglas A., and Julia Wang Miller, eds. *The AIDS Crisis: A Documentary History.* Westport, Conn.: Greenwood Press, 1998. A convenient source of documents on the history of AIDS.

Secondary Sources

Almond, Brenda, ed. *AIDS: A Moral Issue: The Ethical, Legal and Social Aspects.* 2nd ed. New York: St. Martin's Press, 1996. A useful collection of articles exploring aspects of the AIDS crisis.

And the Band Played On. HBO Video, 1993. Based on the book by Randy Shilts, a wake-up call for many on the subject of AIDS.

Bartlett, John G., Ann K. Finkbeiner, and Johns Hopkins AIDS Clinic. *The Guide to Living with HIV Infection.* 4th ed. Baltimore: Johns Hopkins University Press, 1998. An up-to-date book covering all aspects of coping with AIDS.

Gostin, Lawrence O., and Zita Lazzarini. *Human Rights and Public Health in the AIDS Pandemic.* New York: Oxford University Press, 1997. The authors point out that many who suffer from AIDS lack the resources for effective treatment of the disease.

Hooper, Edward, and Bill Hamilton. *The River: A Journey to the Source of HIV and AIDS.* Boston: Little, Brown, 1999. A long and compelling book. Its thesis is that HIV jumped from simians to humans through the administration of oral polio vaccine in Africa in the 1950s. Controversial but powerful arguments.

Smith, Raymond A., ed. *Encyclopedia of AIDS: A Social, Political, Cultural, and Scientific Record of the HIV Epidemic.* Chicago: Fitzroy Dearborn, 1998. A useful reference source.

Starr, Douglas. *Blood: An Epic History of Medicine and Commerce.* New York: Knopf, 1998. A fascinating book that covers many subjects, including scandals connected with HIV-tainted blood.

Sturken, Marita. *Tangled Memories: The Vietnam War, the AIDS Epidemic, and the Politics of Remembering.* Berkeley: University of California Press, 1997. A thoughtful book on how people make their history through objects like the AIDS Memorial Quilt and the Vietnam Memorial in Washington, D.C.

Ward, Darrell E. *The AmFAR AIDS Handbook.* New York: W. W. Norton, 1998. Information on a wide variety of topics presented in summary form (some of it technical).

Watstein, Sarah Barbara, with Karen Chandler. *AIDS Dictionary.* New York: Facts on File, 1998. A useful reference source.

World Wide Web

"AEGIS." *http://www.aegis.com.* A huge site filled with information on AIDS. Includes links to documents and reports of all kinds and links to articles on AIDS-related events around the world.

84. THE ISRAELI INVASION OF LEBANON, 1982

Lebanon, "the Switzerland of the Middle East," with its beautiful capital at **Beirut**, was a favorite holiday spa in the region. After 1949, however, Lebanon's reputation for tolerance and cultural pluralism was severely tested due to an influx of more than 100,000 **Palestinians** who had fled **Israel**. Because of its distinctive cultural and commercial traditions, Lebanon sought neutrality in the ongoing **Arab-Israeli** conflicts.

Starting in 1968, however, Palestinian commandos residing in south Lebanon launched attacks against Israel. By 1970 **Yasir Arafat**, leader of the **Palestine Liberation Organization (PLO)**, had taken up residence in Beirut. The influx of Palestinian refugees upset the delicate political and economic balance among Lebanese **Christians, Muslims**, and **Druze**, a religious community native to Lebanon. Although many Lebanese Muslims supported the PLO attacks on Israel, Lebanese Christians and the Lebanese government did not, and severe tensions between the PLO and Lebanese developed. In 1975 fighting between Palestinians and **Lebanese Christian militia** erupted in Beirut. Soon Beirut became a city under siege, where thousands of civilians were killed in a deadly and complicated power struggle among the PLO, Muslim, and Christian militias. Quickly this fighting spread, and Lebanon dissolved into a civil war that mirrored the tortured politics of the Middle East. **Syria** was quick to take advantage of the chaos by invading northern Lebanon, and Israel increasingly struck PLO targets in southern Lebanon.

Determined to drive the PLO out of Lebanon, on 6 June 1982 Israel mounted a full-scale invasion. Within a week Israeli forces had crossed the **Litani River** and entered Beirut and had inflicted high casualties on Syrian forces in northern Lebanon. Once in Beirut the Israelis, along with **Lebanese Christian Phalange militias**, began a street-by-street removal of PLO forces. On 21 August 1982 a multinational force of **British, Italian, French**, and **U.S**. soldiers entered Beirut to supervise the withdrawal of all remaining PLO forces to **Tunis**. On 14 September, before they could do so, **Bashir Gemayel**, president of Lebanon, was assassinated; in retaliation for this, Phalange militiamen killed hundreds of Palestinians in the Beirut slums of **Sabra and Shatila**.

On 23 October 1983, 241 U.S. Marines and 58 French soldiers, members of the multinational peacekeeping force, were killed in bomb attacks on their barracks. The international force left Lebanon in 1984; Israeli and Syrian forces began a phased withdrawal from Lebanon in 1985, but in 1999 elements of both forces still remained in Lebanon.

Suggestions for Term Papers

1. Although Christians and Muslims play a large role in Lebanese society, the Druze play a critical role as well. Who are the Druze? Why has this religious minority been so powerful in Lebanon's history?

2. Why were Yasir Arafat and the PLO permitted to establish their

headquarters in Beirut in 1970? What role did Egypt and Jordan have in this decision?

3. Investigate the massacre of Palestinians in the slums of Sabra and Shatila in September 1982. Could it have been prevented?

4. Women played very important roles in this war. Read Miriam Cooke's *War's Other Voices* (see Suggested Sources) and write a paper on the ways in which women reporters viewed the war.

5. Evaluate the effectiveness of the multinational force sent into Beirut to escort the PLO forces to Tunis. Did this force accomplish its mission?

6. How could the suicide bomber penetrate the security of the U.S. Marine barracks and kill 241 Marines? Assess the response of the Reagan administration to the massacre.

Research Suggestions

In addition to the boldfaced items, look under the entries for "The Establishment of the State of Israel, 1948" (#43), "Gamal Abdel Nasser and the Suez Crisis, 1956" (#52), "The Six-Day War, 1967" (#66), "OPEC and the Oil Price Shock, 1973" (#75), and "Terrorism in the 1970s" (#78). Search under **Camille Chamoun, Ariel Sharon**, and **Operation Peace of Galilee**.

SUGGESTED SOURCES

Primary Sources

Weir, Ben, and Carol Weir. *Hostage Bound: Hostage Free*. Philadelphia: Westminster Press, 1987. Poignant account of two missionaries captured in Beirut during the Lebanese civil war.

Yermiya, Dov. *My War Diary: Lebanon June 5–July 1, 1982*. Translated by Daniel Amit. Boston: South End Press, 1983. Candid and disturbing views of the Israeli security coordinator, who was shocked by the violence of the invasion.

Secondary Sources

Alin, Erika G. *The United States and the 1958 Lebanon Crisis: American Intervention in the Middle East*. Lanham, Md.: University Press of America, 1994. An overview of why the United States intervened in the earlier crisis.

Avi-Ran, R. *The Syrian Involvement in Lebanon since 1975*. Translated by

David Maisel. Boulder: Westview Press, 1991. An Israeli scholar's views on Syria's Lebanese policies.

Cobban, Helena. *The Making of Modern Lebanon*. London: Hutchinson Education, 1985. The best starting point for Lebanon's history.

Cooke, Miriam. *War's Other Voices: Women Writers on the Lebanese Civil War*. New York: Cambridge University Press, 1988. Powerful evocation of the effects of war on Lebanese society.

Dupuy, Trevor, and Paul Martell. *Flawed Victory: The Israeli Conflict and the 1982 War in Lebanon*. Fairfax, Va.: Hero Books, 1986. A solid military history of the conflict with a good bibliography.

Evron, Yair. *War and Intervention in Lebanon: The Israeli-Syrian Deterrence Dialogue*. Baltimore: Johns Hopkins University Press, 1987. Chapter 4 is a good overview of the 1982 war.

Hiro, Dilip. *Lebanon: Fire and Embers: A History of the Lebanese Civil War*. New York: St. Martin's Press, 1993. A clear analysis of the complicated struggle.

Jansen, Michael. *The Battle of Beirut: Why Israel Invaded Lebanon*. Boston: South End Press, 1983. A good introduction including maps, time lines, and pictures.

Khalide, Rashid. *Under Siege: P.L.O. Decisionmaking During the 1982 War*. New York: Columbia University Press, 1986. Straightforward account of why the PLO elected to leave Beirut in 1982.

O'Ballance, Edgar. *Civil War in Lebanon, 1975–92*. New York: St. Martin's Press, 1998. Shows the long-term effects of the intervention.

85. THE IRAN-IRAQ WAR, 1980–1988

On 17 September 1980, **Saddam Hussein**, president of Iraq, attacked Iran. Although Saddam's motives are not fully known, at least three reasons prompted his attack. First, he wanted to enlarge his power and sphere of influence in the **Persian Gulf** (the war is often called the **First Persian Gulf War**.) Second, he wanted Iranian territory. Third, by launching a preemptive strike against Iran, he would ensure that Iran's **Shiite Muslim** leader, the **Ayatollah Khomeini**, could not inspire Iraq's large Shiite Muslim community to revolt against Saddam.

By 1981 the Iraqi invasion had opened a 730-mile front stretching from Turkey to the Persian Gulf. Slowly the Iranians pushed the Iraqis back. By 1982 Iranian forces were launching counteroffensives and attacking **Basra**, Iraq's second largest city. Iraqi defenses held

Basra, but a grueling war of attrition now ensued. In 1983 Iranian forces, using suicidal human-wave attacks, began to overrun Iraqi defenses and appeared poised to invade southern Iraq. Saddam was so shaken by this prospect that he resorted to the use of **chemical weapons. Hydrogen cyanide, nerve gas**, and **mustard gas** were used to repel the Iranian attacks. The Iranians took countermeasures, and soon they began using mustard gas and **phosgene gas** against the Iraqis.

Throughout the war the numbers favored Iran. Iran's population was 45.2 million compared to Iraq's 15.5 million. Iran mobilized 2.5 million men, while Iraq mobilized 1 million. The Iranian military, despite their three-to-one advantage in manpower, had severe leadership and logistical problems. Khomeini distrusted the Iranian officer corps, and by the 1980s he had purged the military of thousands of its best officers. The Iranian air force, comprised of older U.S.-built aircraft, lacked trained pilots and spare parts and played virtually no role in the war. Artillery, tanks, and even small arms were often in short supply. It was not uncommon for Iranian units to be sent to the front without weapons.

The Iraqi military, though fewer in number, had a superior air force of Soviet-built fighters and maintained air supremacy throughout the war. The Soviet Union also ensured that Saddam Hussein's army had an ample supply of weapons, including multiple-rocket launchers and intermediate-range missiles.

By 1988 momentum appeared to favor Iraq. To protect world oil supplies, the U.S. Navy was now patrolling the Persian Gulf and had clashed with Iranian naval vessels. The Soviet Union had condemned Khomeini's Iranian revolution and announced its commitment to supply Iraq with even more advanced weapon systems. On 18 July 1988, Khomeini accepted a cease-fire. Iranian dead numbered 300,000; the Iraqi dead totaled 135,000. Each side suffered about 750,000 wounded. The war accomplished nothing. It cost Iraq more than $400 billion and Iran more than $600 billion. Saddam Hussein was so impoverished by the war that in 1990 he seized oil-rich Kuwait, igniting a **Second Persian Gulf War**.

Suggestions for Term Papers

1. Why would Saddam's fears of Iraq's Shiite Muslim community persuade him to attack Iran? What justification was there for his fears?

2. Investigate the chemical weapons Saddam used against Iran and report on their effects.

3. Assess Saddam Hussein's military leadership in this war.

4. What stake did the Soviet Union have in the outcome of the war? Evaluate its efforts to protect its interests.

5. Although the United States officially supported Iraq in the war, the Reagan administration supplied some weapons to Iran. How can this seeming contradiction be explained?

6. Review the Reagan administration's "Iran-Contra" policy, in particular its role in promoting U.S. interests in the Gulf region, and report on its success or lack of success.

Research Suggestions

In addition to the boldfaced items, look under the entry for "Ayatollah Ruhollah Khomeini and the Iranian Revolution, 1979" (#80). Search under **Iran-Contra** and **Oliver North**.

SUGGESTED SOURCES

Primary Sources

The Mind of Hussein [videorecording]. Chicago: Films Inc., 1991. A sixty-minute *Frontline* television documentary on Saddam Hussein's wartime policy including excerpts from his speeches and interviews.

United States Congress: Senate Select Committee on Secret Military Assistance to Iran and the Nicaraguan Opposition. *Iran-Contra Investigation: Joint Hearings Before the Senate Select Committee on . . . Covert Arms Transactions with Iran.* Washington, D.C.: Government Printing Office, 1988. These documents focus on the testimony of Lieutenant Colonel Oliver North during the Iran-Contra hearings.

Secondary Sources

Baram, Amatzia, and Barry Rubin, eds. *Iraq's Road to War.* New York: St. Martin's Press, 1993. Several of the essays examine Saddam's motivation for attacking Iran.

Draper, Theodore. *A Very Thin Line: The Iran-Contra Affairs.* New York: Hill and Wang, 1991. A balanced assessment of this debacle.

Hiro, Dilip. *The Longest War: The Iran-Iraq Military Conflict.* New York: Routledge, 1991. A reliable military history of the war.

Karsh, Efraim, and Inari Rautsi. *Saddam Hussein: A Political Biography.*

New York: The Free Press, 1991. Chapters 6 and 7 deal with the war.

Khalil, Simir al. *Republic of Fear: The Inside Story of Saddam's Iraq.* New York: Pantheon, 1990. Examines the totalitarian character of Saddam's rule in Iraq.

Segel, David. "The Iran-Iraq War: A Military Analysis." *Foreign Affairs* 66 (Summer 1988): 946–63. Based on solid research and interviews, Segal shows how the Reagan administration's Iran-Contra policy aided Iran with satellite intelligence photos of Iraqi defenses.

Smolanksy, Oles M., and Betie M. Smolansky. *The USSR and Iraq: The Soviet Quest for Influence.* Durham, N.C.: Duke University Press, 1991. Provides good insights into the troubled relations of these two allies.

Stoessinger, John G. *Why Nations Go to War.* 7th ed. New York: St. Martin's Press, 1998. Chapter 6 focuses on Saddam Hussein's wars.

World Wide Web

"Department of History Map Library" *http://www.dean.usma.edu/history/ dhistorymaps//MapsHome.htm.* Click on "Atlases" for United States Military Academy (West Point) maps of the Iran-Iraq war.

86. CHERNOBYL, 1986

Early in the morning of Saturday, 26 April 1986, the worst nuclear accident of the twentieth century occurred at Chernobyl in the former Soviet Republic of the **Ukraine**. Located sixty-five miles northwest of **Kiev**, Chernobyl was the largest power station in the Soviet Union; it had four nuclear reactors and produced 15 percent of the Soviet Union's electricity. A scheduled daylong experiment was under way when a series of human errors and control malfunctions resulted in a power surge in Reactor 4, producing two explosions. The first explosion blew off the 1,000-ton steel and concrete roof, spewing forth radioactive materials and a plume of radioactive gas 3,000 feet high. It is estimated that 8 percent of the reactor's radioactive material escaped. This would be many times more than the radioactivity released from the atomic bombs dropped on **Hiroshima** and **Nagasaki**. The radioactive debris landed on the roofs of nearby reactors, igniting thirty fires. Inside Reactor 4 one worker was killed in the blast and another died within hours from radiation exposure. Hundreds of firefighters rushed to Chernobyl, where they battled the fires without protective clothing. Within days twenty-nine firefighters died from radiation exposure.

By Sunday, 27 April **Swedish nuclear monitors** had determined that windborne radiation from the Soviet Union was spreading across Scandinavia and western Europe. Belatedly, the Soviet government admitted that an accident had occurred and that 45,000 emergency personnel were at Chernobyl. Between 28 April and 6 May 1986, a heroic "battle for Chernobyl" was under way. To put out the fires, helicopters flew repeatedly over the smoldering reactor, dumping tons of sand, lead, and clay to trap the radiation, smother the flames, and cool the reactor. Later, after the fires were out, a huge steel and cement "sarcophagus" was built to enclose Reactor 4 and seal all gases and vapors. It is estimated that this sarcophagus will have to remain in place for a millennium. By 10 May, 179 villages and 135,000 people had been evacuated from Chernobyl and surrounding areas. Medical teams from throughout the world began treating thousands of people for radiation exposure.

Thirty-one people died in the accident, though the Chernobyl explosion affected more than 1 million people. Six hundred thousand are scheduled twice a year for cancer screening. Thousands of head of livestock were destroyed and millions of acres of farmland, forests, and wetlands have been contaminated by radiation. Although the ultimate costs and consequences of Chernobyl will not be known for some time, there has been an alarming increase in deformed fetuses, abnormal births, mental retardation, and a high incidence of cancers and tumors among the people residing in the Chernobyl area.

Suggestions for Term Papers

1. Read Robert Gale's *Final Warning* (see Suggested Sources) and write a paper commenting on his views on the accident.
2. Despite tightened security, people continue to return to farm, fish, and live in the contaminated zones near Chernobyl. How significant is this problem today?
3. Despite the fact that the RBMK reactor that exploded at Chernobyl has serious design flaws, some are still in operation in the former Soviet Union. Do a report on the nuclear energy policies of Ukraine. Does Ukraine adhere to its nuclear energy policies? Why do you think Ukraine continues to operate RBMK reactors despite their design flaws? Provide reasons for your position.

4. Investigate the health profile of the Chernobyl region today and compare it with other parts of the former Soviet Union.

5. Some experts continue to argue that nuclear energy is cleaner and better for the environment than fossil fuels. Review the arguments on both sides of the question and take a position on the issue. Provide reasons for your position.

6. What is the policy of the United States on nuclear power stations? Write an essay commenting on this policy.

Research Suggestions

In addition to the boldfaced items, look under the entries for "The Breakup of the Soviet Union, 1991" (#91) and "The 1992 Earth Summit in Rio" (#94). Search under **Three Mile Island, Green Parties**, and **RBMK Reactor design**.

SUGGESTED SOURCES

Primary Sources

Chernousenko, V. M. *Chernobyl: Insight from the Inside.* New York: Springer-Verlag, 1991. A candid report by the Ukrainian Academy of Sciences Task Force on Chernobyl.

Gale, Robert Peter. *Final Warning: The Legacy of Chernobyl.* New York: Warner Books, 1988. Gale was an American physician who went to Chernobyl and treated the victims.

Shcherbak, Iurii. *Chernobyl: A Documentary Story.* Translated by Ian Press. Basingstoke: Canadian Institute of Ukrainian Studies, 1989. A good starting point for the key documents.

Secondary Sources

Gould, Peter. *Fire in the Rain: The Democratic Consequences of Chernobyl.* Baltimore: Johns Hopkins University Press, 1990. Lively discussion of the effects of Chernobyl on Europe and the Ukraine.

Liberatore, Angela. *Management of Uncertainty: Learning from Chernobyl.* Amsterdam: Gordon and Breach, 1999. A good retrospective on lessons learned from Chernobyl a decade after the accident.

Mansfield, Jerry W. *The Nuclear Power Debate: A Guide to the Literature.* New York: Garland, 1984. Although dated, this study still remains a good starting point.

Marples, David R. *The Social Impact of the Chernobyl Disaster.* New York:

St. Martin's Press, 1988. A comprehensive discussion of the imme- diate environmental and medical impact of the accident.

Medvedev, Grigori. *The Truth about Chernobyl*. Translated by Evelyn Ros- siter. New York: Basic Books, 1991. Written by a nuclear power expert who had worked at Chernobyl, the book gives a day-by-day account of the tragedy.

Medvedev, Zhores A. *The Legacy of Chernobyl*. New York: W. W. Norton, 1990. A comprehensive account by a leading Russian biologist.

Park, Chris C. *Chernobyl: The Long Shadow*. New York: Routledge, 1989. A geographer's view of the long-term effects of the accident.

Read, Piers Paul. *Ablaze: The Story of the Heroes and Victims of Chernobyl*. New York: Random House, 1993. Dramatic account of the "battle for Chernobyl."

Yaroshinskaya, Alla. *Chernobyl: The Forbidden Truth*. Translated by Michèle Kahn and Julia Sallabank. Lincoln: University of Nebraska Press, 1995. Accessible and fresh assessment of the ecological threats from Chernobyl.

World Wide Web

"Chernobyl: A Nuclear Disaster." *http://library.thinkquest.org/3426/index. htm*. A useful introduction to Chernobyl produced by a team of high school students. Based on information available as of 1997.

87. THE MONTREAL PROTOCOL, 1987

Negotiations on the **Montreal Protocol on Substances that De- plete the Ozone Layer** were completed on 16 September 1987. This path-breaking agreement is the first major international effort to deal with environmental issues that go beyond national boundaries. As such, it is a model for agreements reached in the 1990s and for future agreements.

The main ozone-depleting substances are **chlorofluorocarbons (CFCs)**, invented in the 1920s and used for propellants in aerosol cans, as solvents, and as coolants. Until the 1970s, CFCs were re- garded as highly useful and not harmful. In 1974 **Mario Molina** and **Sherwood Rowland**, chemists at the University of California at Ir- vine, published an article on the possibility that CFCs might cause damage to the ozone layer.

Although the use of CFCs for aerosol sprays was banned in a number of countries at the end of the 1970s, it took the 1985 report by British scientists of a hole in the ozone layer over Antarctica to move negotiations ahead. The result was the Montreal Protocol, which called for industrial countries to cut production and use of CFCs in half by 1998. The protocol was all the more remarkable in that there were not yet enough scientific data to prove extensive damage to the ozone layer or even that CFCs were the major cause.

The protocol was strengthened in meetings in London in 1990, in Copenhagen in 1992, and in Vienna in 1995. Dates for phasing out the production of CFCs and several other chemicals were advanced from the original schedule. The last round of revisions took place in 1997.

The various changes in the Montreal Protocol resulted from periodic reviews by panels of experts. In addition to the outstanding example of cooperation between scientists and public policy makers, industry, after initial resistance, joined in the effort to protect the ozone layer.

While industry worked to find substitutes for the banned CFCs, it also explored completely different ways of accomplishing tasks that CFCs had been used for. For example, instead of expensive solvents made from CFCs to clean circuit boards, some companies used lemon juice, a far cheaper substitute.

The Montreal Protocol has also been successful in dealing with questions of equity in relations between the North and the South. Developing countries were granted a ten-year grace period for phasing out CFCs and other chemicals. Also, a fund was established to help them make the transition.

To date, the Montreal Protocol has been an extraordinarily successful model for international efforts to protect the environment. It has also indicated the importance of environmental issues for questions of international security.

Suggestions for Term Papers

1. Investigate the development of uses for CFCs in the 1950s and 1960s. Why were they regarded as "wonder chemicals"?

2. Determine how much damage has been done to the ozone layer and how long scientists now estimate it will take to recover.

3. Industry and, to some extent, the general public have been slow

to accept the idea of global warming. Yet both groups fairly quickly accepted the idea that the production of CFCs was damaging the ozone layer. Analyze the responses to these two ideas and write a paper accounting for the differences.

4. In 1995 Mario Molina and Sherwood Rowland received the Nobel Prize in Chemistry (Paul Crutzen of Germany's Max Planck Institute also received the prize for work he had done that paved the way for Molina and Rowland). Check newspapers and magazines to see what kind of coverage they received. Did journalists properly recognize the importance of their accomplishment?

5. One important principle used in the negotiations at Montreal is called the "precautionary principle" (the idea that the lack of scientific certainty is no reason to delay action if delay may result in serious or irreversible damage). Read the article on this principle cited in the sources and then apply this principle to the issue of global warming.

6. Do a case study of an industry changing the way a product is designed or made to accommodate the ban on CFCs.

Research Suggestions

In addition to the boldfaced items, look under the entry for "The 1992 Earth Summit in Rio" (#94). Search under **ozone layer, Vienna Convention for the Protection of the Ozone Layer** (1985), **United Nations Environmental Program (UNEP), Ultraviolet-B (UV-B) radiation, Global Environment Facility (GEF).**

SUGGESTED SOURCES

Primary Sources

"Montreal Protocol on Substances that Deplete the Ozone Layer." In Lakshman D. Guruswamy, Geoffrey W.R. Palmer, and Burns H. Weston, eds., *International Environmental Law and World Order*, Supplement of Basic Documents. St. Paul: West Publishing 1994.

Secondary Sources

Cameron, James, and Juli Abouchar. "The Status of the Precautionary Principle in International Law." In David Freestone and Ellen Hey, eds., *The Precautionary Principle and International Law: The Challenge of Implementation*. The Hague: Kluwer Law International, 1996. Discussion of a basic principle now used in dealing with environmental issues.

Cook, Elizabeth. *Ozone Protection in the United States: Elements of Success.* Washington, D.C.: WRI, 1996. A recent review of U.S. efforts to comply with the Montreal Protocol.

French, Hilary F. "Learning from the Ozone Experience." In Lester R. Brown et al., *State of the World 1997.* New York: W. W. Norton, 1997. An excellent review of the diplomatic and technical aspects of the Montreal Protocol and subsequent revisions.

Goodman, Allan E. *The Negotiations Leading to the 1987 Montreal Protocol on Substances that Deplete the Ozone Layer.* Pew Case Studies in International Affairs. Washington, D.C.: The Institute for the Study of Diplomacy, Georgetown University, 1992. An overview that provides a good basis for discussion of the negotiation process.

Lemonick, Michael D. "When Politics Twists Science." *Audubon* 98 (January/February 1996): 110. Congressional efforts to end American support for the Montreal Protocol despite the scientific consensus and long-standing cooperation from industry.

Makhijani, Arjun, and Kevin Gurney. *Mending the Ozone Hole: Science, Technology, and Policy.* Cambridge, Mass.: MIT Press, 1996. An excellent source for all dimensions of the issue.

Nemecek, Sasha. "Rescuing the Ozone Layer." *Scientific American* 277 (November 1997). A fascinating profile of Mario Molina, one of the first scientists to note the possibility of damage to the ozone layer.

Parson, Edward A. "Protecting the Ozone Layer." In Peter M. Haas, Robert O. Keohane, and Mac A. Levy, eds., *Institutions for the Earth.* Cambridge, Mass.: MIT Press, 1994. An excellent study of the efforts to protect the ozone layer.

Rowlands, Ian H. *The Politics of Global Atmospheric Change.* Manchester, U.K.: Manchester University Press, 1995. A very useful discussion that approaches the ozone layer problem from various angles: science, business interests, equity questions, and catalysts for action.

World Wide Web

"The Ozone Secretariat [United Nations Environment Programme or UNEP]." *http://www.unep.org/ozone.* The Montreal Protocol as adjusted through 1999 and many other interesting features and useful links.

88. THE SANDINISTAS AND THE CONTRAS IN NICARAGUA, 1981–1989

Nicaragua, a country the size of North Carolina, had been ruled since 1936 by the Somoza family. Between 1936 and 1979, the Somozas acquired personal land holdings in Nicaragua the size of the state of Massachusetts. In 1979 the **Sandinista National Liberation Front** (Frente Sandinista de Liberación Nacional, or FSLN), the Sandinistas (named for the early twentieth-century Nicaraguan rebel leader, **Augusto Sandino**), drove **Anastasio Somoza** from power and took control of Nicaragua.

Immediately the Sandinistas initiated economic, social, and political reforms. The number of hospitals and schools doubled, a large number of private properties were expropriated, and central economic planning was introduced. **Daniel Ortega**, a key Sandinista leader and a strident Marxist, welcomed close ties with **Fidel Castro's Cuba** and the **Soviet Union**. The newly installed Reagan administration perceived the Sandinistas as rabid Marxists committed to exporting communist revolution throughout Central America. In 1981 **Central Intelligence Agency** (CIA) **Director William Casey** received more than $20 million to begin training an anti-Sandinista force, the **Contras**, to wage war against the Sandinistas. **President Ronald Reagan** authorized the use of CIA contingency funds for this purpose. By 1983 the CIA was training 10,000 Contras and, in clear violation of international law, had mined Nicaraguan harbors. In the 1984 Nicaraguan elections, certified to be freely conducted by international observers, the Sandinistas won 63 percent of the vote.

In 1984 Congress substantially cut funding for the CIA training of the Contras. The Reagan administration decided to secure funding for the Contras from foreign governments such as Saudi Arabia and Brunei. Congressional hearings soon revealed that the U.S. government had illegally sold American weapons to Iran to garner funds for the Contras and that top Reagan officials including **Assistant Secretary of State Elliot Abrams, National Security Adviser James Poindexter**, and Poindexter's aide, Marine **Lieutenant Colonel Oliver North**, had repeatedly lied to Congress about arms sales to **Iran** to fund the Contras' war against the Sandinistas.

Embarrassed by these revelations, the Reagan administration had to accept the 1987 peace plan crafted by Costa Rica's president, **Oscar Arias**, which brought an end to the fighting. In 1990 free elections were held in Nicaragua. **Violeta Chamorro**, an outspoken critic of the Sandinistas, was elected president.

The eight years of fighting between Sandinistas and Contras resulted in 43,000 Nicaraguan casualties. During this period the United States spent millions of dollars funding the Contras and military establishments in **Honduras, Guatemala**, and **El Salvador**. The end result was violence and impoverishment for the people of Central America.

Suggestions for Term Papers

1. What made it possible for the guerrilla army of the Sandinistas to defeat Somoza and take power in 1979?

2. To what extent were the Sandinistas Marxists and their revolution a Marxist revolution?

3. Read Jeane Kirkpatrick's article "Dictatorships and Double Standards" (see Suggested Sources) and write a paper assessing its influence on Reagan administration policy in Nicaragua.

4. During the "Iran-Contra" Congressional hearings Oliver North became a media celebrity. Determine whether he should be considered a "hero" of the Contra cause. Provide reasons for your position.

5. Read about the experiences of the Contras fighting against the Sandinistas in Nicaragua. Write a paper evaluating the tactics and strategy they used.

6. How durable were the Sandinistas' reforms? How many of their reforms remain in contemporary Nicaragua?

Research Suggestions

In addition to the boldfaced items, look under the entries for "The Guatemalan Coup, 1954" (#50), "Fidel Castro and the Cuban Revolution, 1959" (#57), "The Cuban Missile Crisis, 1962" (#64), and "The Overthrow of Salvador Allende in Chile, 1973" (#76). Search under **Cold War** and **Reagan Doctrine**.

SUGGESTED SOURCES

Primary Sources

Borge, Tomás, et al. *Sandinistas Speak*. New York: Pathfinder, 1982. These documents show why the early revolution was so popular.

Chamorro, Violeta Barrios de. *Dreams of the Heart*. New York: Simon and Schuster, 1996. A candid memoir by the former president of Nicaragua.

Gilbert, Dennis, and David Block, eds. *Sandinistas: Key Documents*. Ithaca: Cornell University Latin American Studies Program, 1990. A good insight into the economic and political problems the Sandinistas faced.

Leiken, Robert S., and Barry Rubin, eds. *The Central American Crisis Reader*. New York: Summit Books, 1987. The best starting point for documents on the FSLN, the Contras, and U.S. policy.

Secondary Sources

Burns, E. Bradford. *At War in Nicaragua: The Reagan Doctrine and the Politics of Nostalgia*. New York: Harper and Row, 1987. The Reagan administration accused Burns of spreading "disinformation" about Nicaragua. His book is a powerful indictment of U.S. policy.

Dickey, Christopher. *With the Contras: A Reporter in the Wilds of Nicaragua*. New York: Simon and Schuster, 1987. The best firsthand account of the CIA's guerrilla fighters in Nicaragua.

Kagan, Robert. *A Twilight Struggle: American Power and Nicaragua, 1977–1990*. New York: The Free Press, 1996. The most authoritative study available.

Kinzer, Stephen. *Blood Brothers: Life and War in Nicaragua*. York: G. P. Putnam's Sons, 1991. Based on thirteen years of living in Nicaragua, this is an informed view of daily life under the Sandinistas.

Kirkpatrick, Jeane. *Dictatorships and Double Standards: Rationalism and Reason in Politics*. New York: Simon and Schuster, 1982. The lead article in this collection inspired President Reagan's Central American policy and his support for the Contras.

Lafeber, Walter. *Inevitable Revolutions: The United States in Central America*. 2nd ed. New York: W. W. Norton, 1993. A reliable study by a premier diplomatic historian.

LeoGrande, William M. *Our Own Backyard: The United States in Central America, 1977–1992*. Chapel Hill: University of North Carolina Press, 1998. An exhaustive study of U.S. policy in Central America. Excellent bibliography.

Pastor, Robert A. *Condemned to Repetition: The United States and Nicaragua*. Princeton: Princeton University Press, 1987. A careful account illustrating the long roots of U.S. policy vis-à-vis Nicaragua.

World Wide Web

"The National Security Archive." *http://www.gwu.edu/~nsarchiv*. A nongovernmental collection with documents on Nicaragua.

89. VACLAV HAVEL AND THE "VELVET REVOLUTION," 1989

Czechoslovakia, even with the changes taking place in Poland, Hungary, and the German Democratic Republic (GDR) in the fall of 1989, did not immediately join in the Revolution of 1989 which resulted in the breakup of the Soviet Union and the reunification of Germany. Czechs and Slovaks had responded to **Mikhail Gorbachev**'s call for reform. Dissent had increased in 1987 and 1988, both in the case of **Charter '77**, a group formed after the **Helsinki Conference** to monitor human rights issues, and in the very different case of the Catholic Church, particularly in Slovakia. Nonetheless, **Milos Jakes**, who became the new party leader in 1987, did not have to deal with the kind of economic crises taking place in Poland and the GDR, and maintained order through the fall of 1989.

On 17 November 1989, however, student demonstrators in Prague filled **Wenceslas Square**. The police broke up the demonstration and beat anyone they could find. Angered by the violence, a large crowd, hundreds of thousands of ordinary citizens of all ages, filled the square on 20 November. The crowds grew night after night, and the Czech government found itself responding to events, always at least a step behind.

The center of political gravity moved to the **Magic Lantern Theatre**. There **Vaclav Havel** and others associated with Charter '77 worked to give direction to the opposition movement. They formed a new group called **Civic Forum**. Its counterpart in Slovakia was **Public Against Violence**. On 10 December, a coalition government dominated by non-communists replaced the old government. **Alexander Dubcek**, the heroic figure of the **"Prague Spring,"** emerged from long years of obscurity to lend his presence to what the Czechs began to call the **"Velvet Revolution."** He became chairman of the national assembly, and it elected Havel president unanimously.

Free elections were held the following year in June. Civic Forum and Public Against Violence emerged as the leading parties. Discussions concerning the name of the country, seemingly a very small matter, actually foreshadowed a major issue: the many differences between the Czechs and the Slovaks. By 1993, even as they struggled to establish democracy and free enterprise, Czechs and Slovaks had agreed to the **"Velvet Divorce."** Henceforth, the **Czech Republic** and the **Slovak Republic** would be two separate countries.

Suggestions for Term Papers

1. As a group project, make a presentation on life in Czechoslovakia between 1968 and 1989. In addition to the few actively involved in oppositional politics, what did people do to give meaning to their lives?

2. Read one of Vaclav Havel's absurdist plays and write a report commenting on your reactions to the play and on any connections you see between it and Havel's politics.

3. Compare the "Velvet Revolution" with the German Revolution of 1989. In particular, focus on ways in which Slovakia in the case of the "Velvet Revolution" and West Germany in the case of the German Revolution of 1989 complicated the situations.

4. Examine the political fates of Civic Forum and Public Against Violence in the aftermath of the "Velvet Revolution." Why was neither one able to sustain its initial political power?

5. Vaclav Havel has been by far the most successful political figure coming out of the events of 1989. Study both his activities and his writings since the "Velvet Revolution" and write an essay on factors that might account for his success.

6. Investigate the events leading up to the "Velvet Divorce." Why did the Slovaks decide to do what in many respects was not in their best interests?

Research Suggestions

In addition to the boldfaced items, look under the entries for "The Prague Spring, 1968" (#70), "The Helsinki Accords, 1975" (#77), "Solidarity in Poland, 1980–1990" (#82), and "German Reunification, 1989–1990" (#90). Search under **Jiri Dienstbier, Gustav Hu-**

sak, **Vaclav Klaus, Milan Kundera, Vladimir Meciar, Jan Palach**, and **Obcanske Forum (Civic Forum)**.

SUGGESTED SOURCES

Primary Sources

Havel, Vaclav. *Disturbing the Peace: A Conversation with Karel Hvizdala.* New York: Knopf, 1990. A long, autobiographical interview of Havel. A very useful source.

———. *Letters to Olga, June 1979–September 1982.* New York: Henry Holt, 1989. Letters sent from prison in the period before the "Velvet Revolution." Provides an indication of Havel's philosophy.

Stokes, Gale, ed, *From Stalinism to Pluralism: A Documentary History of Eastern Europe since 1945.* 2nd ed. New York: Oxford University Press, 1996. A highly useful selection of documents that places 1989 in context.

Secondary Sources

Garton Ash, Timothy. *The Magic Lantern: The Revolution of '89 Witnessed in Warsaw, Budapest, Berlin and Prague.* New York: Random House, 1990. Brilliant reporting from an observer who was often at the very center of events.

Kriseova, Eda. *Vaclav Havel: The Authorized Biography.* New York: Pharos Books, 1993. A good introduction to Havel's career as dissident and revolutionary.

Rosenberg, Tina. *The Haunted Land: Facing Europe's Ghosts after Communism.* New York: Random House, 1995. Part One is a fascinating account of some of the problems faced by Czechoslovakia in the aftermath of revolution.

Skilling, H. Gordon. *Charter 77 and Human Rights in Czechoslovakia.* London: George Allen and Unwin, 1981. Good introduction to Charter 77 and Havel.

Skilling, H. Gordon, and Paul Wilson, eds. *Civil Freedom in Central Europe: Voices from Czechoslovakia.* London: Macmillan, 1991. A good source for documents from the period and for informed commentary.

Weschler, Lawrence. "From Kafka to Dreyfus." *New Yorker*, 2 November 1992, 62–63.

———. "The Velvet Purge: The Trial of Jan Kavan." *New Yorker*, 19 October 1992; 66–96.

Wheaton, Bernard, and Zdenek Kavan. *The Velvet Revolution: Czechoslo-

vakia, 1980–1991. Boulder: Westview Press, 1992. An excellent account of events leading up to and during the revolution.

Wolchik, Sharon L. *Czechoslovakia in Transition.* London: Pinter Publications, 1991. A helpful examination of the many changes in Czechoslovakia in the late 1980s.

90. GERMAN REUNIFICATION, 1989–1990

The **German Democratic Republic (East Germany)** experienced a revolution in October and November, 1989. The government could not control or respond adequately to the massive protests in cities like **Leipzig, Berlin,** and **Dresden**. The most dramatic event of that period was the **Fall of the Berlin Wall** on 9 November 1989. At that time, the **citizens' movements** active in the **German Revolution of 1989** still wanted to undertake reform within an independent East Germany. Some in the old **Socialist Unity Party**, renamed the **Party of Democratic Socialism (PDS)** in December, also wanted an opportunity to reform the country. The majority of those who participated in demonstrations that fall in the cities were thinking about unification with the **Federal Republic of Germany (West Germany)**. East Germans wondered why they should chance a new socialist experiment when the West German approach was already available.

Helmut Kohl, the chancellor of West Germany, saw the possibility of unifying East and West Germany and daringly took the lead. With little support from his west European colleagues, and with Soviet leader **Mikhail Gorbachev** still a question mark, this was a brave move. Kohl did have support from **President George Bush** of the United States. He also believed that the continued flow of East Germans into West Germany would harm the West German economy. However, he underestimated the extent of East German economic problems.

The first free elections in East Germany, in March 1990, were for the **Volkskammer** (parliament). West German politicians campaigning for their East German counterparts made unification the main issue. The **Christian Democrats** strongly supported the idea of rapid unification. They won a stunning victory over the **Social Democrats**, who were skeptical about unification. The new government under

Lothar de Maizière plunged into negotiations for the introduction of the **deutsche mark** into East Germany. Kohl contributed a crucial element to the unification process through a meeting with Gorbachev. Germany agreed to pay the Soviet Union a large sum and, in return, the Soviet Union agreed to unification and also to withdraw its troops from East Germany. Additional negotiations between the two Germanies led to full unification in October and free elections in Germany. The coalition of Christian Democrats and **Free Democrats** easily beat the Social Democrats. In the east, only a few delegates from the PDS and almost no one from the citizens' movements were elected. Although some Germans complained that East Germany had been "annexed," unification had been accomplished.

The unification of Germany also led to full sovereignty. In addition to negotiations between East Germany and West Germany, there were the **"2 + 4" talks** involving the two Germanies and the four former allies from World War II, the Soviet Union, Britain, France, and the United States. This resulted in a treaty formally ending the remaining rights held by the four powers in Germany.

Suggestions for Term Papers

1. Investigate the various citizens' movements (for example, Neues Forum, Democracy Awakening) in terms of what they hoped to accomplish and why they failed to convince many other East Germans to work for the same goals.

2. Helmut Kohl was the central figure in the unification of Germany. Report on his career before the events of 1989–1990. Use books by Timothy Garton Ash and Clay Clemens as starting points (see Suggested Sources).

3. For a group project, determine the views of the U.S., French, British, and Russian governments on German unification in 1989–1990 and organize a debate in which teams present each position.

4. Review the unification negotiations between the East Germans and the West Germans in 1990 and write a paper on whether East Germany was "annexed," as some claimed at the time.

5. For decades after World War II, the Soviet Union remained fearful that Germany might unite and once again become a major military power. Why did the Soviet Union decide in 1990 to allow unification to take place, given those long-standing fears?

6. Trace changes in West German opinion about unification from one Bundestag (lower house of parliament) election to the next beginning in 1990.

Research Suggestions

In addition to the boldfaced items, look under the entries for "The Yalta Conference, 1945" (#36), "The Berlin Wall, 1961" (#59), and "The Breakup of the Soviet Union, 1991" (#91). Search under **Neues Forum, Alliance '90, Willy Brandt, Hans-Dietrich Genscher**, and **Margaret Thatcher**.

SUGGESTED SOURCES

Primary Sources

Darnton, Robert. *Berlin Journal, 1989–1990.* New York: W. W. Norton, 1991. Darnton, an expert on eighteenth-century France, shows his reportorial skills to good advantage in *Berlin Journal.*

Gray, Richard T., and Sabine Wilke, eds. and trans. *German Unification and Its Discontents: Documents from the Peaceful Revolution.* Seattle: University of Washington Press, 1996. A most useful collection of documents.

Schneider, Peter. *The German Comedy: Scenes of Life after the Wall.* New York: Farrar, Straus and Giroux, 1991. An ironic look at the post-Wall Germany by a longtime observer.

Uniting Germany: Documents and Debates, 1944–1993. Edited by Konrad H. Jarausch and Volker Gransow. Providence, R.I.: Berghann Books, 1994. Places the unification process in a broad context.

Secondary Sources

Clemens, Clay, and William E. Paterson, eds. *The Kohl Chancellorship.* Portland, Or.: Frank Cass, 1998. Good essays on several aspects of Kohl's political career.

Fulbrook, Mary. *Anatomy of a Dictatorship: Inside the GDR 1949–1989.* Oxford: Oxford University Press, 1995. An excellent history of the German Democratic Republic.

Garton Ash, Timothy. *In Europe's Name: Germany and the Divided Continent.* New York: Random House, 1994. A major book on the German Question. Establishes a useful context for the East German Revolution of 1989 and unification of Germany in 1990.

Jarausch, Konrad H. *The Rush to German Unity.* New York: Oxford University Press, 1994. An excellent introduction.

Leiby, Richard A. *The Unification of Germany, 1989–1990*. Westport, Conn.: Greenwood Press, 1999. A useful and dependable study of the topic.

Maier, Charles S. *Dissolution: The Crisis of Communism and the End of East Germany*. Princeton: Princeton University Press, 1997. The best single book on the topic.

McFalls, Lawrence. *Communism's Collapse, Democracy's Demise? The Cultural Context and Consequences of the East German Revolution*. New York: New York University Press, 1995. Provides extensive survey data indicating the East German mood before and after unification.

Philipsen, Dirk. *We Were the People: Voices from East Germany's Revolutionary Autumn of 1989*. Durham, N.C.: Duke University Press, 1993. A fascinating presentation of the views of political activists in the revolution. Philipsen accepts their perspective uncritically.

Zelikow, Philip, and Condoleezza Rice. *Germany Unified and Europe Transformed: A Study in Statecraft*. Cambridge, Mass.: Harvard University Press, 1997. An authoritative study of the diplomacy involved in the unification of Germany. The 1997 edition contains a useful new preface.

World Wide Web

"The Wall Comes Down." *http:www.cnn.com/SPECIALS/cold.war/episodes/23*. Based on CNN's *Cold War* documentary series, this Web site contains many interesting and useful features.

91. THE BREAKUP OF THE SOVIET UNION, 1991

The end of the **Soviet Union** was also the end of the Russian revolutionary experiment. **Mikhail Gorbachev**, the Soviet leader, first tried *perestroika* (restructuring), *glasnost'* (openness), and *novoye mysl'* (new thinking), then a series of political maneuvers that called into question the monopoly of power by the **Communist Party** and the integrity of the Soviet Union.

Gorbachev's most successful policy was new thinking in foreign affairs. He succeeded in convincing **President Ronald Reagan** of the value of **détente** and began the process of **disarmament**. In the **Soviet bloc** his policies contributed to the **East European Revolutions of 1989**.

Glasnost' was also successful. Soviet citizens enjoyed greater freedom of discussion. The new openness, however, revealed more problems than solutions. And much of the criticism was directed against the Communist Party.

Perestroika, especially in the economic sphere, was unsuccessful. The Soviet economy, skewed toward heavy industry and with only a few sectors competitive with capitalist economies, could not keep pace with technological change. To the end, the bureaucracy resisted the necessary restructuring.

By 1989 Gorbachev had reached an impasse, which he tried to overcome through a fourth policy, ***demokratizatsia*** (democratization). In March 1989 Soviet voters elected the **Congress of People's Deputies** in an election featuring secret ballots and multiple candidates.

Democratization was of limited value as long as the Communist Party retained a monopoly of power. In 1990 and 1991, as Gorbachev tried to use democracy to undermine the strength of the party and the governmental bureaucracy, he also contended with the efforts of the Baltic republics of **Estonia, Latvia**, and **Lithuania** to leave the Soviet Union. In April 1991, however, agreement was reached on a new treaty on the federal structure of the Soviet Union, and signing was set for August.

Before the signing could take place, some party and government officials attempted a coup. **Boris Yeltsin**, the newly elected president of the **Russian Republic**, defied the leaders of the coup and rallied the military behind him. When Gorbachev returned to Moscow, he found political conditions changed. He hesitated to take strong action against the Communist Party and the **KGB**, the secret police. Instead, Yeltsin took the initiative. He and other leaders set up a **Commonwealth of Independent States (CIS)** to replace the Soviet Union. The revolutionary experiment would not likely have survived much longer in any case. It was ironic that Gorbachev, a true believer in the communist system, was the prime mover in its dissolution.

The breakup of the Soviet Union not only marked the end of a revolutionary experiment dating back to 1917 but also the end to the **Cold War** that had done so much to shape world history since the end of **World War II**. The Russian Republic, the main successor state to the Soviet Union, remained a great power but one in transition both politically and economically.

Suggestions for Term Papers

1. Why was Gorbachev so successful in foreign policy matters as leader of the Soviet Union between 1985 and 1991?

2. In 1987 Boris Yeltsin was fired as Moscow party chief and also lost his place in the Politburo. Investigate his career between 1987 and 1991 and determine how he was able to make a political comeback and how one might explain his heroic role in the resistance to the 1991 coup.

3. Review Gorbachev's attempt to make *perestroika* a reality in the Soviet economy. What factors account for his failure here?

4. What role did the three Baltic states, Estonia, Latvia, and Lithuania, play in the unraveling of the Soviet Union? (Pay particularly close attention to the period 1989–1991.)

5. Do a research report on the media's role in the defeat of the coup in 1991. Examine, for example, the coverage by CNN and the use of the fax machine.

6. Examine the history of the Russian Republic from the dissolution of the Soviet Union to the cease-fire in the war with Chechnya (1991–1996) and evaluate the successes and failures of Yeltsin's presidency.

Research Suggestions

In addition to the boldfaced items, look under the entries for "Khrushchev's 'Secret Speech' at the Twentieth Party Congress, 1956" (#51), "SALT I Agreement, 1972" (#74), and "Chernobyl, 1986" (#86). Search under **Edvard Shevardnadze, Egor Ligachev, Nagorno-Karabakh** (Armenian enclave in Azerbaijan), **Strategic Defense Initiative (SDI or "Star Wars")**, and **Afghanistan**.

SUGGESTED SOURCES

Primary Sources

Gorbachev, Mikhail. *The August Coup: The Truth and the Lessons.* New York: HarperCollins, 1991. Gorbachev's version of events.
———. *Memoirs.* New York: Doubleday, 1995. Gorbachev's story, covering all of the important events.

Yeltsin, Boris. *Against the Grain: An Autobiography.* New York: Summit Books, 1990. Yeltsin's story of his life to 1990.

———. *The Struggle for Russia.* New York: Random House, 1994. The saga continues.

Secondary Sources

Dallin, Alexander, and Gail Lapidus, eds. *The Soviet System from Crisis to Collapse.* Rev. ed. Boulder: Westview Press, 1995. An important collection of articles.

Denber, Rachel, ed. *The Soviet Nationality Reader: The Disintegration in Context.* Boulder: Westview Press, 1992. A useful collection of studies of an important topic.

Dunlop, John B. *The Rise of Russia and the Fall of the Soviet Empire.* Princeton: Princeton University Press, 1993. An excellent study of these interrelated topics.

Fish, Stephen M. *Democracy from Scratch: Opposition and Regime in the New Russian Revolution.* Princeton: Princeton University Press, 1995. An interim report; insightful and solid.

Hoskings, Geoffrey A. *The Awakening of the Soviet Union.* Rev. ed. Cambridge, Mass.: Harvard University Press, 1991. A useful survey of the Gorbachev era.

Lieven, Anatole. *The Baltic Revolution: Estonia, Latvia, Lithuania and the Path to Independence.* New Haven: Yale University Press, 1993. A dependable discussion of this vital topic.

Matlock, J. F., Jr. *Autopsy on an Empire: The American Ambassador's Account of the Collapse of the Soviet Union.* New York: Random House, 1995. A massive, well-informed account.

Remnick, David. *Lenin's Tomb: The Last Days of the Soviet Empire.* New York: Random House, 1993. An insightful and highly readable account.

Urban, Michael, with Vyacheslav Igrunov and Sergei Mitrokhin. *The Rebirth of Politics in Russia.* New York: Cambridge University Press, 1997. Up-to-date and well-informed.

Watson, William E. *The Collapse of Communism in the Soviet Union.* Westport, Conn.: Greenwood Press, 1998. A good overview for students, with accompanying biographical profiles and primary documents.

White, Stephen. *Gorbachev and After.* 4th ed. New York: Cambridge University Press, 1992. An excellent summary of the Gorbachev era.

92. NELSON MANDELA AND THE END OF APARTHEID IN SOUTH AFRICA, 1989–1994

At the beginning of the 1980s **Nelson Mandela**, the acknowledged leader of resistance to **apartheid** (a series of laws that segregated blacks from whites), was still in prison, and apartheid seemed impregnable. In actuality, apartheid began to come apart in that decade. **P. W. Botha**, prime minister since 1978, took the first steps when he decided to "reform" apartheid without giving up the actual power held by the whites, especially the **Afrikaners** (descendants of Dutch settlers). Among other measures, Botha introduced a new constitution in 1984 that called for three legislative chambers, one for whites, one for coloureds (mixed race), and one for Indians. Africans had no representation, yet formed 75 percent of the population. Other legislation was passed abolishing the pass laws, which had required blacks to carry pass books with them at all times, and laws banning interracial sex and marriage.

The protest movement that started at the black township of **Soweto (Southwest Township)** in the mid-1970s took on new life in the early 1980s. In August 1983, delegates from hundreds of organizations came together to form the **United Democratic Front (UDF)**. The best-known leader of the UDF was **Bishop Desmond Tutu**. Over the next several years, the UDF and other groups maintained a determined resistance to apartheid. In 1984 Bishop Tutu was awarded the Nobel Peace Prize.

In 1985 Mandela left **Robben Island**, where he was imprisoned, for surgery and did not return. Instead, he was placed in prison on the mainland and began a long series of negotiations with the government, which was attempting to find a way of ending apartheid without surrendering political power. Mandela was careful to maintain close ties with the **African National Congress (ANC)**, the main organization of those resisting apartheid, to forestall any accusations that he had sold out. Mandela and Botha met in 1989, but little came of the meeting.

The seeming impasse was broken by the new prime minister, **F. W. de Klerk**, who staged a virtual coup within the **National Party** against Botha. De Klerk claimed to be moving no faster than the party, but he also talked about a powerful sense of religious calling. In October 1989, Walter Sisulu, a major leader of the ANC, was released from prison. On 11 February 1990, Mandela himself was released from prison.

Over the next four years South Africa moved slowly toward abolishing apartheid and implementing democracy for all inhabitants of the country. One problem was power-sharing versus majority rule. Mandela provided a solution in 1991 when he suggested a multiparty convention to negotiate an interim constitution. Later a constitutent assembly would fashion a constitution, but would be restricted somewhat by binding conventions laid down by the multiparty convention.

The summit meeting of 26 September 1992 in Johannesburg was a turning point. Both within the National Party and the ANC groups existed that wanted to find a way to compromise. Ironically, **Joe Slovo**, long a militant communist supporter of the ANC, took the lead in building the compromise.

Black-on-black violence produced a great deal of tension over the next two years. It seemed to have been caused largely by **Inkatha**, the **Zulu** political organization, with covert backing from some elements of the government. This soured relations between Mandela and de Klerk, but did not prevent the elections of April 1994 from taking place. Apartheid ended and a new, democratic South Africa with Mandela as president, emerged to attempt to deal with the painful legacy.

Suggestions for Term Papers

1. View or read journalists' accounts of life in Soweto in the 1980s and write about what a person your age and gender would likely have experienced.

2. Assess the role played by Bishop Tutu in the struggle against apartheid in the 1980s. What made him such an effective leader?

3. Investigate the efforts of Botha to "reform" apartheid in the 1980s and propose an explanation for the failure of the reform.

4. Assess the crucial role played by Mandela in the late 1980s and early 1990s in finding a way to lead South Africa to democracy.

5. Evaluate de Klerk's motives in his efforts to end apartheid and

establish a democratic system that would protect the rights of the white minority.

6. Survey the progress made by South Africa between the 1994 elections and those in 1999. What problems remain?

Research Suggestions

In addition to the boldfaced items, look under the entry for "Apartheid in South Africa from the 1950s to the 1970s" (#58). Search under **apartheid** and **Afrikaners**.

SUGGESTED SOURCES

Primary Sources

Johns, Sheridan, and R. Hunt Davis, Jr., eds. *Mandela, Tambo, and the African National Congress: The Struggle Against Apartheid, 1948–1990. A Documentary Survey.* New York: Oxford University Press, 1991. An excellent collection of documents connected with the history of the ANC.

Mandela, Nelson. *Long Walk to Freedom: The Autobiography of Nelson Mandela.* Boston: Little, Brown, 1994. Mandela's story of how he outlasted apartheid.

Secondary Sources

Brewer, John D. *After Soweto: An Unfinished Journey.* New York: Oxford University Press, 1987. A thoughtful discussion of events to that point.

Eades, Lindsay. *The End of Apartheid in South Africa.* Westport, Conn.: Greenwood Press, 1999. A good overview for students, with accompanying biographical profiles and primary documents.

The Long Walk of Nelson Mandela. Distributed by PBS Home Video, 120 minutes, 1999. A good introduction to the life and accomplishments of Mandela.

Murray, Martin. *South Africa: Time of Agony, Time of Destiny. The Upsurge of Popular Protest.* New York: Schocken Books, 1987. A well-informed study of protests against apartheid.

Mzamane, Mbulelo. *The Children of Soweto.* Reading, Mass.: Addison Wesley Longman, 1995. An important study of the core group of the resistance to apartheid in Soweto.

Sampson, Anthony. *Mandela: The Authorized Biography.* London: HarperCollins, 1999. The best biography available.

Sparks, Allister. *Tomorrow Is Another Country: The Inside Story of South Af-*

rica's Road to Change. New York: Hill and Wang, 1995. The best book on the series of negotiations that ended apartheid and brought democracy to South Africa.

Thompson, Leonard. *A History of South Africa*. New Haven: Yale University Press, 1990. An excellent introduction to South African history. A good place to begin.

World Wide Web

"The Mandela Page." Part of the African National Congress Web site. *http://www.anc.org.za/people/mandela*. Links to speeches and statements, including the 1993 Nobel Peace Prize acceptance speech, and to the ANC documents archives.

93. THE DISSOLUTION OF YUGOSLAVIA IN THE 1990s

To decrease ethnic rivalries after the death of **Marshal Tito**, ruler of **Yugoslavia** between 1945 and 1980, the seat of government of Yugoslavia in the 1980s rotated among the six autonomous republics of **Serbia, Croatia, Bosnia-Herzegovina, Macedonia, Slovenia**, and **Montenegro**. But this system of rotation soon proved unworkable, and in 1991 Croatia and Slovenia declared their independence from Yugoslavia. Serbia, the largest of the republics, tried to forestall further dissolution, but in March 1992, after a referendum boycotted by most of its Serbian minority, the Muslim-dominated Republic of Bosnia-Herzegovina also declared its independence from Yugoslavia.

At the time of the 1992 referendum on independence, the 4 million Bosnians were divided into a population that was approximately 44 percent Muslim, 31 percent Serbian, and 17 percent Croatian, with the remainder composed of **Gypsies, Albanians**, and other Balkan or western European people. Beginning in the spring of 1992, brutal internecine fighting broke out among the Muslim, Serbian, and Croatian populations in Bosnia.

The practice of **"ethnic cleansing"**—the removal and killing—of a targeted population was used by all groups against their enemies. Two of the most grotesque examples of mass killing took place in **Srebrenica** in July 1995, when Bosnian Serb troops, under the command of **General Ratko Mladic**, with the support of **Slobodan Mil-**

osevic, president of Serbia, invaded a United Nations **"safe haven,"** held **UN peacekeepers** hostage, and executed 7,000 Muslim men. It was the worst atrocity in Europe since the **Holocaust**. On 4 August 1995, **Franjo Tudjman**, president of Croatia, ordered 200,000 Croat soldiers in **Operation Storm** to cleanse 40,000 Serb soldiers and 150,000 Bosnian Serbs from the Serb-held **Krajina** region of western Bosnia.

On 14 December 1995, after three long years of fighting, the **Dayton Peace Agreement** was signed. This provided for a peacekeeping force led by **NATO** to enforce a truce that divided Bosnia into two parts: the **Federation of Bosnia and Herzegovina** for the Muslims and Croats, and **Republika Srpska** for the Bosnian Serbs.

While the Dayton agreement reduced violence in Bosnia, early in 1999 **Kosovo**, a Serbian province with a large **Muslim Albanian** population, exploded in violence. Ethnic cleansing of **Kosovars** by Serbs resulted in hundreds of thousands people fleeing Kosovo for **Albania** and **Macedonia** and prompted **NATO** aircraft to attack Serbia.

Suggestions for Term Papers

1. How might one account for violence between people who have lived next to one another for years without significant problems? Survey the accounts in the primary sources (see Suggested Sources) for possible explanations.

2. Investigate the plight of women in this conflict. Explain why rape became one of the preferred tactics of ethnic cleansing in Yugoslavia.

3. Review what happened at Srebrenica. Why were the UN peacekeepers unable to stop the killing?

4. When Serb soldiers killed Muslims, they quite often referred to them as "Turks." Examine the historic role of Turkey in the region and explain why Serbs might refer to Muslims as "Turks."

5. One of the most brutal paramilitary leaders of the 1990s was Zeljko Raznayovic, also known as "Arkan." Arkan and his "tigers" killed hundreds of Muslims in Bosnia and Kosovo. In a paper on Arkan, his role in ethnic cleansing, and his relationship with the Serbian military and political leadership, explain how and why he was able to kill with impunity.

6. Assess the effectiveness of the NATO air campaign against Serbia in the spring of 1999.

Research Suggestions

In addition to the boldfaced items, look under the entries for "The Holocaust, 1941–1945" (#34), "Pol Pot and the Cambodian Incursion, 1970–1978 (#72), and "Genocide in Rwanda, 1994" (#95). Search under **Radovan Karadzic** and **International War Crimes Tribunal (The Hague)**.

SUGGESTED SOURCES

Primary Sources

Beljo, Ante, ed. *Bosnia-Herzegovina: Genocide, Ethnic Cleansing in Northwestern Bosnia*. Zagreb: Croatian Information Centre, 1993. First-person accounts describing the killings.

Gutman, Roy. *A Witness to Genocide*. New York: Macmillan, 1993. Chilling firsthand accounts by an award-winning *Newsday* reporter.

Holbrook, Richard. *To End a War*. New York: Random House, 1998. A detailed account of diplomacy by America's chief negotiator at the Dayton Peace Accords.

Mousavizadeh, Nader. *The Black Book of Bosnia: The Consequences of Appeasement: By the Writers and Editors of the New Republic*. New York: Basic Books, 1996. Riveting firsthand reports by journalists of the fighting in Bosnia, along with maps and editorials.

Sudetic, Chuck. *Blood and Vengeance: One Family's Story of the War in Bosnia*. New York: W. W. Norton, 1998. By telling the story of the Celik family's battle to survive, the author (who is a member of this family) has written a compelling book on the tragedy.

Zimmermann, Warren. *Origins of a Catastrophe: Yugoslavia and Its Destroyers—America's Last Ambassador Tells What Happened and Why*. New York: New Times Books, 1996. A candid and revealing account by a longtime student of the region.

Secondary Sources

Honig, Jan Willem, and Norbert Both. *Srebenica: Record of a War Crime*. New York: Penguin, 1997. A damning account of the failure of the UN's mission in the former Yugoslavia.

Peress, Gilles, Eric Stover, and Richard J. Goldstone. *The Graves: Srebrenica and Vukovar*. New York: Distributed Art Publishers, 1998. Grim photographs documenting two brutal atrocities in the region.

Rogel, Carole. *The Breakup of Yugoslavia and the War in Bosnia*. Westport, Conn.: Greenwood Press, 1998. A good overview for students, with accompanying biographical profiles and primary documents.

Rohde, David. *Endgame: The Betrayal and Fall of Srebrenica*. New York: Farrar, Straus and Giroux, 1997. The author won a Pulitzer Prize for his reporting of this atrocity.

Sells, Michael Anthony. *The Bridge Betrayed: Religion and Genocide in Bosnia*. Berkeley: University of California Press, 1996. By focusing on the role of religion, this study provides a useful context to the genocide.

Silber, Laura, and Allain Little. *Yugoslavia: Death of a Nation*. New York: Penguin, 1996. Originally published for a TV documentary, the text is reliable and graphic.

94. THE 1992 EARTH SUMMIT IN RIO

The UN Conference on Environment and Development, often referred to as the Earth Summit, took place in Rio de Janeiro in 1992. Many heads of state and representatives of **non-government organizations (NGOs)** attended the conference. Expectations were high that the conference would produce a number of agreements on important environmental issues.

The main document produced by the conference was **Agenda 21**, an action plan divided into forty chapters. Agenda 21 called for individual governments to draw up national sustainable development economic strategies, that is, economic plans that would not push the environment beyond its natural limits. These plans would permit economic growth without causing irreparable damage to the environment. Since the conference, over one hundred nations have done this, but most reports are long on rhetoric and short on specific goals. To review national plans, the Earth Summit set up the **United Nations Commission on Sustainable Development (CSD)**. Unfortunately, CSD has no budget or regulatory powers.

Two other documents are closely associated with the Earth Summit. One is the 1992 **Framework Convention on Climate Change**. According to it, all countries were to prepare an inventory of greenhouse gas emissions and a national climate plan. Industrial countries were to hold emissions of greenhouse gases at or below the 1990 level by the year 2000. Developing countries were under no obligations, although it was hoped they could move quickly to sources of clean energy. Follow-up meetings in Berlin in 1995 and Kyoto in 1997 accomplished relatively little.

The **Convention on Biological Diversity** (an attempt to slow the rate of extinction of plant and animal species), signed in 1992, has fared better. By November 1996, some 162 countries had ratified it. To date, however, the convention lacks targets, timetables, and enforcement mechanisms.

Also connected with the Earth Summit is the **Global Environment Facility (GEF)**, started as a pilot project before the meeting. In Agenda 21, it is seen as a mechanism for providing support for developing-country environmental projects. It has since become the interim funding arm of the climate and biodiversity conventions. Managed by the World Bank, the **UN Environment Programme (UNEP)**, and the **UN Development Program (UNDP)**, it lacks adequate funding and suffers from a complicated management strategy.

Although the Earth Summit has not and may never fulfill the expectations that existed in 1992, it did call attention to a number of environmental issues and established connections between these issues and development issues. It also created institutions and agreements that may bear fruit in the future.

Suggestions for Term Papers

1. Trace the efforts after the Earth Summit to improve the Framework Convention on Climate Change in 1995 (Berlin) and 1997 (Kyoto). You may wish to select a particular country and follow it in negotiations at the two meetings and in its efforts to construct a national climate plan.

2. Investigate the United Nations Environment Programme (UNEP). What kinds of activities has it been engaged in since the Earth Summit?

3. One issue that bears directly on all the other issues discussed at the Earth Summit is population. Write a report on the Conference on Population and Development in Cairo in 1994.

4. Review the efforts since the Earth Summit to make the Convention on Biological Diversity an effective agreement.

5. Look at projects funded by the Global Environment Facility

(GEF). How successful has it been, and how might its success or lack of success be best explained?

6. Working with a number of other students, organize and stage a mock Earth Summit based on current conditions and policy positions in several of the most important nations. What are the most important concerns, and what kinds of agreements might be possible?

Research Suggestions

In addition to the boldfaced items, look under the entries for "The Montreal Protocol, 1987" (#87) and "The Chinese Economy at the End of the Twentieth Century" (#100). Search under **Earth Summit, World Bank, Stockholm Conference on the Human Environment** (1972), **International Conference on Population and Development** (Cairo, 1994), and **Intergovernmental Panel on Climate Change (UN)**.

SUGGESTED SOURCES

Primary Sources

Clinton, William J., and Albert Gore, Jr. *The Climate Change Action Plan.* Washington, D.C.: White House, 1993. The American national plan.
United Nations. *Agenda 21: The United Nations Programme of Action from Rio.* New York: U.N. Publications, 1992. The basic document produced at the 1992 meeting.

Secondary Sources

Flavin, Christopher. "The Legacy of Rio." In Lester R. Brown et al., *State of the World 1997.* New York: W. W. Norton, 1997. A useful survey of progress made in dealing with the issue of global warming since 1992.
French, Hilary F. *Partnership for the Planet: An Environmental Agenda for the United Nations.* Worldwatch Paper 126. Washington, D.C.: Worldwatch Institute, July 1995. An excellent overview of prospects of international cooperation on environmental problems.
Grubb, Michael. *The Earth Summit Agreements: A Guide and Assessment.* London: Earthscan, 1993. A useful overview of the various documents associated with The Earth Summit.
Weizsäcker, Ernst von, Amory B. Lovins, and Hunter L. Lovins. *Factor Four: Doubling Wealth, Halving Resource Use.* The New Report to

the Club of Rome. London: Earthscan, 1997. An important effort to demonstrate the possibility that action on global warming is not only economically feasible but also economically beneficial.

Wilson, E. O. *The Diversity of Life.* New York: W. W. Norton, 1992. A significant discussion of the importance of biological diversity by one of America's leading authorities on social and environmental questions.

World Wide Web

"Earth Summit Documents." *http://www.ecouncil.ac.cr/ftp/riodoc.htm.* An archive of basic documents available for downloading.

"Earth Summit Watch." *http://www.earthsummitwatch.org.* A good source for up-to-date information on initiatives begun at the Earth Summit.

95. GENOCIDE IN RWANDA, 1994

Rwanda is a central African country with a population of 7 million people. The majority of Rwandans claim membership in one of two ethnic groups: the **Hutu** majority (85 percent of the population) or the **Tutsi** minority (14 percent of the population). Once a Belgian colony, Rwanda gained independence in 1962, but the Belgian colonial experience shaped Rwanda in two key respects. First, in the 1930s Belgian colonial officials issued identity cards classifying all Rwandans as Hutu or Tutsi. This classification system remained in place until 1994. Second, Belgian colonial officials generally favored the Tutsi minority over the Hutu majority.

Following independence there were frequent clashes between Hutu and Tutsi. In 1973 **General Juvénal Habyarimana**, a Hutu, seized power, inaugurating a one-party state that severely limited Tutsi economic and political rights. In 1990 political dissidents founded the **Rwandan Popular Front (RPF)**, a Tutsi-led guerrilla movement committed to bringing political reform to Rwanda. To head off civil war, in 1993 at **Arusha, Tanzania**, President Habyarimana agreed to a multiparty state and recognized the legitimacy of Hutu and Tutsi opposition parties. The United Nations (UN) endorsed the **Arusha Accords** and sent a small military mission, the **United Nations Aid Mission in Rwanda (UNAMIR)**, to **Kigali**, Rwanda's capital, to monitor all parties' compliance with the Arusha Accords. On 6 April 1994, President Habyarimana's plane was shot down, killing all on board. Although it now seems likely that Hutus, dissatisfied with President Habyarimana, shot down his plane, Tutsis were immediately blamed for the presidential assassination.

Starting on 6 April 1994, and continuing for one hundred days, more than 800,000 Rwandans, the majority of whom were Tutsis, were brutally slaughtered. The small UNAMIR force in Rwanda could not stop the killings. **Major-General Roméo Dallaire**, the UNAMIR commander, requested 5,000 troops to stop the genocide, but the UN refused to send them. The United States refused to intervene and refused to support the eight African nations who tried to stop the genocide.

Beginning in the summer of 1994 the RPF, under the leadership of **Defense Minister Paul Kagame**, launched an invasion of Rwanda from **Uganda**, and in August 1994, RPF forces took Kigali and installed **Pasteur Bizimungu** as president. By September 1994 nearly 2 million Rwandans were in refugee camps in Zaire; 800,000 were in refugee camps in Tanzania and Burundi. Although a semblance of order has returned to Rwanda, it remains a devastated and shocked country. The UN has established an **International Tribunal** in Arusha to prosecute the perpetrators of the genocide, and more than 50,000 Rwandans are in jail awaiting trial. Echoes of genocide reverberate in refugee camps in Rwanda, Burundi, and the **Congo** (formerly Zaire). On 28 March 1998, **President Clinton** flew to Kigali and apologized for America's refusal to assist in stopping one of the most concentrated and brutal genocides in history.

Suggestions for Term Papers

1. Some scholars argue that the Belgian colonial legacy in Rwanda, particularly in education, health care, and economic development, was overwhelmingly positive. Write a paper that examines and evaluates Belgian colonial rule in Rwanda.

2. Some anthropologists and ethnologists conclude that the classifications Hutu and Tutsi are artificial. If there were at one time distinct differences between the two tribes, by the 1990s these differences had become blurred through intermarriage. The more important differences may be those having to do with economic status, levels of educations, and political connections. Read about the two tribes and determine whether the classifications used are appropriate. Provide reasons for the position you take.

3. The Rwandan genocide, because of its compressed time frame and brutal methods of killing, was a horrific event. Assess the reasons the United Nations Security Council initially refused to label it genocide.

4. Compare and contrast the UN arguments for intervention in Bosnia-Herzegovina and Kosovo (see #93, "The Dissolution of Yugoslavia in the 1990s") with the UN refusal to intervene in Rwanda. How do you account for the difference?

5. Four years after the killings began, President Clinton flew to Kigali and apologized for America's refusal to stop the genocide. Review U.S. policy during the genocide and write a paper defending or refuting this policy.

6. How successful has the International Criminal Tribunal for Rwanda in Arusha, Tanzania, been in bringing those charged with "crimes against humanity" to justice?

Research Suggestions

In addition to the boldfaced items, look under the entries for "The Holocaust, 1941–1945" (#34), "Pol Pot and the Cambodian Incursion, 1970–1978" (#72), and "The Dissolution of Yugoslavia in the 1990s" (#93). Search under **genocide, human rights**, and **Organization of African States (OAS)**.

SUGGESTED SOURCES

Primary Sources

DesForges, Alison. *Rwanda: The Crisis Continues.* New York: Human Rights Watch Africa, 1995. An objective study that relies heavily on statistics to make its case.

United States Congress. *Rwanda: Genocide and the Continuing Cycle of Violence . . . May 5, 1998.* Washington: Government Printing Office, 1998. Good official documentation of the horrors in 1994 and afterwards.

Secondary Sources

Destexhe, Alain. *Rwanda and Genocide in the Twentieth Century.* Translated by Alison Marchner. New York: New York University Press, 1995. A careful appraisal of the genocide that compares it to others in the twentieth century.

Gourevitch, Philip. *We Wish to Inform You that Tomorrow We Will Be Killed with Our Families: Stories from Rwanda.* New York: Farrar, Straus and Giroux, 1998. A prize-winning account that is the starting point for an understanding of the tragedy.
Keane, Fergal. *Season of Blood: A Rwandan Journey.* New York: Penguin, 1995. A reliable short summary with a helpful chronology.
Prunier, Gérard. *The Rwanda Crisis: History of a Genocide.* New York: Columbia University Press, 1995. A good summary of the early killings.
Ratner, Steven R. *Accountability for Human Rights Atrocities in International Law: Beyond the Nuremberg Legacy.* Oxford: Oxford University Press, 1997. It has the international statute for crimes against humanity in Rwanda.

96. DOLLY THE SHEEP CLONED, 1997

In 1997 **Ian Wilmut**, an embryologist, and colleagues at the **Roslin Institute** near Edinburgh, produced the first clone of an adult mammal, **Dolly the Sheep**. This important medical breakthrough has many important implications, although the initial response has been interest in and fear of the possibility of cloning a human being.

Cloning, from the Greek work *klon*, meaning "twig," involves the production of genetically identical animals by a process of **nuclear transfer**. The chromosomes from an unfertilized egg are removed and replaced with a nucleus from a donor cell. The nucleus determines almost all the characteristics of the offspring, so that a clone resembles its "parent," the animal from which the donor cell came, rather than the animal contributing the egg.

The possibility of **cloning humans** immediately became a controversy after the birth of Dolly. Unlike the situation in the film *Multiplicity*, however, cloning will not produce an exact replica of the adult. Instead the clone is born and develops through the normal life stages of a human. For this reason, the personality of a human clone may differ considerably from its "parent." Although many scientists and other commentators have called for a ban on the cloning of humans, it is possible that humans will be cloned at some point in the near future. The techniques are relatively simple, and any infertility clinic could convert itself quickly into a clinic for cloning humans.

A much more likely prospect than cloning humans is gene manipulation for the purpose of producing **"designer children."** Research is already under way to find genes responsible for particular diseases. It will be difficult to draw the line between eliminating life-threatening or debilitating diseases and using gene manipulation to produce superior intelligence or desired physical characteristics in children. However, as the film *Gattaca* demonstrates, gene enhancement may still be offset by drive and determination.

Cloning can be used for many purposes. It can be used to change the function of existing genes. Further research in this area may lead to cures for such diseases as **Alzheimer's** and **AIDS**. Cloning may be used to produce undifferentiated (embryonic) cells for use in medical research. It may also be used to improve possibilities for **xenotransplantation** (use of nonhuman organs to replace defective human organs) by, for example, modifying pigs genetically to prevent rejection of an organ by human immune systems. These and other uses raise ethical as well as technical issues.

Suggestions for Term Papers

1. Work on cloning goes back to the 1960s. Investigate earlier efforts at cloning (see Suggested Sources) and write a report on your findings.
2. Write a paper on the work at the Roslin Institute that led to the birth of Dolly the Sheep.
3. Organize a debate on the ethics of cloning human beings or on the ethics of using cloning techniques for medical research and in agriculture.
4. Use newspapers and magazines to research advances in cloning since the birth of Dolly the Sheep.
5. There are indications that Dolly is aging more rapidly than she should. Investigate the possible drawbacks of cloning and write a report.
6. Interview people in your town or take a poll (scientific or unscientific) to determine public opinion about cloning.

Research Suggestions

In addition to the boldfaced items, look under the entries for "The Discovery of the Double Helical Structure of DNA, 1953" (#49), "First 'Test-Tube' Baby Born, 1978" (#79), "The Spread of AIDS in the 1980s" (#83), and "John Paul II's First Twenty Years as Pope,

1978–1999" (#98). Search under **National Bioethics Advisory Commission, Richard Seed**, and **Jeremy Rifkin**.

SUGGESTED SOURCES

Primary Source

Wilmut, Ian, Keith Campbell, and Colin Tudge. *The Second Creation: Dolly and the Age of Biological Control.* New York: Farrar, Straus and Giroux, forthcoming. Dolly's story as told by her creators.

Secondary Sources

Andrews, Lori B. *The Clone Age: Adventures in the New World of Reproductive Genetics.* New York: Henry Holt, 1999. Andrews, an attorney who specializes in reproductive technology, draws the line at cloning humans.

Crichton, Michael. *The Lost World.* New York: Random House, 1997. The sequel to *Jurassic Park*, but perhaps not so unlikely. Scientists are now hoping to clone a woolly mammoth from a perfectly preserved specimen found in Siberia recently.

Gattaca. Distributed by Columbia TriStar Home Video, 1998. A film version of what the future might be like if people were divided between those who were "gene-enhanced" and those who were not. The protagonist, who is not gene-enhanced, shows that drive and determination still count for a great deal.

Kolata, Gina. *Clone: The Road to Dolly and the Path Ahead.* New York: William Morrow, 1998. A highly readable account by a science reporter for the *New York Times*.

McGee, Glenn, ed. *The Human Cloning Debate.* Berkeley: Berkeley Hills Books, 1998. Includes a contribution by Wilmut.

Nussbaum, Martha, and Cass R. Sunstein, eds. *Clones and Clones: Facts and Fantasies about Human Cloning.* New York: W. W. Norton, 1998. A useful collection of articles.

Pence, Gregory E. *Who's Afraid of Human Cloning?* Lanham, Md.: Rowman and Littlefield, 1998. A call for a more reasoned discussion of the possibilities of cloning.

———. *Flesh of My Flesh: The Ethics of Cloning Humans: A Reader.* Lanham, Md.: Rowman and Littlefield, 1998. A very useful collection.

Rifkin, Jeremy. *The Biotech Century: Harnessing the Gene and Remaking the World.* New York: Putnam Publishing Group, 1998. A warning against the dangers of biotechnology by an influential futurist.

Silver, Lee M. *Remaking Eden: How Genetic Engineering and Cloning Will Transform the American Family.* New York: Avon, 1998. This edition contains an afterword. Silver, a molecular biologist at Princeton, believes that reproductive technology of all kinds will be made available for those who want it and are willing to pay.

World Wide Web

"Roslin Institute Online." *http://www.ri.bbsrc.ac.uk*. Click on "Special Topic: Cloning" for a wealth of information.

97. THE ASIAN ECONOMIC MELTDOWN AT THE END OF THE 1990s

Often referred to as **newly industrialized countries (NICs)**, the Asian countries of **South Korea, Taiwan, Singapore**, and **Hong Kong** emerged in the 1960s as powerful industrial economies. By the 1980s these "four tigers" were heralded as economic prototypes not only for developing countries in Africa and Central America but also for mature economies in the developed world.

Despite considerable differences among these countries, they shared several common characteristics. All four countries benefited from the politics of the **Cold War**. First, they benefited from the purchases the United States made in the course of the **Korean War** and the **Vietnam War**. Then, they also profited from western efforts more generally to bolster their economies and to ensure the economic isolation of the **People's Republic of China**. All are small countries; none are blessed with large mineral or natural resources. Each relies heavily on a highly efficient labor force that has nimbly moved from an economy heavily dependent on manufacturing to one focused on banking, information management, and high technology.

Imitating the Japanese, the governments of Taiwan, South Korea, and Singapore worked very closely with banks and multinational companies to plan their economic growth. Hong Kong, however, achieved its stunning success with virtually no government guidance. Despite differing approaches to economic development and markedly different political and legal systems, the economic success of the four tigers was impressive until the mid-1990s.

Starting in 1996 a deep Asian economic recession began in Japan and quickly spread to Malaysia, Indonesia, South Korea, Taiwan, Singapore, and Hong Kong. For three years this Asian economic meltdown caused widespread dislocation, unemployment, and political tension throughout the Pacific region. For the first time Japanese white-collar workers faced unemployment. Korean students studying abroad were forced to return to Korea because their families could not pay their tuition. Despite dire predictions that the world economy would suffer from the Asian meltdown, little economic slowdown occurred outside of Asia. Two factors softened the global effects of Asia's meltdown. First, the U.S. economy continued to expand during this period; the U.S. imported record levels of manufactured goods from Asian producers. Second, by 1998 South Korea had embraced deficit spending and Japan had announced that it would align its banking and financial practices with Western standards. These decisions have restored consumer confidence and signaled to other Asian countries that an economic recovery is under way.

Suggestions for Term Papers

1. One of the hallmarks of South Korea's economy prior to the meltdown was its largely privately owned industrial groups, *chaebols*, such as Samsung, Hyundai, and Daewoo. Do a research project on one of the *chaebols* and write a paper explaining its composition and analyzing its successes and failures.

2. In 1999 the Japanese government announced that it would welcome increased foreign investment in its finanical markets and banking industry, as well as in Internet sales. Use the *Far Eastern Economic Review* and *The Economist* to investigate the problems of foreign companies operating in Japan and write a paper on whether the situation has changed. Provide reasons for the position you take.

3. Singapore has a reputation for order, efficiency, and respect for authority. Write a paper evaluating Singapore's system of government and how it has contributed to its economic growth.

4. South Korea experienced a sharp recession in the meltdown, but by 1999 showed signs that an economic recovery was under way. Examine the steps taken by the government to combat the meltdown and assess their contribution to recovery.

5. Despite the economic meltdown, national security and defense issues loom large. How do such countries as Japan and South Korea view defense and national security issues?

6. To what extent have Japan and the "four tigers" recovered from the economic meltdown?

Research Suggestions

In addition to the boldfaced items, look under the entries for "The Japanese Economic Miracle in the 1950s" (#47) and "The Chinese Economy at the End of the Twentieth Century" (#100). Search under **Park Chung Hee, North Korea, Lee Kuan Yew, Malaysia, Thailand**, and **Indonesia**.

SUGGESTED SOURCES

Primary Source

"Reality Hits Japan." *The Economist* 345 (29 November 1997): 15, 21–23, 41, 77–78. Firsthand reports of the Japanese, South Korean and Asian banking crises.

Secondary Sources

Amsden, Alice H. *Asia's Next Giant: South Korea and Late Industrialization.* New York: Oxford University Press, 1989. An authoritative examination of the key elements of Korea's economy.

"The Devil to Pay." *Far Eastern Economic Review* 160 (5 June 1997): 50–59. A close look at Japanese, South Korean, Malaysian, Indonesian and Hong Kong banking problems.

Garran, Robert. *Tigers Tamed: The End of the Asian Miracle.* Honolulu: University of Hawaii, 1999. This Australian journalist holds failed economic policy and irresponsible foreign investors responsible for the meltdown.

Jomo, K. S. *Tigers in Trouble: Financial Governance, Liberalisation and Crises in East Asia.* London: St. Martin's Press, 1999. Good case studies of the failed economic policies in Malaysia, Korea, and Indonesia.

Mallet, Victor. *The Trouble with Tigers: The Rise and Fall of South-East Asia.* New York: HarperCollins, 1999. Well written analysis of the meltdown's place within the larger context of Asian economic modernization.

McLeod, Ross, and Ross Garnaut, eds. *East Asia in Crisis: From Being a Miracle to Needing One?* London: Routledge, 1999. A dozen case studies illustrating how credit, economic policy, and market collapse affected the meltdown differently throughout Asia.

Scalpino, Robert A., Seizaburo Sato, and Jusuf Wanandi. *Asian Economic Development: Present and Future.* Berkeley: University of California, Institute of East Asian Studies, 1985. Several comparative economic development studies focused on the four tigers are in this collection.

Simone, Vera, and Anne Thompson Feraru. *The Asian Pacific: Political and Economic Development in a Global Context.* New York: Longman, 1995. Chapter 5 focuses on economic development and has an extensive bibliography.

Vogel, Ezra F. *Four Little Dragons: The Spread of Industrialization in East Asia.* Cambridge, Mass.: Harvard University Press, 1991. A good starting point for understanding the special character of these economies.

White, Gordon, ed. *Developmental States in East Asia.* New York: St. Martin's Press, 1988. A strong collection of essays focused on economic development policies.

World Wide Web

"The World Factbook, 1999" *http://www.odci.gov/cia/publications/ factbook/index.html.* This Central Intelligence Agency site is updated yearly.

98. JOHN PAUL II's FIRST TWENTY YEARS AS POPE, 1978–1999

The first Polish pope, **Karol Wojtyla** (1920–   ), was born in Wadowice, Poland, into a middle-class family. As a young man he witnessed the brutal **Nazi occupation** of his homeland and as an adult endured the oppressive rule of the **Polish Communist Party**. After his ordination as a priest, he studied in Rome, then returned to Poland, where he moved quickly up the ecclesiastical ranks and became a cardinal in 1968.

When **Pope John Paul I** died in 1978, Cardinal Wojtyla was elected the first non-Italian pope in 400 years. Taking the name of his predecessor, **John Paul II** pledged to continue the practice of **ecumenism** but also signaled that he would jealously guard doctrinal purity.

John Paul immediately began to travel the world. In his first two decades he embarked on eighty foreign tours and visited more than 120 countries. On tour he drew huge crowds, particularly among young people, whom he asked to embrace fidelity and reject all forms of what he called **"the culture of death."** He has written two books and more than a dozen major "letters to the world" (encyclicals). Two of his most significant encyclicals focusing on late twentieth-century political and social conditions are *Centesimus Annus* and *Evangelium Vitae*. In *Centesimus Annus* (1991), he condemns both Soviet-style communism for its deprivation of **human rights** and **free market capitalism** for its failure to protect the poor and promote human dignity. *Evangelium Vitae* (1995) condemns all forms of "the culture of death," including abortion, euthanasia, contraception, and capital punishment.

John Paul's pontificate remains one of paradox. Inextricably linked to the tragic history of Poland, he has proven to be a tough opponent of dictators and a champion of democracy. Although professing to continue the collegial spirit of Vatican II, he has little tolerance of dissent and has silenced renowned Catholic theologians, such as **Hans Küng** (Switzerland), **Edward Schillebeeckx** (Netherlands), and **Charles Curran** (United States), who have questioned papal authority. John Paul's immediate legacy is at least twofold. First, by appointing 120 members to the **College of Cardinals**, his influence on papal politics and Catholic doctrine will be felt through the first two decades of the twenty-first century. Second, in the 2,000-year history of the papacy only twelve popes have had longer pontificates.

Suggestions for Term Papers

1. Read *Centesimus Annus* (see Suggested Sources). According to Pope John Paul, what is the proper role of the state in a capitalist society? State your own position on the question and provide reasons for taking it.

2. In 1981 a deranged Turkish communist, Mehmet Ali Agca, attempted to assassinate John Paul II in St. Peter's Square. Investigate John Paul's response and his subsequent relationship with Agca.

3. Evaluate John Paul's role in loosening the Soviet Union's control over eastern Europe.

4. Select one of the theologians disciplined by Pope John Paul II, that is, Küng, Schillebeeckx, or Curran, and do a research project on the issues that led to his censure.

5. Study one of John Paul's major tours and assess its impact on the countries and societies involved.

6. Liberation theology is an important social and theological movement in Third World countries. Investigate John Paul's views on this and assess the influence his opinion has had.

Research Suggestions

In addition to the boldfaced items, look under the entries for "Vatican II, 1962–1965" (#63), "Solidarity in Poland, 1980–1990" (#82), and "The Breakup of the Soviet Union, 1991" (#91). Search under **pope, Vatican**, and **liberation theology**.

SUGGESTED SOURCES

Primary Sources

Bloch, Alfred, and George T. Czuczka, eds. *Toward a Philosophy of Praxis: An Anthology/Karol Wojtyla (Pope John Paul II)*. New York: Crossroad, 1981. A representative collection of John Paul's scholarship.

John Paul II. *Agenda for the Third Millennium*. Translated by Alan Neame. London: HarperCollins, 1996. A good indication why he has been so concerned about papal authority.

———. *Crossing the Threshold of Hope*. Translated by Jenny McPhee and Martha McPhee. New York: Knopf, 1994. An accessible guide to John Paul's optimistic view of life.

———. *Gift and Mystery: On the Fiftieth Anniversary of My Priestly Ordination*. New York: Doubleday, 1997. Reflections on his pastoral obligations.

Miller, J. Michael, ed. *The Encyclicals of John Paul II*. Huntington, Id.: Our Sunday Visitor Publishing Division, 1996. A well-edited edition of twelve encyclicals including *Centesimus Annus*.

Secondary Sources

Bernstein, Carl, and Marco Politi. *His Holiness: John Paul II and the Hidden History of Our Time*. New York: Doubleday, 1996. Argues that John Paul did much to end the Cold War.

Hebblethwaite, Peter. *The New Inquisition? The Case of Edward Schillebeeckx and Hans Küng*. San Francisco: Harper and Row, 1980. A revealing study of how John Paul silenced dissent.

Kwitny, Jonathan. *Man of the Century: The Life and Times of Pope John Paul*

II. New York: Henry Holt, 1997. Shows how universal John Paul's influence has been.

McBrien, Richard P. *Lives of the Popes: The Pontiffs from St. Peter to John Paul II.* New York: HarperCollins, 1997. A short biography by one of John Paul's most consistent critics that includes tables, lists, and bibliographical leads.

Reese, Thomas J. *Inside the Vatican: The Politics and Organization of the Catholic Church.* Cambridge, Mass.: Harvard University Press, 1996. A close examination of the Vatican's organization and finances.

Szulc, Tad. *Pope John Paul II: The Biography.* New York: Scribner, 1995. The most comprehensive English language biography. Strong on the pope's early life.

99. THE INTERNET IN THE 1990s

By any measure, the **Internet** is an extraordinary technological achievement. In 1994, 3 million people were connected to the Internet. By 1997 it had more than 100 million users worldwide.

The Internet, a network connecting many computer networks through the use of a common addressing system and communications protocol, **TCP/IP (Transmission Control Protocol/Internet Protocol)**, came into being in the 1960s. At first it was seen as a means of secure and survivable communication in cases of national emergency. Sponsored by the Department of Defense's **ARPA (Advanced Research Project Agency)**, a small network, **ARPANET**, developed to promote the sharing of super-computers in the United States.

ARPANET began by connecting four universities. By 1971 it networked twenty-three ARPA-funded computer centers together. **Electronic mail (e-mail)** quickly became the most popular application. At the end of the 1970s two graduate students at Duke University, **Tom Truscott** and **Jim Ellis**, and one at the University of North Carolina, **Steve Bellovin**, created the **USENET newsgroups**, which allowed people all over the world to join discussion groups that talked about the Internet and other subjects.

Growth was rapid in the late 1970s and early 1980s, driven by the popularity of e-mail. In 1982 the term "Internet" was used for the first time. In the 1980s, using the common language of TCP/IP, the loose collection of networks that made up ARPANET came together as the Internet. At the same time, the introduction and rapid acceptance of the

personal computer (pc) made it possible for many individuals and corporations to join the Internet.

In 1990 ARPANET was decommissioned. What existed now was a vast network of networks called the Internet. There were 300,000 hosts, where only a few years before, in 1987, there had only been 10,000. The year before, researchers at **CERN High-Energy Physics Laboratory** in Geneva, Switzerland, used **hypertext**, a new computer language, to create what became the **World Wide Web**, a combination of words, pictures, and sounds available through the Internet.

In 1993 **Mosaic**, the first graphics-based **Web browser**, became available. **Marc Andreesen**, who developed Mosaic, formed **Netscape Communications Corporation** the following year. By the late 1990s the World Wide Web had emerged as the major application of the Internet. It is now estimated that more than 320 million Web pages exist, with the number expected to grow 1,000 percent in the next few years.

E-commerce, pioneered by **Amazon.com** and **eBay**, doubled sales in 1998 over 1997 to $7.3 billion. At the end of the century, it is clear that in the space of a few years the Internet and the World Wide Web have begun to change the way people live, learn, work, and shop in many parts of the world.

Suggestions for Term Papers

1. Investigate the early defense-oriented history of the Internet in the 1960s (see Suggested Sources) and write a paper on the technical problems that had to be solved before the Internet could become a reality.

2. E-mail was in many ways a spin-off from the main purposes of the ARPA-funded research. Do a research project on the early days of e-mail, including the development of "netiquette." If possible, conduct interviews with early users of e-mail.

3. The USENET newsgroups were seen as a poor man's ARPANET. Explore the origins of USENET and talk with people about how it is used today.

4. As a group project, do a presentation on how the Internet works and explain the different features we conveniently group together as the Internet.

5. Design a Web page to introduce the Internet to people with no experience on the Web.

6. Do a research paper on e-commerce that explores among other topics the need for sophisticated encryption software.

Research Suggestions

In addition to the boldfaced items, look under the entries for "The Invention of the Computer, 1944–1946" (#39), "First 'Test-Tube' Baby Born, 1978" (#79), and "Dolly the Sheep Cloned, 1997" (#96). Search under **Vannevar Bush (the "Memex"), J.C.R. Licklider, Larry Roberts, Vinton Cerf, Internet Assigned Number Authority, Java, Linux**, and **cyberspace**.

SUGGESTED SOURCES

Primary Sources

Berners-Lee, Tim, with Mark Fischetti. *Weaving the Web: The Original Design and Ultimate Destiny of the World Wide Web by Its Inventor.* San Francisco: HarperSanFrancisco, 1999. Part autobiography, part prophecy, a fascinating book by a major figure in the explosive growth of the Internet in the 1990s.

Bush, Vannevar. "As We May Think." *Atlantic Monthly*, 176 (July 1945): 101–108. Bush presents his ideas about the "Memex," a personal information machine that was the forerunner of today's personal computer and the Internet.

Licklider, J.C.R. *Libraries of the Future.* Cambridge, Mass.: MIT Press, 1965. A pioneering effort to visualize a different way of storing and making available information.

Secondary Sources

Abbate, Janet. *Inventing the Internet.* Cambridge, Mass.: MIT Press, 1999. Probably the best single book available on the origins and growth of the Internet.

Campbell-Kelly, Martin, and William Aspray. *Computer: A History of the Information Machine.* New York: Basic Books, 1996. Places the Internet in the context of computer development. An excellent brief introduction.

Hafner, Katie, and Matthew Lyon. *Where Wizards Stay Up Late: The Origins of the Internet.* New York: Simon and Schuster, 1998. The great man approach. Well-written and carefully researched.

Hauben, Michael, and Ronda Hauben. *Netizens: On the History and Impact of Usenet and the Internet.* Los Alamitos, Calif.: IEEE Computer Society Press, 1997. History from the bottom up of those people who figured out new uses for the Internet and made it the phenomenon it is.

Hudson, David. *Rewired: A Brief and Opinionated Net History.* Indianapolis: Macmillan Technical Publishing, 1997. A good introduction. The author works in the industry but is skeptical of some of the more grandiose claims about it.

Nerds 2.0.1: A Brief History of the Internet. 3 hours., 1998. Distributed by PBS Home Video. An excellent documentary. Some prior familiarity with the topic is useful, however, in viewing it. PBS also has a *Nerds 2.0.1* Web site: *http://www.pbs.org/opb/nerds2.0.1.*

Norberg, Arthur L., and Judy E. O'Neill. *Transforming Computer Technology: Information Processing for the Pentagon, 1962–1986.* Baltimore: Johns Hopkins University Press, 1996. An institutional approach to the history of the Internet.

Rosenzweig, Roy. "Wizards, Bureaucrats, Warriors, and Hackers: Writing the History of the Internet" (review essay), *American Historical Review*, 103 (December 1998): 1530–1552. Rosenzweig does a superb job of sorting out the history of the Internet, showing that it may be approached through biography, through institutional studies, and through studies combining politics and culture. Excellent bibliography.

World Wide Web

"All about the Internet." *http://www.isoc.org/internet-history/#Origins.* At times a little technical, this nevertheless is a useful overview of the Internet's history. Many of the authors played prominent roles in that history. Many interesting links.

"Nerds 2.0.1." *http://www.pbs.org/opb/nerds2.0.1.* Based on the *Nerds 2.0.1: A Brief History of the Internet* documentary, this Web site offers a wide range of introductory material including a timeline, a glossary of terms, and brief identification of many major figures connected with the Internet.

"PBS Life on the Internet Timeline." *http://www.pbs.org/internet/timeline/index.htm.* A useful site with links to other interesting sites on the history of the Internet.

100. THE CHINESE ECONOMY AT THE END OF THE TWENTIETH CENTURY

In 1978, under the leadership of **Premier Deng Xiaoping**, China embraced a series of economic reforms designed to dismantle its Soviet-style economy, adopt elements of a market-driven economy, and encourage economic growth. Deng insisted that China could combine capitalism with socialism in four sectors: agriculture, industry, national defense, and technological development. To promote his reforms, **Special Economic Zones (SEZs)** were established throughout China. These SEZs welcomed foreign investment and provided incentives to Chinese investors to launch new companies.

Initial results of Deng's reforms were most impressive. State participation in the economy decreased while private, cooperative, and individual ownership of businesses dramatically increased. Between 1981 and 1991 China's economy grew at an annual rate of 10 percent; between 1991 and 1995 China enjoyed a growth rate of 12 percent. Yet, China still faced huge problems. Deng's reforms promoted economic growth, but they did not allow for democratic reform. On 3 June 1989, Deng ordered troops and tanks into Beijing's Tiananmen Square to quash the student **pro-democracy** movement. The brutal **Tiananmen Square massacre** of more than 700 demonstrators clearly signaled that, despite economic growth, hard-line communists still controlled China.

By the late 1990s China's economic prospects had dimmed considerably. Even the return of the former British colony of **Hong Kong** in 1997 did not prevent a deep recession. **Jiang Zemin**, Deng's successor, continued Deng's policies, but encountered severe problems. Because of bad loans, by 1998 more than half of China's state banks were insolvent. Twenty million workers in state enterprises were without work, and 120 million Chinese peasants who had left the countryside were ill-housed in its already overcrowded cities. The savage **Yangtze River floods** of 1998 killed more than 3,000 people and affected 250 million people living in its floodplain.

Scholars such as He Qinglian, author of the authoritative *China's*

Pitfall (1998), and Julia Kwong, author of *The Political Economy of Corruption in China* (1998), argue that Deng's reforms have secured economic growth at the price of institutional, political, and financial corruption. Until the corruption is rooted out and true structural reforms compatible with a free market economy are adopted, these scholars insist that China will not repeat the robust economic growth of the 1980s or enjoy true economic development.

Suggestions for Term Papers

1. Investigate Deng Xiaoping's economic policies and write a paper discussing his views of free market capitalism.

2. In 1989 Deng Xiaoping ordered the military into Tiananmen Square to crush the student-led pro-democracy movement. Discuss the political and economic repercussions of this decision.

3. Although China and Japan would seem to be natural trading partners, political problems have interfered at times. Write a paper focusing on the current bilateral trade between China and Japan.

4. In 1997 China reasserted its control over the former British colony of Hong Kong. How has this change of governance affected Hong Kong's economy? How has it affected China's economy?

5. Chinese military armaments, especially missiles, have increasingly become an important export. Write a paper reviewing and assessing the Chinese sale of military hardware to other countries.

6. Coca-Cola, Jeep, McDonald's, and IBM are a few of the American companies that have invested in China's Special Economic Zones. Write a business report on one of these firms covering experience to date in China and prospects for the future.

Research Suggestions

In addition to the boldfaced items, look under the entries for "The Victory of the Chinese Communist Party, 1949" (#46), "The Japanese Economic Miracle in the 1950s" (#47), "The Great Proletarian Cultural Revolution in China, 1966–1976" (#73), and "The Asian Economic Meltdown at the End of the 1990s" (#97). Search under **multinational corporations** and **human rights**.

SUGGESTED SOURCES

Primary Sources

Deng Xiaoping. *Fundamental Issues in Present-Day China*. New York: Pergamon Press, 1987. A good overview of Deng's views of the role of the state in economic planning.

————. "A Market Economy for Socialist Goals." In *Selected Works of Deng Xiaoping. Vol. 3, (1982–1992)*. Beijing: Foreign Languages Press, 1994. The clearest statement of Deng's economic thinking.

Secondary Sources

Ash, Robert F., and Y. Y. Kueh, eds. *The Chinese Economy under Deng Xiaoping*. New York: Oxford University Press, 1996. A good overview of Deng's economic policy.

"China's Economy: Red Alert." *The Economist*, 24 October 1998, 23–26. A crisp analysis of the reasons for China's slow growth rate.

Davis, Deborah, and Ezra Vogel, eds. *Chinese Society on the Eve of Tiananmen: The Impact of Reform*. Cambridge, Mass.: Harvard University Press, 1990. A valuable starting point for understanding Deng's reforms. Excellent bibliography.

Gilley, Bruce. *Tiger on the Brink: Jiang Zemin and China's New Elite*. Berkeley: University of California Press, l998. An astute insight into Jiang's economic and political leadership.

Kwong, Julia. *The Political Economy of Corruption in China*. Armonk, N.Y.: M. E. Sharpe, 1998. Well-researched, critical portrayal of corruption as a way of life in China.

Liu, Binyan Lin, and Perry Link. "A Great Leap Backward?" *New York Review of Books*, 8 October 1998, 19–23. Two China experts review He Qinglian's *Zhongguo de xianjing* [*China's Pitfall*] and provide a good summary of China's economy in the late 1990s.

Nathan, Andrew J. *China's Transition*. New York: Columbia University Press, 1998. An incisive look at the political and economic problems of China after Deng.

Schell, Orville. *Mandate of Heaven: A New Generation of Entrepreneurs, Dissidents, Bohemians, and Technocrats Lays Claim to China's Future*. New York: Simon and Schuster, 1994. Written by a premier China scholar, this is a lively and wide-ranging report on China in the nineties.

Steinfeld, Edward S. *Foreign Reform in China: The Fate of State-Owned Industry*. Cambridge: Cambridge University Press, 1998. A careful examination of the place of China's state-run businesses in its new economy.

Vogel, Ezra F. *One Step Ahead in China: Guangdong under Reform.* Cambridge, Mass.: Harvard University Press, 1989. An in-depth look at Deng's economic and social reforms in one province.

World Wide Web

"The National Security Archive." *http://www.gwu.edu/~nsarchiv.* Good documentation on Tiananmen Square and Deng's policies.

Index

About the Authors

MICHAEL D. RICHARDS is Samford Professor of History at Sweet Briar College. He is the coauthor of *Twentieth-Century Europe: A Brief History* (1998) and has written for a number of reference works. In addition to articles and book reviews for scholarly publications, he writes op-ed pieces for the *History News Service* and his work has appeared in a number of newspapers around the country.

PHILIP F. RILEY teaches in the Department of History at James Madison University. He is coauthor of *The Global Experience: Readings in World History* (1987) and many articles on European history. He is a recipient of the James Madison University Distinguished Teaching Award.